Primary commodity prices: economic models and policy

Centre for Economic Policy Research

The Centre for Economic Policy Research is a registered charity with educational purposes. It was established in 1983 to promote independent analysis and public discussion of open economies and the relations among them. Institutional (core) finance for the Centre has been provided through major grants from the Leverhulme Trust, the Esmée Fairbairn Trust, the Baring Foundation and the Bank of England. None of these organizations gives prior review to the Centre's publications nor do they necessarily endorse the views expressed therein.

The Centre is pluralist and non-partisan, bringing economic research to bear on the analysis of medium- and long-run policy questions. The research work which it disseminates may include views on policy, but the Board of Governors of the Centre does not give prior review to such publications, and the Centre itself takes no institutional policy positions. The opinions expressed in this volume are those of the authors and not of those of the Centre for Economic Policy Research.

Primary commodity prices: economic models and policy

Edited by

L. ALAN WINTERS

and

DAVID SAPSFORD

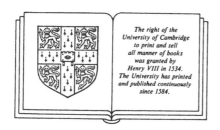

The right of the
University of Cambridge
to print and sell
all manner of books
was granted by
Henry VIII in 1534.
The University has printed
and published continuously
since 1584.

CAMBRIDGE UNIVERSITY PRESS

Cambridge

New York   Port Chester   Melbourne   Sydney

CAMBRIDGE UNIVERSITY PRESS
Cambridge, New York, Melbourne, Madrid, Cape Town, Singapore,
São Paulo, Delhi, Dubai, Tokyo, Mexico City

Cambridge University Press
The Edinburgh Building, Cambridge CB2 8RU, UK

Published in the United States of America by Cambridge University Press, New York

www.cambridge.org
Information on this title: www.cambridge.org/9780521385503

First published 1990

A catalogue record for this publication is available from the British Library

ISBN 978-0-521-38550-3 Hardback

Contents

Figures

Tables

Preface

This volume contains the proceedings of the conference on 'Primary Commodity Prices: Economic Models and Policy', organized by the Centre for Economic Policy Research and held in London on 16/17 March 1989. It formed part of the Centre's programme in International Trade and was supported by Rio Tinto Zinc plc, the European Investment Bank, the Foreign and Commonwealth Office and the Overseas Development Administration. We are extremely grateful to our sponsors for both their financial support and their advice and encouragement in drawing up the programme.

We also wish to thank Alasdair Smith and Richard Portes for encouraging us to run the conference, Wendy Thompson for managing the business arrangements, Andreas Köttering for acting as rapporteur and Jacqui Eggo for ensuring that the conference ran smoothly. Paul Compton, the Centre's Publications Officer, guided this volume to press rapidly and efficiently; he and we were pleased to work with John Black of the University of Exeter, who served as Production Editor. They have kept editors, authors and discussants to CEPR's very tight production schedule, so that these timely, policy-relevant analyses by leading researchers would quickly reach a wide audience.

Conferences are cooperative efforts. We trust that our colleagues, sponsors and readers will find the volume as worthwhile as we have. We believe that the research reported here will communicate to readers the latest thinking on commodity price modelling, encourage researchers to explore new and stimulating paths, and inform current policy debates on price and earnings stabilization. Indeed, if it achieves just one of these aims our efforts will have been well rewarded.

L. Alan Winters
David Sapsford

Conference participants

Michael Bailey   *Rio Tinto Zinc plc*
Robin Bhar   *Rudolf Wolff*
Tony Bird   *Anthony Bird Associates*
Kees Burger   *Free University, Amsterdam*
Vince Cable   *Commonwealth Secretariat*
Philip Daniel   *Commonwealth Secretariat*
Daniel De Roo   *Metallurgie Hoboken-Overpelt*
Leo Drollas   *British Petroleum*
Stephen Dunn   *Rowntree Mackintosh*
George Gawronski   *Organisation for Economic Cooperation and Development*
Gordon Gemmill   *City University Business School*
Surojit Ghosh   *Credit Suisse First Boston*
Linda Gilardoni   *Commodity Research Unit*
Christopher Gilbert   *Queen Mary College, London, and CEPR*
David Harvey   *University of Newcastle-upon-Tyne*
Roland Herrmann   *Institut für Weltwirtschaft, Kiel*
Gerald Holtham   *Shearson Lehman Hutton Securities*
Alison Hook   *Foreign and Commonwealth Office*
Andrew Hughes Hallett   *University of Newcastle-upon-Tyne and CEPR*
David Humphreys   *Rio Tinto Zinc plc*
Mirza Jahani   *Overseas Development Administration*
Richard Just   *University of Maryland*
Paul Kofman   *Erasmus University, Rotterdam*
Andreas Köttering   *St Antony's College, Oxford*
Montague Lord   *Inter-American Development Bank*
Robert Mabro   *Institute for Energy Studies, Oxford*
Alasdair MacBean   *University of Lancaster*
G. S. Maddala   *University of Florida*
David Morris   *International Institute for Cotton*

Stewart Murray *Consolidated Goldfields plc*
David Newbery *Department of Applied Economics, Cambridge, and CEPR*
Theodosios Palaskas *Queen Mary College, London*
Hashem Pesaran *Trinity College, Cambridge*
Louis Phlips *Center for Operations Research and Econometrics, Louvain*
Marian Radetzki *Institute for International Economic Studies, Stockholm*
Prathap Ramanujam *University of Glasgow*
Jim Rollo *Foreign and Commonwealth Office*
David Sapsford *University of East Anglia*
Hidde Smit *Free University, Amsterdam*
John Spraos *University College, London*
Mark Taylor *City University Business School and CEPR*
Pravin Trivedi *Indiana University*
Bruce Trotter *Overseas Development Administration*
Gerhard van Muiswinkel *European Investment Bank*
Jean-Marie Viaene *Erasmus University, Rotterdam*
David Vines *University of Glasgow and CEPR*
E. Lakis Vouyoukas *British Petroleum*
Kenneth Wallis *University of Warwick*
Michael Wickens *University of Southampton and CEPR*
L. Alan Winters *University of Wales, Bangor, and CEPR*

1 Primary commodity prices: an introduction to the major policy and modelling challenges

L. ALAN WINTERS and DAVID SAPSFORD

Primary commodities constitute over 40 per cent of world trade and World Bank figures for 1986 reveal that of the 42 countries with a per capita GNP of less than $1,600, 20 were more than 70 per cent dependent on just two commodities for export earnings. As a result fluctuations in primary export earnings can disrupt LDCs' economic stability and interrupt the flow of finance for development. Primary commodities also play an important role in the behaviour of inflation in the industrial economies. Commodity price volatility has increased almost ninefold during the 1980s. The relationship between commodity prices and world economic activity appears to have broken down – prices were much more depressed than past experience would have suggested – and the relationship with the dollar appears to have shifted as well.

The experience of the 1980s provides an excellent opportunity to test and refine hypotheses about commodity price behaviour and to develop their implications for economic policy and the management of commodity markets. This book reports the proceedings of a major international conference on primary commodity price determination which was held in London during March 1989. The essays and discussants' comments illustrate both the current state of the art in commodity economics and the rich array of alternative approaches which exists. This introduction sets the analytical and policy scenes, places the contributions in their contexts and gives brief non-technical summaries of the principal results. To this end, Sections 1 and 2 outline the major policy and modelling challenges currently faced by commodity economists. Section 3 discusses some of the general econometric issues and developments in commodity economics, while Section 4 illustrates the problems which arise in modelling certain specific commodities: agricultural products, aluminium and oil. Section 5 is concerned with schemes designed to stabilize commodity earnings, while Section 6 presents a brief summary of the major issues to be considered in this volume.

1   The policy challenge

Primary commodities and the forces which determine their prices raise a range of issues which are of concern to economists and policy-makers. Most obviously food, fuels and raw materials account for around half the export earnings of the developing countries as a whole and around 90 per cent of those of sub-Saharan Africa. Moreover, for many individual countries exports are highly concentrated in one or a few specific commodities. For example, around half of developing countries currently earn over 50 per cent of their export revenues from a single primary commodity, while around 75 per cent earn at least 60 per cent from three or fewer primary products. Primary products are also an important source of export earnings for the developed world. Taken together, fully 70 per cent of the world's 125 largest economies depend on primary commodities for more than half of their export earnings.

These data suggest that the evolution of the world trade and prices of primary products is one of the most crucial elements of world economic performance. Moreover for various well known reasons, the quantities traded of most primary commodities tend to grow less rapidly than those of other traded goods, including manufactures. Thus in the long run the only effective response to adverse price trends in primaries is export diversification, and export prices are a vital consideration in developing countries' economic well-being and policy-making.

Primary prices are also critical in the short run, for they appear to fluctuate substantially more than do manufactures' prices. Mostly – although not invariably – price variability results in large swings in export earnings which can be disruptive of investment and growth. The evidence of a long-run link between export fluctuations and the level of economic growth is actually rather ambiguous, but the widespread perception that there is an adverse relationship is sufficient to place the issue firmly on the economist's agenda. Moreover, in the short run, fluctuations in earnings complicate policy-making in developing countries for, in the absence of strong evidence to the contrary, governments are prone to form overly optimistic expectations during price booms. This, in turn, results in uneven patterns of growth, with sharp booms alternating with long periods of austerity and debt accumulation during the periods of apparently unforeseen retrenchment. In addition, the consequences of price fluctuations for private businesses – especially credit-constrained ones – are adverse if not critical, and most firms consider them a significant hindrance to their activities.

The public and private problems of coping with revenue fluctuations have led economists to devote considerable effort to the implementation of schemes to reduce developing countries' fluctuations in export earnings. These efforts have actually had relatively little success – as Chapter 10 below attests – but to many economists stabilization still presents the greatest policy challenge in the field of primaries research.

Commodity price trends and fluctuations are also of importance to industrial countries. First, they produce primaries, and seek to protect their domestic producers from fluctuations – especially in agriculture; second, they consume primaries and find significant swings in their terms of trade disruptive of both real income growth and inflationary expectations. The effects of the oil shocks of the 1970s were confounded by other macroeconomic factors, but it is difficult to deny that they caused OECD countries considerable adjustment costs. Even short-run fluctuations in primaries prices affect the industrial countries. The recovery of the mid-to-late 1980s was strengthened and prolonged by the weakness of commodity prices and at least some commentators have argued that commodity prices are a major factor in OECD countries' inflation (Beckerman and Jenkinson, 1986).

The role of commodity trade in transferring income and transmitting macroeconomic shocks between the developing and the industrial countries is widely recognized at an anecdotal level. A number of formal models of the transmission process also exist, e.g. Currie and Vines (1988) and Klein (1988) – but to date their empirical underpinnings are relatively weak. This is partly because technical progress and unexpected inventory behaviour make it difficult to quantify the effects of industrial countries' aggregate demand on commodity demand and prices. It is also because the potential asset market aspects of commodity price behaviour, deriving from the ease with which they are transferred through time by either storage or deferred extraction, have proved elusive empirically. Whatever the reason, however, it has still proved very difficult to forecast commodity prices with any degree of accuracy and thus very difficult to make allowance for them in global macroeconomic policy-making.

A further important but poorly understood phenomenon is the relationship between commodity prices and exchange rates. Although empirical studies frequently find evidence of a statistically significant relationship between primary prices measured in US dollars and the dollar effective exchange rate, the precise mechanisms involved are not yet fully understood. While nearly all theory suggests that the elasticity of commodity prices with respect to the dollar exchange rates should be below unity (e.g. Ridler and Yandle, 1972), empirical results suggest the contrary. Only recently have explanations of this phenomenon started to emerge in terms of responses to debt problems and mismeasured exchange rates (Gilbert, 1989). Two further complications arise for agents in commodity-dependent countries. First, there is the interaction between commodity prices and the exchange rate, especially when there are effective forward/futures markets for each. Second, the advantages of hedging on forward markets relative to other approaches to stabilization have, to date, been addressed only in simple models using unrealistic symmetric distributions for price and quantity shocks. Chapters 8 and 9 below offer significant extensions to existing partial and general equilibrium models of earnings stabilization, and suggest that considerably more care is needed in assessing the issues at stake than is usually taken.

Until all these various macroeconomic links and puzzles are better understood, proposals such as that to manage the international monetary system via a commodity standard can barely be addressed.

To summarize, commodity markets pose serious challenges to both public and private sector policy-makers. For private participants the criticial issues are the opportunities for profitable commodity trading and the scope for avoiding and coping with risk. Commodity shocks clearly entail risk for market participants and users of primary commodities, and their magnitude and nature are important for decisions on matters such as stock-holding, financial policy, investment in plant (both for producers and users), and even for decisions about whether to undertake certain activities or not. This volume addresses these issues in a series of chapters on price forecasting models. These offer not only some predictive guidance but also a quantification of the remaining uncertainty; moreover, while some of the papers treat short-term dynamics, others identify medium and long-term issues of crucial importance for economic planning.

At a public policy level huge effort (political, economic and administrative) has been put into price and earnings stabilization schemes, and yet questions persist about their feasibility and desirability let alone about the techniques they should use. Macroeconomic policy-makers have to cope with uncertainty about commodity prices both for individual countries and in terms of the transmission of economic shocks. This volume addresses stabilization issues directly in Part III and contributes to efficient forecasting and macro policy by offering clearer insight into commodity price formation and ways of representing it econometrically.

2   The modelling challenge

It is clear from the preceding discussion that primary commodities raise important issues of economic policy for both private agents and public authorities. Commodity markets also generate a number of challenges for economic modellers and commodity analysts. Ultimately modellers and analysts face the same set of issues and contribute to the same set of outcomes as policy economists, but, for them, the immediate issue is the explanation of a number of stylized facts describing recent changes in commodity behaviour.

Although the list of such stylized facts would doubtless vary from one analyst to another, it would likely include such observations as the existence of sharp peaks and flat bottoms to price cycles, the apparent lengthening of lags and possible loss of significance in the relationship between prices and measures of aggregate demand in consuming countries, and the marked increase in the variability of commodity prices during the 1970s and early 1980s, relative to the 1950s and 1960s.[1] Perhaps the most compelling fact, however, has been the persistent inability of existing models to forecast commodity price movements with anything approaching an acceptable degree of accuracy. (See Artis, 1987, for an appraisal of the IMF's forecasting record in this field.)

A potentially informative categorization of commodity analysts is between market participants (including policy-makers, buffer-stock managers, purchasers, sellers, brokers and so forth) on the one hand, and market observers (including academic economists, econometricians and forecasters) on the other. Participants and observers have different priorities in their study of commodity prices, and consequently tend to emphasize different issues and to use different methodologies, but ultimately both groups are concerned with the *same* set of problems: namely, the forces that actually determine the prices of primary commodities. One apparent difference in approach that emerged from the discussion of the papers presented in this volume was the trade-off between information intensity and analytical sophistication. Industry specialists frequently have access to substantial bodies of data about their sectors – see, for example, Chapter 6 below – and are able to extract very considerable amounts of information from them in a relatively straightforward fashion. Observers, on the other hand, frequently have less, and less good, data but devote considerable effort to the econometric analysis of such data. The divergence is more apparent than real, however, for no observer deliberately eschews information and no practitioner consciously uses inappropriate analytical tools. Rather, the difference reflects comparative advantage, on the one hand, and stage of production on the other. Information that was once restricted to market participants – e.g. hourly data on prices and estimated costs of production is periodically extended to observers[2] and techniques of analysis that were once the province of a few cognoscenti – e.g. multiple regression, vector autoregression and cointegration – are gradually (and gratefully) adopted by practitioners. One of the principal purposes of this volume and the conference from which it stems is to encourage just such an interchange. Economics is a policy science (with policy interpreted in both a public and private sense), and good policy derives from the sensible application of the best analysis to the best data.

A major theme of this book is that primary commodity markets provide the ideal test bed for a range of general principles and issues in economics. The 1970s witnessed a revolution in economic thought as economists formulated, adopted, criticized and finally came to terms with the hypothesis of rational expectations. The basic idea of the rational expectations hypothesis is that individual agents do not rely solely on the mechanistic extrapolation of past experience when forming their expectations about the future course of events. Rather they use all available information, including the nature of the economic process and policy pronouncements by governments, at least up to the point where the marginal cost of the acquisition and processing of information equals the expected marginal benefit from its use.

Critics of rational expectations have argued that the hypothesis imposes unreasonable and implausible informational and analytical requirements on individual agents. While such criticism may have some validity the rational expectations paradigm has forced all economists to recognize the importance of forward-looking behaviour and to question the relevance of earlier models of expectations which implied that agents' forecasts could consistently err on one side or the other of actual outcomes. Although a detailed discussion of the merits of rational expectations is outside the scope of this chapter, we note that commodity markets provide an ideal opportunity to test the rational expectations thesis. Macroeconomic tests necessarily refer to aggregations of many goods and very many agents, and are thus rather imprecise about exactly what is being forecast (the retail price index or the price of the individual's consumption basket?) and by whom. Commodity markets, on the other hand, deal with precisely defined products. Moreover, when one considers the Lucas (1976) critique of policy evaluation, the highly informed nature of commodity market participants, plus their sometimes smallness in number, means that such markets provide an ideal opportunity to study whether the pronouncements and behaviour of, say, a buffer stock manager actually exert a significant influence on the behaviour of price via the expectations of market participants.

A major objective of the conference was to bring together people from different sectors with a common interest in commodity markets and problems, in order to explore how they might help each other towards greater understanding. Thus at the end of the day we hope that those whose principal focus of interest is in policy and related matters may have access to the best available techniques, and that econometricians may have increased access to the specialist market knowledge and superior data possessed by practitioners. This is not, by its very nature, an easy task, but as the chapters and discussions in this book illustrate, a degree of interaction was achieved whose fruits, in terms of enhanced understanding of the behaviour of commodity markets, are very significant indeed. The remaining sections of this chapter provide a non-technical guide to the major issues covered by the conference.

3   Econometric analyses

Part I of this book contains chapters by Maddala, Gilbert and Palaskas, and Trivedi. Taken together these papers provide a clear statement of the state of the econometric art in the construction, estimation, interpretation and use of commodity market models.

In Chapter 2 G. S. Maddala (University of Florida) discusses the estimation and use of disequilibrium models (in which one side or the other of the market may be rationed) in the presence of an intervention policy such as a price support. The chapter begins with a review of the various methods by which one may incorporate rational expectations into disequilibrium models and then goes on to discuss the applicability of these methods to modelling commodity markets which are subject to policies such as price supports and buffer stocks. The chapter also examines the usefulness of external indicators of price expectations such as futures prices and survey data.

Maddala's analysis demonstrates that disequilibria significantly complicate the mechanism of expectations formation. However, since agents do take account of market interventions in forming their views of the future, modellers must do so as well. Failure to do so can result in seriously biased estimates of the parameters of economic behaviour. In particular, Maddala suggests that incorporating policy-induced market disequilibrium makes a considerable difference to estimates of the price elasticitity of supply for various primary commodities. He presents an empirical example in which the incorporation of price supports into an estimated commodity market model increases the estimated supply elasticities by about 50 per cent above those which would result from ignoring such interventions. Given the importance of supply elasticities in the assessment of many commodity policies, such differences could clearly be very important indeed.

The theme of expectations in commodity markets is explored in a different context by Christopher Gilbert (Queen Mary College and CEPR) and Theo Palaskas (Oxford University) in Chapter 3. This chapter focusses on the question of incorporating rational expectations into commodity market models and stresses the attractions of fitting price equations as reduced forms of the whole model rather than, as is more usual, as the inverse of a demand for inventories equation. The chapter applies Muth's (1961) rational expectations approach to price formation in primary commodity markets. This approach implies that primary prices respond not only to the current supply-demand balance but also to anticipated future supply-demand imbalances and the rate of interest. These propositions are important for two reasons; first, forward-looking behaviour implies a degree of automatic price stabilization and second, a significant interest rate effect implies the existence of an important link between monetary policy in the developed world and the terms of trade between developing and industrial countries.

Gilbert and Palaskas relate price expectations to current and expected future quantity shocks such as good or bad harvests and the emergence of substitutes. This is a useful and practical approach because shocks to demand and supply are the very thing about which users and producers have most complete information and intuition. In estimating the resulting price equations for a range of six commodities – cocoa, coffee, copper, rubber, sugar and tin – the authors find it difficult to capture the effects of interest rates and inflation upon commodity prices (see also Sapsford, 1988) but discover evidence of significant effects stemming from current and expected future demand-supply imbalances. More specifically, their results confirm earlier evidence, Ghosh et al. (1987), that forward-looking behaviour was important in the copper market. However, they find no evidence of similar effects for the other five commodities analyzed. With the exception of copper, therefore, they conclude that the industry practice of assessing prices in relation to only the current demand-supply balance is not misleading. In interpreting these findings Gilbert and Palaskas note that over their study period copper was the only one of the commodities studied which was *not* subject to any international intervention. Thus indirectly their results add further weight to the points made by Maddala in the preceding chapter. The apparent absence of interest rate effects on commodity prices, raises serious doubts about models of North-South interaction of the sort in which interest rates link industrial countries' monetary policies to developing countries' terms of trade (see, for example, Currie and Vines, 1988).

In the final chapter in Part I, Pravin Trivedi (Indiana University) investigates the roles of commodity stocks and rational expectations in the determination of the prices of perennial crops. Similarly to Gilbert and Palaskas he asks whether a model for perennials benefits from the explicit inclusion of forward-looking variables in the price equation. Trivedi's model allows future dated expectational variables to affect current commodity stocks and prices. In a significant innovation, however, Trivedi argues that agents' responses to certain variables may vary through time. He suggests that given their ignorance about the true state of the world agents are obliged to make as much sense as they can out of the available data, which are both dated and inaccurate. If these data appear very variable or inconsistent they are discounted, while if they are clear and support existing views they are acted upon strongly. Trivedi also argues that in making stock-holding decisions the incentives to over or under-predict demand are asymmetric and thus that responses to positive and negative perceived shocks may differ.

Trivedi's empirical results suggest strongly that such asymmetries and time-variations exist in the markets for tea and cocoa. Given the difficulties of estimating and forecasting in the context of time-varying models, Trivedi doubts the advantages of estimating and using an explicitly forward-looking price equation relative to the more standard market clearing approach in which forward-looking variables appear only in the stock demand equation. The latter approach, if appropriate, has the advantage of being more straightforward to implement for both policy and forecasting purposes. Taken together Gilbert and Palaskas and Trivedi provide only relatively weak evidence of the practical importance of forward-looking variables in price formation, but clear evidence of the complexity of the relationship if they are important.

4   Sectoral studies: food, materials and energy

Part II of the book comprises three chapters on the determination of the prices of particular primary commodities. In Chapter 5, Richard Just (University of Maryland) discusses the modelling of the interactive effects of alternative sets of policies on agricultural commodity prices, while Chapters 6 and 7 explore price determination in the markets for aluminium and oil respectively.

Richard Just's paper investigates a range of methodological issues which arise in modelling agricultural prices. He discusses the various policies that affect prices in the market for agricultural commodities, and proposes a number of general principles to be followed in econometric investigations of agricultural prices. As Maddala argued, modelling the impact of policy on primary prices is complex in sectors such as agriculture; their heavy government intervention, frequent changes in policy regimes, significant international trade, substantial storage activity, competitive markets for productive assets, and concentrated world markets all raise substantial difficulties for the application of standard econometric techniques. Just emphasizes that given the paucity of observations relative to the number of phenomena to be modelled, structural models are to be much preferred to *ad hoc* or flexible specifications for modelling policies of the price or production limit variety. He argues that economists' ability to identify the effects of each set of policies has progressively increased as a result of the commodity and macroeconomic instability that has occurred since the early 1970s; thus provided that sufficient structure is imposed on the data much more informative models of agricultural price formation are now both more feasible and necessary than heretofore.

Just proposes a number of principles for incorporating the various policy forces into agricultural commodity models. He makes two main arguments. First, increased volatility in the agricultural economy calls for the imposition of a considerable amount of *a priori* structure on models in order to capture the global properties of important relationships, and second, that this increased volatility has revealed a number of important international, intersectoral and macroeconomic linkages which, in turn, necessitate a broadening scope of agricultural modelling. In respect of the first of these two messages, it is important to test any *a priori* structure imposed, since quite clearly incorrect structure is not helpful. Other important rules to emerge in this chapter include the necessity of evaluating the model's out-of-sample predictive performance and the need to consider fully the various macroeconomic influences on agricultural commodity prices.

While Just does not address any policy issues directly, he provides a timely reminder of the need to marshall information effectively to answer the question at hand. For some forecasting purposes flexible and agnostic methods are appropriate, but for policy analysis interest usually focusses on particular parameters of behaviour. In order to bring small amounts of data to bear on estimating parameters, economic theory is indispensable.

In Chapter 6 Anthony Bird (Anthony Bird Associates), an aluminium industry consultant, describes a consultant's approach to commodity price forecasting and compares it with the methods adopted in academic enquiries. Bird characterizes the practitioner's approach as *knowledge-intensive* in contrast to what he terms the *logic-intensive* approach commonly adopted by academics. He notes that, while sophisticated techniques are often applied to low frequency and sometimes poorly defined data, consultants in contrast typically use simple techniques on up-to-date, confidential and extensive data. He also argues that one of the main jobs of the commodity market consultant is to check whether producers' expectations are rational and consistent, in contrast to econometricians who typically assume that they are.

To forecast aluminium prices Bird first derives estimates of the costs of production of every aluminium smelter in the world. This is done on the basis of public information about labour costs, the nature of the smelter's contracts with electricity and alumina suppliers (which often relate input prices to the price of the output) and its technical efficiency (which is mainly a function of age). From this information Bird derives a pseudo-supply curve for aluminium – 'pseudo' because of the dependency of input prices on the output price. He notes that exchange rate changes can affect the pseudo-supply curve and hence the final price strongly: because most inputs are priced in local currency, real exchange rates changes can affect both the relative costs of different producers and potentially the absolute costs of marginal producers. Bird's basic argument is that aluminium prices must eventually fall into line with production cost. However, the relevant concept of cost – variable or total cost – changes with the degree of excess capacity in the industry, with total costs being relevant only when pressure on capacity means that new plant is required. Bird recognizes the difficulties of attempting to predict the timing of the convergence of prices to costs, but he argues that although there can be significant periods of exceptionally high or low mark-ups, the basic fact of convergence is inevitable.

Bird's analysis highlights two particular policy issues. First, the eventual convergence of price to cost provides a medium-term peg for price prediction. The models of Part I stress shorter-term phenomena, but are perfectly compatible with the existence of such a peg. For aluminium the long-run supply curve is roughly horizontal over practical ranges of variation, so price is approximately constant in real terms, but this is not a necessary feature of Bird's approach. However, if the supply curve were rising, forecasting the level of demand would be a more important component of price prediction than Bird requires. Second, the use of firm-specific cost data allows a far wider range of exchange rate effects than most primaries models admit.

The difference between Bird's approach and that adopted by Gilbert and Palaskas and Trivedi is one of emphasis. In discussion it was widely agreed that commodity economists should ideally combine information-intensive medium-term models like Bird's with high-frequency dynamic models of the sort explored in Part I. To this end Bird offered to make his historical cost series available to academic researchers.

Chapter 7, by Marian Radetzki (Institute for International Economic Studies, Stockholm), is concerned with long-run price formation in the market for oil. Radetzki first notes that the trend behaviour of the *real* price of oil does not differ in any important respect from that of other commodities. In particular, he shows that over the period 1900 to 1972, the movement of oil prices was not strikingly different from that of either metals and minerals or agricultural commodities. He then argues that the simple and widely discussed Hotelling (1931) rule, according to which the value of the royalty on an exhaustible resource will increase in line with interest rates is an inappropriate model for making oil price predictions. The price of extracted oil is not a royalty, and the rule ignores the roles of unanticipated discoveries and technical progress.

Radetzki next considers four possible influences on oil prices: (a) exhaustibility, (b) monopolistic forces, (c) inter-fuel substitution and (d) technological shocks (in the form of either a moratorium on nuclear power provision or a severe restriction on carbondioxide emissions). He argues that, during the present century price formation in oil has not been perceptibly influenced by exhaustion and that neither is it likely to be over the next two to three decades. On the other hand the inelastic demand for oil, coupled with the geographical concentration of reserves, does provide scope for monopolistic manipulations, even in the long run. Radetzki argues that OPEC has been and *still is* remarkably successful in maintaining oil prices. Marginal costs outside the Middle East are perhaps $18 a barrel in the long run, while those inside this area are only of the order of $1. These values define the bounds of discretion between which OPEC might potentially influence oil prices. Even at the low prices of 1988, it is plain that by cutting output and curtailing the development of new capacity, OPEC has maintained prices well above competitive levels. Although these features make oil unusual it is argued that oil is not unique in this regard since other commodities (including cobalt, niobium, platinum and tin) possess somewhat similar characteristics.

The price of oil – like that of any commodity – will tend to be depressed by the emergence of substitutes and/or the reduction of demand. Radetzki suggests that commercial and technological breakthroughs in respect of natural gas may accelerate the substitution of gas for oil, dampening oil price rises and diluting OPEC's monopolistic power. Similarly, he argues that a nuclear moratorium, the discovery of a new transportation technology, or a global reduction in fossil fuel use prompted by the greenhouse effect would all have a far greater effect on oil prices than would OPEC's behaviour. In view of oil's extraordinary weight in world trade and significance to the world economy, the repercussions of such shocks in the oil market would be much greater than the consequences of similar shocks affecting other primary commodities.

5   Commodity stabilization schemes

Considerable ingenuity has been exercised over many years in the construction and implementation of schemes to stabilize the earnings of primary commodity producers in the face of highly volatile commodity prices. As noted in Section 1 above, many middle to low income countries depend on commodity exports as their main source of foreign exchange and development funds. For these countries fluctuations in commodity earnings pose a variety of threats to the economy, including a cycle of boom and austerity (not least in public expenditure), the disruption of investment and development plans, fluctuations in the distribution of income, and periodic debt-servicing crises. Many of these problems arise from the failure of agents and governments to recognize permanent price changes, and particularly from the formation of over-optimistic expectations in the price boom; in this sense commodity price fluctuations are not the direct cause of the ensuing economic difficulties. However, until economists can be much more accurate in their identification of trends and shifts in commodity prices it is difficult to deny that effective stabilization would ease the problems of economic management in developing countries. Part III of this book addresses the problems of earnings stabilization both in theory and in practice.

Andrew Hughes Hallett (University of Newcastle and CEPR) and Prathrap Ramanujam (University of Glasgow) compare futures markets with price stabilization schemes as means of export earnings stabilization. They relax many of the statistical restrictions which usually characterize such contrasts and consequently produce very much more complex criteria for choosing between schemes. In particular they allow the statistical distributions of prices and quantities to be both skewed and/or leptokurtic. Skewness is an important feature of price distributions, because of the commonly observed patterns of sharp peaks followed by long flat troughs.

Despite the algebraic complexity Hughes Hallett and Ramanujam derive applicable rules for choosing between alternative schemes. They conclude that under no circumstances can either stabilization or futures markets be guaranteed to dominate the other. Rather it is necessary to consider each case separately. The higher moments of the price and quantity distributions are important in this context, as are the correlation between price and quantity and the price elasticity of demand for the commodity in question. In simple symmetric models they demonstrate that where the correlation between price and quantity is positive, or demand is elastic, hedging in futures markets reduces the variance of price by more than price stabilization does.

The paper takes the objective of variance reduction as given, and thus does not conduct a full welfare analysis of the two stabilization schemes. However it shows how trade-offs between the mean and variance in earnings can be handled, and also demonstrates, using the distributions of world prices and quantities, that significant variance reductions are possible. Indeed the results suggest that while hedging is preferable to price stabilization for jute and cocoa and vice versa for coffee and copper, the difference between policies is much less than the differences between some policy and no policy. That is, doing something seems more important than what (out of the two options) you do.

Futures markets are explored in a different context in Chapter 9 by Paul Kofman, Jean-Marie Viaene and Casper de Vries (Erasmus University, Rotterdam). These authors clarify the relationship between primary commodity prices on the one hand, and exchange rate volatility on the other. In order to achieve this, they construct a model with two countries, two periods, and three agents – a home commodity producer, a foreign consumer and a currency speculator. They solve this in a general equilibrium framework to obtain explicit solutions for market clearing prices after allowing for the effects of exchange rate volatility in both spot and futures prices. Although primary commodities are produced domestically, their prices are typically denominated in foreign currency (most commonly the US $), with the consequence that primary producers face *both* price and exchange rate uncertainties. The authors argue that such double risks are a frequent problem in the real world and that for countries heavily dependent on a few primary commodities, general equilibrium interactions between prices and exchange rates are important. Their analysis shows for the first time how general equilibrium considerations can be taken into account, in the integration of the commodity and the foreign exchange markets.

The chapter explores a number of different scenarios, one of the most interesting of which is a decrease in the (exogenous) volatility of the exchange rate. The authors find that once general equilibrium effects are taken into account, decreased exchange rate volatility exerts an influence upon the levels of both prices and output. However, they find that neither effect can be signed *a priori*, although simulations suggest that output will rise, because a rise in the forward exchange rate offsets a potential fall in the futures price of the commodity.

While much of the previous literature on the welfare implications of futures markets has worked in isolation from the international trade context, this chapter is particularly welcome because it sheds light on the role and potential significance of a well-functioning forward exchange market for countries relying to a significant extent on primary commodity production.

In the final chapter, Roland Herrmann, (Institute of World Economics, Kiel), Kees Burger and Hidde Smit (Free University, Amsterdam) provide a detailed quantitative evaluation of the coffee export quota agreement and the natural rubber buffer stock scheme, which it contrasts as means of stabilizing developing countries' foreign exchange receipts with the IMF's Compensatory Financing Facility (CFF) and the EEC's STABEX scheme. Although it is well known from theoretical arguments that compensatory financing schemes are superior to buffer stock or export quota policies, the authors argue strongly that in assessing their relative merits schemes must be evaluated on the basis of their *actual* performance rather than their theoretical properties. The findings of this chapter challenge some widely held views on commodity stabilization. For instance, the analysis suggests that in practice, the coffee agreement is little more than a price support scheme and that, while the rubber scheme did produce a degree of price stabilization, this was more as a result of commodity-specific conditions than of the general virtues of intervention.

Herrmann, Burger and Smit also conclude that the official compensatory financing schemes have failed to stabilize foreign exchange receipts significantly, but have instead served primarily as a means of income transfer to certain arbitrarily favoured developing countries. They find some evidence to suggest that STABEX had been marginally stabilizing in respect of developing countries' export earnings on average, while the IMF's CFF scheme appeared to be slightly destabilizing. Viewed as a transfer mechanism, the authors argue that STABEX may be slightly more attractive than the CFF since it does not impose any conditionality on the use of the funds and contains a rather larger grant element.

The failure of such schemes stems partly from the details of their administration, e.g. the operational difficulties of identifying revenue shortfalls and the time delays on disbursements, but also from their concessionary rates of interest. The latter encourage countries to delay repayments – that is to treat the schemes more like medium-term funds than emergency borrowing – so that they often have no scope for increased borrowing when it is necessary. Finally, it is plausible that STABEX, and even to some extent CFF, divert funds from alternative aid or stabilization schemes. Thus their ineffectiveness is a serious policy issue. That said, however, it must be recognized that particular countries have gained significantly from their existence.

6 Conclusions

Commodity prices are one of the most important determinants of world economic performance. They influence the stability of developing countries' incomes, industrial countries' inflation, and world investment and growth. They also figure prominently in private sector business decisions: producing, consuming and trading firms all have much to gain from fully understanding commodity markets. Despite the importance of commodity prices, however, economists still have a poor record in explaining, forecasting or compensating for them. This volume contains a series of papers illustrating the latest thinking on the modelling and policy aspects of commodity markets.

Perhaps the most important message of the volume is the need to extend the information set that economists use in explaining commodity prices. The role of expectations about future shocks must be recognized; government policy must be modelled explicitly, particularly where it induces market disequilibrium; the effects of macroeconomic shocks on commodity prices must be allowed for; firm or plant-specific cost data provide a firm underpinning for price predictions; the technology of user industries must be examined, as must market structure; unrealistic assumptions about price distributions must be avoided; general equilibrium interactions must be factored in, and the implementation as well as the theory of policy must be considered. All of these extensions to current practice are potentially important, and the remaining challenge is to discover which are crucial to answering which questions. While it is desirable to tackle the extensions more than one at a time, no practical model can encompass them all, so approaches to commodity modelling will continue to differ according to the issues under investigation. What this conference and volume have shown, however, is that practitioners and observers have much to offer each other both within and between groups.

At the policy level a number of lessons have emerged. First, the relationship between commodity prices is complex and difficult to identify. The papers in Part I show the empirical difficulties, and Radetzki discusses some of the economic problems. This conclusion suggests that macroeconomic transmission is more subtle than global modellers frequently assume. Second, there is scope for earnings stabilization policies, although in this volume we have not proved that they are desirable. Policies must, however, pay regard to the distribution of prices to be stabilized and to the details of their administration. Simplistic theoretical models are not the basis on which to cure economic problems. Third, economists and policy-makers must exercise extreme caution in using current estimates of economic parameters. Both Maddala and Just show that estimates based on incorrect models can be highly misleading.

NOTES

1 Chu and Morrison (1982, p. 119), for example, calculate that the variance of the rate of change of commodity prices was about nine times greater during 1971–82 than during the period 1958–71.

2 See, for example, Tony Bird's offer to make his data available for academic research, p. 151 below.

REFERENCES

Artis, M. J., (1987) 'How Accurate is the World Economic Outlook? A Post Mortem on Short-term Forecasting at the International Monetary Fund', December, The World Economic Outlook Staff Studies.

Beckerman, W. and T. Jenkinson (1986) 'What Stopped the Inflation? Unemployment or Commodity Prices?', *Economic Journal* **96**, 39–54.

Chu, K. Y. and T. K. Morrison (1982) 'The 1981–82 Recession and Non-Oil Primary Commodity Prices', *IMF Staff Papers* **31**, 93–140.

Currie, D. and Vines, D. (eds) (1988) *Macroeconomic Interactions between North and South*, Cambridge: Cambridge University Press.

Ghosh, S., C. L. Gilbert and A. J. Hughes Hallett (1987) *Stabilizing Speculative Commodity Markets*, Oxford: Oxford University Press.

Gilbert, C. L. (1989) 'The Impact of Exchange Rates and Developing Country Debts on Commodity Prices', *Economic Journal* **99**, 773–84.

Hotelling, H. (1931) 'Economics of Exhaustible Resources', *Journal of Political Economy* **39**, 139–75.

Klein, L. R. (1980) 'Some Economic Scenarios for the 1980's', *Scandinavian Journal of Economics* **83**, 479–96.

Lucas, R. E. Jr (1976) 'Econometric Policy Evaluation: A Critique' in K. Brunner and A. H. Meltzer (eds), *The Phillips Curve of Labour Markets, Carnegie-Rochester Conference on Public Policy* **1**, 19–46, Supplement to *Journal of Monetary Economics*, Amsterdam: North Holland.

Muth, J. (1961) 'Rational Expectations and the Theory of Price Movements', *Econometrica* **29**, 315–35.

Ridler, D. and C. A. Yandle (1972) 'A Simplified Method of Analysing the Effects of Exchange Rate Changes on Exports of a Primary Commodity', *IMF Staff Papers* **19**, 669–78.

Sapsford, D. (1988) 'Internationally Traded Primary Commodities: A Model of Price Determination', *Applied Economics* **20**, 439–52.

I   Econometric Analyses

2 Estimation of Dynamic Disequilibrium Models with Rational Expectations: the Case of Commodity Markets

G. S. MADDALA*

> A commodity is something that hurts when you drop it on your big toe, or smells bad if you leave it out in the sun too long.
> *Barron's*, 27 June 1983

The aims of this paper are:

(1) to outline some methods of incorporating rational expectations into disequilibrium models;
(2) to discuss the applicability of these methods in the modelling of commodities characterized by market interventions like price supports and buffer stocks; and
(3) to review the usefulness of other sources of price expectations like survey data, futures prices and Bayesian vector autoregressions, if the methods suggested here cannot be implemented.

1 Sources of disequilibrium

The methodology used for incorporating rational expectations into disequilibrium models depends on the particular sources of disequilibrium. In commodity modelling the sources are the different methods used for price stabilization: McNicol (1978, p. 25), for instance, lists the following types of market intervention.

(1) Purchase alone, with the material held in storage indefinitely or disposed of in a way that does not affect market price.
(2) Purchases coupled with restrictions on supply.
(3) Purchases and sales without any restriction on supply.
(4) Restrictions on supply alone.
(5) Purchases and sales coupled with restrictions on supply.

The US agricultural programs provide examples of the first two. A support price program is one of purchase alone. Soil bank and acreage

21

control come under category (2) since they limit the output. Item (3) on the list is a pure buffer stock program. This involves no use at all of restriction on supply. Since these programs introduce limits on prices and/or quantities, estimation of the models would, in general, involve the use of limited dependent variable models.

If currently there is governmental intervention in a market, the policy questions asked are what the prices and quantities would be if the intervention were to be stopped. To answer the question, when one is estimating the model, the limits imposed on prices and quantities have to be taken into account in the estimation procedure.

On the other hand, if currently there is no governmental intervention, and the policy question is what the prices and quantities would be if some intervention were to take place, the estimation procedure would not involve the use of limited dependent varibles. But at the simulation stage, if the model involves any expectational variables, one has to derive the relevant expressions for these, taking into account the limits on prices and quantities imposed by the government intervention.

2   Rational expectations in limited dependent variables models

The incorporation of (Muthian) rational expectations in limited dependent variable models was first suggested in Chanda and Maddala (1983).[1] This model was later applied in Shonkwiler and Maddala (1985) to analyse the price support program in the US corn market for the period 1952 to 1981. Since the model highlights some problems that are likely to be encountered in incorporating rational expectations in disequilibrium models, we will review the model here and then consider other types of intervention in the commodity markets. The model for price support programs is as follows:

$$S_t = a_1 P_t^* + a_2 W_t + e_{1t} \quad \text{supply function}$$
$$D_t = b_1 P_t + b_2 X_t + e_{2t} \quad \text{demand function} \tag{1}$$

P_t, S_t and D_t represent market price, quantity supplied and quantity demanded, respectively. W_t and X_t represent supply and demand shifters, and P_t^* represents the rational expection of product price at the time production decisions are made. The error terms e_{1t} and e_{2t} are assumed to be IN(0, σ_1^2) and IN(0, σ_2^2), respectively.

Under a price support program, let P_t^s denote the exogenously determined price support announced at the time production decisions are made. We will assume that producers realize that the expected price must equal or exceed the support price, i.e., $P_t^* \geq P_t^s$.

If the market clearing price P_t is not less than the support price P_t^s, then we have an equilibrium model and if Q_t is the quantity transacted, we have $Q_t = D_t = S_t$. To derive the rational expectation of P_t^* in this model, we observe that

$$P_t^* = E(P_t | \text{Information at } t - 1)$$

In equations (1) equating D_t to S_t we get

$$a_1 P_t^* + a_2 W_t + e_{1t} = b_1 P_t + b_2 X_t + e_{2t} \tag{2}$$

Taking expectations of both sides we get $a_1 P_t^* + a_2 W_t^* = b_1 P_t^* + b_2 X_t^*$ where W_t^* and X_t^* represent expectations of the supply and demand shifters at the time production decisions are made. Solving for P_t^* we get

$$P_t^* = (a_1 - b_1)^{-1}(b_2 X_t^* - a_2 W_t^*) \tag{3}$$

This is the expression we would use for P_t^* if there were no price support program. The estimation of the model proceeds by substituting this expression in equations (1) and estimating the model jointly with the appropriate equations determining W_t^* and X_t^*, which are usually obtained from autoregressive specifications for W_t and X_t: see Wallis (1980) and Pesaran (1987).

Under a price support program, the producers get the support price P_t^s if the price support is effective, and they get the market equilibrium price if it is over P_t^s. Let us initially assume that W_t and X_t are known at the time production decisions are made. If π_t is the probability that the market equilibrium price is above P_t^s, then using the expression for P_t from (2) we get

$$\pi_t = \text{Prob}\left[\frac{1}{b_1}(a_1 P_t^* + a_2 W_t - b_2 X_t + e_{1t} - e_{2t}) > P_t^s\right] \tag{4}$$

and since P_t^* itself depends on π_t, one cannot get an explicit expression for P_t^*. If P_{1t}^* is the rational expectation of P_t conditional on the assumption that the market price would be greater than P_t^s, then P_t^* is given by

$$P_t^* = \pi_t P_{1t}^* + (1 - \pi_t) P_t^s \tag{5}$$

To obtain P_{1t}^* we have to take expectations of both sides in equation (2) but the expectation of the error term would not be zero since the expectation is conditional on $P_t > P_t^s$. This conditional expectation, in turn, will involve P_t^*. To see this, note that from (4) we have

$$\pi_t = \text{Prob}\left[\frac{e_{1t} - e_{2t}}{b_1} > \frac{b_1 P_t^s - a_1 P_t^* - a_2 W_t + b_2 X_t}{b_1}\right]$$

$$= 1 - \Phi(C_t) \tag{6}$$

where

$$C_t = \frac{1}{b_1 \sigma} (b_1 P_t^s - a_1 P_t^* - a_2 W_t + b_2 X_t)$$

$$\sigma^2 = \text{Var} \left(\frac{e_{1t} - e_{2t}}{b_1} \right) \tag{7}$$

and we use $\phi(\cdot)$ and $\Phi(\cdot)$ to denote, respectively, the density function and distribution function of the standard normal. Also, $P_{1t}^* = E(P_t | P_t > P_t^s)$. From (2) we have

$$P_t = \frac{1}{b_1} [a_1 P_t^* + a_2 W_t - b_2 X_t + e_{1t} - e_{2t}] \tag{8}$$

When we take expectations conditional on $P_t > P_t^s$, note that since $P_t > P_t^s$ implies $\pi_t = 1$, we have from (5)

$$E(P_t^* | P_t > P_t^s) = P_{1t}^*$$

The preceding analysis is appropriate if X_t and W_t are known at the time production decisions are made. If they are not known, let X_t^* and W_t^* be their expectations. Write

$$W_t = W_t^* + u_{1t}$$
$$X_t = X_t^* + u_{2t}$$

Then equation (4) has to be changed to:

$$\pi_t = \text{Prob} \left[\frac{1}{b_1} (a_1 P_t^* + a_2 W_t^* - b_2 X_t^* + e_{1t} - e_{2t} \right.$$

$$\left. + a_2 u_{1t} - b_2 u_{2t} > P_t^s \right]$$

Thus, equation (7) has to be changed to[2]

$$C_t = \frac{1}{b_1 \sigma} (b_1 P_t^s - a_1 P_t^* - a_2 W_t^* + b_2 X_t^*)$$

$$\sigma^2 = \text{Var} \left(\frac{e_{1t} - e_{2t} + a_2 u_{1t} - b_2 u_{2t}}{b_1} \right) \tag{7'}$$

With this change, the other expressions are the same as before. For the purpose of estimation, we have to add prediction equations for W_t and X_t. One particular specification is a simple autoregression:

$$W_t = \gamma_1 W_{t-1} + u_{1t}$$
$$X_t = \gamma_2 X_{t-1} + u_{2t}$$

Now, taking expectations throughout in equation (8), conditional on $P_t > P_t^s$, we get

$$P_{1t}^* = \frac{1}{b_1}(a_1 P_{1t}^* + a_2 W_t^* - b_2 X_t^*) + \sigma \frac{\phi(C_t)}{1 - \Phi(C_t)} \qquad (9)$$

The solution of equations (5), (6), (7') and (9) gives P_t^*. As can be readily seen one cannot get an explicit or even an implicit expression for P_t^*. One feasible alternative is to argue that equations (5), (6), (7') and (9) imply that

$$
\begin{aligned}
P_t^* &= f(W_t^*, X_t^*, P_t^s) \quad \text{if} \quad P_t > P_t^s \\
&= P_t^s \qquad\qquad\quad \text{otherwise}
\end{aligned}
\qquad (10)
$$

where $f(W_t^*, X_t^*, P_t^s)$ is a non-linear function of X_t^*, W_t^* and P_t^s. In practice, we would take this to be a quadratic function in these variables and estimate equation (10) by the Tobit method. The predicted value of P_t^* from this equation could serve as an initial value in any iterative estimation of the model.

For estimation purposes we have to note that the model is like a switching regression model with endogenous switching. Let us partition the sample observations into two sets:

ψ_1: the set of observations for which the market price is equal to or above the support price

ψ_2: the set of observations for which the market price is less than the support price

For the first set we have an equilibrium model with Q_t, P_t as the endogenous variables. For the second set we have a disequilibrium model with D_t, S_t as the endogenous variables (with P_t^s substituted for both P_t and P_t^* in equations (1)).

If $f_1(Q_t, P_t)$ and $f_2(D_t, S_t)$ are the joint densities of the endogenous variables in the two regimes, respectively, the likelihood function is given by

$$L = \prod_{\psi_1} b_1 f_1(Q_t, P_t) \cdot \prod_{\psi_2} f_2(D_t, S_t) \qquad (11)$$

The Jacobians of transformation are b_1 and 1, respectively, in the two regimes. Note that because we have an endogenous switching model, the probabilities $\pi_t = \text{Prob}(P_t > P_t^s)$ do not occur in the likelihood function as discussed in Maddala and Nelson (1974) and Maddala (1983). In equation (11), we substitute P_t^s for P_t and P_t^* in $f_2(D_t, S_t)$. As for $f_1(Q_t, P_t)$ the question is what value of P_t^* we should substitute. In Shonkwiler and Maddala (1985) the estimation was done by the substitution of P_t^* from equation (3), that is, from the equilibrium model. In a way this is a perfect foresight model, the foresight referring to whether the price supports are going to be effective or not.

A correct procedure would be to substitute the expression (9) for P_{1t}^* in place of P_t^* in $f_1(Q_t, P_t)$. This is because P_{1t}^* is the appropriate expression for the rational expectation of P_t in this regime. The maximum likelihood estimation would proceed with the initial estimation of equation (10) by the Tobit method and then using an iterative procedure as in Fair and Taylor (1983). Equation (9) can be seen to involve a Heckman-type correction. Note, however, that it involves C_t and from equation (7') we note that C_t involves P_t^*, which, in turn, involves P_{1t}^* through equation (5). Thus, an iterative solution is quite intricate. On the other hand, if we use P_t^* obtained from the Tobit estimation of equation (10) and use it in the expression for C_t, then the iterative solution becomes much simpler.

3   An extension to dynamic models

The preceding model can be extended to include lagged variables as well. In the literature on disequilibrium models, excess demand and excess supply from the previous time period are used as explanatory variables in the equation for the current demand and supply, respectively, to account for what is known as spill-over effects. See Laffont and Monfort (1979), Dagenais (1980) and Orsi (1982). In our model there will be spill-over effect as well, except that it is only the supply function that is affected. Note that there is no excess demand in any time period. There is only excess supply because of the price support program. The excess supply can be measured by the amount of governmental purchases or the amount of farmers' storage that is subsidized. This acts as a depressant on the current supply because of the indirect expected effect on the future support price. Unlike the case of the dynamic disequilibrium models discussed by the others, we do have information on the amount of excess supply as well as information on the sample separation. The only change, therefore, that we need to make in the model discussed here is that in the first equation in (1), we need to add an additional explanatory variable $(S_{t-1} - D_{t-1})$ which is the excess supply from the previous period.

There are two types of model one can consider: one with exogenously fixed price supports and the other with price supports adjusting with a lag to the excess supply in the previous period. The first model would be formulated as follows

$$S_t = a_1 P_t^* + a_2 W_t + \lambda(S_{t-1} - D_{t-1}) + e_{1t}$$
$$D_t = b_1 P_t + b_2 X_t + e_{2t} \tag{12}$$

There is no excess demand to spillover in the demand function. In the supply function note that the lagged excess supply $S_{t-1} - D_{t-1}$ is observed.

The second model with price supports adjusting with excess supply would consist of equations (1) and the following equation

$$P_t^s = P_{t-1}^s + \lambda(S_{t-1} - D_{t-1}) + e_{3t} \tag{13}$$

In this case the price support at time t is not exogenously announced at time $t - 1$. The producers would have to predict it from the last period's data. If there is a mechanical rule for the adjustment of price supports then equation (13) would not have an error term and λ would be known. In this case P_t^s is exogenously given. If this is not the case, equation (4) needs to be adjusted with the expression for P_t^s from (13) substituted. In equation (5) we substitute the expectation of P_t^s from (13) for P_t^s. Since the details involve just more algebraic expressions and can be worked out, they will be omitted here.

4   Policy implications

One question that might be asked is: is all this complicated estimation procedure worth the effort? If one is interested in simulating the effects of the removal of (or change in) the price support program, one needs to have a reliable set of estimates of the parameters in the model. The estimates of the parameters in model (1) ignoring price supports are not the right ones to use. In practice, how much difference does it make? The results in Shonkwiler and Maddala (1985) suggest that incorporating the price supports and estimating the model (under the restrictive perfect foresight assumption) produces higher estimates (by about 50%) for the coefficient of the expected price P_t^* in the supply function.[3] See the results in Table 2.1. No simulations were, however, attempted to study the effects of the removal of price supports and how much difference this estimation makes in this case. What was done was to test some of the theories (notably, that of Turnovsky, 1983) regarding the relationship between futures price, current spot price and expected spot price. The expected price P_t^* derived from the model was used for this purpose.

Turnovsky employs a rational expectations framework to analyse futures markets for storable commodities. He specifies the optimal behaviour of risk-averse producers and speculators to derive spot and futures prices. For equilibrium in the futures market, the demand and supply of futures contracts by both producers and speculators must be equal. This leads to the futures price determination equation of the form

The calculated rational expectation

$$Q_t = -10.01 + 1.163 P_t^* + 0.5159 \hat{W}_t$$
$$\quad (2.61) \quad (0.156) \quad (0.041)$$

$R^2 = 0.949$ $DW = 1.97$

Futures price as the expectation

$$Q_t = -5.552 + 0.7930 FP_t + 0.5361 \hat{W}_t$$
$$\quad (2.71) \quad (0.130) \quad (0.046)$$

$R^2 = 0.935$ $DW = 1.72$

The Tobit approximation to the expectation

$$Q_t = -8.294 + 0.8158 P_t^* + 0.4576 \hat{W}_t$$
$$\quad (3.56) \quad (0.199) \quad (0.055)$$

$R^2 = 0.905$ $DW = 1.39$

Table 2.1 Single equation least squares comparisons of the supply equation
(Figures in parentheses are asymptotic standard errors)

$$FP_{t+1} = b_1 P_t + b_2 P_{t+1}^*$$

where P_t is the current spot price, and P_{t+1}^* is the expected spot price. Turnovsky argues that, in general, $b_1 + b_2 < 1$. His analysis, however, does not consider the existence of price supports. In Maddala and Shonkwiler (1985) this equation was estimated with the expected spot price derived from the model with price supports and rational expectations. The resulting estimates gave $b_1 = 0.872$, $b_2 = 0.212$ and $b_1 + b_2 = 1.084$ with a standard error of 0.023. Thus, $b_1 + b_2$ was significantly greater than 1, possibly because of price supports (see, however, footnote 3 for the limitations of the empirical analysis).

Mackinnon and Olewiler (1980) undertake a disequilibrium estimation of the demand for copper and find substantial changes in the parameter estimates when the disequilibrium model is used as compared with the OLS estimates. The disequilibrium in their model occurs from the US producers charging their customers a price lower than the free market LME price and rationing the supply. Mackinnon and Olewiler do not model the supply side of the market and do not incorporate rational expectations. The supply side is brought in indirectly by considering the US producer price as an endogenous variable (i.e., considering it in its reduced form). With this procedure it is difficult to incorporate rational expectations. No policy conclusions are drawn in the paper.

Ghosh, Gilbert and Hughes Hallett (1987, Chapter 4) construct a more extensive model of the world copper market and discuss a rational expectations model of the copper price, but within the context of an equilibrium model (Ghosh et al., p. 100). The 'two-price system' (US producer price being different from the LME price) is handled by adopting an area disaggregation (US and non-US). The production behaviour of the US mines which cater for a largely local market is different from that of non-US mines which produce for distant export markets. Unlike the other studies, there is a discussion of the policy implications of the incorporation of rational expectations in the model (Ghosh *et al.*, p. 345, 'Dynamic Policy Responses Under Rational Expectations'). Ghosh *et al.* study the effect of a buffer stock purchase on the market price and find a significantly weaker policy response in the rational expectations model than in the naive expectations model. This suggests that greater magnitudes of intervention are needed under rational expectations to achieve the same degree of price stability.

5 Buffer-stock models

In the previous sections, we talked of the price support program and the incorporation of rational expectations into models with price supports (or price floors). The buffer-stock program involves price floors and price ceilings. If the price were at, or below, the floor price, the buffer-stock manager would buy, subject to the availability of funds, until the price returned to the floor. At the ceiling price he would sell, subject to the availability of stock. Between the floor and ceiling price (called the reference prices) he would do nothing. In addition to the price limits, the buffer stock is usually limited in size and/or total borrowing of the buffer-stock manager.

The reference prices are usually set by political bargaining which may be only slightly influenced by informal forecasting. It makes sense to have some automatic adjustments in the reference prices, if the market prices are outside those limits for a long period and/or buffer stock purchases or sales are high. In the case of natural rubber, the International Rubber Agreement has provisions for lowering or raising the reference price by 5 percent if the average daily indicator market price is either below the lower intervention price or above the upper intervention price over the six months before the review. There is also a stock trigger. If buffer stock purchases or sales of 300,000 tons take place, the reference price is automatically adjusted down or up by 3 percent unless a special vote decrees otherwise (MacBean and Nguyen, 1987, p. 187).

The details of the buffer stock agreements are unusually complex. Anderson and Gilbert (1988) discuss in detail the case of tin. Gordon-Ashworth (1984) details the history of buffer-stock agreements for tin (pp. 116–20), natural rubber (pp. 198–200) and cocoa (pp. 227–30), and minor attempts and failures with several other commodities. Anderson and Gilbert (1988, pp. 31–4) also point out some problems of information, that the details of the operations of the buffer-stock manager were not known to the public. 'When the buffer-stock manager suspended operation and revealed his situation, it came as an almost universal surprise.'

Assuming that such informational problems do not exist, it is not difficult, in theory, to generalize the methods outlined in the previous sections for price control program, to the case of buffer-stock operations. In this respect, the case of natural rubber appears to be the most amenable to analysis. It does not have the complication of the buffer-stock manager operating in the futures market as in the case of tin. It does not have the problem of frequent breakdown as in the case of cocoa.

If P_t^f is the floor price (lower limit), P_t^c is the ceiling price (upper limit) and P_t the market price, then the price suppliers get will be P_t if the buffer-stock manager is inactive, P_t^f if he is buying and P_t^c if he is selling.

Let π_1 be the probability that $P_t < P_t^f$
and π_2 be the probability that $P_t > P_t^c$

Then, the rationally expected price will be

$$P^* = (1 - \pi_1 - \pi_2) P_{1t}^* + \pi_1 P_t^f + \pi_2 P_t^c \tag{14}$$

where P_{1t}^* is the rational expectation conditional on

$$P_t^f \le P_t \le P_t^c$$

This equation is analogous to equation (5). As before, the model in its simplest version, would contain a demand function, a supply function depending on the expected price P_t^*, with a specification of P_t^c and P_t^f. Functions depicting private stock demand the private stock supply could also be added.[4] The main complicating factor is the derivation of an expression for P_t^* in the supply functions.

Consider for simplicity the model in equations (1). We now have 3 regimes:

ψ_1: $P_t^f \le P_t \le P_t^c$: These are the equilibrium points and P_t and Q_t are endogenous.

ψ_2: $P_t > P_t^c$: In this case we substitute P_t^s for P_t and P_t^* in the demand and supply functions, respectively, and treat D_t and S_t as the endogenous variables.

ψ_3: $P_t < P_t^f$: In this case we substitute P_t^f for P_t and P_t^* and treat D_t and S_t as the endogenous variables.

The likelihood function corresponding to (11) is

$$L = \prod_{\psi_1} b_1 f_1(Q_t, P_t) \cdot \prod_{\psi_2} f_2(D_t, S_t) \cdot \prod_{\psi_3} f_3(D_t, S_t) \tag{15}$$

The derivation of expressions for π_{1t} and π_{2t} would be similar to (6), and the derivation of P_{1t}^* would be similar to equation (9). Since the extensions are straightforward, the details will be omitted. The expressions are given in Maddala (1983, p. 331). The dynamic models in Section 3 can also be extended to cover changes in reference prices as in the Rubber Agreement.

The preceding is the case of a pure buffer-stock program. Usually, these are also augmented by export quotas, production controls, etc. Needless to say, the analysis gets very complicated. Furthermore, where all these interventions exist and are changing every year, it is questionable how many observations we would have for estimation purposes and whether all the complicated estimation producers are worthwhile.

6   The usefulness of rational expectations in commodity models

The price support model discussed in Sections 2 and 3 and the buffer-stock models discussed in Section 5, suggest that it is not difficult, at least in theory, to incorporate rational expectations into models of disequilibrium. The results quoted in Section 4 suggest that in cases of disequilibrium, it makes a substantial difference to the parameter estimates of the models if disequilibrium is taken into account, and it also makes a substantial difference to policy conclusions if we incorporate rational expectations into the models (Ghosh *et al.*, 1987). All this is fine but one basic question is how justifiable is the assumption of the so-called 'rational' expectations:

$$P_t^* = E(P_t | I_{t-1})$$

on which all this analysis is based?

This condition of informational unbiasedness, implicit in the estimation of all the rational expectations models has recently been criticized by Stegman (1985) and others. It has been noted that the optimal forecast is not the conditional mean when the loss function is asymmetric. Survey data on expectations, such as the Livingston and Goldsmith-Nagan survey data, typically indicate that individuals hold biased expectations. This evidence has been typically taken to indicate irrationality or that survey data are somehow wrong or irrelevant. Ashley and McTaggert (1988) show that it is rational (in the sense of maximizing expected utility) to bias one's forecast towards zero whenever the distribution of forecast errors is non-degenerate, i.e., has positive variance. This variance might arise from an attempt to quantify the uncertainty in a description of the relevant part of the economy. Alternatively, it could arise from sampling variance in the estimated coefficients of an econometric model.

What this suggests is that where relevant survey forecasts of prices are available, it might be worthwhile to incorporate them in the econometric modelling of commodity markets rather than derive the 'rational' expectation, which anyhow depends on the particular model considered by the econometrician.[5] Unlike the Livingston data on expectations of inflation, where the individuals giving the forecasts are not directly affected by the forecast error, the price expectations of producers of commodities are the forecasts on which they actually make the supply decisions. Thus, the survey forecasts are directly relevant. The incorporation of survey forecasts simplifies greatly the estimation of disequilibrium models (with price supports, buffer stocks and other interventions in commodity markets). The methods outlined in Maddala (1983, pp. 326–34) and Quandt (1988, pp. 72–6) for models with controlled prices can be directly applied here since the price expectations from survey data are exogenous.

Another alternative to survey data on price expectations is information from the futures markets, and the question is how useful the futures prices are as proxies for price expectations. This is what we discuss next. Again, if futures prices can be shown to be useful, then we are back in the comfortable situation where price expectations can be treated as exogenous.

7   The usefulness of futures prices in commodity models

Peck (1985, pp. 55–64) reviews the evidence on the usefulness of futures prices as forecasts of future spot prices. The study by Leuthold and Hartman (1979) on hog prices compared futures prices with forecasts from a purposely simple recursive model of supply and demand for hogs and found that their simple model predicted subsequent prices consistently better than futures prices did. They report 125 percent and 141 percent rates of return from trading futures based on their naive forecasting model.

The case with storable commodities, however, is different. Here the futures prices have been found to perform better in forecasting subsequent spot prices. Tomek and Gray (1970) provide evidence on corn and soybeans. They compare the pricing of the new crop futures contracts before planting dates with their subsequent harvest prices. Their evidence shows no significant difference between the pre-planting and expiration quotation of the futures. Just and Rausser (1981) provide more general evidence that futures prices predict subsequent prices as well as the forecasts of several of the well-known forecast firms. Goss (1986) considers the predictive ability of futures prices for copper, zinc, tin and lead. For copper, tin and lead (but not zinc) he finds that futures prices are unbiased predictors of delivery date spot prices.

There are some other studies that argue the other way. Stein (1981, p. 231) states that 'Prior to four months to maturity, the futures price is a biased and worthless estimate of the price to maturity.' Maddala and Shonkwiler (1985) also find that the expected price derived from the disequilibrium model has better explanatory power (in the supply equation) than the futures price.[6] There is also some other evidence that futures prices are not good proxies for expected future cash prices in the presence of governmental programs (see Peck, 1985, p. 63).

Several theoretical arguments have been advanced why it may be unrealistic to assume that futures prices reflect all the available information in the market. See Bray (1981) and Grossman and Stiglitz (1980). The basic argument is that there is a free-rider problem which leads to an erosion of futures markets as a means for processing and disseminating information. If the prices are such that prices convey all information that informed traders collect, other traders can get the information free by just observing market prices. Hence, speculative markets can exist only if they are informationally inefficient.

Streit (1983) also presents some reasons why futures prices cannot be regarded as expected prices. His argument is that traders who establish positions in the futures market do so precisely because they consider the current price to be a wrong forecast of the price at maturity of a contract and, hence, of the future spot price (or the futures price at any earlier data at which they intend to close out). Similarly, those who are prepared to hold the opposite position must have expectations that diverge both from those implicit in the traded price and those held by the other side of the market. In this case, during the period of contract, trading at 'false' prices determined by divergent beliefs or expectations is the rule. Streit argues that the prices at which transactions take place before the maturity of the contract represent wrong forecasts of future market conditions to traders who make transactions at those prices. The implicit forecasts are acceptable only to those who refrain from trading at those prices. As far as changes in prices indicate changes in information, those who trade tend to disagree that the observable price changes reflect accurately the changes in information. From these observations, Streit concludes that the usual econometric approach of inferring from the aggregate performance of commodity futures markets how expectations are actually formed is basically invalidated. He suggests segmenting the futures market according to types of transactions and positions taken and analyzing segmented expectations (Streit, 1983, p. 8).

The major conclusion that emerges from the review of the empirical and theoretical literature on futures prices and price expectations is that futures prices are likely to be poor proxies for price expectations in commodity markets. This is particularly so in markets subject to interventions typically used for commodity price stabilization.

8   The inter-relatedness of commodity prices

One empirical fact that cannot be ignored in commodity market models is that the prices of largely unrelated raw commodities have a persistent tendency to move together. This puzzling fact has been confirmed and tested in a recent paper by Pindyck and Rotemberg (1988). They consider the monthly price changes for seven unrelated commodities: wheat, cotton, copper, gold, crude oil, lumber and cocoa, and use US average monthly cash prices for 1980–5. They show that this co-movement of prices is well in excess of anything that can be explained by the common effects of past, current or expected future values of macroeconomic variables such as inflation, industrial production, interest rates or exchange rates. The implication of this is that in the formation of price expectations, the movement of prices of even unrelated commodities should be take into account or a proxy like the CRB (Commodity Research Bureau) price index should be used.[7]

This suggests an alternative way of deriving expressions for expected prices, to be used in the modelling of commodity markets. This is to obtain the predicted values from a (Bayesian) vector autoregression that includes all commodity prices or at least the CRB index in addition to the price of the commodity considered.

9   Conclusions

One of the major elements of economic models of commodity prices is the supply response to producers' price expectations. Since producers' price expectations are unobservable, empirical analysis of commodity prices must rely on proxies for the expectational variables. Commonly used proxies include extrapolations of past price data, as in the adaptive expectations models, and information from futures prices.

An alternative route is to use rational expectations (model consistent expectations). The use of rational expectations in models of commodity prices, however, is complicated because of the presence of several governmental interventions in the commodity markets, such as price supports, export quotas and so on.

From the point of view of policy analysis, the important questions relate to an investigation of the effects on prices if the governmental interventions are scrapped or relaxed. It has been found that it makes a considerable difference to the estimated supply elasticities, if the model used incorporates the interventions and the consequent market disequilibrium into the modelling effort. Some empirical examples are cited in the paper to support this point.

The paper has suggested methods of incorporating rational expectations (model consistent expectations) into commodity models characterised by different kinds of interventions (Sections 2, 3 and 5). Where practicable, one should use these methods to derive the implied rational expectations of the price variables that determine the behaviour of the suppliers.

However, in many instances this may not be a feasible strategy because of the complexity of the market interventions and paucity of data. Furthermore, theoretical arguments have also been advanced to suggest that the Muthian type of expectations are not rational (in the sense of maximizing expected utility). In view of this, some alternative procedures for deriving expectations need to be investigated.

The paper discusses three such alternatives:

(1)   survey data,
(2)   futures prices, and
(3)   Bayesian vector autoregressions.

Survey data are likely to provide a potential source. The objections that have been raised in the econometric literature against the use of survey data from the Livingston, Goldsmith-Nagan and other surveys are based on the validity of the Muthian type of rationality, which is questionable. Thus, it is argued, that survey data on expectations will be useful, particularly so in the case of commodity markets where the agents responding to the survey are closely involved in the supply decisions.

After reviewing the empirical evidence and theoretical arguments, it was concluded that futures prices are likely to be poor proxies for price expectations. In any case, this is something that needs to be investigated on a commodity by commodity basis.

Finally, the excess co-movement of commodity prices suggests that Bayesian vector autoregressions are a useful method of generating values for price expectations.

NOTES

* I would like to thank Hashem Pesaran for pointing out an error in equation (7′) in the version presented at the CEPR conference.
1 Quandt (1988, pp. 145–7) discusses models with rational expectations under disequilibrium. The paper by Chanda and Maddala (1983) is discussed there but the corrections to the paper are not noted. Another unpublished paper by Chanda and Maddala on 'Estimation of Disequilibrium Models With Inventories Under Rational Expectations' is outlined on p. 146.

2 In the original version presented at the conference the terms u_{1t} and u_{2t} were missing from the expressions for π_t and σ^2. This error was pointed out by Hashem Pesaran.
3 The expression for P_{1t}^* used in that paper is not the correct one. The correct expression is given in equation (9) in this paper. A re-estimation of the model, making this correction, dropping the perfect foresight assumption and correcting equation (7'), produced broadly similar results. For instance, in Table 2.1, for the first equation the coefficient of P_t^* was 1.393 with a standard error 0.302 and the coefficient of W_t was 0.494 with a standard error 0.073. Thus, the price response is slightly higher. Also, the standard errors are higher as would be expected. Detailed results will be presented in a forthcoming paper.
4 MacBean and Nguyen (1987) Appendix H, pp. 392–4, consider a simple model consisting of these equations for their simulations. However, the supply function depends on lagged price, P_{t-1} not expected price P_t^*.
5 That is why some prefer to call the expectations 'model consistent' rather than 'rational' though there is a certain aura attached to the latter term (which increases the chances of the paper being published).
6 With the calculated expected price from the disequilibrium model, the estimation of the supply function gave $R^2 = 0.949$, $DW = 1.97$. With the futures price, the results were $R^2 = 0.935$, $DW = 1.72$. See Table 2.1. Note, however, the limitation mentioned in footnote 4.
7 In their model of the copper market, Ghosh et al. (1987) include an equation for the aluminum price.

REFERENCES

Anderson, R. W. and C. L. Gilbert (1988) 'Commodity Agreements and Commodity Markets: Lessons From Tin', *Economic Journal* **98**, 1–15.

Ashley, R. and D. McTaggert (1988) 'Rationally Biased Expectations', Department of Economics, Virginia Polytechnic Institute and State University, June.

Bray, M. (1981) 'Futures Trading, Rational Expectations, and the Efficient Markets Hypothesis', *Econometrica* **49**, 575–96.

Chanda, A. K. and G. S. Maddala (1983) 'Methods of Estimation for Models of Markets With Bounded Price Variation Under Rational Expectations', *Economics Letters* **13**, 181–4. Erratum in *Economics Letters* **15**, 195–6.

Dagenais, M. G. (1980) 'Specification and Estimation of a Dynamic Disequilibrium Model', *Economics Letters* **5**, 323–8.

Fair, R. C. and J. B. Taylor (1983) 'Solution and Maximum Likelihood Estimation of Dynamic Non-Linear Rational Expectations Models', *Econometrica* **51**, 1163–85.

Ghosh, S., C. L. Gilbert and A. J. Hughes Hallett (1987) *Stabilizing Speculative Commodity Markets* Oxford, Oxford University Press.

Gordon-Ashworth, F. (1984) *International Commodity Controls: A Contemporary History and Appraisal* Croom Helm, London.

Goss, B. A. (1986) 'The Forward Pricing Function of the London Metal Exchange', in B. A. Goss (ed.), *Futures Markets: Their Establishment and Performance* New York, New York University Press.

Grossman, S. J. and J. E. Stiglitz (1980) 'On the Impossibility of Informationally Efficient Markets', *American Economic Review* **70**, 393–408.

Just, R. E. and G. C. Rausser (1981) 'Commodity Price Forecasting With Large-Scale Econometric Models and the Futures Market', *American Journal of Agricultural Economics* **63**, 197–208.

Laffont, J. J. and A. Monfort (1979) 'Disequilibrium Econometrics in Dynamic Models', *Journal of Econometrics* **11**, 353–61.

Leuthold, R. M. and P. A. Hartman (1979) 'A Semi-Strong Form Evaluation of the Hog Futures Market', *American Journal of Agricultural Economics* **61**, 482–9; and 'Reply' **62**, 585–7 (1980).

MacBean, A. I. and D. T. Nguyen (1987) *Commodity Policies: Problems and Prospects* Croom Helm, London.

Mackinnon, J. G. and N. D. Olewiler (1980) 'Disequilibrium Estimation of the Demand for Copper', *Bell Journal of Economics* **11**, 197–211.

Maddala, G. S. (1983) *Limited Dependent and Qualitative Variables in Econometrics* New York, Cambridge University Press.

Maddala, G. S. and F. D. Nelson (1974) 'Maximum Likelihood Methods for Models of Markets in Disequilibrium', *Econometrica* **42**, 1013–30.

Maddala, G. S. and J. S. Shonkwiler (1985) 'Futures Prices, Price Expectations and Supply Response in Agricultural Markets Subject to Price Supports', Working Paper, CSFM-105, Center for the Study of Futures Markets, Columbia Business School.

McNicol, D. L. (1978) *Commodity Agreements and Price Stabilization* D.C. Heath, Lexington, Massachusetts.

Orsi, R. (1982) 'On the Dynamic Specification of Disequilibrium Econometrics: An Analysis of Italian Male and Female Labor Markets', CORE Discussion Paper, 8228.

Peck, Ann E. (1985) 'The Economic Role of Traditional Commodity Futures Markets', in Ann E. Peck (ed.), *Futures Markets: Their Economic Role* Washington, D.C., American Enterprise Institute.

Pesaran, M. H. (1987) *The Limits to Rational Expectations* Oxford, Basil Blackwell.

Pindyck, R. S. and J. J. Rotemberg (1988) 'The Excess Co-Movement of Commodity Prices', Working Paper, no. 2671. Cambridge, Massachusetts, National Bureau of Economic Research.

Quandt, R. E. (1988) *The Econometrics of Disequilibrium* Basil Blackwell, New York.

Shonkwiler, J. S. and G. S. Maddala (1985) 'Modelling Expectations of Bounded Prices: An Application to the Market for Corn', *Review of Economics and Statistics* **64**, 634–41.

Stegman, T. (1985) 'On the Rationality of the Rational Expectations Hypothesis', *Australian Economic Papers* **24**, 350–5.

Stein, J. (1981) 'Speculative Price: Economic Welfare and the Idiot of Chance', *Review of Economics and Statistics* **63**, 223–32.

Streit, M. E. (1983) 'Modelling, Managing and Monitoring Futures Trading: Frontiers of Analytical Inquiry' in M. E. Streit (ed.), *Futures Markets* Oxford, Basil Blackwell.

Tomek, W. G. and R. W. Gray (1970) 'Temporal Relationships Among Prices on Commodity Futures Markets', *American Journal of Agricultural Economics* **52**, 372–80.

Turnovsky, S. J. (1983) 'The Determination of Spot and Futures Prices With Storable Commodities', *Econometrica* **51**, 1363–87.

Wallis, K. F. (1980) 'Econometric Implications of the Rational Expectations Hypothesis', *Econometrica* **48**, 49–74.

Discussion

M. HASHEM PESARAN*

This paper presents a review of Maddala's earlier work on the incorporation of rational expectations in disequilibrium models and discusses the relevance and usefulness of direct observations on expectations such as survey data or future prices in the econometric analysis of commodity prices. The paper is in two parts. The first part (Sections 2–4) deals with the technical econometric issues that arise in rational expectations models with a limited dependent variable. These types of models are especially suitable for the analysis of markets subject to price support schemes and buffer-stock programs. The second part (Sections 6–8) gives a commentary on the usefulness of the REH in modelling commodity markets and briefly discusses three other procedures for the derivation of price expectations; namely, survey data, futures prices and (Bayesian) vector autoregressions. The overall recommendation of the paper is that one should use rational expectations in preference to the other methods of expectations formation in modelling commodity markets, although Section 6 suggests some misgivings concerning the Muthian form of the REH utilized in the first part of the paper.

I welcome Professor Maddala's approach and agree with his emphasis on rational expectations modelling of commodity markets. The limited dependent variable – rational expectations (LD–RE), model originally put forward in Chanda and Maddala (1983), provides a useful framework for the analysis of market interventions. Its strength lies in the fact that it permits policy analysis in a theoretically consistent manner not possible when survey data or futures prices are used as proxies for price expectations. The same criticism also applies to price expectations derived by the vector autoregressive method where there is no feedback from the policy model to the expectations formation mechanism.

The use of survey data or future prices as proxies for price expectations in the estimation of limited dependent variable models is also subject to an important shortcoming not mentioned in the paper. The claim that the use of survey expectations or future prices results in considerable simplification of the estimation problem rests crucially on the assumption that price expectations derived from these sources are free from measurement errors. In reality expectations derived from surveys or other sources can be subject to serious measurement or sampling error problems, (see, for example, Pesaran, 1985, 1987) and once this is acknowledged the estimation of limited dependent variable models entails estimation of non-linear error-in-variables models which is far from straightforward. See, for example, Fuller (1987) and Hausman *et al.* (1988). It is no longer valid to replace the unobserved price expectations by future prices or by survey expectations and then proceed with the estimation as if they were the 'true' measurements. Estimation by the non-linear instrumental variable method will also be inappropriate and does not yield consistent estimates (see Amemiya, 1985).

In view of these difficulties associated with the use of survey expectations in the limited dependent variable models, the development of an appropriate method for the estimation of the LD–RE models seems to be of particular importance. Such a method is reviewed in the paper but unfortunately suffers from an important shortcoming. The problem lies with the use of the switching regression framework (10), as an alternative to solving equations (5), (6), (7′) and (9) for the price expectations, P_t^*. Under rational expectations P_t^* will not depend on P_t, and therefore it is not clear how P_t^* could possibly follow a switching specification such as equation (10) in which the value of P_t^* is assumed to depend on whether $P_t > P_t^s$ or not. To see this let (in Maddala's notations)

$$Z_t = b_1^{-1}(a_2 W_t - b_2 X_t)$$
$$e_t = b_1^{-1}(e_{1t} - e_{2t})$$
$$\gamma = a_1/b_1$$

and notice that under the usual assumptions concerning the slopes of the supply and demand equations we have $\gamma < 0$. Now use (9) to solve for P_{1t}^* in terms of P_t^*, namely

$$P_{1t}^* = (1 - \gamma)^{-1} \left\{ Z_t^* + \frac{\sigma\phi(C_t)}{1 - \Phi(C_t)} \right\} \tag{A1}$$

where

$$Z_t^* = b_1^{-1}(a_2 W_t^* - b_2 X_t^*)$$
$$C_t = \sigma^{-1}[P_t^s - \gamma P_t^* - Z_t^*]$$

and σ is defined by (7′). Substituting (6) in (5) and using the expression for P_{1t}^* given above we now have

$$P_t^* = (1 - \gamma)^{-1}[Z_t^* + \sigma\phi(C_t)] + [P_t^s - (1 - \gamma)^{-1}Z_t^*]\Phi(C_t)$$
$$= F(P_t^*) \tag{A2}$$

which is the *implicit* function in P_t^* whose derivation is suggested by Maddala (p. 25) not to have been possible.

With the help of (A2), it is now easily seen that $F(P_t^*)$ is continuous and differentiable in P_t^* and unlike the approximation (10) adopted by

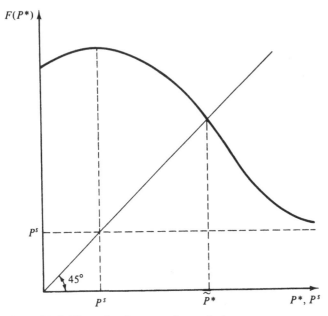

Figure 2A.1 The rational expectations solution

Maddala does not involve a switch point. Moreover, under the assumption that $\gamma < 0$ it can be shown that equation (A2) does in fact possess a *unique* solution for P_t^*.

To establish that $P_t^* = F(P_t^*)$ has a unique solution consider the graph of function $F(P^*)$ in relation to the 45° line in Figure 2A.1, and also note that under the REH; $P_t^* \geqslant P_t^s$.[1] The necessary and sufficient condition for $P_t^* = F(P_t^*)$ to have a unique solution is satisfied if over the range $P_t^* \geqslant P_t^s$, the graph of $F(P_t^*)$ intersects the 45° line only once. But for $\gamma < 0$ and $P_t^* > P_t^s$ we have

$$\frac{\partial F(P_t^*)}{\partial P_t^*} = \frac{-\gamma^2}{(1-\gamma)}\,\phi(C_t)(P_t^* - P_t^s) < 0 \tag{A3}$$

which establishes that $F(P_t^*)$ is a monotonically decreasing function of P_t^* and therefore can intersect the 45° line only once. So if there is a solution to equation (A2) it will be unique. To prove the existence of a solution we need also to show that $F(P_t^s) > P_t^s$. Using (A2) and (A3) we also have (for $\gamma < 0$)

$$\lim_{P_t^* \to \infty} F(P_t^*) = P_t^s$$

$$\partial F(P_t^*)/\partial P_t^* \big|_{P_t^* = P_t} = 0$$

and

$$\partial^2 F(P_t^*)/\partial P_t^{*2}\Big|_{P_t^* = P_t} = \frac{-\gamma^2}{\sigma(1-\gamma)} \phi\left[\frac{(1-\gamma)P_t^s - Z_t^*}{\sigma}\right] < 0$$

Hence, the function $F(P_t^*)$ has a maximum at $P_t^* = P_t^s$ and then declines monotonically to reach its lower bound value P_t^s as P_t^* is allowed to deviate from P_t^s without bounds. This in turn implies that $F(P_t^s) > P_t^s$ and therefore establishes that $P_t^* = F(P_t^*)$ has a unique solution that exceeds the support price, P_t^s.

The above results also suggest a relatively simple method of estimating the parameters of the LD–RE models. Start with some initial estimates of the parameters. Solve the equation $P_t^* = F(P_t^*)$ given by (A2) numerically for the unique solution of P_t^*, say $\tilde{P}_t^*$, by a suitable iterative method such as the method of 'successive substitution' (see Figure 2A.1). Then estimate the standard Tobit model

$$\begin{aligned}
P_t &= \gamma\tilde{P}_t^* + Z_t + e_t, \qquad P_t > P_t^s \\
&= P_t^s \qquad\qquad\qquad \text{otherwise}
\end{aligned} \tag{A4}$$

to obtain new estimates of the structural parameters, taking the expectations series $\tilde{P}_t^*$ as given.[2] Using these new estimates obtain a new solution of $P_t^* = F(P_t^*)$ and repeat the process until convergence is reached.[3] In the case where the support price is not operative (i.e. $P_t^s \to \infty$), the expression for $\tilde{P}_t^*$ reduces to the equilibrium rational expectations solution $P_t^* = (1-\gamma)^{-1}Z_t^*$ and the estimation procedure simplifies to a standard estimation problem extensively discussed in the rational expectations literature (see, for examle, Pesaran, 1987, Chapter 7).

An alternative computationally less burdensome procedure would be to adopt a Heckman-type procedure and estimate the regression

$$P_t = \gamma\tilde{P}_t^* + Z_t + \frac{\sigma\phi(\tilde{C}_t)}{1 - \Phi(\tilde{C}_t)} + \text{Error} \tag{A5}$$

for the observations $P_t > P_t^s$ by the OLS method to obtain new estimates of the structural parameters. In this equation the Mill's ratio $\phi(\tilde{C}_t)/[1 - \Phi(\tilde{C}_t)]$ is computed at $\tilde{C}_t = \tilde{\sigma}^{-1}(P_t^s - \tilde{\gamma}\tilde{P}_t^* - Z_t^*)$, where $\tilde{\gamma}$ and $\tilde{\sigma}$ are the initial estimates. This procedure can also be iterated until convergence is achieved. The computation of the standard errors of the parameter estimates is not, however, a straightforward matter and should also take account of the dependence of P_t^* on the structural parameters via equation (A2). This is true irrespective of whether the Tobit or the Heckman-type procedure is employed. The solution and the estimation methods proposed here can be readily extended to the buffer-stock model discussed in Section 5 of the paper. The details of these and other extensions and an application of the estimation procedure outlined here will be given in a forthcoming paper.

NOTES

* In preparing this comment I have greatly benefited from discussion with Hossein Samiei.
1 This result follows immediately from the fact that the support price condition $P_t \geqslant P_t^s$ is assumed to be 'common knowledge'.
2 Notice that $\tilde{P}_t^*$ does not depend on P_t and at the estimation stage can be treated in the same way as any other exogenous variable included in the model. To achieve identification we also need to assume that the disturbances e_t, u_{1t} and u_{2t} are independently distributed. u_{1t} and u_{2t} are the errors in the processes generating the exogenous variables W_t and X_t, respectively.
3 In practice one also needs to replace Z_t^* in (C2) by $\tilde{Z}_t^* = b_t^{-1}(a_2 \hat{W}_t^* - b_2 \hat{X}_t^*)$, where $\hat{W}_t^*$ and $\hat{X}_t^*$ are consistent estimates of the expectations of W_t and X_t formed at time $t - 1$.

REFERENCES

Amemiya, T. (1985) 'Instrumental variable estimator for the nonlinear errors-in-variables model', *Journal of Econometrics* **28**, 273–89.
Chanda, A. and G. S. Maddala (1983) 'Methods of estimation for models of markets with bounded price variation under rational expectations', *Economics Letters* **13**, 181–4.
Fuller, W. (1987) *Measurement Error Models*, John Wiley, New York.
Hausman, J. A., W. K. Newey and J. L. Powell (1988) 'Nonlinear errors in variables: estimation of some Engel curves', Economics Department Working Paper 504, M.I.T.
Pesaran, M. H. (1985) 'Formation of inflation expectations in British manufacturing industries', *The Economic Journal* **95**, 948–75.
Pesaran, M. H. (1987) *The Limits to Rational Expectations*, Basil Blackwell, Oxford.

Summary of general discussion

Chris Gilbert pointed out that the issue of policy interventions, such as support prices, buffer stock schemes and the like are crucial in commodity models. He referenced Salant's (1983) paper as a seminal piece in this area. He argued that the focus in these models must be on how to formulate the agent's expectations about whether the intervention authority has the stock and resources to perform according to its terms of reference; that is, the agents look at the sustainability of the stabilization effort. He remarked also that Salant in his paper believes that one cannot stabilize anything which seemed to be clearly incorrect to Gilbert.

Alan Winters held that the support price is part of the structural model and would therefore have to be taken account of in such a manner. Hashem Pesaran argued that if one ignores the complicating structural model as a full account can never be taken of all its intricacies and effects; and if there is a support price, then running a regression on a reduced form, at whatever level of aggregation, would yield biased results. The important matter is to see how far wrong one is. Richard Just, however, held that the US agricultural sector, for example, was not represented accurately in the paper as the programme of the USDA was much more complicated than allowed for.

Subsequent to the general discussion G.S. Maddala disagreed with some of the points raised by Hashem Pesaran. Specifically, he pointed out that he did not mention equation (A2) because he could not derive any analytical conclusions from it and did not see that it led to any substantial simplification in the iterative procedure which he had already used; which was why he said that one could not get even an implicit equation. Maddala expressed some doubts regarding the derivation of (A3), the proof following it and the results relating to to Figure 2A.1, arguing that the dependence of C_t on P_t^* had not been taken into account. Lastly, Maddala defended his switching regression framework, arguing that it does not say that P_t^* depends on P_t but rather that P_t^* is a weighted average of P_t^s and P_{1t}^* with weights depending on π_t, with the consequence that it is a function of exogenous variables only. He also noted that the switching regression model is an endogenous switching model and does not imply that there is a switch in P_t^*. To support this argument he considered the case where one has two variables y_t and z_t and seeks the expectation of y_t. He argued that it is perfectly legitimate to evaluate this expectation conditional on $z_t > c$ and $z_t \leq c$ and obtain a weighted average. He also argued that one can write the conditional likelihoods and obtain a weighted likelihood. This, according to Maddala, in no way implies that the expectation of y_t depends on z_t or that there is a switch in the expectation of y_t.

REFERENCE

Salant, S. W. (1983) 'The Vulnerability of Price Stabilization Schemes to Speculative Attack', *Journal of Political Economy* **91**, 1–38.

3 Modelling Expectations Formation in Primary Commodity Markets*

CHRISTOPHER L. GILBERT and
THEODOSIOS B. PALASKAS

1 Introduction

The traditional textbook paradigm requires that primary commodity prices adjust to clear the market. Since production and consumption are generally inelastic over the short run (certainly periods of one year or less) this suggests that fluctuations in demands (boom or recession in the industrialized countries) or supply (good or bad harvests) may result in considerable price variability. Primary commodity prices are indeed highly volatile, and this has been taken by some as providing a *prima facie* case for price stabilizing intervention.

On the other hand, it is also widely recognized that storage is at least potentially important in these markets, and that the demand for storage might in principle be highly elastic. Private agents will typically buy low and sell high, and this will provide a degree of automatic stabilization via the market. If that is the case, it is not clear that one should expect the public sector to be any more efficient than the private sector in providing the socially optimal level of storage.

Extensive storage by the private sector also has other implications. Agents undertaking storage activities will be conscious of the opportunity cost of the funds that they use for this purpose, and this implies that storage, and therefore also commodity prices, will be sensitive to the rate of interest. Primary commodities will then behave to some extent like financial assets. A rise in the interest rates will imply that investors will seek a higher return on commodity stocks and this will require an initial fall in commodity prices, in the same way that the rise in interest rates also induces a fall in bond and equity prices. The greater the level of stock being carried the higher will be the implicit 'duration' of commodity stocks and the greater the effect of a change in interest rates. This effect of developed country monetary policy on primary commodity prices is central to a number of models which look at interactions between the developed and the developing world (see in particular, Currie *et al*. 1988). One purpose of this paper is to attempt to evaluate the strength of this link.

Storage also has implications for the modelling of commodity prices. Econometric commodity price models employed by academics and by international agencies typically either relate the current commodity price level to current stock levels or relate current changes in commodity prices to the current supply–demand balance. If storage is important, the current price will also depend on current expectations of future market conditions. An important question for academic, agency and industry modellers is how these expectations should be introduced into commodity price models.

Standard storage theory suggests that stockholdings will be determined by expected future prices relative to the current price, taking into account interest and other costs of storage. This suggests modelling the current price as dependent on an expected price in a future period. Software developed for macroeconometric modelling and forecasting may be used to generate a model-consistent (i.e. 'rational') price path which will satisfy an estimated expectational price equation of this sort in every period.

In this paper we argue for an alternative approach. If storage is efficient and extensive, commodity prices should not be expected to vary much except in relation to new information. This implies that future commodity prices are unlikely to be very informative about expected future conditions since expected future prices are jointly determined with current prices and depend on the same information set. Except in periods of backwardation, when temporary or end-year shortages drive a wedge between current and expected future prices, future prices will differ from spot prices only by the carrying cost of storage less any convenience yield from the storage activity. Instead, it is more natural to model prices as responding to current and expected future supply–demand imbalances. Moreover, we believe this procedure is in line with industry practice where the price implications of a current imbalance are considered in the context of expected future imbalances.

Unfortunately, it is only possible to derive an explicit representation of the commodity price in terms of current and expected future market conditions in very simple models. This is clearly a limitation of the approach. On the other hand, it may prove possible to employ price equations whose structure derives from a simple model in which there is no (or only limited) dependence of production or consumption on lagged prices to provide an approximate price model which is robust in a wider class of circumstances. This hope motivates the modelling effort reported in the present paper which was anticipated in work reported in Ghosh *et al.* (1987). In this paper we attempt a more complete and rigorous development of the price formation theory underlying the proposed specification and also attempt a more extensive test of the approach.

2   The Muth equilibrium model

Competitive commodity markets equilibrate in each period but private sector stockholding links current prices to expected future prices. Models which reflect this behaviour were introduced by Samuelson (1957) and Gustafson (1958a, b). Gustafson emphasized the importance of the non-negativity constraint on stocks, but acknowledgement of this constraint results in nonlinear stockholding and price relationships – see Wright and Williams (1982), Miranda and Helmberger (1988) and Gilbert (1985, 1988). An alternative approach, due to Muth (1961) and extended in Pesaran (1987), achieves linearity at the expense of ignoring this constraint. Ghosh *et al.* (1987) attempt an econometric implementation of this approach, but their results are suggestive rather than conclusive. What follows may be seen either as an extension of their work or as an attempt to develop an econometrically implementable version of Muth's (1961) model.

It is convenient to derive the Muth equations within a simple linear model. Ghosh *et al.* (1987) suggested that the functional specification which is linear in all quantities and log-linear in all prices is convenient since it both allows aggregation across market clearing identities and permits linear decomposition of relative price terms. In Ghosh *et al.* (1983) the same authors reported that, on a sample of quarterly data relating to the world copper market, this functional specification appears, on the whole, to fit better than more widely used specifications, and in particular the double logarithmic specification.

Let P_t be the price in period t and let $\bar{P}$ be the mean price over the relevant period. Then write $p_t = \log P_t/\bar{P}$. We may then write consumption C and production Q in this functional specification as

$$C_t = \bar{C}[\xi_{1t} - ep_t] \tag{1}$$

where $\bar{C} = C(\bar{P})$ and

$$Q_t = \bar{Q}[\xi_{2t} + \epsilon p_t] \tag{2}$$

where $\bar{Q} = Q(\bar{P}) = \bar{C}$. Note that at this stage we consider only contemporaneous price responses. The terms ξ_1 and ξ_2 represent the price-independent components of consumption and production respectively, whether deterministic or stochastic.

Stock demand depends on the anticipated discounted capital gain

$$S_t = \bar{S} + \alpha \bar{Q}[p_{t+1|t} - p_t - r_t] \tag{3}$$

where $p_{t+1|t} = E_t p_{t+1}$. This generalizes Muth by including the interest rate which will be important in what follows. Note however that we do not impose a non-negativity constraint and this implies that we must suppose $\bar{S}$ sufficiently large to absorb any desired level of destocking. For an alternative approach see Gustafson (1958,a b), Newbery and Stiglitz (1982), Wright and Williams (1982), Gilbert (1985, 1988), and Miranda and Helmberger (1988). The model is closed by the market clearing identity

$$S_t = S_{t-1} + Q_t - C_t \tag{4}$$

An obvious approach to the model defined by equations (1–4) would be to estimate equation (3) using the McCallum (1976) technique. This involves replacing the expectational term $p_{t+1|t} - p_t - r_t$ by the realization $p_{t+1} - p_t - r_t$ and instrumenting to eliminate the resulting measurement error bias. In practice (see Section 4) this results in very poorly determined estimates of the crucial coefficient α. The cause of this difficulty may be understood by analyzing the realized capital gain from stockholding as

$$p_{t+1} - p_t - r_t = [p_{t+1} - p_{t+1|t}] + [p_{t+1|t} - p_t - r_t] \tag{5}$$

In commodity markets the first, noise, component of the right hand side of (5) dominates the second informative component. The reason for this is that joint determination of the current and expected future prices through the stockholding mechanism ensures that the second term is very small. Indeed, if stockholders are risk-neutral and there is no convenience yield, the discounted expected price change will be zero and the regressor in (3) will be entirely noise.

We therefore prefer to follow a two-stage procedure in which we regress price changes on constructed expectational variables. But unlike conventional two-stage RE models, which suggest regression on expected price change variables, we regress on expected quantity variables. This is the same approach as advocated in Ghosh et al. (1987) who argued that expected future price changes are in general uninformative (since arbitraged to equal storage cost less convenience yield) but that expected future supply–demand balances give an indication of the direction in which the price must adjust if the market is to clear over time. But since that adjustment will eliminate these imbalances, the relevant expected future balances are those calculated at a base price (Ghosh et al. used the lagged price). Alternatively, this approach may be rationalized in terms of estimating the reduced form for the commodity price.

We first derive the reduced form representation for the commodity stock. Write $\xi_t = \xi_{2t} - \xi_{1t}$, which may be interpreted as the market excess supply at the base price $\bar{P}$. Write $s_t = [S_t - \bar{S}]/\bar{Q}$. Then one obtains (see Appendix)

$$s_t = \lambda \left(s_{t-1} + \xi_t - (1 - \lambda) \sum_{i=1}^{\infty} \lambda^i \xi_{t+i|t} - (e + \epsilon) \sum_{i=0}^{\infty} \lambda^i r_{t+i|t} \right) \quad (6)$$

where $\lambda < 1$ is the smaller root of the quadratic

$$y^2 - \left(2 + \frac{e + \epsilon}{\alpha} \right) y + 1 = 0 \quad (7)$$

Equation (6) relates storage linearly to total current supply $s_{t+1} + \xi_t$, expected future excess supplies and current and expected future interest rates.

An advantage of the reduced form representation (6) is that it allows solution for the price process. There are two possible representations, depending whether or not one has data on commodity stocks. If one has stock data then solution of (6) into the market clearing equation (1) gives (see Appendix)

$$p_t = -\frac{1 - \lambda}{e + \epsilon} \left[s_{t-1} + \sum_{i=0}^{\infty} \lambda^i \xi_{t+i|t} \right] - \lambda \sum_{i=0}^{\infty} \lambda^i r_{t+i|t} \quad (8)$$

This representation will often be the most convenient in modelling the prices of individual commodities. In some cases, however, stock data will either be unavailable or insufficiently accurate to be useful; and in general this is likely to be true if one is modelling aggregate commodity price indices. In those cases it is preferable to condition on the lagged commodity price rather than on the lagged stock. One obtains (see Appendix)

$$p_t = \lambda[p_{t-1} + r_{t-1}] - \frac{1 - \lambda}{e + \epsilon} \sum_{i=0}^{\infty} \lambda^i [\xi_{t+i|t} - \lambda \xi_{t+1|t-1}]$$

$$- \lambda \sum_{i=0}^{\infty} \lambda^i [r_{t+i|t} - \lambda r_{t+i|t-1}] \quad (9)$$

This equation exhibits lagged dependence with $\lambda \to 1$ as $\alpha \to \infty$ (i.e. as the market approaches risk neutrality) or as $e + \epsilon \to 0$ (i.e. as demand and supply become very inelastic). In these cases, the price also rises with the interest rate, consistently with the Hotelling (1931) result. In addition the price responds to forward discounted λ-quasi differences in expected market excess supply at the mean price $\bar{P}$ and in the market rate of interest. As $\lambda \to 1$, it is only the innovations in these variables that are important, but as $\lambda \to 0$ the interest rate quasi-difference term vanishes and the price depends only on current period supply and demand. This model therefore encompasses both the standard Marshallian cross model ($\lambda \to 0$) and models which emphasize commodities as assets ($\lambda \to 1$) (see Gilbert, 1985).

In estimating equations of the form (8) or (9) we suppose that interest rates follow a random walk (see Shiller *et al.*, 1983) with the implication that

$$r_{t+1|t} = r_t \quad \text{all } i \geq 0 \tag{10}$$

This assumption allows simplification of (8) to

$$p_t = \alpha - \beta(1 - \lambda)\left[s_{t-1} + \sum_{i=0}^{\infty} \lambda^i \xi_{t+i|t}\right] - \frac{\lambda}{1 - \lambda}(r_t - \lambda r_{t-1}) \tag{11}$$

where $\beta = (1/e + \epsilon)$ and where an intercept α has been included. (It is not sensible to attempt to identify the elasticities e and ϵ from price data). Similarly, (9) becomes

$$p_t = \alpha + \lambda[p_{t-1} + r_{t-1}] - \beta(1 - \lambda) \sum_{i=0}^{\infty} \lambda^i [\xi_{t+i|t} - \lambda\xi_{t+i|t-1}]$$

$$- \frac{\lambda}{1 - \lambda}[r_t - \lambda r_{t-1}] \tag{12}$$

Equation (12) imposes strong restrictions on the price formation process. Most importantly the excess supply and interest rate quasi-difference parameter and the rate at which future market conditions are discounted are restricted to be equal to the coefficient of the lagged dependent variable.

It is standard in the agricultural literature to suppose that production depends on lagged expectations of the current price, rather than on the current price as in (2), and indeed Muth (1961) followed this convention. We show in the Appendix that this modification generates a price function of the same basic form as (12) but with one additional parameter.

3   Exchange rates and inflation

Up to this point we have not been specific as to whether the commodity price P is real or nominal, nor as to the currency or currency basket in which it is denominated. It is apparent that the simple supply–demand model derived from equations (1–4) can only make sense if the price is interpreted as real and if exchange rates are fixed (so that the choice of currency is irrelevant). However, if models of this sort are to be practically useful it is important that they relate to the prices which are actually quoted in the markets, and these will usually be nominal dollar prices.

There are two issues here. First, on the question of deflation, one may state the speculative demand function (3) in either nominal or real terms provided that one defines the interest rate conformably. Thus, if the commodity price P is a nominal dollar price, the interest rate should be nominal, while if the price is real one should use a real interest rate converted from the nominal rate using the rate of change of the price deflator.

The currency (exchange rate) question is a little more complicated. Primary commodity pricees are almost universally quoted in US dollars, and we follow that practice. But the obvious implication is that changes in the value of the dollar may be a major determinant of changes in dollar commodity prices. Ridler and Yandle (1972) proposed a simple market clearing model without storage in which all countries in principle produce and consume all commodities. In that model the dollar commodity price responds negatively with a unit elasticity to an exchange rate index G defined as

$$g = \ln G = \sum_{i=2}^{n} v_i g_i \tag{13}$$

where $g_i = \ln G_i$ and G_i is the exchange rate of country i defined as the number of units of i's currency per dollar and where the United States is country 1 (so that $g_1 = 0$). The weights $\{v_i\}$ are defined by

$$v_i = \frac{w_i e_i + \omega_i \epsilon_i}{e + \epsilon} \tag{14}$$

where $\quad e = \sum_{i=1}^{n} w_i e_i \quad$ and $\quad \epsilon = \sum_{i=1}^{n} \omega_i \epsilon_i$

and where $w_i = C_i/\Sigma\, C_j$, the share of country i in world consumption of the commodity and $\omega_i = Q_i/\Sigma\, Q_j$, the share of i in total production of the commodity. It is important to note that the weights in the Ridler–Yandle index (13) sum to $1 - v_1$. In a conventional dollar exchange rate index, such as the widely used IMF MERM index, the weights of the non-dollar currencies sum to unity. The Ridler–Yandle results imply that the commodity price will respond to changes in the value of the dollar, as measured by these indices, with an elasticity of $-(1 - v_1)$.[1]

Gilbert (1989) generalises the Ridler–Yandle results to take into account the fact that changes in nominal exchange rates may not imply corresponding changes in real rates. If Π_i is the price deflator in country i, and writing $\pi_i = \ln \Pi_i$ and $\pi = \pi_1$, the commodity price responds with unit elasticity to

$$\pi_1 - \sum_{i=2}^{n} v_i(g_i - (\pi_i - \pi)) = \pi - h \tag{15}$$

The real exchange rate $h = \ln H$ may be interpreted as a measure of the departure of the dollar from its Purchasing Power Parity (PPP) value. Under PPP, h would be identically equal to zero and the dollar commodity price would simply rise with the US rate of inflation. However, if prices rise faster in the US than elsewhere, the commodity price will rise more slowly than the US rate of inflation; and *vice versa*.

These results are all derived in a model in which there is no storage, and in which the price therefore clears the market in every period. How, if at all, do they apply in a model in which storage plays a central role? First note that assumption of Uncovered Interest Parity (UIP) implies that the incentive to carry stocks is the same in all countries. Let S_{it} be stock demand in country i and let P_{it} and r_{it} be the local currency commodity price and interest rate respectively. Then analogously with equation (3)

$$S_{it} = \bar{S}_i + \alpha_i \bar{Q}_i [p_{i,t+1|t} - p_{it} - r_{it}] \tag{16}$$

But $\quad p_{it} = p_t + g_{it}$

and, by UIP
$$r_{it} = r_t + g_{i,t+1|t} - g_{it}$$

Hence $\quad S_{it} = \bar{S}_i + \alpha_i \bar{Q}_i [p_{t+1|t} - p_t - r_t] \tag{17}$

which may be aggregated to give (3) with $\alpha = \Sigma \omega_i \alpha_i$.

In considering the effects of exchange rates and inflation we may therefore restrict attention to their effects on the production and consumption equations. Consider the model developed in Section 2 in which there are only contemporaneous effects. The consumption equation for country i analogous to (1) is

$$C_{it} = \bar{C}_i [\xi_{1it} - e_i(p_t + g_{it} - \pi_{it})] \tag{18}$$

and correspondingly for production

$$Q_{it} = \bar{Q}_i [\xi_{2it} - \epsilon_i(p_t + g_{it} - \pi_{it})] \tag{19}$$

Equations (18) and (19) imply that aggregate normalized excess supply x_t (at price P_t) is given as

$$x_t = \xi_t + (e + \epsilon)(p_t - \pi_t + g_t) \tag{20}$$

where $\xi_t = \Sigma \omega_{it} \xi_{2it} - \Sigma w_{it} \xi_{1it}$, e and ϵ are defined in (14) and g_t is the index defined in (13). Solving the model in the same way as in Section 2, the solved representation of the storage function becomes (see Appendix)

$$s_t = \lambda \left(s_{t-1} + \xi_t - (1 - \lambda) \sum_{i=1}^{\infty} \lambda^i \xi_{t+i|t} \right.$$

$$\left. - (1 - \lambda) \sum_{i=0}^{\infty} \lambda^i (r_{t+i|t} - \Delta\pi_{t+i+1|t} + \Delta g_{t+i+1|t}) \right) \qquad (21)$$

where $\Delta\pi_{t+i|t} = \pi_{t+i|t} - \pi_{t+i-1|t}$ and similarly for $\Delta g_{t+i|t}$. Essentially, (21) modifies (6) by introducing the appropriate real rate of interest. Solving (21) into the market clearing identity gives

$$p_t + g_t - \pi_t = - \frac{1 - \lambda}{e + \epsilon} \left[s_{t-1} + \sum_{i=0}^{\infty} \lambda^i \xi_{t+i|t} \right]$$

$$- \lambda \sum_{i=0}^{\infty} \lambda^i \{ r_{t+i|t} - (\pi_{t+i+1|t} - \pi_{t+i|t}) + (g_{t+i+1|t} - g_{t+i|t}) \} \qquad (22)$$

which generalizes equation (8). The corresponding equation which conditions on the lagged price level rather than the stock level is

$$p_t = \lambda[p_{t-1} + r_{t-1}] - \frac{1 - \lambda}{e + \epsilon} \sum_{i=0}^{\infty} \lambda^i (\xi_{t+i|t} - \lambda\xi_{t+i|t-1})$$

$$- \sum_{i=0}^{\infty} \lambda^i \{ (r_{t+i|t} - \lambda r_{t+i|t-1}) - (\Delta\pi_{t+i+1|t} - \lambda\Delta\pi_{t+i+1|t-1})$$

$$+ (\Delta g_{t+i+1|t} - \lambda\Delta g_{t+i+1|t-1}) \} + [\pi_t - \lambda\pi_{t-1}] - [g_t - \lambda g_{t-1}]$$

$$(23)$$

As previously, we suppose that interest rates follow a random walk, and we now make the same assumption about exchange rates with the implication that

$$\Delta g_{t+i|t} = \Delta g_{t+i|t-1} = 0 \quad \text{all } i > 0 \qquad (24)$$

For simplicity, suppose that inflation follows a first-order autoregression

$$(\Delta\pi_t - \overline{\Delta\pi}) = \nu(\Delta\pi_{t-1} - \overline{\Delta\pi}) \qquad (25)$$

where $\overline{\Delta\pi}$ is the sample mean inflation rate. This implies

$$\Delta\pi_{t+1|t} = \overline{\Delta\pi} + \nu^i \Delta\pi_t \qquad (26)$$

These assumptions allow us to write equations (22) in the estimatable form (compare (11))

$$p_t + g_t - \pi_t = \alpha - \beta(1 - \lambda) \left[s_{t-1} + \sum_{i=0}^{\infty} \lambda^i \xi_{t+i|t} \right]$$

$$- \frac{\lambda}{1 - \lambda} r_t + \frac{\lambda\nu}{1 - \lambda\nu} \Delta\pi_t \qquad (27)$$

Similarly, equation (18) gives

$$p_t + g_t - \pi_t = \alpha + \lambda[p_{t-1} + g_{t-1} - \pi_{t-1} + (r_{t-1} - \nu\Delta\pi_{t-1})]$$

$$- \beta(1 - \lambda) \sum_{i=0}^{\infty} \lambda^i(\xi_{t+i|t} - \lambda\xi_{t+i|t-1}) - \frac{\lambda}{1 - \lambda}(r_t - \lambda r_{t-1})$$

$$+ \frac{\lambda\nu}{1 - \lambda\nu}(\Delta\pi_t - \lambda\nu\Delta\pi_{t-1}) \tag{28}$$

An alternative expression for (28) is

$$p_t + g_t - \pi_t = \alpha + \lambda[p_t + g_{t-1} - \pi_{t-1} + r_{t-1}]$$

$$- \beta(1 - \lambda) \sum_{i=0}^{\infty} \lambda^i(\xi_{t+i|t} - \lambda\xi_{t+i|t-1}) - \frac{\lambda}{1 - \lambda}(r_t - \lambda r_{t-1})$$

$$+ \frac{\lambda\nu}{1 - \lambda\nu}\Delta^2 \Pi_t \tag{29}$$

4   Results

We have used the model developed in Sections 2 and 3 to examine price formation for six primary commodities: cocoa, coffee, copper, (natural) rubber, sugar and tin. The data are annual covering the period 1963–75, although a shorter sample is used for coffee because of the more recent (1972) start of the disappearance (i.e. consumption) series. For the agricultural commodities, production and consumption are on a crop year (October to September) basis, while for the two metals data relate to the calendar year.

The prices, which are nominal, are end-period prices, defined as averages for December for the two metals, and as July averages of the nearby future for the agricultural commodities. The decision to model end of period prices is prompted by Working's observation that the use of annual averages can introduce apparent lagged dependence even if the original (unaveraged) series are random (Working, 1960). The choice of these particular end-period prices reflects the fact that while metals tend to trade at or near the LME (London Metal Exchange) cash price, the nearby price tends to be the dominant indicator price in soft commodities. The exchange rate and producer price indices are also end of period and relate to the same month. Data sources and definitions are given in the data appendix of Gilbert and Palaskas (1989). A disadvantage of the use of annual data for non-crop commodities (copper and tin in this study) is that it involves loss of a very considerable amount of information, although the choice of crop years appears natural for agricultural commodities.

	Dependent Variable : $S/\bar{C}$					
	Sample: 1965–85					
	Cocoa	Coffee	Copper	Rubber	Sugar	Tin
Durbin–Watson integration order statistics						
$S_t/\bar{C}$	0.63	0.19	0.29	0.11	0.14	0.38
$p_{t+1} - p_t - r_t$	1.77	2.20	2.87	2.42	1.99	1.59
Estimated equations (no lagged dependent variable)						
Intercept	0.39	1.01	0.20	0.40	0.53	0.19
	(0.00)	(0.11)	(0.03)	(0.02)	(0.03)	(0.06)
$p_{t+1} - p_t - r_t$	0.22	0.98	0.18	0.03	0.01	− 0.75
	(0.10)	(0.64)	(0.16)	(0.10)	(0.07)	(0.39)
s.e.	0.10	0.47	0.11	0.06	0.12	0.15
D.W.	0.89	1.45	0.54	0.18	0.13	2.00
$\chi^2(5)$	11.25*	8.35	19.10*	23.70*	24.85*	3.85
Estimated equations (lagged dependent variable included)						
Intercept	0.17	0.19	0.06	0.03	0.03	0.04
	(0.07)	(0.08)	(0.03)	(0.02)	(0.04)	(0.06)
$S_{t-1}/\bar{C}$	0.57	0.45	0.80	0.93	0.97	0.77
	(0.17)	(0.16)	(0.13)	(0.05)	(0.09)	(0.27)
$p_{t+1} - p_t - r_t$	0.18	0.28	0.13	− 0.04	− 0.02	− 0.03
	(0.08)	(0.31)	(0.09)	(0.02)	(0.02)	(0.24)
s.e.	0.08	0.21	0.06	0.01	0.05	0.08
D.W.	1.43	2.00	1.21	1.75	1.89	2.16
$\chi^2(4)$	4.80	8.0	9.00*	4.00	12.44*	2.99
s.d. (dep. var.)	0.15	0.10	0.06	0.11	0.12	0.10

Table 3.1 Estimated speculative stock demand functions

Notes: coefficient standard errors in parentheses: $\chi^2(r)$ is the Sargan instrument validity test (asterisk indicates significance at the 95% level). The instruments for $p_{t+1} - p_t - r_t$ are: $TREND_t$, y_t, Y_{t-1} $S_{t-1}/\bar{C}$ and $p_t - p_{t-1} - r_{t-1}$.

In Table 3.1 we report instrumental variable (IV) estimates of the speculative stock demand equation (3) with the actual price change replacing the expected change (as in McCallum, 1976). Stocks are end-period conformably with the price. Superficially, the estimates of the basic equation with no lagged dependent variable appear reasonable – the stock demand parameter α is positive, the expected sign, for five out of the six commodities, and is significantly so for cocoa. However the very low Durbin–Watson statistics on the copper, rubber and sugar equations indicate misspecification and imply that inference is invalid. The source of the problem may be seen by inspection of the integration order Durbin–Watson statistics at the head of the table. These statistics indicate that in each case (except, possibly, cocoa) the stock variable is I(1), while the actual price change is I(0). It is therefore not logically possible that the latter variable can explain the former (see, for example, Engle and Granger, 1987).

One possible 'solution' to this problem is to add a lagged dependent variable to the regression. This might be justified by appeal to the standard partial adjustment model. In each case this gives a dramatic improvement in fit, but now the estimated α coefficients divide equally between positive and negative, and again only the coefficient in the cocoa equation is significantly different from zero at the 95% level (note that a one-tailed test is appropriate here). These estimates reinforce our view that there is little to be gained from direct estimation of the stock demand equation. This problem arises we believe because commodity stock series are incomplete, due to poor reporting, but also include transactions and precautionary stocks which do not fit our simple model.

We turn now to estimates of equations (27–29). This exercise required that we generate values for the expected supply–demand balances $\xi_{t+i|t}$. These values were generated from production and consumption equations estimated by single equation methods and are reported in Gilbert and Palaskas (1989). The expected supply–demand balances $\xi_{t+i|t}$ were generated over a ten-year horizon for each observation by simulating production and consumption forward for ten years with the price set at its sample mean value. Future values of exogenous variables were generated by first-order autoregression.

It may be noted firstly that the commodity production and consumption equations do contain lagged prices, implying that the model developed in Sections 2 and 3 is not strictly appropriate; and that the equations are non-expectational. Clearly it would be correct to model commodity production and consumption as depending on distributed lags of rational expectations of future prices, and to use a price equation which is conformable with that specification. That exercise would however be very complicated, and in any case it would be necessary to approximate in order to obtain a second-order difference equation if an analytic price equation is to be derived. We do not judge that exercise to be worthwhile.

The equations reported in this paper were all estimated by Nonlinear Least Squares (NLLS). It is well-known that OLS applied to equations containing constructed regressors, such as the $\xi_{t+i|t}$ variables, will give rise to consistent but inefficient coefficient estimates which suffer from biased standard errors (see, for example, Pagan, 1984). This problem arises from

| | Dependent Variable: $p_t + g_t - \pi_t$ | | | | | |
	Cocoa	Coffee	Copper	Rubber	Sugar	Tin
α intercept	7.404	-10.013	2.665	10.009	1.561	0.422
	(0.911)	(4.677)	(0.925)	(1.113)	(5.579)	(0.557)
λ	-0.972	-0.850	0.915	-0.174	0.946	0.752
	(0.059)	(0.099)	(0.074)	(0.529)	(0.336)	(0.170)
β $(1-\lambda)[s_{t-1} + \Sigma\lambda^i\xi_{t+i|t}]$						
	1.072	0.996	0.390	1.431	0.404	-0.231
	(0.151)	(0.433)	(0.135)	(0.159)	(0.516)	(0.160)
$\dfrac{\lambda}{1-\lambda}\, r_t$	-0.493	-0.459	10.764	-0.148	17.519	3.032
$\dfrac{\lambda\hat{\nu}}{1-\lambda\hat{\nu}}\, \Delta\pi_t$	-0.256	-0.243	1.770	-0.108	1.947	1.106
Sample	67–85	74–85	63–85	64–85	63–85	63–85
s.d. (dep. var.)	0.358	0.481	0.428	0.428	0.328	0.218
R^2	0.768	0.578	0.704	0.821	0.258	0.251
s.e.	0.183	0.345	0.246	0.145	0.567	0.198
D.W.	2.323	1.982	1.541	2.378	1.269	1.208
Log-likelihood	-10.53	-13.57	-19.88	-1.28	-39.91	-14.82

Table 3.2 NLLS estimates of equation (27)

Note: Coefficient standard errors in parentheses.

non-sphericality of the disturbances and will apply at least as severely to NLLS estimation. Alternative estimators are the McCallum (1976) Instrumental Variables (IV) estimator and Maximum Likelihood (ML) – see Pesaran (1987). However, no simple IV estimator is available for non-linear equations of the sort we need to estimate. We therefore re-estimated a subset of our equations by ML to check for robustness.

We use the TSP nonlinear Three Stage Least Squares routine (asymptotically equivalent to Full Information ML) to estimate jointly the price, production and consumption equations. We should expect the ML coefficient estimates to differ little from the NLLS estimates since both are consistent, but would expect to find differences in the estimated coefficient standard errors. In fact the ML estimates, which we do not report, exhibited very different coefficient estimates but had similar estimated standard errors. This strongly suggests misspecification in either the price or in the production and consumption equations. While there may be merit in utilizing ML estimation on a model which one knows to be well-specified, we prefer in this exploratory work to rely on the NLLS estimates.

	Dependent Variable: $p_t + g_t - \pi_t$					
	Cocoa	Coffee	Copper	Rubber	Sugar	Tin
α intercept	0.428	0.262	$-$ 0.194	0.025	$-$ 1.311	0.708
	(0.203)	(0.337)	(0.081)	(0.087)	(0.528)	(0.291)
$\lambda\ p_{t-1} + g_{t-1} - \pi_{t-1} + (r_{t-1} - \hat{\nu}\Delta\pi_{t-1})$						
	0.352	0.486	0.533	0.302	0.432	0.474
	(0.196)	(0.246)	(0.113)	(0.227)	(0.225)	(0.201)
$\beta\ (1-\lambda)\Sigma\lambda^i\,\nabla\xi_{t+i|t}$						
	$-$ 2.697	$-$ 1.409	4.013	3.828	6.679	$-$ 0.402
	(0.936)	(1.126)	(1.331)	(1.822)	(6.200)	(0.778)
$\dfrac{\lambda}{1-\lambda}\ (r_t - \lambda r_{t-1})$						
	0.543	0.945	1.141	0.433	0.760	0.901
$\dfrac{\lambda\hat{\nu}}{1-\lambda\hat{\nu}}\ (\Delta\pi_t - \lambda\nu\Delta\pi_{t-1})$						
	0.698	0.698	0.698	0.698	0.698	0.698
Sample	67–85	74–85	63–85	64–85	63–85	63–85
s.d. (dep. var.)	0.358	0.480	0.428	0.328	0.643	0.218
R^2	0.436	0.400	0.638	0.495	0.325	0.339
s.e.	0.293	0.411	0.270	0.245	0.554	0.185
D.W.	1.601	1.730	1.837	1.951	1.579	2.038
Log-likelihood	$-$ 19.84	$-$ 16.28	$-$ 22.08	$-$ 18.87	$-$ 38.58	$-$ 13.36

Table 3.3 NLLS estimates of equation (28)

Note: standard errors in parentheses; $\nabla\xi_{t+i|t} = \xi_{t+i|t} - \lambda\xi_{t+i|t-1}$

In Table 3.2 we report estimates of equation (27) which conditions on the lagged stock variable. These estimates use an extraneous estimate for the inflation autoregression coefficient ν obtained by OLS estimation of equation (25). This gave

$$\Delta\pi_t = 0.015 + 0.698\Delta\pi_{t-1}$$
$$(0.012)\ (0.163)$$

$$R^2 = 0.456 \quad \text{D.W.} = 1.82 \quad \text{s.e.} = 0.041$$
sample 1962–85

The estimated copper and sugar equations appear well-defined and compatible with the forward-looking theory (λ is estimated significantly greater than zero), but the estimates from the other four equations are difficult to reconcile with the theoretical model.

The estimates reported in Table 3.3 use the same procedure to estimate equation (28) which conditions on the lagged price variable rather than the lagged stock variable. The equations for copper and sugar are again compatible with the theory and in these estimates the same is true of that for rubber, although λ differs significantly from zero only in the copper equation. For both copper and rubber, a higher R^2 is obtained by conditioning on the lagged stock level but this results in a marginal loss in fit in the sugar equation. If the estimates in Tables 3.2 and 3.3 may be regarded as alternative consistent estimates of the same parameters we should expect little difference between these estimates. It is therefore disturbing that the estimated λ coefficients are uniformly lower and the estimated β coefficients for these three commodities are uniformly higher in Table 3.3 than in Table 3.2.

Equations (27) and (28) impose strong restrictions on the interest rate and inflation coefficients which depend on λ and on the imposed value for ν. It is therefore interesting to investigate whether the relatively poor performance of equations (27) and (28) is the result of these restrictions. A further relaxation of the restrictions imposed by the model is possible by dropping the requirement that stocks carried forward from the past should have the same depressing effect on prices as current excess supply. A reason for supposing that this restriction might not hold in the data is poor quality of stock data (which would tend to impart a downward bias to the estimated stock coefficient) or incomplete coverage of the stock series (which would have the opposite effect). This suggests examination of an equation specified as

$$p_t + g_t - \pi_t = \alpha - \beta_1 s_{t-1} - \beta_2 \sum_{i=0}^{\infty} \lambda^i \xi_{t+i|t} - \gamma r_t + \theta \Delta \pi_t \qquad (30)$$

Estimates of equation (30) are reported in Table 3.4. The likelihood ratio test against the corresponding Table 3.2 estimates shows that the restrictions in the Table 3.2 estimates are rejected (at the 5% level) only for coffee and sugar. However, only in the case of copper do the estimated coefficients all take the predicted sign. Relaxation of these restrictions therefore does little to save the model.

It is notable that both the coffee and tin markets have been regulated for most (coffee) or all (tin) of our sample period by international agreements which might be considered successful in terms of their own objectives – see Gilbert (1987). In a regulated market stockholders and speculators will need to base their price expectations on the anticipated behaviour of the regulatory authority – see Ghosh *et al.* (1987) and Anderson and Gilbert (1988). Our model omits these factors and it is therefore perhaps not surprising that its explanatory power is poor for these two commodities.

	Cocoa	Coffee	Copper	Rubber	Sugar	Tin
	Dependent Variable: $p_t + g_t - \pi_t$					
α intercept	7.794	4.613	1.770	9.113	12.510	1.094
	(1.310)	(6.609)	(1.218)	(1.686)	(7.477)	(1.283)
λ	− 0.985	0.403	0.780	− 0.761	0.857	0.681
	(0.099)	(0.246)	(0.123)	(1.024)	(0.317)	(0.330)
β_1 s_{t-1}	1.139	0.263	0.316	1.298	1.493	− 0.057
	(0.210)	(0.608)	(0.159)	(0.248)	(0.711)	(0.338)
β_2 $\sum \lambda^i \xi_{t+i|t}$	0.863	− 1.357	0.960	1.590	7.480	− 0.374
	(0.368)	(0.778)	(0.614)	(1.186)	(2.601)	(0.500)
γ r_t	− 0.575	17.747	1.047	1.737	− 8.482	− 0.493
	(2.567)	(4.749)	(3.098)	(1.485)	(5.375)	(3.040)
θ $\Delta \pi_t$	− 0.430	− 2.049	0.221	0.872	2.731	0.300
	(0.931)	(2.597)	(0.916)	(0.801)	(1.811)	(1.015)
Sample	67–85	74–85	63–85	64–85	63–85	63–85
s.d. (dep. var.)	0.774	0.481	0.428	0.328	0.643	0.218
R^2	0.775	0.777	0.773	0.867	0.639	0.316
s.e.	0.199	0.308	0.232	0.137	0.440	0.205
D.W.	2.275	2.994	2.224	2.260	1.848	1.359
Log-likelihood	− 10.23	− 9.75	− 16.71	− 4.20	− 31.41	− 13.83
Likelihood ratio $\chi^2(2)$	0.60	12.76	1.34	6.27	17.0	1.98

Table 3.4 Estimates of equation (30)

Note: Coefficient standard errors in parentheses. The likelihood ratio test is against the corresponding estimates in Table 3.2.

International commodity agreements have also been in force for part or all of our sample in the cocoa, rubber and sugar markets. However, the cocoa and sugar agreements have probably had very little influence on prices, and the rubber agreement, which has had some success in stabilizing prices, only came into operation at the end of 1980 which is near the end of our sample. It is therefore possible that the fact that we do not model the effects of international stabilization in these three markets also accounts for the poor to mixed performance of the theory but the argument seems less convincing than in coffee and tin. On the other hand, the single market (copper) where the theory does appear to offer a good explanation of price movements in the sample is the one market that we investigate in which there has been no intervention of any kind.

The econometric work reported in this paper was motivated (see

Section 1) by the question of the extent to which there is evidence of forward looking behaviour in primary commodity markets which will imply a degree of automatic price stabilization; and also the question of the extent to which these prices are influenced by changes in financial markets, and in particular the rate of interest. We need therefore to address explicitly these questions in relation to the three commodities (copper, rubber and sugar) where the econometric estimates offer some support for the theory.

Consider first the *copper* market. It is apparent from the estimates reported in Tables 3.2–3.4 that the forward looking parameter λ is always significantly greater than zero, and this does imply forward looking behaviour in this market. This supports the findings of Ghosh *et al.* (1987). On the other hand, the estimates in Table 3.4 suggest that the lagged stocks have a smaller effect on prices than current and anticipated future excess supply. Furthermore, the Table 3.4 estimates fail to show any evidence of either interest rate or inflation effects on the (real) copper price. Thus suggests simplification of the Table 3.4 equation to give

$$p_t + g_t - \pi_t = 1.571 - 0.295 s_{t-1} - 0.907 \sum_{i=0}^{10} 0.801^i \xi_{t+i|t}$$

$$(0.925)\ (0.133) \qquad (0.544)\quad (0.098)$$

Sample 1963–85 $R^2 = 0.771$ s.e. = 0.221   D.W. = 2.291
Log likelihood = − 16.83
Likelihood ratio test against Table 3.4 equation, $\chi^2(2) = 0.22$

The simplification is clearly accepted. The equation provides strong evidence of forward looking behaviour, but no evidence of any interest rate effect.

Now consider the *rubber* equation. None of the estimated equations suggests a positive value for λ but there is weak evidence in Table 3.4 for interest rate and inflation effects. Our simplified equation is

$$p_t + g_t - \pi_t = 9.167 - 1.300[s_{t-1} + \xi_t] - 1.608 r_t + 0.674 \Delta \pi_t$$
$$(1.217)\ (0.180) \qquad\qquad (1.479)\quad (0.557)$$

Sample 1964–85 $R^2 = 0.844$ s.e. = 0.139   D.W. = 2.179
Log likelihood = − 5.95
Likelihood ratio test against Table 3.4 equation, $\chi^2(2) = 3.50$

Again the simplification is acceptable, but this equation although consistent with the theory cannot be said to offer support for it.

Finally we consider the estimated *sugar* equation. Again there is no strong evidence for forward looking behaviour in the Table 3.4 estimates where λ is estimated as negative, although there is evidence in these estimates for an inflation effect and for a lower coefficient on lagged stocks than on current excess supply. We therefore chose as the simplified specification

$$p_t + g_t - \pi_t = 10.842 - 1.267s_{t-1} + 5.637\xi_t + 3.437\Delta\pi_t$$
$$(3.996)\quad(0.383)\qquad(2.443)\quad(1.991)$$

Sample 1963–85 $R^2 = 0.503$ s.e. $= 0.488$ D.W. $= 1.553$
Log likelihood $= -35.07$
Likelihood ratio test against Table 3.4 equation, $\chi^2(2) = 7.32$

Although the likelihood ratio test indicates a rejection relative to the Table 3.4 estimates this is due to elimination of the unacceptable negative λ coefficient. Again the estimated equation provides no evidence either of forward looking behaviour or for the influence of interest rates.

5   Conclusions

We have attempted in this paper to develop and apply the Muth (1961) rational expectations model of price formation on primary commodity markets. The Muth model implies that commodity prices should respond not only to the current supply–demand balance but also to anticipated future supply–demand balances and to the rate of interest. These propositions are important since forward looking behaviour implies a degree of automatic price stabilization; and because if the interest rate does impinge in a quantitatively significant way on these markets it implies an important link from monetary policy in the developed world to the terms of trade of the developing world.

We investigated these propositions using annual data for six commodities – cocoa, coffee, copper, rubber, sugar and tin. Ghosh *et al.* (1987) had previously found evidence of forward looking behaviour in the copper market and we confirmed this result. On the other hand, we were unable to reproduce this result for the other five commodities we investigated. It is notable that copper is the only commodity in this group which was not subject to any international intervention during the period we considered, and it may therefore be that a model which takes these interventions into account may be more successful. Alternatively, our negative results may simply reflect the fact that our production and consumption models were insufficiently realistic to pick up future supply–demand balances. This explanation appears plausible for rubber and sugar where the current supply–demand balance was important in explaining price movements, but we have to admit that our models for cocoa, coffee and tin were completely unsuccessful. In the cases of coffee and tin there are strong reasons for supposing that this was due to the inability of our model to account for the effects of international intervention.

This research therefore gives limited support to the view that it is important to take anticipated future market conditions into account in assessing the price prospects in primary markets. This is true in copper, but in other markets we do not find evidence that industry practice of assessing prices in relation only to the current supply–demand situation would be misleading. In no case did we find a successful model in which there were clearly defined and quantitatively significant interest rate effects on commodity prices. This does imply that academic commentaries, such as Currie *et al.* (1988), which suggest that interest rates link developed country monetary policy to developing country terms of trade may be guilty of giving an excessive role to an influence which in reality is only of second-order importance.

APPENDIX: THE MUTH MODEL
From (1), (2) and (4)

$$s_t = s_{t-1} + \xi_t + (e + \epsilon)p_t \tag{A1}$$

Planned stocks $\hat{s}_{t+1|t}$ are given as

$$\hat{s}_{t+1|t} = s_t + \xi_{t+1|t} + (e + \epsilon)p_{t+1|t} \tag{A2}$$

Subtracting (A1) from (A2) gives

$$\hat{s}_{t+1|t} - 2s_t + s_{t-1} = (\xi_{t+1|t} - \xi_t) + (e + \epsilon)(p_{t+1|t} - p_t - r_t) \tag{A3}$$
$$+ (e + \epsilon)r_t$$

Now substitute (3) into (A3) to give

$$\hat{s}_{t+1|t} - \left(2 + \frac{e + \epsilon}{\alpha}\right)s_t + s_{t-1} = (\xi_{t+1|t} - \xi_t) + (e + \epsilon)r_t \tag{A4}$$

Write the left hand side of (A4) as

$$(1 - \lambda_1 L)(1 - \lambda_2 L)\hat{s}_{t+1|t}$$

Then $\lambda_1 + \lambda_2 = 2 + \dfrac{e + \epsilon}{\alpha} > 2$

and $\lambda_1 \lambda_2 = 1$

Take $\lambda_1 > \lambda_2$ without loss of generality. Then it follows that

$$\lambda_1 > 1 > \lambda_2 > 0$$

Write the stable root $\lambda_2 = \lambda$ so that $\lambda_1 = 1/\lambda$. Then

$$(1 - \lambda_1 L)(1 - \lambda_2 L)\hat{s}_{t+1|t} = -\frac{1}{\lambda}(1 - \lambda L^{-1})(1 - \lambda L)s_t$$

This allows us to multiply (A4) through by $-\dfrac{\lambda}{1 - \lambda L^{-1}}$ to obtain

$$s_t = \lambda s_{t-1} - \lambda \sum_{i=0}^{\infty} \lambda^i \{(\xi_{t+i+1|t} - \xi_{t+i|t}) + (e + \epsilon)r_{t+i|t}\} \tag{A5}$$

Note that

$$\sum_{i=0}^{\infty} \lambda^i(\xi_{t+i+1|t} - \xi_{t+i|t}) = (1 - \lambda) \sum_{i=1}^{\infty} \lambda^{i-1} \xi_{t+i|t} - \xi_t$$

allowing us to rewrite (A5) as

$$s_t = \lambda \left[s_{t-1} + \xi_t - (1 - \lambda) \sum_{i=1}^{\infty} \lambda^{i-1} \xi_{t+i|t} - (e + \epsilon) \sum_{i=0}^{\infty} \lambda^i r_{t+i|t} \right]$$

which is equation (6).

To obtain the associated price equation solve (A6) into (A1) to give

$$(e + \epsilon)p_t = -(1 - \lambda) \left[s_{t-1} + \sum_{i=0}^{\infty} \lambda^i \xi_{t+i|t} \right] - \lambda(e + \epsilon) \sum_{i=0}^{\infty} \lambda^i r_{t+i|t} \quad (A7)$$

This is equation (8). Similarly, in period $t - 1$

$$(e + \epsilon)p_{t-1} = -(1 - \lambda) \left[s_{t-2} + \sum_{i=0}^{\infty} \lambda^i \xi_{t+i-1|t-1} \right]$$

$$- \lambda(e + \epsilon) \sum_{i=0}^{\infty} \lambda^i r_{t+i-1|t-1} \quad (A8)$$

Use (A1) to eliminate s_{t-2} to give

$$\lambda(e + \epsilon)p_{t-1} = -(1 - \lambda) \left[s_{t-1} + \lambda \sum_{i=0}^{\infty} \lambda^i \xi_{t+i|t-1} \right]$$

$$- \lambda(e + \epsilon)r_{t-1} - \lambda^2(e + \epsilon) \sum_{i=0}^{\infty} \lambda^i r_{t+i|t-1} \quad (A9)$$

Subtracting (A9) from (A7) gives

$$p_t = \lambda(p_{t-1} + r_{t-1}) - \frac{1 - \lambda}{e + \epsilon} \sum_{i=0}^{\infty} \lambda^i(\xi_{t+i|t} - \lambda \xi_{t+i|t-1})$$

$$- \lambda \sum_{i=0}^{\infty} \lambda^i(r_{t+i|t} - \lambda r_{t+i|t-1}) \quad (A10)$$

which is (9).

Now consider the model in which (2) is replaced by

$$Q_t = \bar{Q}[\xi_{2t} + \epsilon p_{t|t-1}] \quad (A11)$$

in which production depends on the lagged expectation of the current price. Excess supply x_t at the price $\bar{p}$ is given as

$$x_t = \xi_t + ep_t + \epsilon p_{t|t-1} \quad (A12)$$

It is clearly not restrictive in this linear model to suppose that there is no lagged response in consumption. A useful device is to define the 'generalized stock level' as σ where

$$\sigma_t = s_t + \epsilon p_{t+1|t}$$

This generalized stock may be interpreted as the total availability of the commodity at the start of period $t + 1$ resulting both from storage decisions (s_t) and production decisions taken in period t. To obtain the generalized storage function, we write (3) in terms of r_t:

$$\sigma_t = (\alpha + \epsilon)(p_{t+1|t} - p_t - r_t) + \epsilon(p_t + r_t) \quad (A13)$$

We also need to rewrite (A1) in terms of σ. After some manipulation one obtains

$$\sigma_t = \rho(\sigma_{t-1} + \xi_t) + (\rho e + \epsilon)p_t + \epsilon r_t \qquad (A14)$$

where $\rho = 1 + \epsilon/\alpha$. Multiply (A14) through by α and difference to obtain the planned level $\hat{\sigma}_{t+1|t}$ as

$$\alpha\hat{\sigma}_{t+1|t} - (2\alpha + \epsilon)\sigma_t + (\alpha + \epsilon)\sigma_{t-1} = (\alpha + \epsilon)(\xi_{t-1|t} - \xi_t)$$
$$+ [(\alpha + \epsilon)e + \alpha\epsilon](p_{t+1|t} - p_t - r_t) + \alpha\epsilon r_{t+1|t} + (\alpha + \epsilon)er_t, \qquad (A15)$$

(compare (A3)). Multiply (A15) through by $(\alpha + \epsilon)$ and substitute from (A13) to give

$$\alpha(\alpha + \epsilon)\hat{\sigma}_{t+1|t} - [(\alpha + \epsilon)(2\alpha + e + \epsilon) + \alpha\epsilon]\sigma_t + (\alpha + \epsilon)^2\sigma_{t-1}$$
$$= (\alpha + \epsilon)^2(\xi_{t+1|t} - \xi_t) - \epsilon[(\alpha + \epsilon)e + \alpha\epsilon]p_t + \alpha\epsilon(\alpha + \epsilon)r_{t+1|t}$$
$$+ [(\alpha + \epsilon)^2 e - (\alpha + \epsilon)e\epsilon - \alpha\epsilon^2]r_t \qquad (A16)$$

Now substitute for p_t from (A12) into (A14) to give (after cancellation)

$$\hat{\sigma}_{t+1|t} - \left(2 + \frac{e + \epsilon}{\alpha}\right)\sigma_t + \sigma_{t-1} = (\rho\xi_{t+1|t} - \xi_t) + \epsilon r_{t+1|t} + \epsilon r_t \qquad (A17)$$

which is exactly analogous to (A4). Solving in the same way obtains

$$\sigma_t = \lambda\sigma_{t-1} - \lambda \sum_{i=0}^{\infty} \lambda^i \{(\rho\xi_{t+i+1|t} - \xi_{t+i|t}) + \epsilon r_{t+i+1|t} + \epsilon r_{t+i|t}\} \qquad (A18)$$

Noting that

$$\sum_{i=0}^{\infty} \lambda^i(\rho\xi_{t+i+1|t} - \xi_{t+i|t}) = (\rho - \lambda) \sum_{i=0}^{\infty} \lambda^{i-1}\xi_{t+i|t} - \xi_t$$

we may rewrite (A18) as

$$\sigma_t = \lambda\left[\sigma_{t-1} + \xi_t - (\rho - \lambda) \sum_{i=1}^{\infty} \lambda^{i-1}\xi_{t+i|t} - \epsilon r_t - (\lambda e + \epsilon) \sum_{i=1}^{\infty} \lambda^{i-1}r_{t+i|t}\right] \qquad (A19)$$

Derivation of the associated price process again follows the same pattern as in the simple model. Substitute (A19) into (A14) to obtain

$$p_t = -\frac{\rho - \lambda}{\rho e + \epsilon}\left[\sigma_{t-1} + \sum_{i=0}^{\infty} \lambda^i\xi_{t+i|t}\right] - \frac{\lambda e + \epsilon}{\rho e + \epsilon} \sum_{i=0}^{\infty} \lambda^i r_{t+i|t} \qquad (A20)$$

which generalizes (8). Similarly, in period $t - 1$, we obtain (using (A14))

$$\lambda p_{t-1} = -\frac{(\rho - \lambda)}{\rho e + \epsilon}\left[\sigma_{t-1} + \lambda\rho \sum_{i=0}^{\infty} \lambda^i\xi_{t+i|t-1}\right]$$
$$- \lambda r_{t-1} - \frac{\rho\lambda(\lambda e + \epsilon)}{\rho e + \epsilon} \sum_{i=0}^{\infty} \lambda^i r_{t+i|t+1} \qquad (A21)$$

Subtract (A21) from (A20) to give

$$p_t = \lambda(p_{t-1} + r_{t-1}) - \frac{\rho - \lambda}{\rho e + \epsilon} \sum_{i=0}^{\infty} \lambda^i(\xi_{t+i|t} - \rho\lambda\xi_{t+i|t-1})$$

$$- \frac{\lambda e + \epsilon}{\rho e + \epsilon} \sum_{i=0}^{\infty} \lambda^i(r_{t+i|t} - \rho\lambda r_{t+i|t-1}) \qquad (A22)$$

Equations (A22) relaxes (9) in two respects: the coefficient of the expectational quasi-differences in equation (8) is restricted to be equal to the coefficient λ on the lagged dependent variable, while in (A22) this equality is replaced by an inequality restriction (since $\rho \geq 1$); and equation (A22) does not impose any restriction (for e and ϵ unknown) on the magnitude of the overall interest rate effect.

In a multiple currency world, (A1) is replaced by (A22)

$$s_t = s_{t-1} + \xi_t + (e + \epsilon)(p_t + g_t - \pi_t) \qquad (A23)$$

Analogously to (A4), we obtain

$$\hat{s}_{t+1|t} - \left[2 + \frac{e + \epsilon}{\alpha}\right] s_t + s_{t-1} = (\xi_{t+1|t} - \xi_t)$$

$$+ (e + \epsilon)[r_t - (\pi_{t-1|t} - \pi_t) + (h_{t+1|t} - h_t)] = (\xi_{t+1|t} - \xi_t) + (e + \epsilon)r_t^* \qquad (A24)$$

Proceeding as previously with r^* replacing r gives the stock equation (21). To obtain the price equations (22) and (23) note that (A10) is replaced by

$$(p_t + g_t - \pi_t) = \lambda(p_{t-1|t} + g_{t-1} - \pi_{t-1} + r_{t-1}^*)$$

$$- \frac{1 - \lambda}{e + \epsilon} \sum_{i=0}^{\infty} (\xi_{t+i|t} - \xi_{t+i|t-1}) - \lambda \sum_{i=0}^{\infty} \lambda^i (r_{t+i|t}^* - r_{t+i|t-1}^*) \qquad (A25)$$

Equation (29) is obtained by noting that

$$- \lambda \Delta \pi_{t|t-1} + \lambda \sum_{i=0}^{\infty} \lambda^i (\Delta \pi_{t+i+1} - \lambda \Delta \pi_{t+i+1|t-1}) = - \lambda \nu \Delta \pi_{t-1}$$

$$+ \frac{\lambda \nu}{1 - \lambda \nu} (\Delta \pi_t - \lambda \nu \Delta \pi_{t-1}) = \frac{\lambda \nu}{1 - \lambda \nu} \Delta^2 \pi_t \qquad (A26)$$

NOTES
* We have benefited from comments made at the conference, in particular those of the discussant Ken Wallis. Part of the material was contained in a paper given at the 25th International conference of the Applied Econometric Association on International Commodity Market Modelling, Washington D.C., 23–25 October 1988. The research was financed by the ESRC under grant B00232191.
1 Gilbert (1989) shows that the high weight of the Canadian dollar in the MERM index results in commodity price elasticities with respect to this index which, in certain cases, exceed unity.

REFERENCES
Anderson, R. W. and C. L. Gilbert (1988) 'Commodity agreements and commodity markets: lessons from tin', *Economic Journal* **98**, 1–15.

Currie, D., D. Vines, T. Moutos, A. Muscatelli and N. Vidalis (1988) 'North–South Interactions: a general equilibrium framework for the study of strategic issues', in D. Currie and D. Vines (eds.): *Macroeconomic Interactions between North and South*, Cambridge University Press.

Engle, R. F. and C. W. Granger (1987) 'Co-integration and error correction: representation, estimation and testing', *Econometrica* **55**, 251–76.

Ghosh, S., C. L. Gilbert and A. J. Hughes Hallett (1983) 'Tests of functional form in dynamic econometric models: some empirical experience', *Empirical Economics* **8**, 63–9.

Ghosh, S., C. L. Gilbert and A. J. Hughes Hallett (1987) *Stabilizing Speculative Commodity Markets*, Oxford, Oxford University Press.

Gilbert, C. L. (1985) 'Efficient market commodity price dynamics', World Bank, Commodity Studies and Projections Division, Working Paper 1985–4.

Gilbert, C. L. (1987) 'International commodity agreements: design and performance', *World Development* **15**, 591–616.

Gilbert, C. L. (1988) 'The dynamics of commodity stocks and prices and the specification of econometric commodity price models', Institute of Economics and Statistics, Oxford mimeo.

Gilbert, C. L. (1989) 'The impact of exchange rates and developing country debt on commodity prices;, *Economic Journal* **99**, 773–84.

Gilbert, C. L. and T. Palaskas (1989) 'Modelling expectations formation in primary commodity markets', Department of Economics, Queen Mary College, Working Paper No. 192.

Gustafson, R. L. (1958a) 'Carryover levels for grains: a method for determining amounts that are optimal under specified conditions', USDA, Technical Bulletin, no. 1178.

Gustafson, R. L. (1958b) 'Implications of recent research on optimal storage rules', *Journal of Farm Economics* **40**, 290–300.

Hotelling, H. (1931) 'The economics of exhaustible resources', *Journal of Political Economy* **39**, 139–75.

McCallum, B. (1976) 'Rational expectations and the natural rate hypothesis: some consistent estimates', *Econometrica* **44**, 43–52.

Miranda, M. J. and P. G. Helmberger (1988) 'The effects of commodity price stabilization programs', *American Economic Review* **78**, 46–58.

Muth, J. F. (1961) 'Rational expectations and the theory of price movements', *Econometrica* **29**, 313–35.

Newbery, D. M. and J. E. Stiglitz (1982) 'Optimal commodity stockpiling rules', *Oxford Economic Papers* **34**, 403–27.

Pagan, A. R. (1984) 'Econometric issues in the analysis of regressions with generated regressors', *International Economic Review* **25**, 221–47.

Pesaran, M. H. (1987) *The Limits to Rational Expectations*, Oxford, Blackwell.

Ridler, D. and C. A. Yandle (1972) 'A simplified method for analyzing the effects of exchange rate changes on exports of a primary commodity', *IMF Staff Papers* **19**, 559–78.

Samuelson, P. A. (1957) 'Intertemporal price equilibrium: a prologue to the theory of speculation', *Weltwirtschaftliches Archiv.* **71**, 181–219; reprinted in P. A. Samuelson: *Collected Scientific Papers* (J. E. Stiglitz ed.) **2**, 946–84.

Shiller, R. J., J. Y. Campbell and K. L. Schoenholtz (1983) 'Forward rates and future policy: interpreting the term structure of interest rates', *Brookings Papers on Economic Activity* **1**, 173–217.

Working, H. (1960) 'Note on the correlation of first differences of averages in a random chain', *Econometrica* **28**, 916–18.

Wright, B. D. and J. C. Williams (1982) 'The economic role of commodity storage', *Economic Journal* **92**, 596–614.

Discussion

MONTAGUE J. LORD

Chris Gilbert and Theo Palaskas have suggested a useful approach to the application of the theory of rational expectations to the empirical analysis of price determination in commodity markets. The most important innovation of the paper lies in the formulation of expectations concerning quantities, rather than prices. Despite the limitations of the initial results, the concept is plausible in that economic agents anticipate the effect on future inventory levels from lagged production responses. Price expectations therefore reflect quantity expectations in commodity markets with inventories.

Gilbert and Palaskas have also provided valuable insights into the process by which the theory they set forth provides an accurate representation of the underlying data generating processes in commodity markets. Those who argue that econometric models are not intended to be an accurate description of the real world have not had to confront policy makers who must base their decisions on forecasts generated by economists who rely on these types of econometric models for their projections. For this reason, it would be useful if the authors would eventually provide the usual performance tests of their model using 1986–8 data.

Having made these general remarks, and since I agree with the theory set forth by the authors about the way in which expectations are formed, I will direct my specific comments to extensions of the model, in the light of my own interests.

Reduced form models

Gilbert and Palaskas estimate structural equations for production and consumption and then proceed to estimate their alternative price equations. The question arises as to whether to estimate market prices from a reduced form equation or from a system of equations in their structural form. The first stage estimation of quantity expectations does not preclude the second stage estimation of the structural form of the model specified in the study.

Ultimately, the answer to this question depends on the purpose of the models. If models are aimed at policy applications, then it would be appropriate to estimate the system of equations in its structural form if it is to have a wide range of applications. This applies, for example, to market intervention schemes. In this case, export quotas or buffer stocks are used as instruments to achieve a given target. This type of model also applies to trade liberalization schemes which affect the level of consumption in commodity markets.

Models estimated in their reduced form are useful in forecasting applications, however. In this field, we need to consider two major applications for commodity models: short-term projections of one year or less for trading purposes, and long-term projections for planning and investment strategies. In short-term projections, data availability is an advantage in time-series models; in long-term projections, the key issue is whether the models can capture the underlying cyclical behaviour of markets for non-perishable commodities. These cyclical patterns arise in commodity markets because producers often take several years to react fully to price changes, and consumers of raw materials and basic, pre-processed foods take time to adjust to price changes. In the following section we consider how this behaviour can be characterized within the modeling framework set forth by Gilbert and Palaskas.

Extensions of the Gilbert–Palaskas model

The empirical results of Gilbert and Palaskas suggest the existence of a non-contemporaneous response to prices in either production or consumption of the six commodities covered by their study. Thus the incorporation of the lag structure in the estimated equations for consumption and production would be likely to improve the empirical results for market prices. For this reason it would be particularly useful to be able to estimate their 'Model with Lagged Response' in the Appendix to their paper.

Consider a simplified representation of equations (1) and (13), but where their functional specification is either linear or log-linear:

$$C_t = \xi_{1t} - \gamma p_t \tag{1}$$

$$Q_t = \xi_{2t} + \epsilon p_{t-n} \quad \text{where } n > 0 \tag{A11}$$

$$S_t = \bar{S} + \alpha \bar{Q}(p_{t+1|t} - p_t - r_t) \tag{3}$$

$$S_t = S_{t-1} + Q_t - C_t \tag{4}$$

Setting actual stocks in equation (4) equal to desired stocks in equation (3), and using Gilbert and Palaskas' equation (A19) in the first stage of the estimation procedure, yields:

$$p_t = 1/\gamma[Q_t - \Delta S_t - \xi_{1t}] \tag{A22a'}$$

if the functional specification for C_t and Q_t is linear, and

$$p_t = [(Q_t - \Delta S_t)/\xi_{1t}]^{-1/e} \qquad (A22b')$$

if the functional specification for C_t and Q_t is log-linear.

The system of equations to be estimated would therefore consist of (3), (A11), and either (A22a') or (A22b'). This formulation does not remedy the problem of estimating ρ in Gilbert and Palaskas' equation (A19), however. Nor does it simplify the calculation of the reduced form equations for stocks when production and consumption are specified as log-linear equations. Instead, it suggests an approach to estimating the second stage so that the model captures the feedback effects between prices and quantities that give rise to observed cyclical behaviour in commodity markets. This approach permits an examination of price formation in terms of the dynamics underlying the data generating processes of the six primary commodities covered in the Gilbert–Palaskas study, rather than in terms of their analysis of a model where only contemporaneous effects are considered in the market clearing identity.

Conclusion

To sum up, Gilbert and Palaskas provide a credible explanation of how expectations are formulated in commodity markets and offer a number of insights on how to implement empirically the theory they set forth. What their results underscore is the need for further exploration of the dynamics underlying the structural form of the equations in this type of modelling framework.

KENNETH S. WALLIS

This is an interesting exploratory study, the revised version of which incorporates a number of my previous comments, as the authors note. Two broad issues remain for discussion.

First, at the technical level, it is not clear that the solution for the price process is the most appropriate representation to choose for empirical implementation in models with unobserved forward expectations variables. Several methods are available for the direct estimation of equations containing forward expectations, and this has the advantage that fewer auxiliary hypotheses are required. In contrast, if the explicit solution form is used, a joint hypothesis is under test, and when interpreting the results it is often difficult to disentangle the basic model from the auxiliary hypotheses that are required. Two such hypotheses employed in the present case are that interest rates follow a random walk and that uncovered interest parity holds. That the variance of interest rates increases without bound is *a priori* implausible, and the hypothesis of uncovered interest parity is generally rejected in empirical tests. It might then be prudent to adopt an empirical approach which does not rely on such assumptions. It should be emphasized that this reservation concerns the econometric implementation of models with explicit forward-looking variables, and it is not an argument against the formulation and use of such models. In policy analysis in other areas of economics such models are proving most helpful, and the same can be expected in commodity markets. In macroeconomics, for example, they provide a natural framework within which such issues as the credibility and sustainability of policy, and the consequences of the possibility of the eventual reversal of an intervention, can be fruitfully considered.

This leads into the second question, namely, what is the appropriate strategy for modelling markets subject to intervention. The authors offer a kind of counterfactual strategy: the Muth competitive equilibrium model is extended to incorporate stockholding; its empirical performance is found to be disappointing; this is explained by the fact that markets have been regulated. Surely a more productive strategy would be to incorporate known institutional features into the models from the beginning. Of course this may require a more commodity-specific approach, if the nature of the regulation and the policy instruments employed differ across commodities. But the models that are eventually estimated may then represent a closer approximation to the data generation process, and hence be more helpful in further policy analysis. In particular, they may offer answers to standard counterfactual questions, such as what if a different policy had been pursued or, indeed, what if no intervention had occurred, which models built as if no intervention had occurred do not begin to answer.

Summary of general discussion

Leo Drollas wondered why there should be so much worry about the accuracy of directly measured stock series when they can be generated from benchmark figures. Gilbert responded that such data can be highly misleading because of the cumulation of measurement errors: generating stock data was a possible but not always advisable route to take. Drollas also pointed out that Gilbert's paper considered only speculative stocks, either ignoring the precautionary demand for commodity stocks or subsuming them under demand; this is an unwarranted procedure in the oil sector where the precautionary demand makes up an important part of total stocks.

Louis Phlips asked whether the exclusion of the convenience yield could not be rectified by a simple device such as a quadratic function, the derivative of which would be linear. In response, Gilbert asserted that the convenience yield would be better represented by a hyperbolic function. He summarized the distinction between the two by pointing out that the hyperbolic function yields a stable root in the difference equation and that the convenience yield in such a function will not be influenced by the extent of backwardation in the market; whereas a quadratic description of convenience yield is useful in allowing linearity in the model and the simple incorporation of interest rates.

Michael Wickens pointed out that dynamics and rational expectations are compatible; that is to say that setting up a model in a dynamic form does not inhibit the specification of rational expectations. However, Gilbert explained that even in the Appendix the dynamics had to be restricted so as to get second-order representations and to avoid higher-order difference equations.

Mark Taylor said he expected significant ARCH effects in a forward looking model as the one discussed here. He was therefore interested in seeing not only conditional first moments being considered, but also the inclusion of conditional second moments, e.g. forecast errors, and the modelling of heteroscedasticity by means of an ARCH representation. Gilbert pointed out that one of the response parameters in the model (alpha) does in fact contain the price variance in its denominator. He said he had looked at ARCH processes, which can be picked up, but with such a small sample it was not clear whether they merely reflected large residuals.

4 The Prices of Perennial Crops: The Role of Rational Expectations and Commodity Stocks*

PRAVIN K. TRIVEDI

1 Introduction

The general question of price determination is complex since it involves issues concerning the structure of markets in which a commodity is traded and whether these conditions can lead to disequilibrium. For commodities like tea and cocoa, and perhaps also other tree crops, there is a widespread presumption that price determination conforms to the basic paradigm of competitive markets, at least as a good first-order approximation. If this position is accepted, 'price equations' should correspond to the standard 'law of supply and demand' in which the change of price is a function of the gap between market demand and supply.

The elementary static market model consisting of supply and demand equations plus the equilibrium condition, will determine three endogenous variables, viz., quantity demanded, quantity supplied and the price. If an inventory accumulation identity is added to the model, so that equality of production and demand period by period is no longer required, the basic picture does not change if a new equilibrium condition is added which stipulates that the prevailing price must be such that inventories are willingly held. When inventories are included a price equation is not necessarily required to close the model.

The original research objective which instigated the present paper was intended to develop a satisfactory representation of the price formation process in the context of global econometric models for perennial crops like cocoa and tea (Akiyama and Trivedi, 1987).[1] An important question in this regard is whether inclusion in such models of an explicit price equation incorporating future expectational variables would constitute an improvement over the currently more popular approaches; see, for example, Adams and Behrman (1976), Hwa (1985), Burger and Smit (1988) and Manger (1988).

In global commodity models, comprising blocks of supply and demand equations, including demand for inventories, no structural price equation is required if market clears in each period. The price may be obtained by solving for the value which clears the market. In one variant of this approach the inventory equation is 'inverted' to yield a price equation[2], and inventories are then determined as a residual from the supply-demand identity. Nevertheless, so long as it is assumed that inventories at the end of the period are willingly held, this is still a model in which price adjusts to clear the market each period and in which an explicit price equation is not necessary.

Implementation of the above scheme has sometimes generated inconsistencies. Viewed as equilibrium price models some formulations (Adams and Behrman, 1976; Hwa, 1985) are unsatisfactory because they include both partial adjustment stock-holding *and* price equations, implying that the model may generate price paths that entail unplanned inventory accumulation. In other cases global agricultural commodity models are internally consistent, but have not adequately reflected forward-looking speculation which is sometimes thought to characterize inventory adjustment behaviour (Muth, 1961; Ghosh, Gilbert and Hughes Hallett, 1987). The so-called 'speculative demand for inventories', which makes inventory demand depend upon expected future change in price, introduces future dated endogenous variables and leads to significant analytical and computational complications, especially if one adopts the rational expectations equilibrium concept. However, since the latter is a more general equilibrium concept it seems interesting to consider how it might be implemented in a global commodity model, what problems arise from such an attempt and whether the operational versions of such models lead to significant improvement over its antecedents.

The rest of the paper is organized as follows. Section 2 derives an equilibrium price adjustment equation consistent with rational expectations in the context of a 'linear prototype' of a global commodity model which incorporates intertemporal demand for inventories. This model generates a price equation in which expectations about future price, in turn based on expectations about future excess demand, can play a role. It then considers the possibility that market participants cannot directly observe inventories, and hence must base their behaviour on a proxy for them. This Section suggests that agents' responses to certain variables may be temporally unstable; it grafts a Kalman filter model of learning and/or information revision on to the model of price behaviour and has interesting testable econometric consequences. Section 3 exploits the insights of Section 2 in the specification and estimation of price-inventory equations for three perennial crops, viz., tea, cocoa and vegetable oils. These empirical examples are intended to furnish evidence on whether forward-looking behaviour adds significantly to one's understanding of why or when inventory positions have a significant impact on price movements. Section 4 concludes with a general discussion of this approach and a comparison with other approaches.

2   Some issues of specification

In extending these basic ideas to a global dynamic model of a perennial crop, several complications need to be considered. First, there is the complication arising from the existence of a production lag or a gestation lag. Production is determined in part by price expectations held in the past about the current price level. The second complication arises when the existence of demand for inventories (consisting of a transactions component and a speculative component) is introduced. The latter component, in the usual specification, depends upon the difference between the prevailing market price and the expected future price of that commodity. There is an intimate connection between the current price and the expected, past, current and future prices. The third complication arises from the hypothesis of rational expectations which implies certain restrictions on the equations of the model and on the errors of expectation.

If commodity market disequilibria last for relatively short time periods, the assumption of rational expectations has considerable appeal. In such a model one may wish to characterize the response of the equilibrium price level to stochastic demand and supply shocks using the rational expectations solution to the model. Such an exercise can involve complications in a global commodity model which would necessarily contain a large number of exogenous variables (both on the demand and on the supply side) and which is highly likely to be nonlinear. Furthermore, within a global model the demand and supply equations would be specified in terms of local consumer and producer prices which in turn would reflect the effects of local taxes, exchange rates and so forth. 'The price' which clears the market, however, is the average world price. In that sense 'the price equation' of the model should be specified to explain the average world price. The model-closure equation in conjunction with the rest of the model determines the average world price.[3]

I begin with a linear prototype model. The rational expectations solution to this model is the theoretical price equation used as the (admittedly rather loose) basis for the empirical price equation.

2.2 The linear prototype

The linearized model of world demand and supply is similar to Muth's inventory model and consists of the following equations:

$$Q_t = \gamma_1 P_t + \gamma_2 P_t^e + \psi_1 X_{1t} + u_{1t} \quad \text{(production)} \tag{1}$$

$$Q_t^d = -\beta_1 P_t + \psi_2 X_{2t} + u_{2t} \quad \text{(demand)} \tag{2}$$

$$P_t^e = E[P_t | I_{t-1}] \quad \text{(expectations)} \tag{3}$$

$$H_t^d = \delta_1(P_{t+1}^e - P_t) + \delta_2 Q_{t+1}^{d,e} \quad \text{(inventory demand)} \tag{4}$$

$$H_t = H_{t-1} + Q_t - Q_t^d \quad \text{(market clearing)} \tag{5}$$

$$H_t^d = H_t \quad \text{(market clearing)} \tag{6}$$

The current meaning of the symbols is as follows:

Q : World production
Q^d : World demand for consumption
P : World price
P_t^e : World price for period t expected in period $t - 1$
X_{1t}, X_{2t} : Vectors of exogenous variables
H_t : Inventories at the end of period t
$Q_{t+1}^{d,e}$: World demand for period $t + 1$ expected in period t
H_t^d : World demand for inventories
u_{1t}, u_{2t} : Stochastic disturbances
I_t : Information set at time t

It is not necessary for present purposes to provide a detailed justification of equations (1) and (2) which are consistent with standard theory. Assume δ_1, δ_2, β_1, γ_1, γ_2, to be positive. To preserve the homogeneity property of the demand and supply functions the price variable appearing in such equations should be the real price. In the context of a world demand and supply model the appropriate deflators to use in (1), (2), and (4), respectively, will be different and will be functions of the general world price level and exchange rates in the producing, consuming and stock-holding countries. At the theoretical level the simplifying assumption is made that the deflators are all the same, implying that the price variable(s) in different equations are the same. An alternative possibility is to interpret P as the nominal price but to include the relevant deflators and exchange rates as exogenous variables in all equations where the price variable appears. To ensure homogenity the parameters of the equation would then be subject to additional restrictions.

Equation (4) is a variant of the standard inventory equation used in the supply of storage literature (Weymar, 1968). The first term on the right-hand side is the speculative component. Strictly speaking this component should depend upon the expected price change net of the cost of storage (usually proxied by an interest rate variable), but for simplicity storage costs are ignored. It is assumed $\delta_1 > 0$. Some derivations of the demand for speculative inventories show the coefficient δ_1 to be a nonlinear function of higher moments of the distribution of P but this possibility is also ignored. The second term in (4) reflects transactions demand for inventories which produce a positive convenience yield. The demand for inventories for transactions purposes depends upon expected future consumption demand, denoted $Q_{t+1}^{d,e}$.

Equation (4) may be interpreted as a price equation. Combining (4) and (6) and normalizing on P_t leads to

$$P_t = (1/\delta_1)H_t + P_{t+1}^e + (\delta_2/\delta_1)Q_{t+1}^{d,e}$$

$$= -(1/\delta_1)H_t + \left(1 - \frac{\beta_1 \delta_2}{\delta_1}\right)P_{t+1}^e + (\delta_2/\delta_1)(\psi_2 X_{2,t+1}^e + u_{2,t+1}^e)$$

$$(7)$$

whence it is seen that the period t price will depend, *inter alia*, upon (factors which drive) expected future price and on the expected future values of X_2. Equation (7) is 'structural' in the sense that its parameters have a behavioural interpretation. However, if additional parametric assumptions about the process generating future values of X_2 are substituted into (6), then the resulting equation contains some parameters which are not 'structural' in one sense. Sometimes when a futures market exists, the futures price is used as a proxy for P_{t+1}^e; if a proxy variable for $X_{2,t+1}$ can also be found, then (7) could be estimated directly. However, the holding identity implies a definitional relationship between the future price, the current price and the carrying cost, so the interpretation of the results will not be straightforward. If no futures price variable is available, estimation may be approached indirectly by first solving the model to obtain a reduced form solution for P_{t+1}^e and then substituting it back into (7) to produce a pseudo-structural equation for P_t.

2.3   Solution of the model

The solution approach follows Pesaran (1987). Combining (1)–(6) and solving for P_t yields the following linear equation:

$$P_t = \lambda P_{t-1} + \alpha P_{t+1}^e + \beta P_t^e + v_t \qquad (8)$$

where λ, α, β and v_t are defined as follows:

$$\lambda = \delta_1 d^{-1}$$
$$d = \gamma_1 + \beta_1 + \delta_1$$
$$\alpha = (\delta_2 \beta_1 - \delta_1) d^{-1}$$
$$\beta = (\delta_2 \beta_1 - \gamma_2 - \delta_1) d^{-1}$$
$$v_t = [\delta_2 u^e_{2,t+1} - \delta_2 u^e_{2t} + u_{2t} - u_{1t} - \psi_1 X_{1t}$$
$$+ \delta_2 \psi_2 (X_{2,t+1} - X^e_{2t}) + \psi_2 X^e_{2t}] d^{-1}$$

The superscript e denotes expectation conditional on I_{t-1}. Note that the stochastic demand and supply disturbances, the current and expected future values of X_2 and the current value of X_1 all appear as components of v_t. The explicit solution of the equation (8) depends upon the roots of the quadratic equation

$$\alpha \mu^2 - (1 - \beta) \mu + \lambda = 0. \tag{9}$$

Although there are several cases to consider, a special case of some interest is one in which equation (9) has two real roots μ_1 and μ_2, $\mu_1 < 1$ and $\mu_2 > 1$. This is sometimes referred to as the 'regular' case.

The general solution for P_t involves a 'backward' and 'forward' infinite series in v_t. If no further restrictions are imposed, such a solution need not be unique, but there are a number of ways of achieving uniqueness. One is to assume that the stochastic process generating input variables in the difference equation (8) is stationary. In this case a unique stable 'forward' solution will exist. To show this explicitly define the process

$$v_t = (1 - \alpha \mu_1)^{-1} \sum_{i=0}^{\infty} \mu_2^{-i} E(v_{t+i} | I_t) \tag{10}$$

and assume that this is a realizable stationary process. Then using arguments given by Pesaran (1987) it can be shown that the unique reduced form forward solution for P_t is given by

$$P_t = \mu_1 P_{t-1} + v_t - \omega E(v_t | I_{t-1}) \tag{11}$$

where $\omega = (\delta_2 \beta_1 - \gamma_2 - \delta_1) / [(\delta_2 \beta_1 - \delta_1) \mu_2]$

(10) and (11) show that P_t is determined by current and expected future values of the X_1 and X_2 and of μ_{1t} and μ_{2t}.

If the stochastic process generating the exogenous variables X_1 and X_2 can be specified explicitly, then it may be possible to replace the last term in equation (11) by an expression in terms of observable variables only. Some commonly used assumptions include the following: X_t is generated by (A1) random walk with a drift, (A2) a first-order autoregression, and (A3) random walk with a first-order moving average process. Under assumption A1 the future values of exogenous variables are obtained by adding a constant to the known current value. So the reduced form equation ends up with only current dated exogenous variables in it. Under assumption A2 the future dated values of X_1 and X_2 can also be reexpressed in terms of the current values. Given assumption A3 the optimal forecasting procedure is to use the adaptive expectations formula causing the lagged values of X_1 and X_2 to appear in the equation though the usual transformation may be applied to eliminate them.

2.4   Derivation of a 'semi-structural' price equation

A 'semi-structural' price equation is obtained as follows. Using (11)

$$P^e_{t+1} = E[P_{t+1}|I_t] = \mu_1 P_t + (1 - \omega) E[v_{t+1}|I_t] \tag{12}$$

which is then substituted into (7) and the equation rearranged. This yields a forward-looking price equation:

$$P_t = \left(1 - \mu_1 + \frac{\mu_1 \beta_1 \delta_2}{\delta_1}\right)^{-1}$$

$$\left[- \delta_1 H_t + (1 - \omega)\left(1 + \frac{\beta_1 \delta_2}{\delta_1}\right) E(v_{t+1}|I_t) \right.$$

$$\left. + \left(\frac{\delta_1}{\delta_2}\right)(\psi_2 X_{2,t+1} + u_{2,t+1}) \right] \tag{13}$$

To turn (13) into an estimatable equation the simplest procedure would be to replace the terms excluding $H(t)$ by a linear function of the current values of X_1 and X_2 and any other variable which is useful for forecasting future demand and supply shocks.

The use of the descriptor 'semi-structural' is intended to contrast two approaches to modelling prices. In the first, only supply and demand equations are modelled, allowing for all agents' forward-looking behaviour, and there is no explicit price equation. In the second a price equation derived from an underlying structural model is included in the model and may even be estimated entirely on its own by one who wants to study price determination independently of other components of the model. The remainder of this paper examines some difficulties in using the second approach.

2.5   Uncertain market response to anticipated inventories

This and the subsequent Section are intended to provide a theoretical explanation of why the response of price to inventories may be temporally unstable. In many commodity markets aggregate demand may be very stable but supply shocks often lead to market imbalance. The market response to such an imbalance will depend upon, first, the clarity with which the inventory situation is perceived, and, second, on the (implicit or explicit) loss function that market participants use to form their inventory estimates. An econometrically testable implication of this theory is that the coefficient of the inventory variable in the price equation will be temporally unstable. This is tested in later sections.

The analysis up to this point has followed convention and has assumed that all relevant aggregate variables are observed without error by the market participants. Stocks may be held at many locations throughout the producing and consuming countries so it is not surprising that even published estimates are thought to be unreliable. It is more realistic to assume that in many markets the month-to-month variations in inventories will be very imperfectly measured. Moreover, published information about inventories is typically available only with a lag. Hence market participants whose inventory plans depend upon knowledge of current inventory would need to form estimates.

Therefore, we shall consider a model of how market participants learn about and form estimates of current inventories and the implications of the learning process for the behaviour of prices.

Assume that the true level of inventories is unobserved and market participants infer that level using a signal extraction mechanism. They observe a variable, denoted H_t^*, a proxy for the true unobserved inventory level, denoted H_t; knowledge of the stochastic process generating the former is used to make estimates, denoted $\hat{H}_t$, of the latter.

Following many previous treatments, signal extraction may be considered using a state–space representation, see Harvey (1987). Let

$$H_t^* = H_t + \xi_t \tag{14}$$

be the measurement equation, and let

$$H_t = \phi_1 H_{t-1} + \eta_t \quad 0 < \phi_1 < 1 \tag{15}$$

be the transition equation, where ξ_t and η_t are respectively i.i.d. normal mutually uncorrelated disturbances with zero means and variances σ_ξ^2 and σ_η^2 respectively.[4] Let $\hat{H}_{t-1}$ be the minimum mean square error (MMSE) predictor of H_{t-1}: $E(H_{t-1}|I_{t-1}) = \hat{H}_{t-1}$ and var $(\hat{H}_{t-1}) = \Sigma_{t-1}$. Using standard results from Kalman filter theory (see Harvey, 1987, pp. 286–9) we have the prediction equations

$$\hat{H}_{t|t-1} = \phi_1 \hat{H}_{t-1} \tag{16}$$

and $\quad \Sigma_{t|t-1} = \phi_1^2 \Sigma_{t-1} + \sigma_\eta^2 \tag{17}$

which are used to predict the values of $H_{t|t-1}$ and $\Sigma_{t|t-1}$. Once the proxy variable H_t^* becomes available the predictions can be recursively updated using the following relations:

$$\hat{H}_t = \hat{H}_{t|t-1} + \Sigma_{t|t-1}[H_t^* - \hat{H}_{t|t-1}]/f_t \tag{18}$$

$$\Sigma_t = \Sigma_{t|t-1} - \Sigma_{t|t-1}^2/f_t = \Sigma_{t|t-1} - K_t\Sigma_{t|t-1} \tag{19}$$

$$f_t = \Sigma_{t|t-1} + \sigma_\zeta^2 \tag{20}$$

where $K_t = \Sigma_{t|t-1}/f_t$ $\qquad\qquad\qquad\qquad\qquad\qquad\qquad$ (21)

The coefficients in the updating equations are time-variant, but in the special case where the updating process has a convergent solution, the updating formula (18) reduces to the steady-state updating equation

$$\hat{H}_t = (1 - K)\hat{H}_{t|t-1} + KH_t^* \tag{22}$$

where $K = 1/(1 + \sigma_\zeta^2/\hat{\Sigma})$ is the weighting coefficient, which by analogy with adaptive expectations may also be thought of as a coefficient of adaptation.

Consider the econometric implications of the foregoing analysis. Substitution of either (18) or (22) into the price equation (13) yields useful and econometrically testable insights into the relation between the inventory level and price. When the signal extraction (learning) process has not converged, the response of price to inventories will vary over time, reflecting partly the changes in the variance of the observed proxy and partly the variance of the predicted value around its conditional mean. Improved information about H_t based on H_t^* will increase the absolute size of response of price to the stock variable. Also if the variance of H_t is large, or if H_t shows high persistence, the corresponding value of K will be larger and this in turn will imply a stronger interdependence between price and inventory level. Conversely, the presence of noisy proxies and/or highly variable inventory levels will tend to reduce the impact of inventories on price. In a nonstationary situation such a response will vary over time for a given commodity and may vary also between commodities.

The argument of the preceding paragraph can be further reinforced as follows. In equation (15) true inventories have a stationary 1AR representation. Though this leads to considerable technical simplification, the alternative that H_t follows a non-stationary process, e.g. 1AR with unit root, is both interesting and relevant since aggregate inventory levels do seem to exhibit trends; see Figures 4.2 and 4.6. The detailed derivation of the signal extraction mechanism for this case is beyond the scope of this paper, but as Kohn and Ansley (1987) observe, 'The major difficulty in handling the model with nonstationary components is that the distribution of observations is not defined unless assumptions are made about the initial values because they affect the correlation structure of the whole series.' Thus if H_t is nonstationary initial conditions play a special role in producing estimates of the unobserved variable. Rational agents would be aware that inaccurate estimates of initial conditions (reflecting poor information) lead to poor estimates of inventory levels. Hence it is questionable whether in such a case prices will respond strongly to estimated inventories. The discussion suggests that different initial conditions may account for the time-varying price response to inventories.

2.6 Alternative loss functions

There is also reason for expecting agents to respond to inventories asymmetrically as well as in a non-constant fashion. The argument so far has been carried out in terms of a Kalman filter which has a minimum mean squared error (MMSE) property. Though MMSE is an attractive optimality property, it presumes a quadratic loss function which has no intrinsic merit. It symmetrically penalizes both over- and under-estimation of prediction (signal extraction) errors. The result that prices would respond less strongly to inventories when the agents' estimate of the latter is subject to higher variance reflects the characteristics of the underlying loss function. However, other loss functions, such as the asymmetric linear-exponential (LINEX) function proposed by Varian (1975) and investigated by Zellner (1986), and the zero-one loss function used in the theory of mode regression, are also plausible candidates.[5]

Would the previous conclusion apply if the agents had a different loss function? Is it possible that under other loss functions agents might use upward biased estimates of the unobserved variable and hence respond *more* strongly to an uncertain signal? Could this explain episodes of panic overbidding that might induce temporary surges in prices of commodities following supply shocks? These are plausible and interesting hypotheses which should ideally be investigated using high frequency data. Temporal instability of inventory–price relationship is just a broad implication of this theory.

Some special examples suggest that under alternative plausible loss functions optimal point predictions (of $\hat{H}_t$) could be upward or downward biased relative to those obtained under a squared error loss function. Zellner (1986) provides analysis of estimation and prediction under an asymmetric LINEX loss function. Let D denote scalar estimation error; then the LINEX loss function is $L(D) = b[\exp(aD) - aD - 1]$ where $a \geq 0$, and $b > 0$. This involves a scale parameter (b) and a shape parameter (a). For small values of a the function is almost symmetric, but when $a > 1$ the function is quite asymmetric with overestimation penalized more than underestimation. Under LINEX loss 'biased' point predictions are optimal and the bias can be positive or negative, depending on the relative costs of under- and over-estimation.

When market participants attach relatively higher costs to under-estimating inventory levels (that is, high costs to not being able to service production or shipments efficiently), they will use conservative estimates of actual inventories, or upward biased estimates of their desired inventories, causing price surges on occasions when a shortfall in supply is expected. Subsequently as supplies increase, the initial price surges will be followed by a 'collapse', but the collapse will be slower and more drawn out. Such movements seem to be an important feature of commodity price movements over short periods of time, although in annual data time aggregation may smooth out such features.

In conclusion, the idea that current inventory level is unobservable, and that market participants base their reactions on an estimate which is optimal relative to their loss functions allows us to rationalize theoretically asymmetric and time-variant relationships between price and inventory behaviour. The two aspects may be present jointly or separately in a given commodity market, and may be mutually reinforcing or cancelling. We shall now examine some empirical evidence to throw further light on the issue.

3 Empirical evidence

The objective of this section is to investigate the strength and stability of the relationship between the nominal price and inventory level, and the importance of future values of exogenous variables in the price equation based on the model developed in Section 2. I shall discuss the price–inventory equation of the type (13) which has been estimated for tea, cocoa, coconut oil and palm oil using annual data. But before doing so the time series structure of exogenous variables will be analyzed in order to consider the usefulness of any derived equations for making predictions.

Following Nickell (1985) and others one may consider a family of ARMA type time series models with or without unit roots (see Diebold and Nerlove, 1988) as possible characterizations of exogenous variables in price equations. It is useful to first generalize this type of model to allow for the presence of outliers or interventions (Tsay, 1986).[6] The latter can be pulse effects, which enter in the form of dummy variables for single periods, or step effects, which enter as dummy variables for a sequence of periods. Many of the supply and demand shocks in commodity markets can be usefully characterized as pulse or step impulses, for example crop

Exogenous variable	Period	DF	ADF-'*t*'	*H*-test	*N*-test
EXW3	1958–83	− 1.15	− 1.23	6.40	*
TYT	1958–83	0.08	− 0.28	*	35.20
EUROINT	1951–85	0.36	− 0.32	6.90	*
LMUV	1951–85	0.079	0.90	*	*
LGRDW	1952–85	0.14	3.30	*	3.43
LPINDX	1959–83	− 2.58	− 1.22	*	*

Table 4.1 Unit root tests on selected exogenous variables

* denotes a value insignificant at 10% or higher level.
EXW3   : Exchange rate (weighted mean for UK, India and Sri Lanka)
TYT   : Coffee price denoted in US$
EUROINT: Eurodollar interest rate
MUV   : Manufacturing unit value index
GRDW   : Cocoa grindings
PINDX   : Demand share-weighted index of vegetable oils and fats
L in front of variable name denotes log.
Source: All data were obtained from the IECCM Division of the World Bank.

damage due to adverse weather, exchange-rate shocks, or changes in marketing arrangements such as the establishment of a buffer stock scheme or a general commodity agreement.

Since the random walk characterization has attracted much attention in the literature recently, the exogenous variables appearing in the price equations were examined for the unit root property. In almost all cases the hypothesis that the series were 1AR with a unit root could not be rejected using the Dickey–Fuller tests. Details are given in Table 4.1. The hypothesis that a better characterization of the series might be provided by further including dummy variables in the model was also tested and the details are given in Table 4.2.

To apply the Dickey–Fuller (DF) unit root tests first-order autoregressive models without constant or trend were estimated. For a regression in levels the DF test statistic is $n(r − 1)$, where n is the sample size and r is the estimated autoregressive coefficient. This value is given in the column headed DF in Table 4.1. To account for possible serial correlation two lagged changes were added to the regression ('augmented Dickey–Fuller procedure') and a '*t*-test' performed on the autoregressive coefficient; this value is reported in the column headed ADF '*t*'-test in Table 4.1. The critical values of these tests are given in Fuller (1976), Tables 8.5.1 and 8.5.2. For $n = 25$, the null hypothesis of unit root cannot be rejected against the alternative of stationarity for any of the six series with the possible exception of LPINDX.

Variable	Time series structure	Intervention variables
EXW3	First difference = constant	+ four intervention effects Pulse type: 1968, 1976 Step type: 1974, 1980
TYT	Log first difference	= 1MA error + four intervention effects Pulse type: 1967, 1974, 1983 Step type: 1973
EUROINT	First difference = constant	+ error + 0 intervention effects
LMUV	First difference = constant	+ 1MA + 1 intervention effect Pulse type: 1950
LGRDW	Level = constant	+ 2 intervention effects Pulse type: 1948 Step type: 1963
LPINDX	First difference = 1MA	+ 0 interventions

Table 4.2 Time series models for exogenous variables

Notes and *Source* as Table 4.1.

To guard against the possibility that the test outcome is sensitive to the presence of dummy variable type effects in the series, we first carried out a test of heteroskedasticity (*H*-test) and non-normality (*N*-test).[7] The heteroskedasticity test is chi-squared with one degree of freedom and the non-normality test is chi-squared with two degrees of freedom. The tests indicate the presence of one or the other problem in at least half the cases. The models were therefore reestimated allowing for automatic detection of the presence of 'intervention' effects.

Table 4.2 summarizes qualitatively the results of this exercise for a number of time-varying exogenous variables. The exchange-rate variable in the tea equation, for example, can be satisfactorily modelled as a random walk with drift provided one allows for the pulse and step type interventions. This implies that much of the potential uncertainty about future values of exogenous variables would stem from temporary or permanent 'jumps' in values. The exchange rate (*EXW3*) and the coffee price (*TYT*) variables in the tea price equation are of this type, the latter perhaps reflecting the effects of supply shocks.

These results strongly support the hypothesis that most of the exogenous variables in our model may be characterized as random walks with interventions. That is, the best forecast of a future value is the current vaue, plus an adjustment for an 'intervention'. Whether the latter is

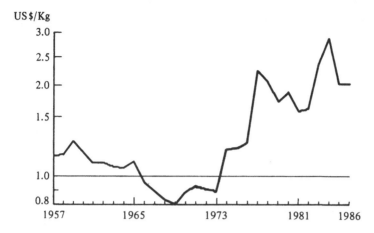

Figure 4.1 Log of world tea prices (US$/Kg)
(Note logarithmic scale on vertical axis)

predictable is debateable and the answer is likely to be case-dependent. The price equation estimated in this paper assumes that these 'jumps' are unpredictable. If the innovations in exogenous variables are largely of the unpredictable kind, the rational expectations approach to modelling prices will not work well. A further implication is that the appearance of current or lagged exogenous variables in the price equation as predictors of future dated variables is not necessarily a weakness but it is a source of ambiguity.

3.2   The price equation for tea

The empirical counterpart of nominal price is *WPRICE* which denotes the weighted average of the price of tea at four auction centres – Calcutta, Cochin, Colombo and Mombasa – denominated in US dollars per Kg.; see Figure 4.1. The weights used are shares in the total value of tea traded with the qualification that dust tea is excluded. The price *includes* export taxes and cesses which are important in Sri Lanka and which have been imposed periodically in India.

The deflator is the ratio of weighted CPI for the United Kingdom, India and Sri Lanka divided by the weighted exchange rate for the same three countries denoted *EXW3*. The weights are the total tea stocks held in each of the three countries, expressed as a proportion of the total stocks in the three countries combined. The rationale for this index is as follows. Firstly, it is broadly true that proportionately the largest amount of tea stocks are held in India, Sri Lanka and the United Kingdom. Since the stocks data for other countries are somewhat fragmentary the simplifying

---

Estimate of equation for *LWPRICE* by Instrumental Variables

Sample: 1959–1983

$$LWPRICE = -0.971 \; TWSL + 1.597 \; EXW3 + 0288 \; TYT$$
$$(0.2931) \qquad (0.2006) \qquad (0.0831)$$

$$-0.021 \; TREND + 0.382 \; TYT \, (-1) + 3.393$$
$$(0.01086) \qquad (0.1010) \qquad (1.3621)$$

INSTRUMENTS USED: *LWPRICE* (-1), *III* (-1), *TWSL* (-1), *TYT* (-1)
RSS = 0.1501   DW = 1.552   OLS–R^2 = 0.92
Mean = 0.201;   S.D. = 0.320

Estimate of equation for *LPICCO* by Instrumental Variables

Sample: 1959–1985

$$LPICCO = -0.857 \; LSTKW + 0.011 \; EUROINT - 0.051 \; EUROINT \, (-1)$$
$$(0.1562) \qquad (0.0153) \qquad (0.017)$$
$$+ 1.447 \; LMUV + 37.344 \; LGRDW - 2.604 \; LGRDWSQ - 129.0$$
$$(0.1451) \qquad (17.3378) \qquad (1.2228) \qquad (60.994)$$

INSTRUMENTS USED: *LPICCO* (-1), *LSTKW* (-1), *LGRDW* (-1),
                              LGRDWSQ (-1)
RSS = 0.4081   DW = 1.423   OLS–R^2 = 0.97

Table 4.3 Estimate of *LWPRICE* and *LPICCO* by instrumental variables
(Standard errors are given in parenthesis)

WPRICE
: weighted average of the price of tea at four auction centers – Calcutta, Cochin, Colombo and Mombasa – denominated in US dollars per Kg.
TWS   : Total 'world' inventory variable
TREND   : Time
III   : The ratio of weighted CPI (CPI3) for the United Kingdom, India and Sri Lanka divided by the weighted exchange rate for the same three countries (EXW3)
PICCO   : World cocoa price
STKW   : World cocoa bean stocks
GRDWSQ: GRDW²
L in front of a variable name denotes log.

Source: All data were obtained from the IECCM Division of the World Bank.

assumption is adopted that total 'world' stocks equals stocks in the United Kingdom, India and Sri Lanka; which implies that the equation (4) represents inventory demand in those three countries alone. It follows that the appropriate deflator is the three-country weighted CPI, denoted *CPI3*. Secondly, since *WPRICE* is expressed in US dollars an exchange rate conversion is required. Therefore, *CPI3* is divided by *EXW3*, which denotes a weighted average of exchange rates in the three countries – the weights being the same as those used for constructing *CPI3*.

The dependent variable in the price equation is (log of) *WPRICE*, denoted *LWPRICE*, and not $WPRICE \times EXW3/CPI3$. If the latter were used, the equation would explain the *real* price of tea. This would be equivalent to specifying a homogeneous-of-degree-zero inventory equation. However, given the approximations implicit in the construction of *CPI3* and *EXW3* it does not seem appropriate to impose the homogeneity assumption. Instead *CPIE/EXW3* has been included as an independent variable on the right-hand side.

The proxy variables for the future-dated exogenous variables in the price equation should be the aggregate world counterparts of the exogenous variables which enter the demand and production equations for individual countries. On the supply side the most important exogenous variables are time trend, various country-specific price deflators and exchange rates, and subsidies. On the demand side, time trend has also been found to be an important explanatory variable, being a proxy for, *inter alia*, growth in per capita income and changes in taste. Another exogenous variable included in some demand equations is the price of coffee, though this variable has not been found to be particularly important. Nevertheless, it may have special value in forecasting future demand disturbances, i.e., in calculating $E(u_{2,t+1} | I_t)$. That is, the importance of the coffee price variable may derive not only from its power to predict the future coffee price, which probably has a rather small direct impact on tea consumption, but also from its usefulness as a predictor of future demand disturbances[8] $(u_{2,t+1}, i \geqslant 1)$.

The *WPRICE* equation estimated for the model is log-linear. The exogenous variables included $III (= CPI3/EXW3)$, *TYT*, $TYT(-1)$, *TWS* and a time trend. The variable *CPI3/EXW3* is included because of its role as a deflator in the inventory equation. Its inclusion can also be justified on the argument that its current value may be useful for predicting future values which belong in the price equation. (This gives yet another reason for not imposing the homogeneity constraint.) *TYT* denotes the coffee price variable denominated in US dollars.

Figure 4.2 shows the behaviour of the log of *TWS*. Since *TWS* is endogenous, the equation was then estimated by the generalized instrumental variable method.[9] Whether ordinary least squares or instrumental variables are used, it is found that the current and lagged coffee price variable is extremely important in explaining *WPRICE*. The same is also true for the deflator *CPI3/EXW3*. The total 'world' inventory variable *TWS* has the expected negative coefficient. However, recursive least squares and recursive instrumental variable estimates of the equation

000 tons

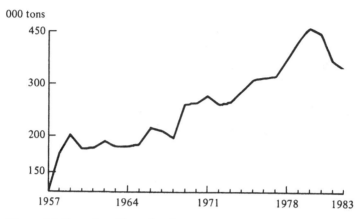

Figure 4.2 Log of world stocks of tea

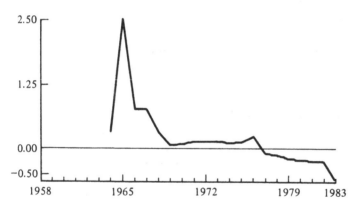

Figure 4.3 Plot of the coefficient of *TSWL* based on recursive regression

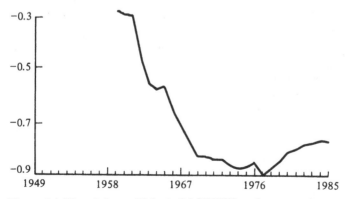

Figure 4.4 Plot of the coefficient of *LSTKW* based on recursive regression

show, see Figures 4.3 and 4.4, that the size and sign of the coefficient of *TWS* depends upon relatively few observations and is unstable. The *a priori* acceptable negative coefficient reflects predominantly the influence of the last few observations, especially the surge in the world price of tea following the imposition of export quotas for quality tea by India in 1983. The fragility of this coefficient is consistent with a generally weak relationship between price and inventory that might be expected if speculative considerations are unimportant, except on rather special occasions, for whatever reasons.[10]

3.3   Price equation for cocoa

The price equation for cocoa is an extension of the work of Akiyama and Duncan (1982) and the price equation in the global cocoa model at the World Bank. The dependent variable is log of world cocoa price (*LPICCO*), the explanatory variables are world cocoa bean stocks (*LSTKW*), manufacturing unit value index (*LMUV*), grindings (*LGRDW*), a demand variable, which enters quadratically and lagged and current interest rates (*EUROINT*); Figures 4.5 and 4.6 show the recent behaviour of *LIPCCO* and *LSTKW*. The current and/or past values of exogenous variables are taken as appropriate proxies for their unknown future values given our earlier results about their time series structure. All coefficients have *a priori* expected signs; but that of *LMUV* is somewhat larger than the expected value of approximately unity under the hypothesis that *LMUV* and *LIPCCO* are cointegrated variables. This equation has a better fit over the sample period and is considerably more robust than the *LWPRICE* equation, though there remains some possibility of serially correlated residuals. In particular, recursive least squares and/or recursive instrumental variable estimates of the coefficient of *LSTKW* does not show more variation than expected under the hypothesis of parameter constancy. It is interesting to note also that the inventories for cocoa are generally presumed to be subject to a smaller measurement error than for tea.

Our conclusion is that for cocoa more than for tea there is evidence of a price sensitive intertemporal demand for inventories. Nevertheless, given that current dated variables serve as predictors of their future values is a source of ambiguity in the interpretation of the results.

3.4   Price equations for coconut oil and palm oil

In this section some further difficulties confronting the application of the 'semi-structural' rational expectations approach will be considered.

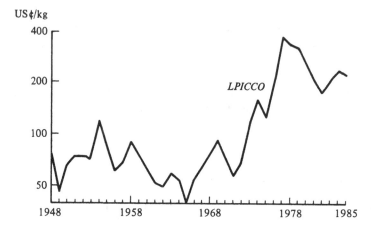

Figure 4.5 Log of price of cocoa (US¢/Kg)

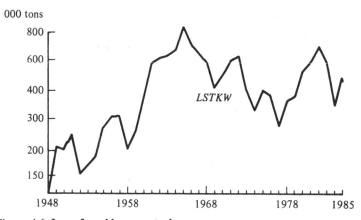

Figure 4.6 Log of world cocoa stock

Though from an empirical viewpoint the analysis is preliminary, some hitherto unexplored issues will be emphasized.

The case of coconut and palm oil provides an interesting contrast to the two previous examples. A major difference is that the demand, supply and stockholding behaviour of these commodities may be best analyzed in the context of a global disaggregated model for vegetable oils, which would also include groundnut and soybean oil. That is, whereas most econometric models of beverages implicitly assume separability and neglect substitutability between beverages, substitution between alternative types of vegetable oils is very important on the demand side (Goddard and Glance, 1988; Griffith and Meilke, 1979; Suryana, 1986).

Consider the implications. Any actual or expected demand or supply disturbance will affect all related prices. If the 'semi-structural' price equations are desired then one must derive a vector version of equation (13) in Section 2.4. Consequently, each individual price equation will involve 'own' inventories as well as inventories of substitutes. Further, the solution of such an equation and the subsequent replacement of future-dated exogenous variables by proxies will introduce into any one price equation a rather large number of variables. There is justification for the complaint one sometimes hears from commodity modelers that the price equation ends up 'collecting' too many variables. If this argument is valid, one should expect that a 'semi-structural' price equation for coconut oil or palm oil specified analogously to those given above either will be unwieldy or unstable.

To throw some light on these observations some cointegration tests (see Engle and Granger, 1987; Hall, 1986) were performed on the vegetable oil (coconut, palm and soybean) price and inventory data to see whether inventories have an important influence on the price of coconut and palm oil. I test for cointegration between the three nominal price variables *LPCCO*, *LPPLP* and *LPSBO* and three inventory variables *LESCCO*, *LESPLO* and *LESSBM*, making nine combinations of cointegrating regressions. The null hypothesis of non-cointegration would imply the absence of a linear (equilibrium) relationship between variables.[11] The hypothesis that prices and inventories of vegetable oils are jointly determined implies that the null hypothesis of non-cointegration should be rejected more often when the cointegrating regression includes more inventory variables.

The first step in testing for cointegration is to check whether the variables are integrated of order 1, I(1); for the subset of I(1) variables cointegrating regressions are estimated and the residuals from the regressions tested for stationarity (I(0) property). If the residuals are not I(0), the hypothesis of non-cointegration is accepted, which implies either that the hypothesized relationship does not exist, or that (as in Hall, 1986) a larger set of cointegrating variables is called for.

Table 4.4 provides details of the tests. All six variables display the I(1) property, but the cointegration tests tend to accept the non-cointegration hypothesis. Using 5% critical values for samples of 100, which finds cointegration too often for samples of 25 like ours, the CRDW offers weak evidence of cointegration, while the more powerful ADF test finds no evidence in its favour at all. There is, however, a weak tendency for non-cointegration to come closer to rejection as additional inventory variables are included.

A brief attempt was made to model the price behaviour of palm oil and

Variable	DF test	ADF 't-test
LPCCO	− 0.03	− 0.09
LPPLO	− 0.012	− 0.05
LPSBO	0.003	0.016
LESCCO	0.039	0.62
LESPLO	0.162	2.14
LESSBM	0.21	2.02
5% critical values for sample size 25	− 7.3	− 1.95

TESTS OF COINTEGRATION

Variables	CRDW	ADF-'t'-test
LPCCO, LESCCO	0.94	− 1.83
LPCCO, LESCCO, LESPLO	1.35	− 0.51
LPCCO, LESCCO, LESPLO, LESSBM	1.36	− 2.67
LPPLO, LESPLO	0.87	− 1.03
LPPLO, LESPLO, LESCCO	0.77	− 1.55
LPPLO, LESPLO, LESCCO, LESSBM	0.69	− 1.61
LPSBO, LESSBM	0.82	− 1.47
LPSBO, LESSBM, LESCCO	0.78	− 2.24
LPSBO, LESSBM, LESCCO, LESPLO	0.73	− 1.98

Table 4.4 Unit root tests on price and inventory variables

Critical values: Engle and Granger give the 5% critical values (sample size 100) of 0.386 and − 3.17 for CRDW and ADF respectively, for a cointegrated pair: for three variables (see Hall, 1986) the value are 0.367 and − 3.13.

PCCO : Price index of coconut oil
PPLO : Price index of palm oil
PSBO : Price index for soybean oil
ESCCO: End-period stocks of coconut oil
ESPLO : End-period stocks of palm oil
ESSBM: End-period stocks of soybean meal
L in front of a variable denotes log.

Source: All data were obtained from the IECCM Division of the World Bank.

coconut oil econometrically. The basic form of the equation was as before but some variants which take account of interdependence arising from substitution possibilities on the demand side were also considered. None of the equations fitted well, and none offered evidence of any significant relationship between price and inventories. In particular neither the real interest rate variable nor the index of manufacturing prices had any explanatory power. Including predictors of future demand induced marginal improvement in the equation for palm oil, but none for coconut oil. In neither case were the results such as to suggest that there exists a strong relation between price and inventory movements.[12]

4   Implications for global econometric commodity models

The two preceding sections have considered the nature of intertemporal demand for inventories. Theoretical reasons have been given why such demand may have either an insignificant or, on occasions, an exaggerated impact on prices, and empirical examples have been given to support either position. In this section I shall consider the implications of these results for the specification of the price equation in a global commodity model.

We have examined some weaknesses in empirical versions of the 'semi-structural' forward-looking commodity price equations based on rational expectations. An alternative to this approach is the conventional market-clearing approach modified to allow for forward-looking behaviour on the supply and demand side.[13] This paper leans towards this alternative.

Several recent econometric models of commodities, for example, Burger and Smit (1988), Manger (1988), Akiyama and Trivedi (1987), begin by specifying the price equation as an inverted inventory demand equation. Typically such equations are over-parameterized, often because at the post-simulation stage variables are added just to improve the tracking performance. My own experience in joint work with Akiyama (Akiyama and Trivedi, 1987) is that the price equation tends to be somewhat unstable. Neglect of forward-looking inventory behaviour or the fundamentally unstable nature of such forward-looking behaviour are possible reasons for instability. The first is not necessarily very important if the relevant exogenous variables have simple time series characterizations. Some *a priori* reasoning and empirical evidence suggest that the largely unpredictable pulse- and step-type innovations that characterize exogenous variables may be inadequately modelled. Further, the potential for an unstable speculative demand for inventories has been insufficiently emphasized in the literature.

Whether the current price level reflects intertemporal inventory demand is a difficult hypothesis to test. Suppose, however, that an acceptable test procedure based on a 'semi-structural' equation has been devised and that an unambiguous conclusion is reached. What are the implications for modelling price behaviour in a global model?

The first possible outcome is that there is no identifiable speculative or price-sensitive demand component of inventories and that the latter are largely held for purposes of efficient production and/or shipment scheduling. Nevertheless, inventories perform a market clearing and buffer role in the sense that willingly held inventories absorb the difference between aggregate demand and supply. In this case it is not possible to specify an explicit price equation in the model. Rather the model should solve for price and inventories through market clearing equations. If a price equation were included in such a model it would surely be linked to the rest of the model and, in simulation, may generate a time path inconsistent with that implied by the fundamental supply and demand equations. I understand that such problems are the major reason why several commodity models have eschewed explicit price equations in recent years;. see, for example, Akiyama and Varangis (1988).

The second possibility is that there is evidence of a speculative demand. It still does not follow that a 'semi-structural' price equation is required. One could introduce forward-looking exogenous variables into the inventory equation. An important example here is the case of frost damage to coffee supply in Brazil. Frost affects the following year's supply, not this year's, and so in this case survey information will be available regarding its impact. Indices based on such information could be constructed and introduced as explanatory variables in the inventory equations to reflect inter-temporal demand. Once again no explicit price equation would be needed. This suggests that survey measures of expectations about future quantities, as well as probability of the occurrence of certain kinds of discrete events, may have a potentially useful role in modelling intertemporal inventory demand.[14] Such a step is very much in the spirit of the rational expectations approach which emphasizes the importance of expected future inventories on current demand. It is not necessary to embrace the 'semi-structural' approach to benefit from this insight.

The 'semi-structural' price equation given in Section 2 will be particularly unwieldy when we face the task of modelling the price-inventory behaviour of a commodity for which many substitutes exist. The example of vegetable oils considered in Section 3 illustrates this point. The more disaggregated the model the less appropriate will be the 'semi-structural' approach.

For a variety of reasons global commodity models tend to be annual rather than monthly models. While speculative inventory behaviour may be important in the short term, its neglect in annual models may not be a serious misspecification.

A difficult case in practice may be the one in which the intertemporal stock demand is an exceptional but important event. That is, while 'normally' there may be no speculative demand for inventories, exogenous events of uncertain impact could trigger such demand from time to time. The importance of such episodes may be considerable because the resultant price rises may be huge relative to normal movements, and may in turn stimulate other actions (such as investment) by producers. Neglect of such a possibility in structural or 'semi-structural' econometric models will lead to poor predictions on precisely those occasions when users might want to depend upon them. However, this issue has not been faced in models of perennial crops in a systematic manner so one does not know how widespread or important it is.

The consequences for econometric modelling of speculative demand for inventories have been considered, and we have argued that, for research into price determination, in the case of many commodities the focus should be on detailed and accurate modelling of the demand and supply side of perennial crops. These conclusions are relevant to model-based policy analyses. For understanding the role of important exogenous and policy variables the 'semi-structural' equation, even when it embodies the valuable insights of rational expectations, may prove to be unwieldy indirect, and of limited usefulness. For a range of important policy-related issues such as the impact of commodity taxes, production and investment subsidies and exchange-rate policies on world production and prices, the alternative approach is both direct and potentially more informative.

NOTES

* This paper owes much to discussions with and comments of Takamasa Akiyama of the World Bank arising from and subsequent to our earlier collaboration on this subject; see Akiyama and Trivedi (1985, 1987). I am also grateful to Don Larson for his advice and help in respect of the price and inventory data for vegetable oils and for general discussions regarding the modelling of price and inventories in this areas. My discussants at the Conference, Mike Wickens and David Newbery, and Alan Winters made perceptive comments which have influenced the revisions incorporated in the present version. However, I retain all responsibility for the contents of this version.

1 Typically such models contain several price equations, often one for each major producing region. However, typically also most such price equations link regional prices to some central 'world price'. This is 'the' price which econometric models seek to explain.

2 Ghosh et al. (1987) explain the motivation for inverting the inventory demand equation thus: 'Typically this equation is inverted to express price in terms of stocks since otherwise, in forecasting or model simulation the price is forced to move too much in order to clear the market. This is a consequence of the incompleteness and inaccuracy of stock data which result in poorly fitting stock demand equations. The inversion approach, on the other hand, results in equations which suffer from errors in variable bias, and gives forecasts that are too smooth.' Reasons other than inaccuracy of stock data may also be relevant, e.g., inappropriate functional form of the stock equation which may imply overly restrictive response of price to stocks.

3 Linkage equations connect the average world price with local prices.

4 A more general transition equation may be considered, but for the present purpose this is unnecessary.

5 This loss function implies constant finite loss when the error is outside some specified range and zero loss when it is not.

6 The time series package AUTOBOXP allows automatic or interactive fitting of models with two types of interventions, viz., pulse effects and step effects. See AUTOBOX PLUS: User's Guide Version 2.0 (1987) *Automatic Forecasting Systems*, Hatboro, Pennsylvania.

7 The null hypothesis of homoskedasticity is tested against the alternative that the variance of observation *i* is proportional to the square of the expected value. For testing non-normality the test is the Bera–Jarque test. Both tests are score tests.

8 Disaggregated demand equations produce some evidence of substitution, but not overwhelming evidence. Nevertheless, the apparent high usefulness of the latter in predicting tea prices is a little surprising. A simple explanation is that large shocks to coffee prices induce expected substitution and price changes in tea; alternatively, beverage prices could be cointegrated.

9 Estimation of equations involving future dated variables has been thoroughly discussed by Wickens (1986).

10 That is, learning may be highly imperfect, or market participants may have an asymmetric loss function for prediction errors, or the demand for inventories may largely reflect efficient production scheduling considerations.

11 See Hall (1986) for a detailed application of this approach.

12 Similar results apply to natural rubber, but evidence of actual substitution seems more limited (Burger and Smit, 1988, and Manger, 1988). These studies also fail to suggest significant forward-looking inventory behaviour.

13 Estimation of structural equations by instrumental variable methods is perfectly feasible as demonstrated by Wickens (1986).

14 Pesaran (1987) has forcefully argued for greater reliance on survey measures of expectations.

REFERENCES

Adams, F. G. and J. R. Behrman (1976) *Econometric Models of World Agricultural Commodity Markets: Cocoa, Tea, Coffee, Wool, Cotton, Sugar, Wheat, Rice*, Cambridge, Massachusetts: Ballinger.

Akiyama, T. and R. C. Duncan (1982) 'An Analysis of the World Cocoa Market' Commodities Study and Projections Division Working Paper No. 1983, The World Bank.

Akiyama, T. and P. K. Trivedi (1987) *A Global Tea Model: Specification Estimation and Simulation*, World Bank Staff Commodity Working Paper No. 17.

Akiyama, T. and P. K. Trivedi (1985) 'Specification of the Price Equation in a Prototype Model of a Perennial Crop', unpublished seminar paper, Commodities Studies and Projection Division, The World Bank.

Akiyama, T. and P. Varangis (1988) 'Impact of the International Coffee Agreement's Export Quota System on the World Coffee Market'. Paper presented at the XXVth International Conference on International Commodity Market Modelling, Applied Econometrics Association, World Bank, Washington, D.C., October 1988.

Burger, K. and H. P. Smit (1988) 'Long-term and Short-term Outlook for the Rubber Market'. Paper presented at the XXVth International Conference on International Commodity Market Modelling, Applied Econometrics Association, World Bank, Washington, D.C., October 1988.

Diebold, F. X. and M. Nerlove (1988) 'Unit Roots in Economic Time Series', forthcoming in T. H. Fomby and G. F. Rhoades, Editors, *Advances in Econometrics: Co-Integration, Spurious Regression, and Unit Roots*, Greenwich, Connecticut: JAI Press.

Engle, R. F. and C. W. Granger (1987) 'Cointegration and Error Correction: Representation, Estimation and Testing', *Econometrica* 55, 251–76.

Fuller, W. (1976) *Introduction to Statistical Time Series*, New York: John Wiley.

Ghosh, S., C. L. Gilbert and A. J. Hughes Hallett (1987) *Stabilizing Speculative Commodity Markets*, Oxford: Clarendon Press.

Goddard, E. W. and S. Glance (1988) 'Demand for Fats and Oils in Canada, US and Japan'. Unpublished paper, University of Guelph, Ontario, Canada.

Griffith, G. R. and K. D. Meilke (1979) 'Relationships Among North American Fats and Oils Prices', *American Journal of Agricultural Economics*, 61(2).

Hall. S. G. (1986) 'An Application of Granger–Engel Two-step Procedure to UK Aggregate Wage Data', *Oxford Bulletin of Economics and Statistics* 48, 229–39.

Harvey, A. C. (1987) 'Applications of the Kalman Filter in Econometrics', Chapter 8 in T. Bewley, Editor, *Advances in Econometrics, Fifth World Econometric Congress, Vol. 1*, Cambridge University Press.

Hwa, E. C. (1985) 'A Model of Price and Quantity Adjustments in Primary Commodity Markets', *Journal of Policy Modelling* 7, 305–38.

Kohn, R. and C. Ansley (1987) 'Signal Extraction for Finite Non-stationary Time Series', *Biometrika* 74, 411–21.

Manger, J. (1988) 'Econometric Analysis of the World Rubber Market'. Paper presented at the XXVth International Conference on International Commodity Market Modelling, Applied Econometrics Association, World Bank, Washington, D.C., October 1988.

Muth, J. (1961) 'Rational Expectations and the Theory of Price Movements', *Econometrica* 29, 315–35.

Nickell, S. J. (1985) 'Error Correction, Partial Adjustment and All That: An Expository Note', *Oxford Bulletin of Economics and Statistics* 47, 119–30.

Pesaran, M. H. (1987) *The Limits of Rational Expectations*, Oxford: Blackwell.

Suryana, Achmad (1986) 'Trade prospects of Indonesian Palm Oil in the International Markets for Fats and Oils', Unpublished Ph.D. Dissertation, North Carolina State University.

Tsay, R. S. (1986) 'Time Series Model Specification in the Presence of Outliers', *Journal of American Statistical Association* 76, 132–41.

Varian, H. R. (1975) 'A Bayesian Approach to Real Estate Assessment', in *Studies in Bayesian Econometrics and Statistics in Honor of Leonard J. Savage*, eds. S. E. Fienberg and A. Zellner, Amsterdam: North-Holland, pp. 195–208.

Weymar, F. H. (1968) *The Dynamics of the World Cocoa Market*, Cambridge: MIT Press.

Wickens, M. R. (1986) 'The Estimation of Linear Models with Future Rational Expectations by Efficient and Instrumental Variable Methods', Center for Applied Economic Policy Research Discussion Paper No. 111.

Zellner, A. (1986) 'Bayesian Estimation and Prediction Using Asymmetric Loss Functions', *Journal of American Statistical Association* 81, 446–51.

Discussion

DAVID M. NEWBERY

It is clearly useful to be able to forecast commodity prices, and also to be able to describe the statistical properties of commodity price series (e.g. as in Cuddington and Urzua, 1987, 1989). If the price follows a pure random walk, then price stabilization is likely to be futile, and intertemporal consumption smoothing difficult. More to the point, it is helpful to know how persistent price shocks are for making durable investment plans and current consumption decisions. How should one best model commodity price determination in order to address such questions? Is it sufficient to model demand and supply, and pay relatively little attention to inventory behaviour, or can one use information on inventory levels and the assumption of rational expectations to obtain a better model? Trivedi explores these questions in a workmanlike way (though one somewhat daunting to those unfamiliar with the latest econometric techniques). He finds the results mixed – price equations with inventories are somewhat unstable for tea, not bad for cocoa (where stocks are more accurately observed), and poor for edible oils, where there are important substitution possibilities in demand.

One of the problems with inventory equations is that inventories are held for speculative and transactions reasons by private agents, as well as for buffering prices under international commodity agreements. The motives behind each are different. Speculative demands for annual carryover are likely to be low in most years, and, more crucially, since they cannot become negative, will be a non-linear function of supplies or prices (Newbery and Stiglitz, 1979). Buffer stocks will depend on the intervention rule followed by the buffer agent, and may induce speculative attacks by private agents, so that aggregate stocks may be dominated by the speculative or buffering motive in different periods. The non-linearity (non-negativity) in the inventory equation means that prices changes are likely to be non-normally distributed – if carryovers fall to zero, prices may rise suddenly to great peaks, but current excess supplies will be carried forward and the price falls muted. Stockouts (of speculative stocks) will sever the intertemporal price dependencies and autoregressive structure, further complicating the analysis of the time series. Small wonder that modelling inventory behaviour in a simple linear form is fraught with difficulties. (Though the use of logarithms of prices and stocks may avoid this difficulty, it is harder to relate the estimated equations to the simple structural model of the text).

The conclusions of the paper are primarily addressed to commodity modellers. It would have been helpful to have had some comments on what we have learned about commodity price instability, the confidence with which we can forecast, and the time horizon over which such forecasts are useful, and what are the prospects for stabilization.

REFERENCES

Cuddington, J. T. and C. M. Urzua (1987) 'Trends and Cycles in Primary Commodity Prices', Working Paper, Economics Department, Georgetown University.

Cuddington, J. T. and C. M. Urzua (1989) 'Trends and Cycles in the Net Barter Terms of Trade: A New Approach', *Economic Journal* **99**, 426–42.

Newbery, D. M. and J. E. Stiglitz (1979) *The Theory of Commodity Price Stabilization*, Oxford University Press.

MICHAEL R. WICKENS

It is always a pleasure to comment on a piece of applied econometrics by Pravin Trivedi because it is invariably interesting, has a firm base in economic theory, has up-to-date and carefully executed econometrics and is well written. This paper is no exception. In fact, when the need rises, such as being a discussant, I can think of no better person to disagree with.

I am very sympathetic to the main aim of this paper, which I take to be the introduction of forward-looking expectations into commodity modelling. When Greenfield and I were working on the coffee market back in 1970 we recognized the need to take account of multi-period optimization in the decisions of consumers and especially of producers in agricultural commodity models. At the time the technology for doing this was rather primitive. The fashion was to eliminate all unstable roots by assuming static expectations with the result that one finished up with a backward-looking model whose dynamics were determined by the stable roots. With the development of rational expectations, or, less strong, model-consistent expectations, instead of having a contemporaneous, static target one can introduce a forward-looking target. This is a much less restrictive assumption and it opens up a number of interesting avenues of enquiry, such as optimal private inventory policy and the role of a buffer stock agency.

Rather than derive the behavioural equations of the model formally, in this paper they are stated in an *ad hoc* manner. The model is then reduced to a single equation which is called a 'semi-structural' price equation, and is estimated on data for tea, cocoa, coconut oil and palm oil. There are several things about this approach with which I shall take issue.

The commodities studied are tree crops but the model is more suited to field crops as it ignores the dynamic structure of the supply function. There is now ample evidence of the importance of the long lags of supply in tree crops and I would have thought that this should be taken into account. In fact, very little attention is paid to the particular characteristics of the particular commodity in the equation estimated apart from the prices of substitutes. In a similar vein the exogenous demand variables are treated very casually as trends rather than actual demand. I wonder, therefore, what is the point of estimating equations such as these when one could expect to do better by taking account of specific commodity characteristics. Maybe it is to see how well a completely general approach fares. A less charitable interpretation is that it is another example of the dreadful methodology practised occasionally by many of the world agencies, such as the World Bank, in which every country is treated like every other and given the same model. It may be quick and it may be equitable, but it isn't good economics.

After all the various substitutions have been made, despite the more general theoretical underpinnings of the model, the final equation estimated is virtually indistinguishable from something that might have been estimated twenty years ago. In particular, the structure is submerged and virtually lost and there are no explicit expectations terms. The apparent justification offered for working with (only) a price equation appears in a footnote. Reference is made to the argument of Ghosh *et al.* for inverting the inventory equation to obtain a price equation on the grounds that otherwise price has to 'move too much in order to clear the market'. In my view this is a spurious argument as the market clearing price is determined within the whole structural model in which both price and inventories are endogenous.

It would be far better to estimate a structural model than a single reduced form price equation. It would then be possible to test the individual equations for misspecification rather than throw all the misspecification into one equation from which its source is difficult to detect. This will help re-specification too. I would also carry out proper cointegration tests of the structural equations. This would help detect any misspecification in the long-run structure.

Estimating the structural equations also has the merit of permitting the expectations variables to be estimated explicitly. There is no need to solve the model for the expectations prior to estimation. This can be done for forecasting purposes after the structure has been estimated. At present all the benefits of starting with a carefully specified expectations structure are completely lost. Who knows what role any particular variable is playing in the price equation estimated? I would then use a single equation GMM estimator as this takes account of both simultaneity and the error structure caused by the presence of rational expectations.

Perhaps I have been rather hard on my old friend Pravin. My remarks are possibly a counsel of perfection permitted only in my required role as a hyper-critical discussant. Let me end, therefore, by repeating my earlier judgment that this is a very good piece of work, and one which I am sure will be of value in the development of commodity modelling.

Summary of general discussion

The bulk of the discussion focused on estimation and modelling methods. Trivedi opened the general discussion by responding to Michael Wickens' proposal that models should take much more account of individual commodity market information. He argued that the price equation should be embedded in a full commodity model precisely so that the specifics and relevant details of any market could be included as exogenous variables. The question addressed in his paper, however, was whether such a price equation is in fact required or whether an inverted stock equation would do.

Richard Just questioned the applicability of the rational expectations paradigm to these models; actual decision makers seemed to operate without rational expectations if the costs of compiling them seemed too high. In such a case the formation of rational expectations would not be worth the agent's while, particularly in periods of volatile prices. Several participants replied that, while the rational expectations hypothesis in its strong form may be strictly inapplicable, it remains the best empirical method of coping with forward looking behaviour.

Christopher Gilbert argued in favour of reduced-form equations, claiming that structural modelling fails to take account of the poverty of data. If one is interested in forecasting prices (as for example the World

Bank and commodity traders are) then modelling the price equation directly is preferable to modelling the stock demand equation with inferior data.

Mark Taylor made the following proposal with respect to the question of single equation versus full information estimation: first estimate the single equation by instrumental variable techniques, then estimate the full information system and compare the two by means of the Haussman test. This would reveal any inconsistency due to misspecification elsewhere in the model.

II Sectoral Studies: Foods, Materials and Energy

5 Modelling the Interactive Effects of Alternative Sets of Policies on Agricultural Prices

RICHARD E. JUST

1 Introduction

Understanding agricultural prices is a complex and highly evolutionary process. In most countries, agricultural prices are more highly regulated than other prices. Thus, understanding the effects of domestic agricultural policy is crucial. This problem is complicated by frequent revisions not only in the levels of policy instruments but also by changes in the active set of instruments. Moreover, each major new agricultural price swing over the last several decades has drawn attention to an additional set of policy instruments that has important spillover effects on domestic agriculture. These sets of policy instruments include domestic macroeconomic policy, foreign agricultural policy, and foreign macroeconomic policy as well as domestic regulation of other sectors.

This paper discusses the role of alternative sets of policy instruments in determining agricultural commodity prices, evaluates alternative approaches for modelling agricultural commodity prices, and briefly discusses some empirical experience. Some of the points in the paper are substantiated by specific examples while others are offered simply as a summary of intuition and experience. The two main messages of the paper are (1) that increasing volatility in the agricultural economy calls for imposing more structure in estimation in order to capture the global properties of important relationships and (2) that increased volatility has revealed many important international, intersectoral and macroeconomic linkages that necessitate an ever broadening scope in agricultural modelling.

2 Domestic agricultural policy instability

The most important variable on the supply side that drives agricultural crop prices is acreage planted. Acreage of some of the most important crops depends heavily on government policy. The set of instruments through which agricultural policy is administered has been subject to frequent change. The US feed grain program serves as a major example.

During the 1950s, these grains (e.g., maize and sorghum) were regulated only by price supports which were occasionally at ineffective levels. At times in the early 1960s they were also regulated by binding farm-level acreage limitations (allotments). Beginning in the mid-1960s, these programs became voluntary so that each farmer received the price support only when electing to plant within the allotment. Later, minimum feed grain acreage diversion levels were specified under which part of each farm's base acreage had to be removed from production of a specified set of commodities for eligibility in the program. At times, farmers have been offered a per acre payment for diverted land and occasionally an additional per acre payment has been offered for land voluntarily diverted beyond the minimum. For several years in the mid-1970s, the commodity boom tended to make the feed grain program ineffective. Since 1977, support has been tied to a farmer-owned reserve under which grains enter the reserve at the price support level, generally do not come out of the reserve until prices rise to a release price, and must come out at the call price (all three levels are policy instruments). In addition, farmers' voluntary decisions to put grains into the reserve are affected by the extent of interest subsidy provided to farmers on loans made against the reserves. Beginning in 1983, payments to farmers began to be made in kind.

The point of this brief review, which omits many other minor changes, is that policy regimes have changed so often that only a few annual observations are available under each policy regime. Thus, from a purely objective standpoint, econometric identification is technically impossible in many policy regimes given the number of other variables such as input prices and technological change that interact with policy instruments in determining acreage. This leads to the first principle of this paper.

> PRINCIPLE 1. *Empirical modelling and understanding of commodity prices in heavily regulated industries with frequent changes in policy regimes is possible only by imposing substantial subjective and theoretical structure on the data.*

An example can serve to make this point. Early on, acreage response was modelled as an *ad hoc* linear function of market price and support price, $A = A(P_m, P_s)$. Because of high collinearity of the two, however, this approach often led to an implausible sign on one or the other. More plausible and useful results have been found by specifying acreage following $A = A(P_f)$ with farm commodity prices following the kinked relationship $P_f = \max(P_m, P_s)$ even though the market price is an uncertain variable at the time of the acreage decision whereas the price support is not (Just, 1973).

Limited dependent variable models have also been suggested to address problems where mandatory allotments may or may not be binding depending on economic conditions (Chambers and Just, 1982b). Nevertheless, the typical approach to modelling acreage response in the presence of voluntary programs is to specify a linear acreage equation with

$$A = A(\pi_c, \pi_n, \pi_a, A_{-1}, G_v) \tag{1}$$

where π_c is anticipated short-run profit per acre under (voluntary) compliance with government programs, π_n is anticipated short-run profit per acre under noncompliance, π_a is anticipated short-run profit per acre from production of competing crop(s), A_{-1} is lagged acreage representing production fixities, and G_v is the government payment per acre for voluntary diversion beyond the minimum (see, e.g., Rausser, 1985; Love, 1987). In this formulation, the levels of profit under compliance and noncompliance are assumed to pick up the change in voluntary compliance.

A common-sense approach which imposes more structure on the data is as follows. Suppose first that free market acreage follows $A = A_f(\pi_n, \pi_a, A_{-1})$. Then when government programs are voluntary, the nonparticipating component of acreage can be assumed to follow this free market equation on the nonparticipating proportion of farms so nonparticipating acreage is

$$A_n = (1 - \phi) A_f(\pi_n, \pi_a, A_{-1}) \tag{2}$$

where ϕ is the rate of participation in the diversion program.

Using common sense and an assumption of constant returns to scale which often provides a reasonable approximation for agriculture, participation in a voluntary program and access to its price subsidies would not be attractive unless the acreage limitations were effective. Thus, the participating acreage is, for practical purposes, determined by program limitations with

$$A_p = B\phi(1 - \theta) - D(G_v) \tag{3}$$

where B is the program base acreage, θ is the minimum proportion of base acreage required to be directed for participation, and D describes additional voluntary acreage diversion beyond the minimum as a function of the payment per acre for additional diversion. The estimating equation for total acreage given the participation level is obtained by combining (2) and (3),

Crop	Model definition (equation)	Estimation period	Forecast period	Standard error within sample (million acres)	Standard error post-sample (million acres)
Wheat	(1)	1962–82	1983–86	4.41	14.90
Wheat	(4)	1962–82	1983–86	3.32	6.21
Wheat	(4), (5)	1962–82	1983–86	[b]	9.07
Feed grain	(1)	1962–82	1983–87	1.73	6.40
Feed grain	(4)	1962–82	1983–87	6.26	6.38
Feed grain	(4), (5)	1962–82	1983–87	[b]	5.50

Table 5.1 **The performance of structural versus *ad hoc* models: the case of US wheat and feed grain acreage**[a]

[a]See the text for equations which define the various models.
[b]No within sample error is computed since the model is derived by combining the estimated equations corresponding to (4) and (5).

$$A_t = B\phi(1 - \theta) - D(G_v) + (1 - \phi)A_f(\pi_n, \pi_a, A_{-1}) \tag{4}$$

where $D(\cdot)$ and $A_f(\cdot)$ follow linear specifications.

To determine the level of participation in this framework, each farmer i is assumed to participate if anticipated profit per acre (given diversion and diversion payment considerations) is greater under compliance than under noncompliance ($\pi_c^i > \pi_n^i$). Assuming that individual perceived profits differ by an amount characterized by an appropriate random distribution across farmers, the participation rate at the aggregate level can be represented by a logistic relationship with[1]

$$\ln \frac{\phi}{1 - \phi} = \phi^*(\pi_n, \pi_c). \tag{5}$$

To illustrate the difference in performance of the approach in equation (1) compared to that in equations (4) and (5), both were used to estimate acreage response of wheat and of feed grains in the US over the period 1962–82 and then to forecast acreage in the 1983–86 period. (See Just, 1989, for a detailed specification of the models and data used for the analysis.) The results are given in Table 5.1. The results for equation (4) take the participation rate as exogenous whereas the results where the model is specified as equations (4) and (5) include forecasting errors for the participation rate as well.

In the case of feed grains, the *ad hoc* formulation in (1) leads to a much smaller standard error in the sample period than the structural form in (4) even though the structural form performs better than the *ad hoc* form in *ex ante* forecasting of the post-sample period. The model combining equations (4) and (5) obtains an even lower standard error. In the case of wheat, the structural form fits the sample data better than the *ad hoc* form and performs substantially better in *ex ante* simulation. These results suggest

> SUBPRINCIPLE 1.1. *When theory or intuition has strong implications for nonlinearities, kink points, boundary values, etc., estimation of heavily structured relationships based on theory and intuition leads to better understanding of commodity prices than flexible (unstructured) relationships necessary for objective identification.*

The superior performance of the structural model carries through when errors in forecasting the participation rate are also considered. The reason the structural form can outperform the *ad hoc* model even in the sample period is that nonlinearities and kinks in response over a wide range of policy parameters put a premium on global properties of the function. The participation rate over the sample period ranges from zero (a kink point) to near 90 percent in others. As a result, the effects of profits with an without compliance cannot be well represented by a smooth approximating function following (1). This substantiates

> SUBPRINCIPLE 1.2. *When policy instruments vary widely, a plausible global relationship consistent with the intuitive structural role of policy is preferred to locally flexible functional representations.*

Next, consider the role of government policy in demand. In many countries, the government has become involved in buying agricultural commodities and thus adds an additional component of demand to the usual components of food, feed, inventory, etc. Changes in government policy can have distinct and discrete effects on the structure of both public and private demand.

> SUBPRINCIPLE 1.3. *Disaggregating demand by its various components (food, feed, inventory, etc.) with a separate component for government commodity purchases can permit inclusion of more structure in demand and aid understanding of commodity price behaviour.*

In one sense, this subprinciple says little more than that use of more disaggregated data leads to better understanding of how a system works. Econometric investigators of agricultural commodity markets have long found that disaggregations of demand into food, feed, export, and inventory components leads to better understanding of total demand because the additional data allows identification of the role of as many exogenous variables for each component as could be identified for total demand in a total demand formulation. For example, consider a demand system for a given commodity of the form

$$Q_i = Q_i(P_m, X_i) \qquad\qquad Q_f = Q_f(P_m, X_f)$$
$$Q_x = Q_x(P_m, X_x) \qquad\qquad Q_m = Q_m(P_m, X_m) \qquad (6)$$
$$Q_{m,-1} + A_t \cdot Y_a = Q_i + Q_f + Q_x + Q_m$$

including the supply–demand identity where the -1 subscript represents a one period lag and

> Q_z = quantity demanded with $z = i$ for food/industry, $z = f$ for
> feed, $z = x$ for export, and $z = m$ for market stocks
> X_z = exogenous variables which determine the relevant demand.

Clearly, if all of these demands are aggregated into a total, $Q_t = Q_i + Q_f + Q_x + Q_m$, then the resulting demand equation, $Q_t = Q_t(P_m, X_i, X_f, X_x, X_m)$ may not be identified for econometric purposes even though all of the individual demands are. Furthermore, regardless of identification, information is lost as a result of aggregation so econometric estimators of total demand are inefficient compared to estimators of the disaggregated demand system. The same principle applies to the role of, say, a government inventory demand equation, $Q_g = Q_g(P_m, X_g)$, which includes an additional set of exogenous factors, X_g.

Another reason for estimating government demand separately is to include the theoretical and intuitive structure associated with various policy interventions which can give a model better global properties as discussed above on the supply side. These considerations may call for limited dependent variable models. Alternatively, qualitative definitions of right hand side variables may suffice. For example, in the case of government acquisition of feed grains in the US, one finds

$$Q_g = 0.3873 + 0.5838\ Q_{g,-1} + 39.85\ \max\{0,\ (1.1\ P_s - P_m)\ \phi\}$$
$$(0.38) \quad (9.04) \qquad\qquad (7.74)$$
$$+\ 20.37\ D - 0.1172\ T_1 + 1.821\ T_2 + 0.5981\ T_3$$
$$(6.90)\ (-0.09) \qquad (1.33) \qquad (0.45)$$
$$R^2 = 0.927,\ \bar{R}^2 = 0.919,\ DW = 1.42,\ \text{Sample} = 1973{:}1\text{–}1987{:}3$$

where D is a policy variable reflecting the payment-in-kind program of 1983, the T_i are quarterly dummy variables, other variables are as defined above and t-ratios are in parentheses (see Just, 1989, for a complete definition of variables and data sources).[2,3] This equation captures the qualitative relationship whereby stocks are not turned over to the government until market price falls to near the government support level but are increasingly turned over as the market price falls below that level (note that only grain produced under voluntary compliance with the program is supported so the market price can fall below the support price). Here the price variable is highly significant as compared to standard cases where a continuous function of market and support prices is used as a term explaining government stocks (see, e.g., Rausser, 1985, where the price term is a ratio of support price to market price and an implicit t-ratio of 1.48 is obtained in an otherwise similar equation).

3   Domestic macroeconomic policy

Traditionally, the consideration of policies in the study of agricultural prices did not go beyond domestic agricultural policy. The effects of policies for individual farm products and productive inputs could be investigated entirely in a microeconomic framework. Such a narrow perspective is no longer adequate.

> PRINCIPLE 2. *If international trade, inventory holding, or productive asset holding plays an important role in a commodity market, then understanding the role of the macroeconomy is an important part of understanding a commodity market.*

The narrow microeconomic perspective was perhaps adequate prior to significant events related to exchange-rate determination in the 1970s. However, with the shift away from the Bretton Woods system of fixed exchange rates and the ensuing exchange-rate variability, the importance of macroeconomic policy to the agricultural sector began to be recognized (Schuh, 1974).

The related events caused many analyses of the macroeconomic impacts on agriculture to focus on the effects of exchange rates on agricultural prices. These studies have overwhelmingly found exchange rates to be a dominant force affecting agricultural prices. For example, Chambers and Just (1981) in studying the commodity boom of the 1970s estimate a market system of equations similar to (6) for US wheat, corn, and soybeans where the exchange rate appears as an exogenous variable in the export equation. The resulting reduced-form elasticities of price with respect to exchange rate tend to dominate all others (see Table 5.2). Only lagged inventory (carryin) for wheat and consumer income for corn have larger elasticities in explaining prices. Given sample variation in the exogenous variables (which is small for consumer income), an examination of standardized (beta) regression coefficients (see Goldberger, 1964, pp. 197–8) reveals that exchange-rate variation explains more short-run variation in each price than any other variable except carryin. In the long run where carryin is determined endogenously in the system, exchange-rate variation explains more variation than any other variable.

These results imply that exchange rates play a larger role in agricultural commodity markets than the agricultural policy instruments designed to

		Model	
Exogenous Variable	Wheat	Corn	Soybeans
Lagged Disappearance	0.001	− 0.173	− 0.233
Lagged Inventory	− 1.535	− 1.168	− 0.841
Lagged Exports	0.177	0.101	0.605
Lagged (Expected) Price	− 0.575	− 0.285	− 0.085
Support Price	− 0.563	− 0.227	− 0.047
Exchange Rate	− 1.243	− 1.903	− 2.643
Consumer Income	0.817	− 2.316	− 0.689
Cattle on Feed		0.739	0.601
Pigs on Feed		1.091	
Non US Stocks/Shipments	− 0.212	− 0.213	− 0.031
EEC Threshold Price	− 0.623		

Table 5.2 Estimated reduced-form price elasticities for selected US agricultural commodities[a]

[a]See Chambers and Just (1981) for a complete report of the estimates and complete definitions of variables and data sources.

regulate them. Moreover, at times the two tend to work against one another. For example, several studies have recently found that the effects of macroeconomic policies on agriculture can more than offset its sector-specific policies in terms of the relative price signals guiding producers and consumers (Rausser, 1985; Valdes, 1986). These results substantiate

> SUBPRINCIPLE 2.1. *In a world of exchange-rate volatility, investigation of the effects of sector policy on tradable commodity prices requires considering interactions of policy instruments with exchange rates.*

As the instability of the macroeconomy evolved through the 1970s and early 1980s, the high levels of volatility enabled more linkages between the macroeconomy and agriculture to be identified. Exchange-rate volatility beginning in the early 1970s with the collapse of the Bretton Woods Agreement allowed the importance of exchange rates to be clearly identified empirically about a decade ago. More recently, the sharp swings in interest and inflation rates in the late 1970s and early 1980s have similarly allowed their importance to be identified empirically. The work that identified a strong empirical linkage to agricultural commodity markets through interest rates occurred in the mid-1980s in response to the data with wide variations in interest rates generated in the early 1980s (Rausser, 1985).

Interest rates have their primary effect on agricultural commodity markets through the incentive to carry stocks of storable grains and to adjust breeding herds of livestock. To illustrate the importance of these points, consider the estimated equation for wheat stocks,

$$Q_m = 316.6 + 0.6803\ Q_{m,-1} - 46.84\ P_f - 22.84\ r_m$$
$$(0.94)\quad (5.80)\qquad\quad (-1.85)\quad (-2.24)$$
$$+ 191.7\ D - 140.9\ T_1 - 119.4\ T_2 + 1464\ T_3$$
$$(1.75)\quad (-1.63)\quad (-0.83)\quad\ (8.32)$$
$$R^2 = 0.948,\ \bar{R}^2 = 0.940,\ DW = 1.55,\ \text{Sample} = 1973{:}\ 1\text{--}1986{:}\ 2$$

where all variables are as defined above and t-ratios are in parentheses (see Just, 1989, for a complete definition of variables and data sources). Here, the interest rate is statistically more significant than own price. If one reestimates this equation with data terminating in the second quarter of 1979 just before the interest-rate boom, the t-ratio for the interest rate drops to -0.90. This t-ratio compared to the t-ratio of -2.24 above demonstrates the importance of interest-rate variability beginning about a decade ago in identifying interest-rate effects on agricultural commodity markets. These results suggest

> SUBPRINCIPLE 2.2 *In a world of interest-rate volatility, investigation of the effects of sector policy on storable commodity prices requires considering interest-rate effects on inventory holding.*

The importance of interest rates in agricultural commodity markets is illustrated even more dramatically in livestock markets. Consider the following two estimated equations for breeding hog inventories and pork production,

$$Q_h = 759.2 + 0.9509\ Q_{h,-1} - 23{,}590 P_c/P_p - 32.36\ r_m$$
$$(3.01)\ (24.08)\qquad\quad (-3.83)\qquad (-3.45)$$
$$- 49.00\ T_1 + 120.0\ T_2 - 170.5\ T_3$$
$$(-0.67)\qquad (1.64)\quad (-2.32)$$
$$R^2 = 0.925,\ \bar{R}^2 = 0.916,\ DW = 1.75,\ \text{Sample} = 1973{:}1\text{--}1987{:}4$$

$$Q_p = 864.9 + 2403\ P_c/P_p - 0.1016\ (Q_h - Q_{h,-1}) + 34.70\ r_m$$
$$(2.35)\ (0.40)\qquad (-0.86)\qquad\qquad\quad (3.40)$$
$$+ 0.1456\ Q_{n,-2} + 116.2\ T_1 + 121.6\ T_2 + 203.4\ T_3$$
$$(7.59)\qquad\quad (1.43)\qquad (1.59)\qquad (1.71)$$
$$R^2 = 0.826,\ \bar{R}^2 = 0.802,\ DW = 1.42,\ \text{Sample} = 1973{:}1\text{--}1987{:}4$$

where Q_h is breeding hog inventory, Q_p is pork production, Q_n is new pig crop (which itself is a function of breeding hog inventory with a lag), P_c is corn price, P_p is pork price, other variables are as specified earlier, and t-ratios appear in parentheses (see Just, 1989, for details). The first equation reveals that the interest rate has a significant effect on farmers' willingness to carry breeding herds. (Again, to illustrate the importance of interest-rate variability over the last decade in identifying this coefficient, note that the corresonding t-ratio when using a sample period ending in the second quarter of 1979 is only -1.18.) The second equation, on the other hand, illustrates an important dynamic effect of interest rates on agriculture. A higher interest rate has not only a direct effect of lowering profitability but the associated liquidation of breeding stocks causes short-run meat production to increase thus further reducing profitability. This feeds back in the form of lower meat prices thus tending to cause a short-run overadjustment.

The importance of interest rates in determining the cost of carrying productive assets, however, is only part of the picture. Because productive assets can serve as a store of values in periods of inflation, the role of inflation must also be considered. The flow of funds in and out of agriculture induced by interest rates and inflation can be substantial because agricultural production asset markets are transacted in markets that are highly competitive. For example, agricultural land attracts investment as a store of value in periods of high inflation but funds are drawn away from the financing of land purchases by high real interest rates. The resulting effects on variability of farmers' wealth have been extraordinary over the last fifteen years.

These points are made here on the basis of the study of macroeconomic effects on land prices by Just (1988b) which again illustrates the importance of utilizing structural versus *ad hoc* specifications (SUBPRINCIPLES 1.1 and 1.2). A common econometric approach to explaining land prices is to use an *ad hoc* function of a lag distribution of short-run returns or rents per acre from farming (e.g., Burt, 1984). Alston (1984) generalized this approach to consider interest rates and inflation in a 'capitalization' formula by using an equation with

$$P = \frac{\alpha_0 + \alpha_1 R}{\beta_0 + \beta_1 I} \tag{7}$$

where P is land price, R is a free form 13-period lag distribution on real returns per acre, and I is the real interest rate (16 estimated parameters).

By comparison, it was found that an equation derived almost entirely from theory fits the Alston data better. The equation is of the form

$$P = (1 + f)\frac{(1 - \rho)(1 - \nu\psi)P^* + (1 - \tau)R^* - \beta\Sigma}{1 + \gamma\theta(1 - \tau) + r\eta(1 - \theta)(1 - \tau) + \lambda + X} \tag{8}$$

where f is the rate of inflation, ρ is the rate of transactions cost (commissions, etc.) on land sales, ν is the rate of tax on capital gains, ψ is the proportion of capital gains in land value, P^* is expected real land price after the next production period, τ is the rate of tax on ordinary income (which includes interest income and treats interest expense as a deduction), R^* is expected real returns to farming per unit of land in the next production period including government program payments, β is a coefficient of risk aversion, Σ is the risk (variance) of returns plus capital gains over the next production period, γ is the real rate of interest earned on savings or alternative investments, θ is the proportion of land not financed by debt, r is the real rate of interest paid for farmland mortgage funds, η is a term representing transactions cost in borrowing, λ is the rate of real estate taxation, and X is a term representing opportunity cost associated with imperfections in the capital market (credit limitations).[4] Equation (8) is basically a generalized capitalization formula. The numerator is the returns to ownership corrected for taxes, transactions costs, and risk premium. The denominator is the opportunity cost of capital corrected for taxes, transactions costs, and capital market imperfections.

Data were available for all the terms in this model except β so only one coefficient was estimated.[5] Nevertheless, a better fit of land price data (R^2 of 0.98 versus 0.95) in the Midwestern US was obtained by specifying simple naive expectations of land prices and returns (rational expectations, adaptive expectations, and extrapolative expectations obtained poorer but similar fits).

Admittedly, equation (8) includes many more variables than equation (7). But this is part of the point. The reason more variables can be included in (8) is that the form of the equation is imposed from theory. One cannot hope to obtain plausible signs for so many variables simultaneously by estimating an *ad hoc* or flexible econometric relationship particularly given that many of the variables have minor effects individually. Also, the nonlinearities of variables in (8) are likely to elude an *ad hoc* or flexible econometric approach except as a local approximation. Thus, not only would predictive ability be lost when values of some variables move outside the range of data used for estimation, but the intuitive understanding of how variables interact would be reduced. These results give

> SUBPRINCIPLE 2.3. *In a world of interest-rate and inflation volatility, investigation of commodity prices in sectors with competitive markets for productive asssets requires considering effects of interest rates and inflation on productive capacity.*

Another result obtained with the equation in (8) is that the estimated model changes very little as the sample period is altered (Just, 1988b). This is because the model has only one estimated parameter which is basically a calibrating parameter. Thus, for example, a fit of the model prior to the land boom or prior to the land price decline of the 1980s produces almost the same *ex ante* fit of the 1980s data as an *ex post* fit based on a sample through 1986. This suggests a concept similar to SUBPRINCIPLE 1.2.

The results of this section demonstrate that the effects of macro-economic policy are transmitted to the agricultural sector through exchange rates, interest rates, and inflation in addition to consumer income. The importance of multiple channels of effects suggests

> PRINCIPLE 2.4 *When several macroeconomic variables have a direct role in an individual commodity market, the effects of macroeconomic variables on commodity prices can be meaningfully investigated only by incorporating a model of the macroeconomy that assures consistent levels of macroeconomic variables.*

Many researchers have attempted to measure the influence of changes in macroeconomic variables on agriculture. However, these exercises have often proven to be unreliable because they are based on incomplete macroeconomic models that assume various macroeconomic linkage variables to be exogenous (Farrell, DeRosa, and McCown, 1983). The point here is that macroeconomic linkage variables such as the exchange rate, interest rate, inflation, and consumer income are determined by macroeconomic policies. Since they all appear in models of agricultural commodity markets, plausible implications of commodity market models can only be assured if the macroeconomic linkage variables are set at levels which are mutually consistent given the set of macroeconomic policies available. This is accomplished either by using historically observed levels of macroeconomic linkage variables (which considerably narrows the scope of investigation) or by generating predicted levels from a simultaneous macroeconomic model with specific macroeconomic policy choices.

4   Foreign agricultural policy

Foreign sector-specific policies can also play a crucial role in explaining domestic agricultural commodity prices. Many studies have found that foreign prices, and thus the policies that determine foreign prices, are important in explaining real trends in export sectors (e.g., Ansu, 1985). Chambers and Just (1981) find that the European Community's (EC) threshold price for wheat is statistically the most significant variable explaining US wheat exports in the early 1970s based on the equation,

$$Q_x = 4.396 + 0.2914 Q_{x,-1} - 9.498 P_m - 2.282 E - 0.008416 P_t$$
$$\quad (2.52) \quad (1.74) \quad (-0.82) \quad (-1.18) \quad (-1.82)$$
$$\quad + 0.008831 W - 0.004221 G + 0.2014 T_1 + 0.1764 T_2 - 0.003492 T_3$$
$$\quad (0.81) \quad (-0.61) \quad (1.10) \quad (1.33) \quad (-0.03)$$

Sample = 1969:1–1977:2

where P_t is the EC threshold price, W is stocks of wheat in other major exporters, G is government (Public Law 480) shipments of wheat from the US, other variables are defined above, and t-ratios are reported in parentheses (R^2 and Durbin–Watson statistics are not reported because the market system of equations was estimated by three stage least squares). These conditions are the product of a situation where world agricultural commodity markets are dominated by a relatively small number of very large exporters and where domestic agricultural sectors in these countries are heavily regulated.

A more recent example related to the role of the US wheat sector in the world market can also serve to illustrate the significance of foreign agricultural policies for domestic agricultural sectors. The US is the major exporter of wheat in the world market with a market share of 43 percent (based on 1980–2 data). A number of agricultural economists have argued that because of this dominant share, US wheat price supports act essentially as world price supports (US Department of Agriculture, 1985). Because of this dominant role, a decision to discontinue price supports in the US (such as was considered in 1985) has significant implications for countries attempting to develop domestic wheat production sectors such as Argentina. For example, Gardner (1985) has estimated that curtailing US wheat price supports would cause the world wheat price to decline by 17 percent. Clearly, this foreign policy change could have devastating effects on the domestic wheat policies of a country like Argentina. Similarly, US sugar import policies play an important role in determining the foreign exchange earnings of developing countries that are able to export sugar to the United States (occasionally at prices five times the world level) under its import quotas. These considerations suggest

> PRINCIPLE 3. *Understanding domestic prices of traded commodities that are characterized by concentrated world markets and regulated markets in major foreign exporting countries requires consideration of foreign sector policy.*

5   Foreign macroeconomic policy

In the same way that the results above imply critical dependence of exchange rates on domestic macroeconomic policy, they imply a critical dependence of exchange rates on the macroeconomic policies of foreign trading partners. Evidence of the importance of foreign macroeconomic policy to domestic agriculture is clear from the increased portion of adjustment in world agricultural trade that has involved middle income developing countries in recent years. During the late 1970s when the United States was pursuing a liberal monetary policy that led to devaluation of the dollar, agricultural imports by these countries accounted for almost half of the increased value of US exports. They also accounted for almost half of the decline in 1982 when the United States sharply tightened its monetary policy and the dollar appreciated rapidly (Schuh, 1985). The availability of cheap agricultural commodities as a result of US macroeconomic policy in the 1970s has been cited as a major disruption of efforts to develop domestic agriculture in these countries. These observations emphasize the importance of considering foreign macroeconomic policies pursued by trading partners in formulating domestic agricultural policy.

> PRINCIPLE 4. *Understanding effects of foreign macroeconomic policy on exchange rates can be crucial to understanding variation in domestic commodity prices and the effects of domestic sector policy.*

The difference in responses of US exports to depreciation of the dollar in the early 1970s and mid 1980s gives another example of the role of foreign macroeconomic policy. In the early 1970s, the depreciation of the dollar relative to currencies of major importers lead to a sharp increase in US agricultural commodity prices and exports. The response was not as great to an equal devaluation of the dollar in the mid 1980s because major competing grain exporters followed macroeconomic policies that maintained par with the dollar. That is, while the dollar devalued with respect to importers' currencies, it did not devalue with respect to exporters' currencies as it had in the 1970s. This implies the importance of third country macroeconomic policies.

> SUBPRINCIPLE 4.1. *The set of potentially important macroeconomic policies abroad for explaining domestic commodity prices includes not only those of trading partners but also those of trading competitors.*

These principles collectively imply that consideration of the effects of foreign macroeconomic policies on domestic commodity prices is a complex issue.

6   Overshooting in flexible markets

Increasingly, world markets for agricultural commodities have come to be viewed as more flexible or volatile than those for other sectors of the international economy. Explanations have been advanced associated with the explosion of trading in major futures and commodities exchanges. Commodity futures trading increased 437 percent in the US from 1972 to 1981. In 1980, the volume of futures trading in soybeans was over 32 times the volume of the entire crop (Commodity Research Bureau, 1982). This simultaneous development has raised the issue of whether excess volatility in agriculture is due to excessive speculation by traders using technical rather than fundamental trading rules (see discussion from the session on Excess Volatility in Agriculture in the December, 1988, *American Journal of Agricultural Economics*). While this debate is not closed, empirical results are beginning to suggest that excess volatility in agriculture is largely due to excess volatility in macroeconomic policy; the level of trading activity in agricultural markets is important only insofar as it contributes to their competitive and flexible nature.

As experience has accumulated more studies have realized that monetary policy causes differential rates of inflation among commodity markets due to different degrees of price fixity (Dornbusch, 1976; Hicks, 1974; Okun, 1975; Mussa, 1981; Phelps and Taylor, 1977). Dornbusch (1973) has shown that a monetary shock in an economy with both fixed and flexible prices will cause flexible price markets to overshoot their long-run equilibrium in the short run. Okun argues that the difference in characteristics between manufactured goods and services (customer markets) and basic commodity markets such as in agriculture (auction markets) justifies the fixed-price/flex-price framework. He characterizes customer markets by imperfect competition and differentiated products which make price adjustments sluggish compared to competition and rapid price adjustment in auction markets.

This framework has been applied to agricultural prices by Lawrence and Lawrence (1985). In their general equilibrium model of a dualistic economy, agricultural commodities are traded in auction or flex-price markets while other commodities are traded in customer or fixed-price markets. Primary commodity markets for agricultural goods clear in the short run by price adjustments whereas manufactured goods markets clear in the short run by quantity adjustments. The result of this dichotomy of adjustments is that unanticipated monetary disturbances affect relative commodity prices in the short run even while long-run real effects are neutral. As a result of this fixed-price/flex-price duality, the burden of monetary instability that is otherwise placed on the agricultural sector by virtue of its importance in trade is further exacerbated.

Increasingly, empirical results are verifying the validity of this explanation for agriculture. For example, the elastic response to money supply found by Chambers and Just (1982a) was early evidence in this respect.[6] Lombra and Mehra (1983) also found that money supply has a statistically significant effect on food prices consistent with more flexible price response in the more basic commodity markets. Van Duyne (1982) was the first to specifically use the fixed-price/flex-price model in explaining food prices. More recently, Stamoulis and Rausser (1988) have verified over-shooting for US agriculture in a more complete empirical model paralleling the theoretical model of Lawrence and Lawrence (1985). Cavallo (1985) has found in an analysis of exchange rates in Argentina that monetary and exchange-rate policies have short-run real effects that differ from those in the long run where the law of one price becomes effective. Amranand and Grais (1984) found that the fixed-price/flex-price dichotomy explains general equilibrium adjustments and distributional implications of macroeconomic policy in Thailand. The lessons from these studies are

> PRINCIPLE 5. *Understanding volatility of basic commodity markets requires modelling their flexibility along with the fixity of related markets in a general equilibrium framework.*
> SUBPRINCIPLE 5.1. *Neutrality of monetary policy cannot be imposed on individual commodity markets in the short run.*
> SUBPRINCIPLE 5.2. *Discernment of the source of short-run price adjustments and the extent to which they are a consequence of overshooting is crucial in determining the likelihood of continuation.*

While many of the studies on overshooting focus on monetary policy, similar principles apply to fiscal policy as well. Collectively, they identify some important considerations that tend to be ignored in macroeconomic policy formation. Macroeconomic policy debates focus primarily on macroeconomic variables and measures of aggregate performance. In so doing, the inefficiencies and costs of adjustment imposed on individual sectors through sluggish adjustment in some and overshooting in others are ignored. Variability in macroeconomic policy imposes externalities on individual sectors because these various sector-specific consequences are not taken into account at the level of macroeconomic policy formation (Just, 1988a). Only recently have empirical results been developed that show these effects to be important at the aggregate level (Kormendi and Meguire, 1984 and 1985; Fry and Lilien, 1986).

The same principles of overshooting apply to commodity markets in an international context where the commodity is heavily regulated (fixed) in some counties and unregulated (flexible) in others. Johnson (1973), in his analysis of world agriculture in disarray, argues that some kinds of agricultural policies have characteristics which export instability to world markets. The variable trade levies of the EC are an example. Through variable trade levies, the internal price is stabilized but exports and imports are destablized thus imposing excess instability on world markets (Just, Lutz, Schmitz, and Turnovsky, 1977). Many developing countries also have adopted policies that fix internal price for purposes of assuring cheap food while maintaining production incentives. For example,

Mexico has policies that fix internal farm and consumer prices of agricultural grains with the government relying on world markets to make up the difference. These circumstances suggest another application of the fixed-price/flex-price characterization of market behaviour where the fixed-price markets are characterized by government intervention which prevents price adjustment. These considerations have been examined empirically by Zwart and Mielke (1979) who find that instability of world markets for wheat has been significantly exaggerated as a result of policies that fix internal prices in the EC. Thus, continuation of EC policies has significant implications for commodity price variability in other countries.

> SUBPRINCIPLE 5.3. *Understanding the volatility of basic commodity markets that are subject to various levels of price regulation among countries requires modelling the price and quantity volatility imposed on free market countries by fixed market countries.*

Because these results are realized only by analyzing the specific structure through which foreign policies operate, they underscore the principles of Section 2.

7   Volatility, the increasing endogeneity of exogenous variables and the expanding scope of commodity price models

Many of the sections of this paper recount developments as modelers have realized that some variables previously treated as exogenous must necessarily be treated as endogenous. These realizations include policy variables as well as choices of technology and price linkages to other sectors of the economy. This increasing scope of modelling suggests.

> PRINCIPLE 6. *Commodity modellers should continually seek to endogenize the exogenous variables in existing commodity models and be prepared to revise and refine interpretations accordingly.*

In early efforts to model commodity markets, government involvement was often taken to be exogenous. However, governments rarely leave policy instruments unchanged over a long period of time. Changes in policy are motivated by policy disequilibria that arise when markets do not follow the preconceived conditions that surrounded policy formation (Just and Rausser, 1984). As a result, such unexpected conditions as high food prices, high treasury exposure, or depressed performance of agricultural exports can lead to public pressure that causes an endogenous change in agricultural policy (Rausser, 1982). The volatility of commodity markets in recent times has caused these conditions to develop with increased frequency. When the endogenous nature of government policies is ignored, econometric models cannot give a complete understanding of commodity price formation and behaviour. This leads to

> SUBPRINCIPLE 6.1. *When government involvement in a commodity market is responsive to market conditions or to political conditions that depend on market conditions, endogenous consideration of government behaviour is necessary for adequate understanding of commodity price behaviour. This necessitates understanding the political economy of policy formation.*

The endogeneity of agricultural policy controls was first investigated by Rausser and Freebairn (1974) who found US meat import quotas to be explained by an estimated policy criterion function. Love (1987) and Just (1984) present results that show policy instruments for major US agricultural grain markets to be significantly responsive to lagged market conditions, exchange rates, and government inventory levels. Obviously, if policy instruments follow these relationships, models which treat them as exogenous will give a poor understanding of the sustained effects of various shocks. The limitation of assuming government behaviour to be exogenous is analogous to the limitation of partial equilibrium models in capturing general equilibrium relationships.

Consider next the increasing endogeneity of non-policy variables. For example, agricultural acreage equations have been estimated historically as a function of prices and possibly yields with technology and the cost of input prices assumed fixed. After the volatility of the 1970s and early 1980s, changes in cost per acre were successfully included in econometric equations explaining acreage. Implicitly, these specifications permit variability in technology and input prices but take those changes to be exogenous. More recent results, however, suggest that such specifications are inappropriate.

Based on a Chicago School view of market adjustments, Gardner (1984) argues that the prices of inputs will be bid up until the cost of production is equal to output price. This suggests that the per acre cost of production is not exogenous but rather is responsive to commodity prices. Testing this hypothesis for corn and soybeans obtains

$$C_c = -13.16 + 0.5360\ T + 13.39\ P_c + 0.4212\ C_{c,-1}$$
$$\quad\ (-0.69)\ (2.11)\qquad (5.34)\qquad (3.41)$$
$$R^2 = 0.8179,\ \bar{R}^2 = 0.7930,\ DW = 1.83,\ \text{Sample} = 1962\text{--}1987$$

$$C_s = -14.30 + 0.2211\ T + 3.958\ P_s + 0.4886\ C_{s,-1}$$
$$\quad\ (-1.52)\ (1.87)\qquad (7.08)\qquad (5.61)$$
$$R^2 = 0.9117,\ \bar{R}^2 = 0.8997,\ DW = 2.08,\ \text{Sample} = 1962\text{--}1987$$

where T is a time trend reflecting increases in yield that have roughly followed linear trends over the sample period and P_i is the real price of the respective commodity (see Just, 1989, for details). In each equation, the commodity price is highly significant, confirming that costs of production previously taken as exogenous are responsive commodity prices.

These equations could likely be improved by adding consideration of input prices in a modern cost function framework if collinearity did not prevent identification of separate coefficients. The point, however, is that variables that have previously been treated as fixed or exogenous should be considered endogenous in modelling agricultural commodity markets. Furthermore, there is no reason to expect that future conditions will maintain the same collinearity of output and input prices that makes these equations an adequate representation of production costs. Future conditions may reveal that some of the relationships that cannot yet be identified include additional endogenous variables that must be considered. As further endogenous variables are identified, the policies of other sectors of the economy are also likely to come into play. These kinds of experiences suggest

> SUBPRINCIPLE 6.2. *Understanding commodity prices is limited by past conditions that may not support identification of relationships that will explain future commodity price variations. Increasing commodity market volatility tends to invalidate models limited in scope and identification by historical data.*

The best hope for effective commodity modelling in the case of SUBPRINCIPLE 6.2 appears to be incorporation of structural information based on theory and intuition following the principles of Section 2 when it is available.

8   The scope of economic analysis of agricultural prices

Because of the complexity of the various policy interactions discussed in this paper, adequate policy analysis is difficult if not impossible without a formal framework. However, models that embody all of these interactions are not available. Models are needed that facilitate analysis of agricultural policy, recognizing the complex interactions of agricultural and macroeconomic policies both domestically and abroad. Addressing such policy questions requires modelling a number of components of economic activity both domestically and abroad.

First, a component describing a particular commodity market must be developed both for the country in question and for the (groups of) trading competitors and partners whose policies are important. Each of these must include significant agricultural policy instruments and macroeconomic phenomena related to the effects of exchange rates on trade; the effects of interest rates on storage, investment, and productivity; and the effects of taxes, subsidies, and other barriers on production and trade. In addition, since each country represents substantially less than the total world market, a commodity-specific component may be needed for the rest of the world.

Next to consider the implications of macroeconomic policy, a rest-of-the-economy component must be included for both the country under consideration and the trading competitors/partners. This component is necessary because the effects of macroeconomic policy on agriculture are correlated with those of other sectors; the strength of this correlation determines the magnitude of feedback relationships that govern exchange-rate and interest-rate determination. To reflect this phenomena appropriately, the rest-of-the-economy component must be sensitive to the shares of traded and nontraded goods in the total economy which may require separate modelling.

These considerations seem to require large complex models for studying commodity prices. However, large complex models are limited because intuition and understanding of the mechanism of change is lost. For this reason, an advantageous approach is to specify economic sectors with decreasing detail and increasing aggregation as one moves away from the specific domestic agricultural commodity under consideration rather than using a uniformly detailed general equilibrium specification (Just, Hueth and Schmitz, 1982; Rausser and Just, 1981). Thus, general equilibrium properties can be maintained with greater simplicity and understanding.

The approach advocated here is to develop fairly streamlined models with emphasis on understandability but yet models that cut across all relevant economic variables. This is made possible by using specifications that reduce the number of estimated coefficients, by making maximal use of extraneous information such as theory and intuition, and by using summary variables rather than representative variables. With this approach, models of commodity prices combine some aspects of theoretical analysis with some aspects of econometric and simulation methods. That is, the models can be analyzed under a wider range of conditions and values of certain key parameters as is typical of theoretical analysis while certain other, perhaps better identified, coefficients can be determined econometrically. These suggestions are summarized by

> PRINCIPLE 7. *Models that combine a broad set of phenomena affecting general equilibrium can convey more understanding by incorporating less detail and more aggregation in components less closely related to the commodity market in question and by imposing more intuitive and theoretical structure combining the many variables of importance.*

The development of models that incorporate decreasing detail and increasing aggregation in specifying components of commodity models less closely related to the commodity in question suggests the following subprinciple.

> SUBPRINCIPLE 7.1. *Specific purpose rather than general purpose commodity models are more easily structured to enhance understanding of commodity prices.*

A similar principle is discussed by Rausser and Just (1981) so the point will not be further belaboured here.

With little doubt, the approach of foregoing estimation of numerous coefficients by imposing heavy structure on data through theory and intuition meets with substantial resistance by those advocating the traditional concept of 'objectivity' attached to econometrics in theory. However, econometric practice suffers pitfalls whereby objectivity is lost through judicious selection of variables and substantial pre-test estimation that is not completely reported in the literature (Leamer, 1983). By removing this 'appearance of objectivity' constraint, the researcher is freed to use his intelligence in making sense of the data and to combine in an intimate way the methodology of theory and estimation.

Developing heavily structured models for empirical analysis is much like constructing theoretical models. In principle, an infinite set of alternatives are possible. Without a standard of comparison, there is no reason to expect this process to converge on any representation or understanding of a market particularly when many researchers are involved in similar activities. However, when a heavily structured model can outperform the standard *ad hoc* or flexible models in the literature (supposedly the best economists have to offer) then a degree of empirical validity is achieved that demands attention.

> SUBPRINCIPLE 7.2. *Models that impose heavy structure on the data should be judged on the basis of how well they fit the data and how well they generate ex ante forecasts in comparison to ad hoc and flexible specifications.*

Since this approach also clearly abandons the 'objectivity' that makes econometric and statistical measures of significance valid, another set of criteria are necessary for comparing and selecting models.

> SUBPRINCIPLE 7.3. *If several models fit the data with about equal precision, then plausibility of structure, stability of estimated structure with respect to sample period, and ex ante forecasting ability are appropriate means of model discrimination. All models that satisfy these criteria must be held as potentially valid until additional data is generated under economic conditions that permit discernment.*

An example of a model where these criteria are met is the model of land prices discussed in Section 3.

9   Conclusions

Agricultural commodity prices are affected in major ways by many sets of policies. These sets of policies are subject to frequent change in both the level of policy instruments and the active set of policy instruments. Heavy regulation and frequent changes in active sets of agricultural policy instruments demands heavily structured models for econometric identification. Tradability, storability, concentration of world markets for agricultural commodities, and competitive markets for productive assets cause significant interaction with foreign and macroeconomic sectors which demands general equilibrium considerations. Varying levels of price flexibility among markets must be captured to understand short-run overshooting and volatility. Increasing volatility is expanding the set of policy and price variables that must be considered endogenous in commodity price models. These conditions call for liberal use of theory and intuition in analyzing and understanding commodity price variation. Hopefully, the principles put forward in this paper can be useful toward this end.

NOTES

1 An equation similar to (5) was used by Chambers and Foster (1983) to explain participation in the farmer-owned reserve but was not used further in conjunction with a structural acreage equation such as (4).

2 Of course, other changes can be incorporated into an inventory equation that impose more structure. For example, some of the features of the land price equation discussed below which apply to holding assets can be readily included. The example provided here is merely intended to suggest a simple first step in that direction.

3 Note that throughout this paper the Durbin–Watson (DW) statistic is reported even though it is not strictly applicable in cases with a lagged dependent variable (Nerlove and Wallis, 1966). While appropriate adjustments can be made to correct this problem, the equations are reported only for illustrative purposes. For most of the cases in this paper, calculation of the h statistic which corrects for inclusion of a lagged dependent variable following Durbin (1970) reveals very low significance. Nevertheless, the t-statistics should be interpreted with caution where the DW statistic is low.

4 For brevity, the latter two terms are not explained in detail here; it suffices to say that they are not a major part of the explanation.

5 This statement must be qualified to some extent because some proxy data was used for a few minor variables. A complete statement of the qualifications is omitted here for purposes of brevity.

6 Chambers and Just (1979) present arguments that exchange-rate elasticities should not be tied directly to own price elasticities when cross price elasticities are omitted in estimation. The problem is that the exchange rate affects each of the other prices of traded goods. Even though each of these other prices may be individually unimportant and thus omitted in estimation, the collective exchange-rate effect that comes through all other foreign prices can be important. This implies that the export demand equation must be in the form $Q_x = Q_x(P_m, E, X_x)$ or $Q_x = Q_x(P_m \cdot E, E, X_x)$ if P_m represents a small subset of all traded prices in order to capture the aggregate effects of exchange-rate variation. Chambers and Just (1981) show that these considerations are important for agricultural commodities. Estimated exchange-rate elasticities of US export demand for wheat, corn, and soybeans are all considerably higher than the corresponding price elasticities. Similarly, the reduced

form exchange-rate elasticities of price are greater than 1 for all three commodities (see Table 6.2). Without the flexibility of this export demand specification with respect to the exchange rate, this type of overshooting phenomena cannot be detected.

REFERENCES

Alston, J. M. (1984) 'An Analysis of Growth of U.S. Farmland Prices, 1963–82', *American Journal of Agricultural Economics* **68**, 1–9.

Amranand, P. and W. Grais (1984) 'Macroeconomic and Distributional Implications of Sectoral Policy Intervention: An Application to Thailand', World Bank Staff Working Paper, Washington, D.C., November.

Ansu, Y. (1985) 'External Shocks, Domestic Policies and Structural Change: Kenya 1971–82', unpublished manuscript, World Bank, Washington, D.C.

Burt, O. R. (1984) 'Econometric Modeling of the Capitalization Formula for Farmland Prices', *American Journal of Agricultural Economics* **68**, 10–26.

Cavallo, D. F. (1985) 'Exchange Rate Overvaluation and Agriculture', Background paper for World Development Report 86, World Bank, Washington, D.C., September.

Chambers, R. G. and W. E. Foster (1983) 'Participation in the Farmer-Owned Reserve Program: A Discrete Choice Model', *American Journal of Agricultural Economics* **65**, 120–4.

Chambers, R. G. and R. E. Just (1979) 'A Critique of Exchange Rate Treatment in Agricultural Trade Models', *American Journal of Agricultural Economics* **61**, 249–57.

 (1981) 'Effects of Exchange Rates on US Agriculture: A Dynamic Analysis', *American Journal of Agricultural Economics* **63**, 32–46.

 (1982a) 'An Investigation of the Effect of Monetary Factors on Agriculture', *Journal of Monetary Economics* **9**, 235–47.

 (1982b) 'Qualitative Econometrics and Agriculture', in *New Directions in Econometric Modeling and Forecasting in U.S. Agriculture*, ed. G. C. Rausser, New York: Elsevier North-Holland, Inc.

Commodity Research Bureau (1982) *Commodity Year Book*, New York: Commodity Year Book.

Dornbusch, R. (1973) 'Currency Depreciation, Hoarding and Relative Prices', *Journal of Political Economy* **81**, 893–915.

 (1976) 'Expectations and Exchange Rate Dynamics', *Journal of Political Economy* **84**, 1161–76.

Durbin, J. (1970) 'Testing for Serial Correlation in Least-Squares Regression when some of the Regressors are Lagged Dependent Variables', *Econometrica* **38**, 410–21.

Farrell, V. S., D. A. DeRosa and T. A. McCown (1983) 'Effects of Exchange Rate Volatility on International Trade and Other Economic Variables: A Review of the Literature', Board of Governors of the Federal Reserve System, Washington, D.C., December.

Fry, M. J. and D. M. Lilien (1986) 'Monetary Policy Responses to Exogenous Shocks', *American Economic Review* **76**, 79–83.

Gardner, B. G. (1984) in *Alternative Agricultural and Food Policies and the 1985 Farm Bill*, ed. G. C. Rausser and K. R. Farrell, Giannini Foundation of Agricultural Economics, University of California, Berkeley.

 (1985) 'US Agricultural Policy and Developing Country Agriculture', paper presented at the Allied Social Science Association Meetings, New York, December 28–30.

Goldberger, A. S. (1964) *Econometric Theory*, New York: John Wiley & Sons.

Hicks, J. R. (1974) *The Crisis in Keynesian Economics*, Oxford: Basil Blackwell.

Johnson, D. G. (1973) *World Agriculture in Disarray*, New York: St Martins Press.

Just, R. E. (1973) 'An Investigation of the Importance of Government Programs in Farmers' Decisions', *American Journal of Agricultural Economics* **55**, 441–52.

 (1984) *Automatic Adjustment Rules for Agricultural Policy Controls*, Studies in Economic Policy, American Enterprise Institute for Public Policy, Washington, D.C.

(1988a) 'Exchange Rates and Macroeconomic Externalities in Agriculture', in *Macroeconomics, Agriculture, and Exchange Rates*, ed. P. L. Paarlberg and R. G. Chambers, Boulder, Colorado: Westview Press.

(1988b) 'The Role of Monetary, Fiscal, and Agricultural Variables in Farmland Prices', Working Paper, University of Maryland.

(1989) 'An Econometric Model of Major US Agricultural Commodities', Working Paper, University of Maryland.

Just, R. E., D. L. Hueth and A. Schmitz (1982) *Applied Welfare Economics and Public Policy*, New York: Prentice-Hall.

Just, R. E., E. Lutz, A. Schmitz and S. Turnovsky (1977) 'The Distribution of Welfare Gains from International Price Stabilization Under Distortions', *American Journal of Agricultural Economics* **59**, 652–61.

Just, R. E. and G. C. Rausser (1984) 'Uncertain Economic Environments and Conditional Policies' in *Alternative Agricultural and Food Policies and the 1985 Farm Bill*, ed. G. C. Rausser and K. R. Farrell, Giannini Foundation of Agricultural Economics, University of California, Berkeley.

Kormendi, R. C. and P. G. Meguire (1984) 'Cross-Regime Evidence of Macroeconomic Rationality', *Journal of Political Economy* **92**, 875–908.

(1985) 'Macroeconomic Determinants of Growth: Cross-Country Evidence', *Journal of Macroeconomics* **16**, 141–63.

Lawrence, C. and R. Z. Lawrence (1985) 'Global Commodity Prices and Financial Markets: Theory and Evidence', Working Paper, Columbia University, New York.

Leamer, E. E. (1983) 'Let's Take the Con Out of Econometrics', *American Economic Review* **73**, 31–43.

Lombra, R. E. and Y. P. Mehra (1983) 'Aggregate Demand, Food Prices, and the Underlying Rate of Inflation', *Journal of Macroeconomics* **5**, 383–98.

Love, H. A. (1987) 'Flexible Public Policy: The Case of the United States Wheat Sector', unpublished Ph.D. dissertation, University of California, Berkeley.

Mussa, M. (1981) 'Sticky Prices and Disequilibrium Adjustment in a Rational Model of the Inflationary Process', *American Economic Review* **71**, 1020–7.

Nerlove, M. and K. F. Wallis (1966) 'Use of the Durbin–Watson Statistic in Inappropriate Situations', *Econometrica* **34**, 235–8.

Okun, A. M. (1975) 'Inflation: Its Mechanics and Welfare Costs', *Brookings Papers on Economic Activity*, 351–401.

Phelps, E. S. and J. B. Taylor (1977) 'Stabilizing Powers of Monetary Policy Under Rational Expectations', *Journal of Political Economy* **85**, 164–90.

Rausser, G. C. (1982) 'Political Economic Markets: PESTS and PERTS in Food and Agriculture', *American Journal of Agricultural Economics* **64**, 821–33.

(1985) *Macroeconomics of U.S. Agricultural Policy*, Studies in Economic Policy, American Enterprise Institute for Public Policy, Washington, D.C.

Rausser, G. C. and J. W. Freebairn (1974) 'Estimation of Policy Preference Functions: An Application to US Beef Import Quotas', *Review of Economics and Statistics* **56**, 437–49.

Rausser, G. C. and R. E. Just (1981) 'Using Models in Policy Formation', in *Modeling Agriculture for Policy Analysis in the 1980s*, The Federal Reserve Bank of Kansas City, Kansas City.

Schuh, G. E. (1974) 'The Exchange Rate and US Agriculture', *American Journal of Agricultural Economics* **56**, 1–13.

(1985) 'Strategic Issues in International Agriculture', Working Paper, Agricultural and Rural Development Department, The World Bank, Washington, D.C.

Stamoulis, K. G. and G. C. Rausser (1988) 'Overshooting of Agricultural Prices', in *Macroeconomics, Agriculture, and Exchange Rates*, ed. P. L. Paarlberg and R. G. Chambers, Boulder, Colorado: Westview Press.

US Department of Agriculture (1985) *Agricultural Outlook*, Economic Research Service, US Government Printing Office, Washington, D.C.

Valdez, A. (1986) 'Exchange Rates and Trade Policy: Help or Hindrance to Agricultural Growth?' paper presented at the XIX Conference of the International Association of Agricultural Economists, Malaga, Spain, August 16–September 4.

Van Duyne, C. (1982) 'Food Prices, Expectations, and Inflation', *American Journal of Agricultural Economics* **64**, 419–30.
Zwart, A. C. and K. D. Mielke (1979) 'The Influence of Domestic Pricing Policies and Buffer Stocks on Price Stability in the World Wheat Industry', *American Journal of Agricultural Economics* **61**, 434–47.

Discussion

DAVID HARVEY

It is not my purpose to quarrel with the arguments or logic of this paper, which my co-discussant may wish to deal with, but with which I am largely in agreement. However, it might be noted that it is not always easy to put the principles into practice, especially when policy makers are breathing down one's neck for results! However, there are three major questions which occur to me from a policy analysis perspective.

Modelling domestic policies has been shown to require considerable 'subjectivity' – as the imposition of *a priori* maintained theory and expert intuition – in order to impose sufficient structure on the system of price determination to be able to estimate the basic relationships. How, then, do we demonstrate the credibility/objectivity of the resulting analysis to the policy decision makers who may not care about, know or believe the theory or intuition? Do we need a multiplicity of independent models to obtain objectivity? If so, then discrimination between models becomes of paramount importance, in which case does the theoretical consistency and expert judgement then becomes entirely secondary to the empirical performance of the model, regardless of its abstract elegance, logical consistency or conformity with expert opinion? Part of the point is that professional economists' concept of objectivity (as represented through careful elaboration of theoretical implications) is inconsistent with policy makers' concepts of objectivity (which are seldom well-defined other than as telling stories which their various constituencies can be persuaded to believe).

The impact of domestic monetary, fiscal and foreign exchange macro policy, plus foreign agricultural and macro policy has been demonstrated in this paper to be of overwhelming importance in determining both the level and, more importantly, the stability of domestic agricultural prices, returns and farming incomes (especially when we treat domestic policy as endogenous as Just quite rightly points out we need to do).

On the policy side, however, the concerns are precisely with the level and stability of these domestic variables. Whether or not current versions of public choice theories are capable of demonstrating it, politicians and the political process wish to provide increased incomes and improved stability to the domestic agricultural sectors in order either to promote growth (developing countries) or to minimize adjustment costs of declining sectors (developed countries). An apparent implication of the Just analysis is that a viable policy option (perhaps the only practical and effective option) is to isolate and insulate domestic agricultural sectors from both the macro and foreign influences. Much existing agricultural policy has this as a major effect. How can we convince them otherwise? The current GATT negotiations are a case in point. There is a strong (albeit slightly over-perfect) economic argument in favour of liberalizing agricultural markets. Yet an implication of this paper is that the resulting free market might well be plagued with instability generated through the effects of macro and foreign policy and market-induced shocks (the notion of endogenous policy makes the distinction between these two sources of shocks somewhat blurred). Does this mean that the GATT negotiations will have to move the question of commodity market stability (and associated macro stability) to the top of the agenda in order to achieve any significant steps towards commodity trade liberalization? If so, what implications does the modelling approach which Just advocates have for appropriate policy instruments?

'What a tangled web we weave when first we practice to deceive' seems to be the moral of the analysis. Market intervention, macro and foreign policies feed on one another to create increasingly complex systems of market and policy interaction. However, the theories of rent-seeking and of pursuit and protection of self and group interest around which most of the theory of public choice are built, suggests that the current system of market intervention and other forms of government policy will be difficult if not impossible to overturn without considerable institutional change (especially political institutions which have developed in tandem with rent-capturing institutions). At the considerable risk of making a complicated and highly interactive system model even more complex, does this mean that a completely general system has to include the theories of induced institutional innovation as well as the increasingly conventional theories of induced technical innovation and adoption? How close are we to being able to conceive of such theories and incorporating at least some part of these into the systematic models? As a further (and rather mischievous) question – would such incorporation then justify the Marxist criticism of neoclassical theory that it is predominantly an ideology defending existing vested interests and 'class' structures?

DAVID VINES

My comments will be brief: this is an interesting paper. The author has presented us with a set of seven commandments (although the original paper had thirty!). I will confine myself to just two.

1.   Impose structure

This is in fact one of Just's major themes. It can, however, be used as exhortation to further develop some of the results which he himself presents. I give two rather different examples.

(i) *Interest rate effects.* (See discussion above sub-principle 2.2) If one really does adopt a price overshooting model, as discussed in Section 6, then the equation above sub-principle 2.2 should perhaps be investigated by regressing prices on stocks, not vice versa. Thinking about a full structural model of the problem might have suggested this. The analogy is with foreign exchange markets where, (because the exchange rate is essentially an asset market price) one regresses exchange rates on outstanding asset stocks and interest rates, rather than regressing asset holdings on exchange rates and interest rates.

(ii) *Foreign repercussion effects.* The equation at the beginning of Section 4 in which US exports of wheat depend on the EEC intervention price would not be consistent with the alternative scenario envisaged two paragraphs later in which the US wheat support price acts essentially as a world support price. A full structural model would attempt to disentangle these influences.

The moral with which I am sure Just would agree is: embed even single equation investigation in a wider structural framework.

2.   Think about macroeconomic interactions

The first implication of this is emphasized by Just. One should be careful when doing econometrics that what, at first sight, look like exogenous variables to be used as regressors, are in fact jointly endogenous to agricultural developments. Example: if commodity prices influence inflation and inflation influences interest rates, then interest rates are not exogenous to commodity prices.

The second implication is more tricky and not dwelt on by Just. For many countries, particularly LDCs, agricultural supplies are a major component of macroeconomic aggregates, particularly for example exports. This means that macroeconometric forecasting models (e.g. for use in the design of fiscal and monetary policy) will contain processes which are heavily influenced by agricultural developments (e.g. the export function may be essentially an agricultural supply function). The interconnections between agricultural, micro, analysis and economy-wide, macro, analysis – and the implications of this for the construction of macroeconometric models – has only just begun to be recognized.

Summary of general discussion

Just responded to the comments made by the discussants that in fact he saw a point in increasing the structure of a model; he cited an example of a model with fifteen variables for which only a single parameter had to be estimated. This model turned out to be performing much better than any other he had seen before. Just could not see a problem with having two actors or agents determining the world price, instead of one having to function as a residual while the other dictated the world price. He agreed that induced innovation should be made endogenous where possible.

Chris Gilbert thought that perhaps the North American continent was indeed wide enough to allow econometric practices in one part of the country to go unaffected from quite different methodological pronouncements elsewhere. He referred to Sims (Minnesota) who argued that most models impose too many restrictions. In contrast he, Gilbert, would go along with what Just had set out in his paper and impose restrictions where possible. However, those restrictions require testing since only when they have been shown to be valid may they be imposed, giving structure to the model.

As a rejoinder G. S. Maddala pointed out that there is not just one Minnesota econometric procedure, but two! Minnesota econometrics I, as pronounced by Sims, argues that there are generally too many restrictions imposed on models; while Minnesota econometrics II, associated with

Sargent, argues that there are not enough restrictions imposed on models.

Just agreed that restrictions need to be tested. More important still he felt that it was necessary to test how the model performed outside the sample period. On that note he introduced the possibility that a particular model may not test well when considering its structural restrictions, yet may do well in forecasting outside the sample. Just said he had examples to prove such possibilities. Mark Taylor suggested that while the post-sample adequacy of a model may be a desirable criterion, he would still urge any modeller to also keep track of the in-sample adequacy of the model.

6 Price Determination in the Market for Aluminium*

ANTHONY BIRD

1 Introduction

Consultants and industrial economists think about the world in a quite different way from academics.

First, they have more information. Much of the data available to consultants comes from proprietary studies, which may not be available to academics. And if data is available, academics are often surprisingly unaware of it. For a good recent example of this, see Fama and French (1988).

Second, consultants are less sophisticated in matters of modelling technique. In part, this is because we are simple fellows. But in addition, consultants are severely constrained by the need to present their models and results to clients, who will often be non-economists. Clients distrust forecasts, and will be very quick to reject any findings which are based on a model which they do not understand. It is essential that models are simple and transparent, and that the clients can see the little wheels going round.

Thus consultants use models that have simple logic but which are· knowledge-intensive. This paper describes a forecasting approach of this type, as applied to the aluminium industry; although the detailed specification of a model will not be pursued here. The paper naturally reflects the special features of the aluminium industry; but models using similar methods are in common use by consultants and industrial economists concerned with other metal commodities.

Such models generally work by asking in what way the world would be different if only expectations were formed in a rational and consistent manner, instead of the way that they are. It is clear from this that consultants do not in general *assume* the existence of rational or consistent expectations, as academics do.

* I am grateful to David Humphreys, Surojit Ghosh, Philip Crowson and Alan Winters for comments on an earlier draft of this paper. Any errors which remain are mine.

A further feature of these models is that they yield strong forecasts of the likely behaviour of commodity prices in the medium and long term. They are strong in the sense that any discrepancy between actual prices and model prices causes agents to react, eventually forcing prices back into line.

However, there is great uncertainty about the *timing* of any price corrections. As a result of this, consultants cannot use their medium and long-term models to make predictions about price developments in the short term with any hope of beating the market. Indeed, I am very sceptical of all claims that this is possible.

2   General features of the aluminium industry

This section highlights some important features of the aluminium industry which are reflected in the forecasting approach outlined here. They are points which other economists may need to pay special attention to when using this method to track the price of other commodities.

Aluminium is a simple metal, in two important respects. First, there is a high degree of insulation between the primary and secondary industries, for technical reasons. This insulation has been weakening in recent years, but it still holds in general. Thus it is possible to consider the primary aluminium industry on its own, without the complication of destabilizing feedback which scrap recycling can produce. I shall use 'aluminium' to mean 'primary aluminium'.

Second, most of aluminium's costs are incurred at the processing and not at the mining stage. This has the important consequence that, for practical purposes, aluminium's long-run supply curve is approximately flat. This would not be true for very small or very large increments to supply; but for a wide range of likely rates of growth of demand, aluminium faces a broadly flat long-run supply curve. As we will see, this simplifies the problem of long-run price forecasting.

3   Prior information

Three types of prior information are available – *cost studies on existing plants, cost studies on new plants, and surveys of producer intentions.*

In recent years, the US Bureau of Mines (USBM) has published an extensive series of cost studies, covering both old and new facilities in a range of metal commodities, as part of its Mineral Availability System (USBM, 1987). However, the USBM calculations are rather less successful for the processed commodities such as aluminium than they are for the mined commodities. Accordingly, I shall not rely on the USBM results here.

Instead, I shall rely on a series of consulting studies on the pattern of aluminium production costs which I have prepared for aluminium industry clients annually since 1982. Most major aluminium companies subscribe to reports in this series. We consider first the findings of these studies on *existing smelter economics.*

The reports are based on a model which generates estimates of the cost of production in each smelter in the non-Socialist world. First, an assessment is made of the likely technical operating efficiency of each plant, after taking account of its age, technology, and location. This assessment is based on the results of an engineering model of the aluminium production process. For example, electricity consumption per tonne of metal produced, e, is derived from a relationship such as:

$$e = a(1 - g)^n + b + c$$

where a is the electricity consumption in a new best-practice prebaked smelter, g is the historical rate of decline of specific electricity usage, n is the life of the smelter since construction or major overhaul, b is a dummy variable to reflect the different levels of power consumption in smelters using the now-obsolete Soderberg process, and c is a dummy used in cases where a smelter has been designed with second-best technology (which usually reflects the ready availability of low-cost power). Similar relationships can be derived for other cost components. In some cases, such as labour, the relationships are more complex; systematic country or area differences need to be taken into account as well, and there are also scale economies.

Next, these technical coefficients must be multiplied by the price of each input. A judgement is made of the price at which each smelter is likely to be buying its alumina, after taking account of the relationships between the smelter and the refinery, and of developments in the alumina market; of each smelter's power cost, after allowing for long-term contracts with the electric utility (on average, aluminium smelters buy their power for less than half the price paid by other large industrial consumers); and of wage and maintenance costs and other expenses. It should be noted that these judgements on input prices are derived in a different way from the assessments of operating efficiency; they come from an intelligence-gathering process, rather than a technical model.

These estimates of efficiency and input prices, taken together, then give us an estimate of the total operating costs of each smelter. After that it is a simple matter to calculate country, area, and company averages, and – of particular interest for our present purposes – a cost curve.

There are several ways in which the general accuracy of the cost model can be checked. Predicted electricity usage can be compared with the published industry aggregate figures (IPAI, 1988). Estimated alumina costs can be compared with average value data computed from trade statistics. And there is constant feedback from the aluminium companies themselves, who monitor the readings from the model against the actual figures for their own smelters, and (sometimes) comment on any biases that they observe.

However, it must be remembered that individual plant estimates are based on a model, and not on confidential data supplied by the companies. Indeed, any confidential data is carefully *excluded* from the study. As a result, figures for individual plants can not be expected to coincide exactly with actual operating costs. However, if the results are used in an aggregate form, as a cost curve, it is likely that the results will be very close to the mark. Hilyard (1987) confirms that different consultants do in practice arrive at similar estimates of the current position of the overall cost curve.

Table 6.1, taken from Bird (1988), shows what the pattern of operating costs looked like in mid-1988, on various definitions. Some 13,658 thousand tonnes of capacity has been included in the calculations used to derive these curves. In addition, some 504 thousand tonnes of capacity remained physically in existence and able to produce, although its closure had been announced as imminent. In any use of cost curves, or calculation of the supply–demand balance, account must of course be taken of these graveside-reprieve smelters.

The cost curve thus measured is not strictly speaking the same as a short-run supply curve. This is because some smelters link elements of their input costs to the final price of metal. Such arrangements are common in the free (as opposed to the tied) market for alumina, and from late 1986 onwards they also started to become popular for electricity supply arrangements, especially in the high-cost US industry. Accordingly, if cost curves are to be used to generate an estimate of the short-run cost-justified price, an iterative procedure is needed. Table 5.1 shows that the mid-1988 cost curve would have looked like had metal prices been lower than the 120-cent level seen in mid-year.

It must be stressed that metal-linked cost contracts differ from smelter to smelter. Further, some smelters have a contract of this kind for their alumina but not their electricity; some have these contracts for their electricity but not their alumina; some for both of these cost components; while many smelters do not have metal-linked contracts at all. As a result, calculating the exact impact that these contracts have on the industry's cost curve is a somewhat messy business. A separate allowance must be made for the circumstances of each individual plant.

Further, the terms of these contracts are sometimes complex. For

	Thousands of tonnes of smelter capacity with costs at or below a given level			
	Operating Cost Basis			Avoidable Cost Basis
cents per pound	120-cent metal	75-cent metal	50-cent metal	50-cent metal
21	0	0	0	38
22	0	0	0	38
23	0	0	0	143
24	0	0	0	143
25	0	0	17	547
26	0	0	17	1,038
27	0	0	157	1,266
28	0	0	195	1,413
29	0	17	195	2,194
30	0	17	241	2,699
31	0	157	653	4,180
32	0	195	653	4,935
33	0	195	653	5,631
34	0	195	1,371	6,306
35	30	271	1,451	6,515
36	47	683	1,651	6,900
37	47	683	2,115	7,934
38	572	1,118	2,916	8,467
39	610	1,622	3,333	9,043
40	840	1,958	3,908	10,701
41	840	2,165	4,182	11,008
42	1,293	2,973	5,154	11,159
43	1,767	3,704	5,468	11,518
44	2,074	4,548	6,124	11,734
45	2,651	5,325	7,152	12,484
46	3,045	5,612	8,430	12,866
47	3,697	6,277	8,833	13,282
48	4,407	7,606	9,316	13,367
49	4,699	7,888	9,489	13,427
50	5,410	8,244	10,113	13,427
51	6,536	8,452	10,436	13,562
52	6,986	9,128	10,905	13,562
53	7,586	9,476	11,579	13,633
54	8,196	10,242	12,269	13,658
55	9,173	19,727	12,600	13,658
56	9,578	11,281	12,808	13,658
57	10,453	11,853	13,112	13,658
58	10,738	12,204	13,217	13,658
59	10,841	12,503	13,263	13,658
60	11,181	12,741	13,313	13,658
61	11,400	13,050	13,385	13,658

Table 6.1 (*cont.*)

Thousands of tonnes of smelter capacity
with costs at or below a given level

cents per pound	Operating Cost Basis			Avoidable Cost Basis 50-cent metal
	120-cent metal	75-cent metal	50-cent metal	
62	11,523	13,213	13,385	13,658
63	11,970	13,358	13,574	13,658
64	12,318	13,358	13,574	13,658
65	12,427	13,402	13,574	13,658
66	12,427	13,402	13,574	13,658
67	12,627	13,402	13,574	13,658
68	12,852	13,574	13,574	13,658
69	12,852	13,574	13,574	13,658
70	13,411	13,574	13,574	13,658
71	13,411	13,574	13,574	13,658
72	13,574	13,574	13,574	13,658
73	13,658	13,658	13,658	13,658
Average	52.9 cents	48.8 cents	45.2 cents	36.1 cents

Table 6.1 Aluminium's cost curve

example, the Bonneville power contract, which affects ten smelters in the US, provides that the price of electricity is to be:

– 15 mills at metal prices below 52.7 cents per pound (a mill is one-tenth of a cent)
– for metal prices above 52.7 cents but below 60.7 cents, the electricity price rises by 1 mill for every 1 cent rise in the metal price
– 23.1 mills for metal prices between 60.7 cents and 73.4 cents
– for metal prices between 73.4 and 80.7 cents, the electricity price rises by 0.75 mills for every 1 cent rise in the metal price
– 28.6 mills for metal prices above 80.7 cents.

It should be clear from this account that a metal-linked cost contract is analytically equivalent to a package of options on the metal price – see Bird (1987).

A second complication is that the cost curve thus measured assumes that producers are not attempting to reduce their level of production. If they are, then adjustment costs can become a major burden. Frequently, alumina contracts incorporate a take-or-pay provision; electricity contracts are often subject to a demand charge; and in many areas smelters may be unable to hire and fire labour in accordance with swings in the economic cycle. Accordingly, a smelter's *avoidable* cost in bad times may be significantly lower than its operating costs. Table 5.1 shows that under recession conditions the avoidable cost curve is about 9 cents per pound lower than the operating cost curve. At the right-hand end of the curve (or the bottom of the table) – the part that does the work – the gap between the two curves is rather more marked than this, at about 11 cents per pound.

Once again, the process of calculating the position of the avoidable cost curve is somewhat messy, since allowance must be made for the different circumstances of individual plants. For example, European smelters, who cannot readily fire and re-hire workers at will, tend to find a larger gap between their avoidable and their operating costs than American smelters. One consequence of this is that in a recession smelters do not necessarily close down in accordance with their position on the general operating cost curve; for rankings on the avoidable cost curve may be different.

Once such a model has been set up, it is a simple matter to modify it to produce estimates of the *cost of producing aluminium in a new smelter*. Such a plant will typically be much more efficient technically than an older smelter, and will in particular have lower electricity usage. However, the prices paid for inputs will tend to be higher than those available to older smelters; some of the very favourable power prices paid by older plants are not available to new projects. Thus it is not possible to say *a priori* whether operating costs in a new plant will be higher or lower than in an old plant; although just at present they happen to be a few cents per pound lower.

However, a new plant must bear an additional burden which an old plant need not – capital charges. An existing smelter may of course have capital charges, in the form of interest and depreciation; but these are sunk costs. They do not affect the question of whether a smelter operates or not, and hence do not affect the general economics of the industry. In the case of a new smelter, however, capital charges are very important. Unless the potential owners and their bankers can reasonably expect capital to be recovered and to earn normal profits, a new smelter will not be built. Thus capital charges are a component of long-run marginal cost.

Methods of accounting for capital charges vary widely. And yet, for our present purposes it is essential to have a standard method. Following Merrett and Sykes (1973), Brealey and Myers (1981) and Hatch and White (1986), I assume that:

(1) The debt–equity ratio has no effect on the cost of capital.
(2) Capital costs may be safely modelled by the sinking-fund return

| | US cents per pound | |
	Operating cost	Total cost
Australia	48.3	68.3
Brazil	48.2	68.1
Canada	48.5	68.5
Middle East	46.0	72.6
Venezuela	39.9	59.9

Table 6.2 The economics of new smelters

method, which calculates a composite capital charge to take account of interest, amortization, and normal profit.

(3) The weighted average cost of capital in the aluminium industry can be taken to be 10 per cent, in real terms.

(4) The expected life of a project is 20 years.

These assumptions, taken together, imply an annual capital charge equal to 11.746 per cent of the initial cost of the project.

The capital cost of building a new smelter will naturally vary according to its location, and will be particularly influenced by the availability of existing infrastructure, whether the project is to be built in a developing country or not, and by economies of scale (though these are weak in the aluminium industry). Nevertheless, the range of variation in capital costs is much less than is found in the case of the mined commodities. As a result, it is an acceptable simplification to think of a certain capital cost as being 'typical' in each region of the world.

Table 6.2 shows the pattern of production costs in representative new projects around the world in mid-1988, both before and after allowing for capital charges in the way discussed earlier. Although these calculations have been carried out with actual data on proposed new projects to hand, they do not represent figures for individual projects. Rather, they show the cost levels at which I believe that substantial additional new capacity could in principle come on stream.

The third type of prior information which we must consider is the *announced plans of producers*. These fall into three categories. First, past plans and investment decisions give present capacity, and hence a ceiling to maximum available supply in the short term. Further, since it takes nearly three years to build an aluminium smelter, and a further period to plan it and arrange the financing, we can make projections of maximum available supply running three years into the future with a high degree of accuracy.

Second, aluminium smelters cannot be closed and restarted instantaneously. From a technical point of view, it takes about six weeks to restart an idled potline; and in addition to that companies must hire and train workers, and arrange their raw material supplies. As a result, after considering announcements from aluminium companies it is possible to forecast actual production with a high degree of accuracy three months into the future, and with reasonably good accuracy as much as six months ahead.

Third, producers announce their plans for investment in new smelter capacity some time before construction work commences. As a result of this, it is possible to make projections of total capacity as much as six or seven years into the future. However, these longer-term capacity projections are more tentative than short-term capacity calculations. Many new projects will fail to be completed, often because of the difficulty of raising finance. Alternatively, if demand turns out to be more buoyant than originally projected, it may be possible for expansions to existing smelters to be hurried through more quickly than would be possible with a greenfield project.

In the light of these various announced plans of procedures, we can build up a tolerably accurate picture of the *expectations of suppliers*. Such pictures are regularly compiled by all industry commentators – see for example Bird (1989a).

4   A demand function

All the prior information which we have noted so far comes from the supply side of the industry. Before we can make use of it, we need a demand function as well. We need only sketch this briefly; for detailed model specification is not our main interest here.

I proceed by estimating a series of equations covering aluminium consumption in each major country, and relating it (logarithmically) to industrial production, the price of aluminium relative to the price of other commodities, and seasonal and other dummies. The equations are of the error–correction type. After aggregating the results across the world, I estimate that the long-term elasticity of demand for aluminium with respect to industrial production is about 1.13, working through with a lag of 1–2 quarters. There are some grounds for thinking that this elasticity may be about to decline in the future. I estimate that the long-term price elasticity is about − 0.21, working through with a lag of about six quarters.

It might be thought that this price elasticity is surprisingly low. However, it must be remembered that elasticities are being measured at the raw metal stage of production, since this is what metal market prices relate to. But consumers actually exercise their choices with an eye to the price of semi-finished metal products, which are much less volatile than the raw metal price. Accordingly, any measurement of the price elasticity which is made at the raw metal stage is bound to yield a figure which looks low at first sight.

One important reason for modelling demand is to vet or validate the expectations held by producers, and to determine whether or not they are consistent with what is known about the state of the industry and its likely future growth. In academic circles, it is common to *assume* that expectations of agents have been derived in a way that is consistent with all known data and with the analyst's model of the world. But industrial consultants make no such assumption. Indeed, one way of looking at what consultants do is to say that they attempt to make expectations more rational and consistent than they were initially.

But for the moment we will assume that no conflict has arisen between the findings of the demand model and the expectations of producers.

5   The determination of price

Thus we have prior information on costs and on the expectations of suppliers. We can now ask, what is the price at which all this is consistent? This is normally referred to as the *cost-justified price*. There are three possible cases:

Case 1 – Recession

Assume that economic activity is declining, and that the underlying demand for aluminium is falling with it. Producers face a short-term surplus of metal, and know that they must cut production. Further, they see no need for the construction of new capacity in the foreseeable future.

In this situation, the cost-justified price is given by the intersection of the demand curve and the avoidable cost curve, with this calculated in an iterative manner as explained earlier. Calculations in Bird (1988) suggest that at mid-1988 prices and exchange rates this would imply an aluminium price of about 45 cents per pound.

Case 2 – Stagnation

Suppose that demand is expected to remain unchanged in coming months, and producers plan to keep their present output levels unchanged. Suppose too that there is an adequate margin of spare capacity from mothballed smelters, so that producers do not see the need to invest in new capacity.

In this case, the cost-justified price will be given by the intersection of the demand function with the operating cost curve, again after iteration. Table 1 earlier suggests that this would imply a price in mid-1988 money of about 61 cents per pound.

Case 3 – Boom

Assume now that demand is growing, in such a way that existing capacity will clearly become inadequate soon. New investment is needed, and this implies that the cost-justified price is set by the economics of building a new smelter, inclusive of return on capital.

Firms will have a choice about where to build their new capacity. Just at present, low-cost Venezuela has been favoured by many. However, bankers are very reluctant to finance projects in what they see as a risky and heavily-indebted country. In the light of this, the mortality rate among new projects in Venezuela is likely to be very high. Safer though higher-cost Canada and Australia look likely to attract more investment; and as a result the cost-justified price under boom conditions can be measured at just over 68 cents per pound, at mid-1988 prices and exchange rates.

We may switch between each of these cases, in accordance with our view of the general state of the world. In order to do this, it is necessary to make preliminary forecasts, to establish just how far in the future any need for new capacity might lie.

However, some difficulties can arise at the point of transition from one case to another. For example, we might believe that no new capacity was needed in the short term, so that Case 2 pricing was appropriate; but that it would be needed soon, making the (discounted present value of the) Case 3 price also correct. If these two figures are significantly different, there may be severe strains in the marketplace. It is possible that the volatility of aluminium prices in the 1986–8 period may partly be due to a transition from Case 2 to Case 3 pricing.

Figure 6.1 shows these various mechanisms at work. Curve 1 shows the cost curve calculated at 120 cents; curve 2 at 50 cents; curve 3 is the avoidable cost curve; and curve 4 is the flat long-run supply curve, set by new-plant economics. Note that curve 4 is defined in a different way from curves 1–3, for it includes capital servicing costs, which the other curves do not. Further, curves 1–3 have a vertical section, reflecting the limits of existing capacity; but curve 4 of course does not. Curve 5 is the demand curve, as it was in mid-1988. In this graph the demand curve has been

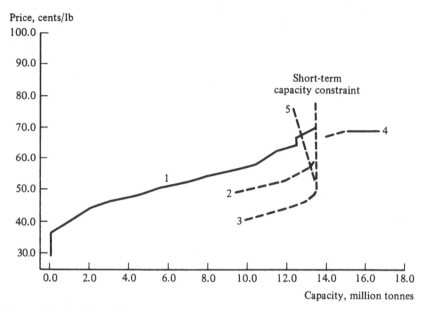

Figure 6.1 Aluminium's cost curve (amount of smelter capacity with costs at or below a given level)

adjusted to put it onto a basis consistent with curves 1–4; that is, production from the graveside-reprieve smelters and net exports from the Socialist countries have been subtracted from published data on consumption.

We have derived the prices in Cases 1–3 as those needed to ensure full consistency between the cost picture, the expectations of producers, and the demand model. However, we can make stronger claims about the figures than this. These are theoretical prices towards which actual prices *must* tend to converge. If they prove at all reluctant to converge, then agents (who dislike holding price expectations which are *very* different from the current price) will react in such a way as to force convergence to take place. For example, in mid-1988 prices were 120 cents per pound, well ahead of their Case 3 cost-justified level. If this state of affairs were to persist for any length of time, then excess profits would eventually trigger a powerful investment boom, which would in time bring prices down through oversupply.

The idea of a 'justified' price level has been applied in many markets: for example, it is common to think of the equilibrium level of an exchange rate, determined perhaps by PPP or trade balance requirements. However, Goodhart (1988) points out that the forces of convergence in such cases are very weak, even difficult to detect at all. It is my belief – more on this in a moment – that the forces of convergence are quite powerful in the case of aluminium, and probably of the other commodities as well. Why should different markets behave in a different fashion in this respect? The best conjecture that I can offer is that the ratio of real people (that is, producers and consumers) to speculators is much higher in the commodity markets than it is in the foreign exchange market. Accordingly, it may be more difficult for fads or fashions to develop in a commodity market than in a foreign exchange or an equity market. However, it is hard to think of a satisfactory way of testing this proposition.

6   The discrepancy between costs and prices

The next step must be to examine the actual movement of aluminium prices against the standard of these cost-justified prices, calculated on one method or another, and see what we can say about the size, timing, and correction of the discrepancies.

Table 6.3 shows the actual aluminium price quarterly since January 1980, as a percentage of the cost-justified level. The prices shown here are those ruling early in the month concerned, and are defined as the transactions price reported by the American trade magazine *Metals Week*. The table also shows the method used to derive the cost-justified price. In early 1980 new plant economics were used as the basis; between October 1980 and October 1986 old plant economics; and from January 1987 onwards the table returns to new plant economics. This is of course a two-tier model of price determination, rather than the three-tier model described earlier; and a strong case can be made for using the third tier, based on the avoidable cost curve, in 1981 and 1982. Unfortunately, the avoidable-cost option was only programmed into the model from 1984 onwards, and avoidable cost curves for the earlier years are not available. In most cases, the ratio of actual to theoretical price was published *at the time*, and has not been revised in the light of later knowledge. The exception is the data for the period October 1980–April 1982, when the cost curve model was under development; theoretical prices for this period have been calculated later, in the light of information available in 1982. Figure 6.2 – from Bird (1989b) – repeats this information, in graphical form.

It is clear at once that the discrepancies between actual prices and cost-justified prices that have emerged have sometimes been very marked indeed. At the troughs in 1982 and 1984 prices fell below the cost-justified level by 30–33 per cent, while at the recent price peak in early 1988 prices were nearly 80 per cent higher than their cost-justified level. And, as

		Based on economics of smelters which are–	Price	Cost	Price as a percent of cost
1980	Jan	new	84.1	68.8	122.2
	Apr	new	82.2	78.0	105.4
	Jul	new	70.9	76.3	92.9
	Oct	old	72.4	64.5	112.2
1981	Jan	old	67.6	65.6	103.0
	Apr	old	66.0	68.4	96.5
	Jul	old	56.7	68.8	82.4
	Oct	old	54.8	68.3	80.2
1982	Jan	old	51.3	69.2	74.1
	Apr	old	47.8	68.7	69.6
	Jul	old	44.1	65.0	67.8
	Oct	old	45.0	67.2	67.0
1983	Jan	old	50.6	67.3	75.2
	Apr	old	64.3	69.5	92.5
	Jul	old	72.1	70.2	102.7
	Oct	old	75.1	70.7	106.2
1984	Jan	old	76.1	70.4	108.1
	Apr	old	68.2	78.3	87.1
	Jul	old	56.1	78.6	71.4
	Oct	old	50.1	71.1	70.5
1985	Jan	old	50.1	65.0	77.1
	Apr	old	52.0	64.5	80.6
	Jul	old	46.9	66.0	71.1
	Oct	old	45.7	61.5	74.3
1986	Jan	old	55.3	61.9	89.3
	Apr	old	61.6	65.0	94.8
	Jul	old	56.7	62.0	91.5
	Oct	old	55.4	61.0	90.8
1987	Jan	new	52.8	59.0	89.5
	Apr	new	65.0	61.5	105.7
	Jul	new	73.3	64.0	114.4
	Oct	new	84.8	62.0	136.7
1988	Jan	new	87.1	62.0	140.5
	Apr	new	155.6	64.5	179.2
	Jul	new	113.2	69.4	163.1
	Oct	new	103.6	70.3	147.3
1989	Jan	new	112.7	70.4	160.1

Table 6.3

The discrepancy between costs and prices

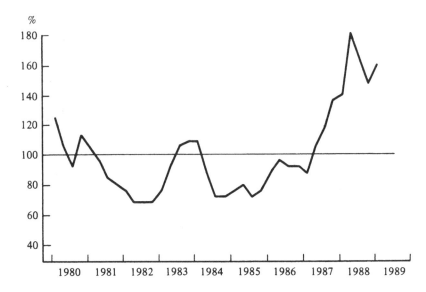

Figure 6.2 The discrepancy between prices and costs (actual prices as percentage of cost-justified level)

argued earlier, any periods of very marked price–cost discrepancy have triggered corrective action on the part of agents. The high prices of early 1980 (and of 1979, not shown in this table) led to a marked increase in plans for investment in new smelter capacity; the low prices of 1982 and 1984 led to cutbacks – and on each occasion these reactions were widely tabulated by industry commentators, and did in time produce the required correction. Just at present, prices have once more risen well above their cost-justified levels, and although this has indeed produced a reaction in the form of the recommissioning of idled smelters and a rise in investment intentions, this response has not yet been powerful enough to bring about any substantial fall in price.

It would be nice if it could be shown that the price–cost discrepancy correlated closely with producer stocks, with consumer stocks, or with data on desired consumer stocks (an index of this was formerly compiled and published by Alcoa). However, although a strong correlation does appear for one or more of these variables over short periods, I have been unable to find an equation whose coefficients are reasonbly stable over the whole period from 1980 to the present.

Thus we have a tool for forecasting the level to which prices are likely to converge in the medium term – indeed must, for agents will make them converge. In the light of this, industry commentators tend not to disagree strongly about medium and longer-term price prospects; Adams (1988) cites a World Bank survey carried out in late-1987 which supports this view.

Although the philosophy of preparing medium and long-term price forecasts is simple, the detailed implementation of models which use this approach can be complex; it is not simply a matter of calculating what the cost-justified price is today, on some measure. At least three additional complications must be taken into account.

First, an assessment must be made of cost pressures in the pipeline, and thus of the likely position of the cost curve and the new-plant economics picture some years ahead. This is particularly important when, as at present, some important cost components (alumina, electricity) are traded at prices that are below their long-run marginal cost.

Second, attention must be paid to possible changes in exchange rates. In a slump or stagnation world, changes in the level of the US dollar tend to have little effect on the cost-justified price, since the right-hand end of the cost curve is dominated by American smelters. This is less true than it was, but it still holds good in general. In a boom world, however, exchange rate changes are a major complication. This is because all new smelters which might be built in the future are outside the US. Thus if the US dollar falls, their costs when measured in dollars will rise by (approximately) the full amount of the depreciation – for very few cost items are themselves dollar goods. Further, the exchange rates of the new aluminium-producing countries are themselves not stable. Accordingly, any forecast based on cost-justified prices in boom conditions must be careful to spell out the exchange rate assumptions that have been used in its derivation.

Third, the forecaster must take account of reaction lags on the part of producers and markets. It is well known that different lag specifications can produce markedly different patterns of behaviour of prices over time; I have a preference for specifications that produce strongly damped cycles.

However confident we may be about our views on prices in the medium and long term, calculations on the cost-justified price tell us little about the likely behaviour of prices in the short term. This is because there are two important things that we do not know. The first uncertainty is that if prices are initially in line with their cost-justified level, we cannot predict with confidence exactly when the next discrepancy will occur. Indeed, it is sometimes difficult to explain just why a particular discrepancy has appeared, even after the event. The 1984 discrepancy is just such a case. It was not associated with any sharp cyclical swing, or any marked imbalance between supply and demand, and was not generally foreseen ahead of the event. It now seems likely that it was triggered by a burst of consumer de-stocking in the face of high real interest rates; but even so it is hard to explain why this discrepancy ever became as large as it did.

Second, we cannot be sure when reactions by agents will come to dominate the marketplace. In a recession, prices may continue to weaken even though plants have been idled and producer stocks are starting to fall. And it is impossible to tell how long it will take for these reactions to iron out discrepancies completely. The correction process over the period October 1984–January 1987 was surprisingly long drawn-out. What we can say is that if prices are excessively high in a Case 3 situation, then it is unlikely that such excessive prices will last for more than about three years, since that is the time needed to build a new aluminium smelter.

This uncertainty over timescales – we have a good idea of what is going to happen to prices, but we don't know *when* – means that a high degree of confidence over eventual price developments is quite consistent with semi-strong form market efficiency.

Although consultants do not publicize errors in their track record for forecasting prices, no consultant or consulting firm of which I am aware does in fact claim to be able to use its analysis of proprietary data to beat the market – with the possible exception of those who are closely associated with broking firms. Sometimes, consultants will be particularly candid on this point; for example, if they are put into a court of law as expert witnesses, giving evidence on oath. Recently – Kentucky Public Service Commission (1987) – three consultants described their track record in forecasting short-term price fluctuations in the following terms:

Frank Yans, Arthur D. Little Inc.:	'humble'
Robins Adams, Resource Strategies Inc.:	'poor'
Tony Bird, Anthony Bird Associates:	'both humble and poor'.

However, although consultants generally believe in semi-strong form market efficiency, there is some academic evidence (Taylor, 1986) of weak-form market inefficiency in the past. It must be said that this evidence is not conclusive in the face of the very large volume of evidence from earlier studies that markets in general are efficient, at least in the weak sense; but nevertheless the evidence exists.

But it is possible to reconcile these two positions. Recall that there has been a dramatic increase in the availability of computing power in recent years, and – especially since 1986 – in the willingness of financial firms to invest heavily in that computer power and in quantitative people. Accordingly, it may be the case that if we apply the techniques and knowledge available *today* to the historical record, we may seem to be able to exploit profitable trading opportunities. This may hold whether we use Taylor's time-series methods, or the structural models using prior information described here. However, it would be most unsafe to argue from that that such techniques could be counted on to yield profitable trading opportunities in the future. Put another way, statistical evidence of market inefficiency in the past is not a good enough reason to believe that the market is inefficient *today*.

7 Concluding remarks

This paper has given an account of the knowledge-intensive approach to commodity price forecasting which is in widespread use among practitioners. It differs markedly from the logic-intensive models which are common amongst academics. However, it is important to realize that the differences are matters of emphasis only; the two approaches are not in any sense incompatible in principle. In my opinion, there is room for considerable progress to be made in blending these two approaches in future research. Reflecting this, I would be prepared to make available historical data on cost patterns and producer intentions to academic researchers who wished to make use of it.

REFERENCES

Adams, R. (1988) 'Economic cost analysis of the aluminium industry'. Unpublished paper presented at Metal Bulletin's Fifth International Aluminium Conference, Caracas, November 1988.
Bird, A. P. (1987) *Evaluating Variable-Rate Power Contracts Linked to Metal Price – a New Approach*. London, Anthony Bird Associates.
(1988) *Aluminium Production Costs 1988*. London, Anthony Bird Associates.
(1989a) *Aluminium Analysis*. London, Anthony Bird Associates, January 1989.
(1989b) *Aluminium Annual Review*. London, Anthony Bird Associates, March 1989.
Brealey, R. and M. Myers (1981) *Principles of Corporate Finance*. New York, McGraw-Hill.
Fama, E. F. and K. R. French (1988) 'Business cycles and the behaviour of metals prices', *Journal of Finance* **43**, 1075–93.
Goodhart, C. A. E. (1988) 'The foreign exchange market: a random walk with a dragging anchor'. *Economica* **55**, 437–60.
Hatch, J. E. and R. W. White (1986) 'A Canadian perspective on Canadian and United States capital market returns 1950–1983'. *Financial Analysts Journal* **42**, 60–8.
Hilyard, M. (1987) 'State of the bauxite/alumina/aluminium industry and outlook'. *IBA Quarterly Review* **13**, 24–37.
IPAI (1988) *Electrical power utilisation – annual report for 1987*. London, International Primary Aluminium Institute.
Kentucky Public Service Commission (1987) 'An investigation of Big Rivers Electric Corporations's rates for wholesale electric service: Case no 9885'. *Transcript of evidence*. Frankfort, Ky.
Merrett, A. J. and A. Sykes (1973) *The Finance and Analysis of Capital Projects*. London, Longman, second edition.
Taylor, S. (1986) *Modelling Financial Time Series*. Chichester, John Wiley and Sons.
US Bureau of Mines (1987) 'An Appraisal of Minerals Availability for 34 Commodities'. *Bulletin* 692.

Discussion

DAVID HUMPHREYS

Tony Bird's paper provides a coherent explanation of how aluminium prices form and how therefore one can set about forecasting them for the medium/long term. It also provides some useful insights into the considerable (and not always particularly helpful) differences in the analytical approaches of academic and industrial economists. While academics tend to use data extensively, industrial economists use it intensively. If a particular series does not exist then the industrial economist may have to create it, as Tony does with his cost data. In a sense, his problem *is* the data; and no amount of sophisticated manipulation can substitute for it.

I should like to make three points on the paper; one on the principle of cost-justified pricing; a second on the derivation of the demand function; and a third on aluminium price formation on the LME.

That prices must converge in the medium term towards a cost-justified level may well be the case, but the forces of convergence are not only those contained in the paper. It is important to recognize that prices and costs are not independent but closely interact with each other. When prices are weak and falling, *and are expected to remain weak*, producers are forced to cut costs in order to stay in business. Conversely, when prices are way above costs there is a tendency to catch up on deferred spending, and for management to become more lax. More important, many costs, including alumina and energy but even in some cases wages, have become contractually related direct to metal prices, as recognized in the paper. The tendency to link input costs with prices has probably gone furthest in the United States. The interdependence of prices and costs reduces the validity of the concept of a cost-justified price.

Figure 6A.1, based on the work of one of Tony's competitors, shows the comparative movement of prices and marginal costs in real terms since 1979. It shows two measures of marginal cash costs, respectively 75 per cent and 90 per cent along each successive year's cumulative cost curve. It clearly brings out how real costs are reduced between 1984 and 1987. Similar trends are also apparent in most other minerals and metals.

When prices substantially exceed marginal costs, however these are defined, as they clearly do today, there will be a tendency to invest in new capacity. In addition, high prices will tend to moderate demand, again forcing prices and costs back into alignment.

In short, the use of cost-justified pricing needs to be accompanied by an

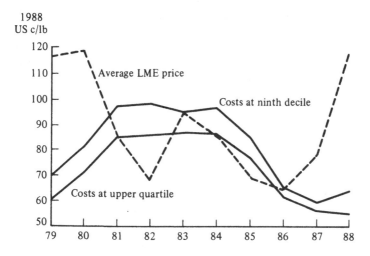

Figure 6A.1 Aluminium costs and prices (US cents per lb. Real 1988 terms)

appreciation of the dynamics of cost-price interaction. Moreover, when considering physical investment in a project, and particularly the financing of such a project, it is not sufficient to look only at the longer-term averages. One has also to consider the extreme price conditions to which serious imbalances in the market can give rise. Just as in a downturn the existence of high stocks can enable prices to fall below the theoretical (avoidable cost) floor, so in boom times, as at present, costs become largely irrelevant. In evaluating one's ability to repay capital on a project, given that one cannot guarantee to bring it in as a boom is beginning, some consideration needs to be given to the possible extremes as well as to the averages.

Nor is it inevitable, incidentally, that an excess of prices over marginal costs will necessarily bring forward new investment in quite the way the paper assumes. If demand is sufficiently strong and the barriers to entry into an industry sufficiently high then it is entirely feasible that prices will exceed marginal costs for extended periods, as indeed happened in aluminium during the 1960s. During these years buoyant demand ensured that additional capacity was regularly required, while entry into the industry was, as it always is, limited by the severe technological and financial demands of establishing aluminium smelters, and the availability of low-cost electric power. In the near term there is also a potential shortage of alumina. The aluminium industry's dependence on electric power is, incidentally, a reason for dismissing the argument in the paper that aluminium's long-run supply curve is approximately flat. Our evidence is that it is no flatter than the supply curves of other metals, including copper.

My second point relates to the demand function. Demand is the determinant of which of the various cost curves is relevant to prices at any time and the mechanism of adjustment for moving between them.

I cannot help feeling that Tony is being a little disingenuous in his treatment of this matter. I have seen some of the equations he uses to deduce demand and have tried a few similar ones of my own. It is not always quite so easy to obtain significant coefficients for these equations as he seems to suggest. The less well integrated aluminium is into the general body of industrial production in a country the less reason is there to expect demand for it to move regularly with industrial production as a whole, and the less well will these equations perform. With prices, it is often difficult to obtain significant coefficients at all, or at least those which provide any sort of a confidence level for forecasting. This said, the method described is probably no worse than many others for forecasting demand – including highly disaggregated sectoral models – and is more cost-effective than most.

For purposes of longer-term price forecasting it would seem unwise to attempt to compute a demand function at all. Far better to assume a balanced market and take the marginal producer as one falling in the range of 90–95 per cent capacity utilization.

My third point concerns price formation on the metal exchanges. Towards the end of his paper Tony makes some remarks on the efficiency of the metal markets and the implications for forecasting. I would agree with his general point that consultants stand little chance of consistently succeeding with their short-term forecasts (for market efficiency reasons) and also that they should not be judged solely on their ability to do so. I would also agree that consultants and other analysts, by providing information to the market in a timely fashion, are contributing to the very efficiency that makes short-term forecasting so difficult.

Two things do slightly confuse me however. One is the remark that while 'consultants generally believe in semi-strong form market efficiency, there is some academic evidence of weak form market inefficiency'. Logically, if a market is weak form inefficient then it must also be semi-strong form inefficient because past price information – the incorporation of which is the test of weak form efficiency – is a subset of contemporary public information – the incorporation of which is the test of semi-strong form efficiency. If the former falls, so must the latter. So far as the substance of the case is concerned, and one could dispute this all day, I incline to the view that probably the aluminium market is not strictly efficient in either weak or semi-strong form. Taylor, whom Bird quotes, has done interesting work demonstrating the existence of short-term 'trending' in commodity prices – possibly evidence of a gradual rather than an instantaneous absorption of information in the market and there is plenty of other academic work which casts doubt on weak form-efficiency too. However, unless such a claim should give undue encouragement to forecasters and speculators alike, I should perhaps add that statistical evidence of inefficiency does not necessarily, in the real world of transactions costs and taxes (not to mention forecasting costs), mean that there is money to be made out of such inefficiency.

My final query derives from a remark on page 146 of Tony's paper. A question is posed on the forces of convergence in different markets. This is left rather in the air but seems to me an idea well worth pursuing. Does the fact that the underpinning of the aluminium contract is a physical commodity make it behave differently from a pure asset market such as the stock market or foreign exchange market? Or is it simply the density of speculation that make the difference as Tony suggests? Or again, is the aluminium market liable to significant inefficiency because there are still ways of trading aluminium other than through the exchanges but essentially only one market if one wishes to trade securities? It is a criticism that has been levelled many times at the aluminium market over the years, that trading was too thin to make it a genuinely representative price indicator. If this is so then potentially it has been giving the wrong signals and undermining the forces of convergence.

Summary of general discussion

David Newbery enquired about the price–cost margin over the lifetime of a typical smelter; he suggested that this may be a crucial indicator in view of the typical price behaviour of many commodities with high peaks and long, flat, troughs. Thus, if positive deviations from cost-justified prices exceed negative ones absolutely then this would promote investment in these industries even if the probability of making a loss appeared high. Those losses would be made good in times of exceptionally high prices. Christopher Gilbert noted, however, that price peaks, though absolutely larger than price troughs, occur less frequently. Bird also noted that there was little evidence of such incentives for investment in the very low prices of old smelters. Bird also enlarged upon his observation that in the aluminium industry an appreciation of the US dollar (the most common concern) leaves the supply curve unaffected in the short run, as currently the high cost producers are still mainly US-based and thus isolated from such an exchange-rate effect. In the long run, however, as the new plants likely to come on stream are foreign (Venezuelan, Australian, Canadian), an appreciation of the US dollar provides an incentive for them to do precisely that.

Gilbert pointed out consultants' advantages in their intimate knowledge and access to current production costs and conditions. If academic modellers had that information they would, however, not necessarily proceed as consultants and industry analysts. Instead, they would estimate the desired level of production and use this in an analytical framework as part of a dynamic adjustment process. Academics are well aware that there are two adjustment processes, namely that of price to costs and that of costs to price. He welcomed Bird's offer to make historical cost curves available; this would allow a direct comparison of the academics' new modelling methods with the industry analyst's supply-demand balance approach.

Marian Radetzki urged that academics should go out and find detailed data themselves, rather than continue to rely on deficient aggregate and low-frequency published series. He was skeptical that collecting such data would be more costly for academics than for consultants and was convinced of the advantages that would flow from new collection efforts.

Hashem Pesaran argued that, since costs merely provided a floor to prices, they would be of little use for the determination of price fluctuations. Bird responded by reiterating that costs serve not only as a floor but as a target to which prices must eventually converge.

7 Long-run factors in oil price formation

MARIAN RADETZKI

The purpose of this study is to discuss some of the factors that are crucial in the determination of long-run international petroleum prices, to explore what impact these factors might have, and to clarify whether the price formation process in petroleum differs significantly from that in other primary commodity markets. The time horizon of the study is the next 2–3 decades. Sections 2, 3, 4 and 5 explore, in turn, the roles of (a) exhaustibility; (b) monopolistic forces; (c) inter-fuel substitution; and (d) future technological shocks, represented here by the possibility of a moratorium on nuclear power, or of severe restrictions on carbon dioxide emissions. However, in order to provide a broader context, and a historical perspective on the subject, Section 1 reviews the prices of petroleum and other primary commodities since the beginning of the present century.

1 The historical evidence of prices: oil and other primary commodities

Figures 7.1–7.4 depict indices of real prices between 1900 and 1986 for oil, metals and minerals, non-food agricultural commodities and food commodities.[1] An ocular inspection of the oil price developments reveals a gentle downward slope beginning after the first world war, and ending in the early 1970s, when, in the view of a majority of economists,[2] the OPEC cartel drove up prices to historically unprecedented levels. The slow downward slope is interrupted by a much steeper temporary decline in the latter half of the 1940s, caused by the opening up of the rich Middle East oil resources on a large scale. The exports from this region rose from 4.5 million tons, 9 per cent of the global total in 1938, to 51.6 million tons and 37 per cent in 1950.[3]

Comparisons with other commodities reveal a considerable short-run stability in petroleum prices over a large part of the period studied, as compared to the price indices of major non-oil commodity groups. This

157

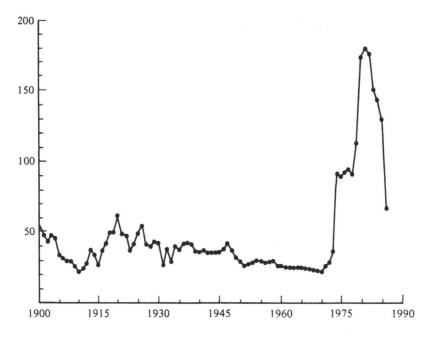

Figure 7.1 Index of the real price of oil (1977–9 = 100)

Figure 7.2 Index of the real prices of metals (1977–9 = 100)

Figure 7.3 Index of the real prices of non-food agricultural commodities (1977–9 = 100)

Figure 7.4 Index of the real prices of food commodities (1977–9 = 100)

	Intercept a	Time coefficient b	Regression statistics $\bar{R}^2$	SEE	DW
Oil	− 0.838 (− 16.73)	− 0.007 (− 5.62)	0.30	0.21	0.46
Metals and minerals	0.336 (6.62)	− 0.001 (− 9.47)	0.55	0.22	0.32
Agricultural non-food	0.326 (6.72)	− 0.010 (− 8.38)	0.49	0.21	0.34
All food	0.016 (0.39)	− 0.005 (− 4.66)	0.22	0.17	0.44
Tropical beverages	− 1.124 (− 17.48)	0.006 (3.85)	0.16	0.27	0.35
Food excluding tropical beverages	0.241 (5.59)	− 0.006 (− 5.94)	0.32	0.18	0.45

Table 7.1 Results of regressions of deflated commodity prices on time, 1900–72

(t values in parentheses)

could be because of the peculiarities of the oil price quotation or of the market structure characterizing oil. The posted Saudi crude price has been used in the graph between 1948 and 1984. In the 1950s and 1960s, this quotation was changed very infrequently. It is quite likely, however, that the smoothness has other explanations, and would have remained even if other price series were employed. Between the 1930s and the 1970s, the oil market was dominated by an oligopoly of multinational firms, and, as is typical for such a market structure,[4] there was a considerable reluctance among its members to change prices at frequent intervals.

An important issue that needs to be illuminated is whether the long-run trend in real oil prices deviates in any important way from the trends exhibited by other major commodity groups. Oil being an exhaustible resource, one might expect its prices to move up over time, in relation to renewable raw materials.

Results of regressions of real commodity prices on time, using the model $\ln P_i = a + bt_i + u_i$, where P is the deflated commodity price, t is the time trend, and u the error term, are presented in Table 7.1. To avoid the very strong distortions caused by the OPEC cartel, the regressions cover only the 1900–1972 period. In addition to (a) oil, regressions have been run for (b) metals and minerals, (c) agricultural non-food commodities, and

(d) food commodities. Furthermore, the food group has been subdivided into (e) tropical beverages, and (f) other food.

The adjusted $\bar{R}^2$ values of the regressions are not impressively high. With the exception of metals and minerals, more than half the variation in prices is explained by factors other than time. Relatively low $\bar{R}^2$ values are to be expected in equations covering a long period, and having only the exponential trend as their explanatory variable. The t values indicate that the time coefficients are significant. The DW statistics indicate substantial serial correlation, making it difficult to draw far-reaching inferences from the equations. But then, the main purpose of the statistical exercise is merely to provide a context to help clarify whether the oil trend has been exceptional.

All the major commodity groups recorded trend declines in their real prices over the period covered by the regressions. The agricultural non-food index exhibits the sharpest decline, a full 1 per cent per year, while the average price fall for the metals and minerals group is only 0.1 per cent. One can surmise that an expanded geographical spread of primary commodity production, along with increasing productivity of labour, and of the natural resources used in commodity production, have permitted producers to reduce costs, despite the manyfold increases in the volume of output recorded during the period. A further subdivision of the food index yields the only instance of rising real prices: 0.6 per cent per year for the tropical beverages group.

Most of the non-oil commodity price trends experience only small changes when the regressions are extended until 1986. The metals and minerals index is an exception, however. On account of depressed metal prices after 1974, the trend decline rises to 0.8 per cent in a regression that covers the period 1900 through 1980.[5]

Oil does not appear exceptional in our comparisons with other commodities. The trend price decrease recorded for oil, 0.7 per cent per year for the 1900–1972 period, emerges as neither particularly high or especially low. In this respect, developments in the oil market are not different from those that occurred in other major commodity markets.

2   The role of exhaustibility for petroleum prices

In 1980, oil prices were approaching their peak, after an historically unprecedented tripling in real terms in the early 1970s, followed by a further doubling towards the end of the decade. At that time, there was a virtual unanimity among economic analysts and policy makers that oil prices would continue to rise over the rest of the century, and possibly beyond, by some 2–3 per cent per year in real terms.[6] This view persisted

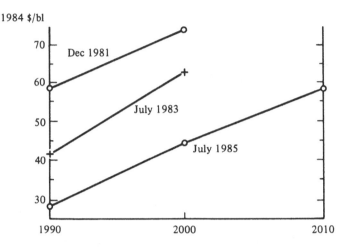

Figure 7.5 Consensus of oil price forecasts made in 1981, 1983 and 1985 (constant 1984 $/barrel). *Source*: **International Energy Workshop of IIASA, reported in** *New York Times* **22 September 1985.**

into the mid-1980s, despite substantial price falls after 1981. The consensus of oil price forecasts, compiled by the International Energy Workshop at IIASA in 1981, 1983 and 1985, reproduced in Figure 7.5, continued to indicate rising real petroleum prices to 1990 and 2000, running in parallel, but at successively lower levels, due to the declining starting points in the forecast exercises.

Retrospectively it is evident that these forecasts went monumentally wrong. Common to them all was a belief that the demand and supply responses to changing energy prices would be very slow and very small, that the global energy resource base was not very expandable, and that technological progress would have little impact on the cost of marketable energy products. The major OPEC oil producers were believed to be uninterested in expanding capacity and output, given the perceived low utility of additional income in these countries. The projected increases in demand would tally with future supply only if prices rose substantially over the forecast period.

The studies went wrong because both demand and non-OPEC supply proved far more price elastic than the forecasters had assumed. As demand declined and supply outside the cartel expanded, the high price was maintained for some time by large scale reductions in OPEC deliveries. In 1986, the ability of OPEC to withhold supplies was weakened, and prices fell to about half of the average level between 1980 and 1985, and have since remained at the lower level.

A perverted notion of the Hotelling rule seems to have constituted a crucial element in all these studies. The uniformity of the assumptions about a 2–3 per cent rate of increase in real price is hard to explain other than by the perception that the price of oil, an exhaustible resource, must appreciate by the real rate of interest. Once the price path was set with the help of Hotelling, the oil forecasters adjusted their analysis of future demand and supply, to vindicate that such a path of prices was needed to assure market equilibrium.

Using Hotelling in this way was, of course, a misconception. The exhaustible resource theory claims, with impeccable logic, that in an environment of utility and profit maximizing agents who use an unchanging technology to exploit a natural resource from a given and uniform stock, the value of a unit of that unexploited resource, i.e. the royalty, will rise at the rate of interest.[7] The relationship is commonly referred to as the Hotelling rule.

The following analysis concludes that the rule applies only to very special circumstances which are seldom encountered in the real world. In addition, it is argued that those who use the Hotelling rule as a guide to petroleum price developments, made an unwarranted jump in their analysis, from the price of the resource in the ground to the price of the extracted product in the market. It will be shown below that the prices of the two need not move in parallel.

Given the fundamental role that the theory of resource exhaustion appears to have played in the faulty forecasts, it is important to ask what, if any, relationship can be established between the exhaustible nature of oil on the one hand, and price formation in the oil market, on the other.

The discussion can instructively be divided into two steps. *First*, what is the impact of exhaustibility on the royalty, i.e. on the value of the undeveloped resource in the ground? And *second*, is there a detectable uniform relationship between the value of the resource deposit in the ground, and the price of the finished marketable product?

As noted, for the Hotelling rule to hold in the straightforward way indicated by theory, the undeveloped resource must be of a uniform quality, and of a finite and known size.[8] If the quality is uneven in the Hotelling world, there will be as many royalty levels as qualities, all rising at the rate of interest. Economic logic asserts that the best quality with the highest royalty will be exploited first. As that quality is depleted, there will be a downward adjustment in the average level of the rising royalties. Still, the royalty on a deposit of a given quality will rise over time at the rate of interest, so it might be economical to defer exploitation and let such a deposit appreciate in the ground.

Discovery of new deposits through exploration normally introduces further complications to the time path of royalties. Since discovery adds to the stock of unexploited resource in the ground, the unit cost of discovery must correspond to the unit value of that resource, i.e. to the royalty. If the royalty rises at the rate of interest, the correspondence will be maintained only if the cost of discovery increases in equal measure. This obviously holds in the real world only in exceptional cases. It is hard to model the rate at which discoveries are made and the costs involved. From time to time there are unanticipated breakthroughs in discovery, when a given exploration expenditure results in massive finds. The gradual unfolding of massive oil deposits in the Middle East in the 1940s is an example of such a spurt. The cost of discovery then falls, and so does the royalty in consequence. Hence, the Hotelling rule breaks down. With unanticipated discovery, even the assertion that the royalty on a deposit of a given quality rises at the rate of interest will cease to hold.

A further doubt about the validity of the Hotelling rule arises when technological improvements are introduced. These work in several ways. Consider first the technology of exploration. With unchanged technology one could premise that the cost of discovery will rise over time on the Ricardian argument that it is necessary gradually to move exploration to less promising territories. In this scheme of things, spurts in discovery can be regarded as *ad hoc* aberrations whose impact evens out in the long run. These premises cease to hold when technological progress is introduced. With improvements in exploration technology, the unit cost of discovery of a given quality deposit need not rise at all, and may even fall over time.

Consider second the technology of exploitation. Technological progress can lead to wholesale shifts in the cost of exploiting different kinds of deposits, changing the quality ranking among them, and invalidating the theoretical uniform percentage increases in royalties over time. At the turn of the century the highest quality deposits of copper consisted of small high-grade veins; the best iron ore deposits were the ones located close to the steel mills. Technological breakthroughs in mass mining methods and in bulk transport made it much more economical to extract copper from more meagre but much larger sulphide deposits, and iron ore from landscapes of high-grade ores in faraway places like Brazil and Australia. The royalty on the most valued deposits of earlier times fell to zero; the royalty on the deposits exploited in more recent times has not grown perceptibly, because of the huge discoveries in past decades.

The above analysis indicates that any relationship between the value of exhaustible resources in the ground, and the rate of interest, is tenuous and unstable. Hence, it is not surprising that we lack empirical observations confirming that royalties on exhaustible resource deposits rise at the rate of interest over extended periods of time.

The second step in the analysis, i.e. the establishment of a relationship between the royalty on the one hand, and the finished natural resource product, on the other, may seem superfluous, if no meaningful time-path for royalties can be established. It suffices to note that cost-reducing change in the technology of exploitation can compensate or even over-compensate for any systematic cost increases due to rising royalties or augmenting cost of discovery. Judging from the negative trends in the long-run prices of exhaustible resource products in the course of the present century, such overcompensation must have been common.

It may now be instructive to recapitulate. In a realistically formulated theoretical world, the Hotelling rule, where the price of the resource in the ground rises at the rate of interest, emerges as a very special, not a general case. In the real world, we have no empirical evidence of unexploited exhaustible resource prices systematically rising at the rate of interest. The evidence suggests that exploited exhaustible resource materials like crude oil experience gently falling price trends. What conclusion, if any, can be drawn from this about the role of exhaustibility for petroleum prices?

The answer is precious little. From past history we can conclude that technological progress, coupled possibly with luck in exploration, have overwhelmed any impact that exhaustibility and depletion may have had on crude prices. For the future, a case can clearly be constructed where the cost of discovery rises, not necessarily by the rate of interest, but by more than the technologically induced reduction in the cost of exploitation. If these conditions persist, the rising royalty will push the costs and prices of crude oil upwards over time. But this is only one of several possible scenarios, and it is not supported by the evidence from the past. Another, equally likely scenario for the very long run is that the fate of oil will follow that of European coal in the course of the present century: the emergence of superior substitutes will diminish the demand for oil, and suppress the need for additional discovery. Instead of rising continuously, and pushing prices upwards, royalties will then shrink into insignificance.

In conclusion, therefore, it does not seem possible to establish unambiguously whether exhaustibility and depletion will have any perceptible impact on petroleum price in the coming two to three decades with which this paper is concerned.

3   Monopolistic elements in the petroleum market

The present section takes a look at the petroleum market in isolation, and explores the scope for producers to reap monopolistic profits by managing supply. The focus of attention is on the long run. In the following section, the vista is widened, and price formation in the oil market, competitive or monopolistic, is related to the price developments of substitute products.

1985 marked the end of a 12-year period of very high oil prices. Early in 1986, the price of petroleum (North Sea Brent) declined by almost 50 per cent to about $14 per barrel. Measured in other major currencies like the Yen or DMark, the fall was even greater and exceeded 60 per cent. Since then, price variations have been considerable, but the average has barely exceeded $15.

The common view after the price had fallen was that the cartel had collapsed. A more careful look at the circumstances characterizing the oil market after 1985 indicates that this was not the case at all. Leaving aside the controversy whether OPEC acted as a cartel in 1973–74 and in 1979–80,[9] it suffices to note that the OPEC members have kept 8–10 million barrels per day, almost one-third of their total production capacity, inactive during 1986–88. Most of this capacity had variable costs below those of major non-OPEC producers e.g. those operating in the US and in the North Sea. The latter had no economic incentive to close down existing operations on any large scale unless prices fell below $5 per barrel.[10]

Without the supply restraint exercised by OPEC in the 1986–88 period, price would therefore have settled at $5 or below, instead of the $15 average that has actually prevailed. OPEC would have been producing at its full capacity of almost 30 million barrels per day, with the non-OPEC output sharply reduced, to assure equilibrium between supply and demand. In any historical perspective, a commodity producer group which succeeded in withholding one-third of its supply capacity, thereby raising prices to three times the competitive market level, would be deemed an extraordinarily successful cartel.

In a short- to medium-term perspective stretching into the mid-1990s, the monopolistic elements of the international petroleum market hinge on the relatively low price elasticity of demand, the heavy concentration of petroleum supply available for exports, and the preparedness to collaborate developed among the OPEC producers over the past decades.

The concentration of actual and readily available potential export supply of petroleum is depicted in Table 7.2. The six Middle-East OPEC countries accounted for more than half the actual surplus of production over consumption from major exporting areas. The cartel aggregate of 13 countries generated almost three-quarters of the total.

The importance of OPEC emerges even more starkly when the potential surplus of capacity over consumption is considered. Admittedly, the capacity data are uncertain and vague. But while Mexico, the UK, Norway and the Socialist Countries operated close to their technical

(Million barrels per day)

	Capacity	Prod	Cons	Surplus 1	Surplus 2
OPEC Mideast	19	13.1	2.1	11.0	16.9
OPEC other	10	5.9	1.5	4.4	8.5
OPEC total	29	19.0	3.6	15.4	25.4
Mexico		2.9	1.6	1.3	
North Sea		3.7	1.8	1.9	
SCs		15.9	13.8	2.1	
Total of above		41.5	20.8	20.7	

Table 7.2 Production and capacity to supply petroleum in excess of domestic requirements, by major exporting areas in 1987
Notes:
Surplus 1 = production − consumption.
Surplus 2 = production capacity − consumption.
SCs = Socialist Countries.
Capacity figures for non-OPEC areas have not been found. However, these areas have been asserted to produce reasonably close to their total capacity in the year shown.
Sources: BP Statistical Review of World Energy, 1988. Petroleum Intelligence Weekly, several issues. US Energy Information Administration, *International Energy Annual 1986.*

capacity limits, the members of the OPEC cartel have for a number of years carried a huge excess capacity from which additional surpluses could be generated. With relatively short notice, the OPEC countries could increase their export surplus to 25 million barrels per day, thus providing more than 80 per cent of the global total.

These figures demonstrate the power that the cartel wields in the international petroleum market. While OPEC's share in world production has been reduced in the past decade to less than a third, most non-OPEC oil is domestically consumed, and the cartel continues to hold a very dominant position in the exported supply. This position is used to reap huge monopoly profits for the cartel members.

How lasting is OPEC's or its Middle East members' market power? That depends on the degree of ambition in the cartel's market management. The high prices that prevailed between 1974 and 1985 created incentives for a fast expansion of capacity and output outside OPEC in the non-Socialist world. That output had remained stagnant for a number of years, but started to rise, with a lag, in response to the higher prices. Between 1976 and 1985, non-OPEC supply outside the Socialist Countries rose by 55 per cent, or from 16.3 to 25.3 million barrels per day.[11] This expansion diluted the cartel's market power. In order to defend the price levels of the early 1980s, the cartel had to reduce its output, from 31.5 million barrels in 1979, to 17.2 million in 1985. With falling demand for their output, there was no incentive to expand capacity in the OPEC countries. In fact, neglect to maintain existing installations may have resulted in some capacity shrinkage.

It is probable that a prolonged defence of the 1980–85 price level would have led to continued growth of non-OPEC supply. Together with shrinking demand, this would have further reduced OPEC's market share, ultimately making the high price policy uneconomical to the cartel even in the short run.

Interestingly, after prices fell in early 1986, the non-OPEC supply has ceased to grow, and demand expansion has resumed, thus providing a widened scope for OPEC sales, increasing both the absolute volume and the market share of the cartel.

The time period since the price fall is far too short to permit any conclusions about definite trend reversals. Nevertheless, a continuation of the tendencies that have emerged after 1985 will result in a gradual increase in OPEC's utilization of existing capacity. If that capacity remains unchanged, the need for supply management will dwindle, and disappear completely, maybe towards the end of the century, when full capacity utilization by OPEC members becomes consistent with the $15 price. Without supply management, one could then talk about a competitive market in which OPEC production is intramarginal and reaps substantial rents on account of its superior resource base.

The argument about a competitive market, used in the preceding paragraph, hinges on the assumption of constant OPEC capacity. When that assumption is relaxed, and capacity is permitted to change, competition among profit maximizing agents implies that capacity should increase through investment in the most economical deposits, until the expanded production has driven prices down to a level where additional investments yield no more than the normal capital return.

As already noted, investment behaviour in the petroleum market over the past 15 years has been very different from what one would expect in a competitive market. In the late 1970s, the total incremental cost to produce an additional barrel per day was about $8 in the US, but less than $0.15 in Saudi Arabia.[12] Yet, a lot of investment activity took place in the US, and hardly any in Saudi Arabia. In 1985, an average of 963 oil rigs were operated in Texas and Louisiana in the United States. In Saudi Arabia, with about the same surface area, but a vastly superior potential, only ten rigs were in place.[13] In 1985, the whole of OPEC operated no more than 290 rigs. By 1987, the number had fallen to 186. This was only 7.5 per cent of all the rigs operated in the non-Socialist world. Yet, more than 80 per cent of the non-Socialist world oil reserves were located in OPEC countries.[14]

More to the point, the cost of establishing and maintaining oil production capacity varies enormously, not only between the US and Saudi Arabia, but among all oil producing countries. Adelman[15] reckons that a price of around $20 (1985 dollars) would be needed to sustain the current non-Socialist world production levels outside OPEC in the long run. His calculations, based on conservative assumptions about currently identified petroleum reserves, also show that within a ten-year period, five OPEC members in the Middle East (Iraq, Iran, Kuwait, Qatar and Saudi Arabia) could establish and operate profitably a lasting capacity of 49 million barrels per day, at prices below $1 (1985) per barrel. The whole of OPEC could create a sustainable and profitable capacity of 64 million barrels, at prices of $5 (1985). This can be compared with the 1987 capacity of 19 million barrels in the Middle East, and 29 million for all of OPEC, or with production, amounting to 13 million in the Middle East and 19 million in the whole of OPEC, or with the entire non-Socialist world output in that year, of 44 million barrels per day.

The unwillingness of the OPEC countries to use their extraordinary resource potential for expanding production capacity after the mid-1970s, has been an important, although not binding, component of the cartel's policies to manage supply.

Adelman's figures show that in a competitive petroleum market, the huge Middle East resource potential would suffice as the only source for capacity expansion over a very long period of time. They also indicate that in competitive market conditions, much of the US and North Sea capacity would be forced to close prematurely, because a brisk and highly profitable expansion in OPEC countries would keep prices below the variable costs in North America and Europe.

The exceedingly uneven quality and geographical concentration of oil deposits provides great scope for profitable monopolistic coordination in the long run, through restricted access to the rich parts of the resource base for capacity expansion. Psychologically, the management of long-run supply through investment restraints is probably easier to accomplish than management of supply in the shorter run through cuts of production from existing capacity. The former merely involves deferral of decisions about the future, while the latter requires immediate and highly visible action.

The present paper does not provide scope for the complex investigation to determine the extent of profitable monopolistic market power of those who control the rich petroleum resources. It suffices to state that their profits will be raised by long-run restrictions in supply that push prices substantially above the $5 (1985) or less, that could be expected with competitive market behaviour. It can be conjectured that at these higher price levels (maybe $10–12 in constant 1985 dollars corresponding to about $4 in constant 1970 dollars) the long-run price elasticity of demand is below absolute 1.[16] Hence, maximization of profit or revenue by the owners of the rich resources will make a significant non-OPEC output profitable too.

Neither does the paper provide scope for clarifying the precise nature of the objective function that the members of the long-run cartel would pursue, nor for resolving the institutional issues that such collaboration would involve. Despite impressive intellectual efforts devoted to the issue, there is no believable model of OPEC behaviour even for the past,[17] but this does not imply that long-run collaboration will be difficult to establish. Public control of petroleum production in OPEC countries limits the number of decision making units that need to be involved, thus facilitating the management of investments. A historical experience worth noting in this context is that where the external market preconditions for monopolistic profits exist, they will be utilized by the suppliers, irrespective of prevailing institutional relationships.[18]

The simple conclusion emerging from the analyses of this section is that monopolistic forces are likely to influence petroleum prices also in the long run, stretching a decade or two into the next century. The reason is the very skewed petroleum resource base which provides considerable scope for monopolistic profits through restrained supply. In this respect, the petroleum market is unusual. Most other commodity markets offer little scope for profitable monopolistic coordination over extended periods of time. The potential degree and power of monopolistic coordination therefore warrants careful consideration in long-run analyses of petroleum prices.

4   Interfuel substitution and petroleum prices

The possible emergence of competitive substitutes for oil could dampen oil price developments, and impose a constraint on the monopolistic power of the countries richly endowed with oil resources.

Undoubtedly, the emergence of oil as a major source of energy in the 1930s, when it first exceeded 20 per cent of global primary energy consumption[19] and the fast growth in its share of the total to over 40 per cent during the following four decades, imposed an effective cap on the price of coal. One can speculate that in the absence of competition from oil, coal prices would have been substantially above their actual record over this period. Since oil could conceivably encounter similar competition in future decades, with its price kept down by the emergence of alternative energy sources, it is important to explore the mechanics of the process, and the preconditions and likelihood for it to occur.

The impact of relative prices on inter-fuel substitution is quite tricky to disentangle; the recursive impact of substitution on prices is even trickier. The following analysis deals mainly with the second issue. The picture is painted with a very broad brush.

In approaching the subject, it may be instructive first to consider that relative price between oil and the substitute energy raw material, say steam coal, which will assure both materials an unchanging share of the total energy market. The international market share of oil was expanding, that of coal contracting in the 1960s, when oil and coal had roughly the same price per unit of energy.[20] The reverse was true between 1974 and 1985, when coal could be had at a discount to oil of more than 50 per cent, measured in energy equivalents.[21] Somewhere in between, maybe at an oil/coal price ratio of 2:1 (expressed in energy equivalents), a competitive neutrality will occur. The competitive advantage of oil over coal in certain markets (transport fuels) will then be balanced by its competitive disadvantage in others (electricity generation), so that the overall market share of each remains constant. In practice, this neutrality is hard to determine, and even harder to observe, because of quality differentials in each material, because transport costs will result in shifting price ratios in different geographical areas, and because technical change will affect the relative competitiveness of the two materials over time.

Abstracting from these ambiguities, we may conclude that the higher the actual price ratio is above the competitive neutrality, the greater will be the pressures to substitute coal for oil. As a result, there will be a close relationship between the oil/coal price ratio, and the relative growth of demand for each of the two materials.

For such substitution to make a significant dent in the growth of demand for oil, it is not enough that the price ratio is substantially different from competitive neutrality. Another precondition is that the competing material's initial market share is substantial. If it is not, then even a very fast growth of its market will have little impact on oil, until that market share has attained a substantial size.

If both preconditions hold for a material which is a close substitute to oil, the share of that material's overall energy market will grow. At the same time the share of oil will decline, and the absolute growth of the oil market will be suppressed. If the price ratio remains unchanged, the growth of market share for the substitute will continue until it has replaced oil completely in those market segments where it has a competitive advantage.

However, the price ratio is not likely to remain unchanged during the process. In particular, there are reasons to believe that a slowdown in oil demand growth will weaken petroleum prices.

Consider first the case of a competitive petroleum market. It was argued in Section 2 that depletion would not impact perceptibly on petroleum prices within the time horizon of the present study, because any cost increase due to a deterioration in the physical resource base was likely to be dwarfed by cost-reducing technological progress in exploration, extraction and processing. This, at least, is what historical evidence suggests.

Suppose, however, that demand growth for oil accelerates to twice or four times the historical rate. A reasonable case can then be argued that cost-reducing technical progress will lag behind cost-increasing deterioration of physical resources, resulting in an upward push of cost and price. An equally reasonable case can be argued in the opposite direction: when substitution arrests the growth of demand for oil, then the likelihood is that technical progress will be faster than resource deterioriation, resulting in reduced costs and prices. In this way, the introduction of competitive substitutes for oil on a large scale could well depress oil prices below what they would have been in the absence of such substitution.

It must be underlined that the above argument points to a reasonable likelihood, not to a definite certainty. For instance, the effects we discuss might not occur at all if there is a causal relationship between the rate of growth of oil demand, and the rate of cost-reducing technological progress in the oil industry. Also, there may be downward cost shifts like that triggered by the discovery of the rich Middle East resource base. Such events will disturb the tendency towards rising costs caused by fast demand expansion.

Consider second, the case of a monopolistic petroleum market. A slowdown in demand growth is even more likely to depress oil prices in this case. The emergence of an aggressive substitute will increase the price elasticity of demand for the colluding producers' output, thereby reducing the scope for profitable monopolistic coordination at each point in time. Fearing a shrinkage of their market, the producers' long-run price ambitions are likely to be set below those that would prevail in the absence of the substitute.

The relationship between relative oil prices and degree of substitution is recursive. With weaker oil prices, the extent of substitution will be less far reaching, and the ultimate share of oil in the total energy market greater than if oil prices remain unchanged.

If the conjectures formulated in Section 3 about oil prices averaging about $10–12 (1985 dollars) in the next couple of decades turn out to be correct, what then are the prospects for powerful substitutes for oil emerging in the energy markets?

Nuclear energy might have developed into such a substitute, if all the rosy expectations held about this energy source in the 1960s and early 1970s had become true. As events turned out, nuclear power costs have risen, because of safety concerns and ensuing regulation. In addition, public fear and apprehension have come to constitute an absolute restraint on nuclear expansion. For these reasons, nuclear energy is unlikely to develop into an aggressive substitute for oil in the time span under consideration.

Neither is coal likely to eat itself much further into the markets for oil. Analyses of the end-century coal supply potential[22] suggest delivered prices in the major industrialized centres of $35–42 per ton (1985 dollars), corresponding to $7–9 per barrel of oil equivalent. Such prices will not make coal into a formidable competitor to oil, when oil prices are $10–12.

There remains natural gas. Its resource base is less well defined than that for oil and coal,[23] but what is known indicates a very large and expandable supply potential at costs and prices that are highly competitive with the price of oil prevailing in the late 1980s.[24] The technologies of extraction, transport and use of gas are claimed to be inefficient, either because they are old, or because they are oil-based, and not appropriately adapted to gas.[25] The technological development potential, and the scope for reducing costs is therefore considerable. As a result, the competitively neutral price ratio between oil and gas is particularly unstable. The technical change in prospect for gas and a reduction of entry barriers facing producers and consumers of gas, caused by economies of scale and inflexible institutional arrangements in many countries, could substantially increase the competitiveness of this energy material.

Gas might therefore conceivably emerge as a formidably competitive substitute for oil towards the end of the century, provided a number of things turn in its favour. If it did, it could reduce the monopolistic power of petroleum producers. Whether in fact gas will assume this role in the course of the coming decades, remains an open question.

The present section can now be concluded. We have discussed the preconditions for, and mechanics under which substitution might suppress the future prices of oil. It is concluded that neither nuclear power nor coal commands the required competitive advantage, but that natural gas could possibly play that role, if a number of developments turn in its favour. If so, then oil prices at the end of the present century and beyond could turn out to be lower than the conjecture of $10–12 (1985 dollars) formulated in an earlier section. Developments in the gas market are therefore important to consider when the long-run prospects for oil prices are analyzed.

5   Technological shocks and the price of oil

All of the above assumes a reasonably normally functioning world. In reality, events may, or are even likely to, stray away from the normal path in the extended period under scrutiny.

The number of possible abnormal scenarios with strong and lasting impacts on the price of oil, either upwards or downwards, is infinite. In the following paragraphs we choose to consider briefly the consequences for oil prices of two entirely plausible technological shocks. The first involves an abrupt and complete dismantling of the world's nuclear power after one or a few very severe accidents with nuclear reactors. The second consists of the reactions to a sudden awareness that the greenhouse effect has immediate, undesirable and drastic effects on the world's climate. The details of total energy consumption by fuel in 1987 and forecast 2000, displayed in Table 7.3 may serve as an instructive base in the treatment of both shocks.

Nuclear power in the non-Socialist world in the late 1980s corresponds to some 7 million barrels of oil per day, less than current excess capacity in the OPEC group. The removal of that energy supply in the nearby future would give the oil cartel a tremendous moral boost, and greatly facilitate its ability to manage supply. There is considerable uncertainty about the way the cartel would utilize its strengthened market position. Its members have certainly learnt from past experience, and it is by no means given that they would act in the same way as they did in response to the political events of 1979–80 which triggered the second oil crisis. In principle, they could replace the entire energy shortfall simply by expanding the utilization of existing capacity, but such an outcome is unlikely. Instead, oil price levels like those prevailing in 1981, or even higher, would probably emerge, as energy consumers substituted oil for nuclear power.

However, the period of high prices would probably not be as extended as the one that began in 1974. The recency of the preceding energy crises has established a readiness to respond that was not there at all in the mid-1970s. A new crisis would immediately arouse frantic efforts to expand non-OPEC oil capacity. The results would be speedy, since the physical and human capital needed for the purpose was built up early in the 1980s, and can be mobilized with short notice. The crisis would also give rise to intensive activity to expand natural gas and coal supply, and to save energy use. In these endeavours too, the world of the late 1980s is far better prepared to act than it was 12 years earlier.

	1987		2000	
	Million bpd oil	%	Million bdp oil	%
Oil	45.4	44.5	52.9	40
Natural gas	18.6	18.3	25.1	19
Coal	22.5	22.1	30.4	23
Hydro, solar etc	8.3	8.2	13.2	10
Nuclear	7.0	6.9	10.6	8
Total	101.8	100.0	132.2	100

Table 7.3 Non-Socialist world consumption of primary commercial energy

Note: The consumption of hydro and nuclear is expressed as the oil input required to generate the corresponding amount of electricity.

Sources: BP Statistical Review of World Energy, 1988; Chevron, *World Energy Outlook*, October 1987.

Hence, it is probable that the scrapping of nuclear power in, say, 1990, would boost OPEC's market power and cause an oil price explosion, but it is also likely that the tightness in world energy markets would be overcome well before the end of the decade, weakening OPEC's clout, and resulting in falling oil prices.

The impact on the oil market would be greater and more enduring, if instead, nuclear power were to be eliminated through a sudden decision at the end of the century. By that time, nuclear is expected to account for a larger share of total energy consumption in the non-Socialist world. Also, assuming a surprise-free world energy scenario for the 1990s, there would be little excess capacity in OPEC to draw on, in order to dampen an energy shock in 2000. Finally, a large part of the human and physical capital stock needed to expand energy production, that was built up in the early 1980s, would have ceased to exist by the end of the century, if oil prices in the 1990s remained relatively low.

The second technological shock to be considered would have an opposite impact on oil. An urgent programme to slow down global carbon dioxide emissions could be pursued at different levels of ambition and speed. Its impact on the energy sector in general, and on the oil market in particular, would differ correspondingly. Any such programme would involve two basic reactions. The first would be to reduce the use of fossil fuels, and especially those causing the greatest emissions per unit of energy. Coal would be hardest hit, but a significant decrease of the overall emission levels would certainly require severe cuts in petroleum use too. Natural gas would be the least affected among the fossil fuels.

Hydro and nuclear power would receive a strong boost, as efforts were mounted to compensate for part of the fossil shortfall. But since fossil fuels account for very dominant shares of total energy consumption, it would not be feasible to replace any large cut in their use by expansion of other energy sources within the time span of a decade or two. Hence, the second basic reaction would be to mount large-scale energy saving programmes.

Both reactions would have a negative impact on oil demand and oil prices. In the extreme, the use of oil as an energy material might collapse, leaving the demand for feedstocks in the chemical industry as the major oil market, with prices declining towards the production cost of the rich and abundant resources in the Middle East. The value of all other resources of oil in the ground would then fall to zero.

6   A summary of conclusions

Except for its size in terms of value, the international market for oil does not appear to be exceptional in any important respect, in comparison with the markets for other commodities. The historical development of oil prices between 1900 and 1972 was not strikingly different from that for metals and minerals, or for agricultural commodities.

Our analyses reveal that price formation in oil during the present century has not been perceptibly influenced by exhaustion. Neither is it likely to be affected by this factor over the two to three decades into the future which constitute the time horizon of the present study. The unimportance of exhaustion for price developments is not exclusive to oil. It is equally applicable to virtually all primary commodities.

The low price elasticity of demand for oil combined with a concentration of its production, provides scope for monopolistic manipulation. The extreme geographic concentration of the most economic resource base for this material makes it possible for producers to exert monopolistic power even in the long run, provided that they are not overambitious. These features make oil unusual, but in no way unique among commodities. Metals like cobalt, niobium, platinum and tin possess somewhat similar characteristics.

Like the price of any commodity, the price of oil will tend to be suppressed by the emergence of competitive substitutes. The study suggests that fortuitous technological and commercial breakthroughs in natural gas might greatly speed up the substitution of gas for oil. The ensuing slowdown in the expansion of oil demand would dilute the monopolistic power of oil producers, and dampen oil price developments.

Future technological shocks could impact strongly on petroleum prices over long periods of time. The study considers briefly the oil price explosion that would ensue if there were a sudden nuclear moratorium, and the possible collapse of oil prices if the adverse consequences of the greenhouse effect led to global restrictions on fossil fuel use. Oil stands out among primary commodities by its extraordinary weight and importance to the world economy. The economic repercussions of technological shocks affecting oil, such as those discussed in this study would therefore be much more severe than the consequences of similar shocks affecting any other primary material.

NOTES

1 Nominal oil prices have been obtained by splicing three different series, viz., (a) 1900–1948: US domestic average prices at wellhead, as provided in Manthy (1978), Table MP–3; (b) 1948–1984: Posted Saudi Arabian light crude prices. Data for 1948 and 1949 are from Adelman (1972), table V–1. Data for 1950–1984 are from World Bank (1986); and (c) 1984–1986: North Sea crude, spot quotations. The figure for 1984 refers to oil from the Forties field, as given in British Petroleum (1988), June. The figures for 1985 and 1986 are for Brent oil, as given by the IMF's monthly statistical compilations of commodity prices. All other nominal commodity price indices, as well as the deflator to obtain real prices (the US index of wholesale prices of manufactures) have been obtained from Grilli and Yang (1988), Appendix Table 1.
2 Gately (1984).
3 Darmstadter, *et al.* (1970).
4 Scherer (1980).
5 Grilli and Yang (1988).
6 Forecasts of price rises of such magnitude were made, amongst others, by US Energy Administration (1980), EXXON (1980), World Bank (1981), and Stobaugh (1982). The UN Economic Commission for Europe (1978) anticipated the real unit supply cost of oil to rise by 117 per cent in the 1980s, and by a further 12 per cent in the 1990s.
7 Hotelling (1931).
8 Fisher (1981).
9 Gately (1984).
10 Adelman (1986a).
11 British Petroleum (Annual), several issues.
12 Adelman (1986b).
13 Adelman (1986a).
14 OPEC (1988).
15 Adelman (1986a).
16 This conjecture is supported by several studies reviewed in Pindyck (1979).
17 Gately (1984).
18 MacKie-Mason and Pindyck (1986).
19 Darmstadter *et al.* (1970).
20 The record of coal prices in that period is blurred. The price equivalence

emerging in Swedish import statistics of the time suggests that the same price ratio may have held through northwestern Europe.
21 OECD (1987); British Petroleum (Annual), several issues.
22 Doyle (1988).
23 Percebois (1986).
24 MIT Energy Laboratory (1985, 1986).
25 Rogner (1988).

REFERENCES

Adelman, M. A. (1972) *The World Petroleum Market*, Resources for the Future, Washington, D.C.
Adelman, M. A. (1986a) 'The competitive Floor to World Oil Prices', *The Energy Journal*, October.
Adelman, M. A. (1986b) 'Scarcity and World Oil Prices', *The Review of Economics and Statistics*, August.
British Petroleum (Annual) *BP Review of World Gas*.
British Petroleum (1988) *BP Statistical Review of World Energy*.
Darmstadter, J. et al. (1970) *Energy in the World Economy*, Resources for the Future, Washington, D.C.
Doyle, G. (1988) 'The International Coal Trade and Price Outlook', IEA Coal Research, London.
EXXON (1980) *World Energy Outlook*, December.
Fisher, A. C. (1981) *Resource and Environmental Economics*, Cambridge University Press, London.
Gately, D. (1984) 'A Ten-Year Retrospective: OPEC and the World Oil Market', *Journal of Economic Literature*, September.
Grilli, E. R. and M. C. Yang (1988) 'Primary Commodity Prices, Manufactured Goods Prices, and the Terms of Trade of Developing Countries: What the Long Run Shows', *World Bank Economic Review*, January.
Hotelling, H. (1931) 'The Economics of Exhaustible Resources', *Journal of Political Economy*, April.
Mackie-Mason, J. K. and R. S. Pindyck (1986) 'Cartel Theory and Cartel Experience in International Mineral Markets', in H. D. Jacoby (ed.), *Energy Markets and Regulations: What Have We Learned?*, MIT Press.
Manthy, R. S. (1978) *Natural Resource Commodities – A Century of Statistics*, Resources for the Future, Washington, D.C.
MIT Energy Laboratory (1985, 1986) 'International Natural Gas Trade Project', MIT Energy Laboratory Reports no 85–013, 86–005 and 86–010, Cambridge Mass.
OECD (1987) *Coal Information 1987*.
OPEC (1988) *Facts and Figures*, 1988 edition.
Percebois, J. (1986) 'Gas Market Prospects and Relationship with Oil Prices', *Energy Policy*, August.
Pindyck, R. S. (1979) *The Structure of World Energy Demand*, The MIT Press, Cambridge, Mass.
Rogner, H. H. (1988) 'Technology and the Prospects for Natural Gas', *Energy Policy*, February.
Scherer, F. M. (1980) *Industrial Market Structure and Economic Performance*, Rand McNally, Chicago.

Stobaugh, R. (1982) 'World Energy to the Year 2000', in D. Yergin and M. Hildebrand (eds), *Global Insecurity: A Strategy for Energy and Economic Revival*, Houghton Mufflin.

UN Economic Comimssion for Europe (1978) *Coal 1985 and Beyond.*

US Energy Information Administration (1980) *1979 Annual Report to Congress*, July.

World Bank (1981) *World Development Report 1981*, September.

World Bank (1986) *Commodity Trade and Trade Trends*, 1986 edition.

Summary of general discussion

E. Lakis Vouyoukas opened the discussion by putting the quoted assertion by Adelman into perspective. Whereas it may be true that much of the Middle Eastern oil could be pumped out of the ground at costs of below $1 per barrel, such a situation would never occur in practice, as demand would rise far above the 60 million barrels per day available at that cost. Thus $1 is not a sustainable competitive equilibrium price. Nonetheless, at today's demand marginal units of oil are available at $1 per day. On the question of substitution he felt that the key was between the static sector and the transport sector. A series of nuclear accidents leading to the immediate cessation of all nuclear generation would not be nearly as beneficial to the oil sector as a new transport invention leading to significant reductions in petrol consumption per mile would be damaging. The latter prospect appeared much more likely than the former.

Robert Mabro stressed the need to take the structure of the oil industry into account in analyzing price trends, especially its huge capital costs and long gestation lags. Thus, he argued, equilibration is an extremely long process, and it is not clear that we have yet worked through the adjustments to the shocks of 1973–74 and 1978–79.

III Stabilization Schemes

8 The Role of Futures Markets as Stabilizers of Commodity Earnings

ANDREW J. HUGHES HALLETT and
PRATHAP RAMANUJAM

1 Introduction

Countries which produce primary commodities face rapidly fluctuating prices and revenues from their output and exports. Many of the producing countries, particularly those middle income or poor countries in the third world, depend on commodity exports as their primary source of foreign exchange, employment and development funds. Moreover they are typically dependent on the exports of just one or two commodities, and are therefore unable to diversify away from those price and earnings risks. For example, World Bank figures for 1986 show that out of 42 countries with GNP per head of less than $1,600, 20 were more than 70% dependent on just two commodities for export earnings. Revenue fluctuations can severely restrict growth by interrupting income levels and the flow of development funds in countries which are highly indebted and unable to borrow from the capital markets in order to smooth their revenues. Yet the indebted countries have increasingly relied on commodity exports for servicing their debts.

This paper examines the statistical distribution of earnings from commodity market sales, with arbitrary distributions for market clearing prices and quantities. We are concerned with limiting the impact of demand and supply disturbances by introducing certain rules governing stockholding, or by committing certain quantities to be bought/sold at a known price on the futures market, or by purchasing options to buy/sell at preannounced prices. The producers' decision is then to select an 'intervention' rule which improves the earnings distribution, typically either in terms of raising average earnings or of reducing their variance.

Previous work in this area has been concerned with a general welfare analysis and the ranking of particular rules. Although the welfare approach may appear to be more general, it has in practice required a number of restrictions – the main ones being normally distributed prices and quantities, unbiased markets, no stockholding, and arbitrarily assigned degrees of risk aversion. Those restrictions are inconsistent both with the data and with *a priori* reasoning. We examine the consequences of relaxing them in terms of producers' earnings – the mean and variance of export earnings being the main concern of policy makers in the LDCs and of the international agencies who oversee the flow of development funds to those countries. We use a *non-parametric* approach to avoid any dependence on particular distributional or model specifications.

Commodity market stabilization therefore becomes a matter of choosing a stockholding rule, a futures market position, or an options pricing scheme, in order to transform the earnings distribution. The first step is to identify conditions under which earnings can actually be stabilized. The second stage is to determine optimal intervention rules, optimal hedging rules, or optimal options contracts and to examine how far they would stabilize earnings. This paper provides practical illustrations of this taken from the Coffee, Cocoa, Jute and Copper markets.

The third stage would be to draw parallels between these stabilization rules and the kind of buffer stock or financial stabilization schemes which have been proposed in the past. In particular, options contracts operate to produce something similar to the bandwidth control rules which have been used in certain markets and recommended for UNCTAD's Integrated Commodity Programme, while futures contracts produce outcomes very similar to certain income support schemes operated in national agricultural markets and in the EEC's 'Stabex' scheme (and to a lesser extent the IMF's Compensatory Finance Facility). It is important to determine how close these parallels are because the main argument against any form of market stabilization is that producers can achieve the same results by adopting appropriate positions in competitive futures and spot markets. The difficulty with this is threefold: a complete set of contingency markets does not exist for most commodities; most of the LDC producers who are in need of earnings stabilization are now severely credit constrained; and production lead times are often long relative to the term of the futures contracts, so that rolling contracts over to 'insure' prices over the production period just substitutes basis risk for price risk (Ghosh *et al.*, 1987). But if we can design support schemes which will effectively reproduce the outcomes of the hedging or options strategies that would have been undertaken on the contingency markets, then we can get the desired outcomes even when those markets are non-existent or incomplete, or credit is not forthcoming.

This paper investigates the extent to which commodity earnings may be stabilized, but it does not provide the welfare justification for doing so. Obviously if stabilization changes the earnings distribution, it may also generate incentives to change the pattern of demands and supplies and hence transfer income between different groups of agents. It is simply assumed here that the necessary welfare evaluations have been undertaken and approved, and that the producers/policy makers now wish to know how to generate the earnings stability that they need. Earnings stability is defined in terms of the variance of random fluctuations about mean or trend values. Hence our hedging or stabilization rules are designed to 'buy' certainty or predictability, rather than to induce stability in the sense of modifying the systematic part of earnings. Similarly the question of whether the underlying prices are statistically stationary, stationary with discrete jumps, or trending, plays no role here since we are concerned with random fluctuations about some deterministic trend or cycle.

2 Stabilization strategies

2.1 Market versus non-market stabilization schemes

In this paper we compare market mechanisms to non-market mechanisms for stabilizing commodity prices or earnings. By hedging on the futures markets, a producer uses existing market instruments to protect himself against price fluctuations which are beyond his control. He does that by trading some of his output in advance of its actual production at prices known at the moment of trade. By choosing the quantity which he agrees to deliver at a fixed price, the producer is able to alter the price and earnings distributions which he faces in a desirable way, but leave the price and earnings distributions for the rest of the market unchanged.

With a price stabilization programme, however, the producers (or some market authority) have to create intervention instruments which are designed to alter the market-generated price and earnings distributions themselves. That will affect the entire market, not just the producers who decide to take advantage of the scheme.

Both approaches work entirely within the existing market framework in that neither the market's supply or demand function is suspended. Operating on futures markets is a genuine free market solution – no extra players are introduced to constrain the producers' and consumers' activities. A price stabilization programme, on the other hand, involves modifying the interactions within a free market and hence an extra 'player' whose activities constrain those of the producers and consumers. That extra 'player' might be a market authority or a coalition of producers large enough to influence market prices by operating a buffer stock. Strictly speaking, therefore, this approach depends on solving a 3 or more player game[1] in which the market authority is an explicit player. However, in common with all the literature on this topic, we simplify that solution by assuming that the parameters governing market responses are not significantly affected by the buffer stock operations.

Both hedging and price stabilization should be contrasted with the possibility of introducing production controls designed to raise or stabilize revenues and prices. Control schemes of that nature go outside the market mechanism because they involve changes to, or the suspension of, the market's supply function. Such arrangements have neither been easy to sustain nor notably successful. They are not considered here.

2.2　The market invariance assumption

We assumed at the start that the necessary welfare evaluations had been undertaken and approved. The problem is then to determine (and compare) optimal hedging and price stabilization rules. That, as it turns out, requires estimates of the first four moments of the joint price-quantity distribution. Thus, where the policy problem is one of creating or providing access to futures market, or where it involves setting up a buffer stock operation, our decision rules should be constructed from the parameters of the new joint probability distribution. Of course that begs the question of how those parameters will change from the old regime. If agents cannot determine the parameters of the new distribution (perhaps because they cannot solve the implied game) but use estimates of the parameters of the old distribution instead, the stabilization results can be no more than an approximation to the correct rule.

It would be interesting to model this implied game explicitly, but its solution is not analytically tractable, which makes any general comparisons between hedging and stabilization quite impossible. Nevertheless there are a number of important cases where using the moments of the existing regime's joint distribution produces either the correct rule or a good approximation to it. Futures markets already exist for many traded commodities. Likewise buffer stock schemes already operate in some commodity markets and in a great many agricultural markets. In these cases the question is whether to continue hedging or renew a buffer stock agreement and, if so, could the current hedging/stabilization rules be improved upon? The case where new hedging opportunities/stabilization procedures are proposed is perhaps more complicated. However none of the rules studied here depends on the parameters of the market's supply and demand functions as such, or on the parameters of producers' and consumers' stockholding, but they do depend on the moments of the price and quantity distributions. Thus even if the insurance offered by futures markets did change price or income elasticities, or substitution effects, it would only change the hedging rule if the increase in supply (say) was not matched by an equivalent increase on the demand side (allowing for any reductions in stockholding given the extra security). Similarly buffer stock interventions would only have to change on average if greater price stability induced greater supply unmatched by greater demand (less any change in overall stockholding). Finally parameter invariance would hold if agents calculated that there would be little advantage in changing their behaviour, or if acquiring the information or means to do so was too expensive, and to the extent that the buffer stock just replaced private sector storage. How much impact all these shifts would have on our decision rules must depend on particular cases, but, with so many conflicting changes, the moments of the price and quantity distributions are likely to be affected significantly less than parameters of the underlying supply, demand and stockholding functions.[2] Hedging or stabilization decisions may be more robust to regime shifts than the underlying responses of the market participants.

2.3   Stockholding

Almost all commodity markets display positively skewed price distributions. Wright and Williams (1982) argue that this is the result of stockholding activities. If the market exhibits excess demand, that can only be met in the short term by running down stocks. Supply is inelastic in the short term and once stocks are exhausted prices will rise very rapidly. If, on the other hand, there is excess supply, agents can accumulate stocks so long as they have sufficient finance. They may not wish to accumulate stocks indefinitely, but they can certainly accumulate more easily than decumulate and they can often hold stocks 'in the ground' or fail to harvest. Hence prices fall by considerably less than they rise in the excess demand case. The implication of that asymmetry is that reducing price variations will reduce average prices, since high prices are reduced by more than low prices are raised (Hughes Hallett, 1986). If that happens more earnings stability will mean lower average earnings.

The same arguments imply that stockholding will generate large third moments from the bivariate price–output distribution. For example, large negative supply shocks are likely to push market prices high above their mean value because stocks and short-run supply responses are inadequate to cope with the excess demand. But a positive supply shock would push market prices below their mean by a rather smaller amount since stocks can absorb the excess supply (at least in the short to medium term). Hence stockholding will imply,

$$\mu_{12} = E(p - \bar{p})(q - \bar{q})^2 > 0 \quad \text{and} \quad \mu_{21} = E(p - \bar{p})^2(q - \bar{q}) < 0$$

It is quite inappropriate to restrict the analysis to symmetrically distributed prices (let alone normally distributed prices) since that would rule out any stockholding and would provide price distributions which fail to match those observed in practice. For that reason, all our analysis is done for the general, distribution-free, case.

2.4   Extensions: speculation and exhaustion

Speculative activity is a feature which is covered only indirectly in our analysis. Gilbert (1988) argues that a large number of speculators in a market where price risks are diversifiable will ensure that the futures price is an unbiased predictor of the corresponding spot price.[3] On the other hand, in a world where spot and futures price are jointly determined and where there is little or no speculative activity, the futures price will be generally biased (Turnovsky 1983, Kawai 1983). For most of our analysis we assume unbiasedness, which may be a reasonable approximation for many commodity markets where there are many traders including speculators and where risks are likely to be diversifiable. However, for markets where there are only a few speculators and less diversifiability because of a concentration on a few commodities and a lack of markets for alternative financial assets, we consider the implications of a systematic bias in the futures price. It turns out not to make any difference to stabilizing incomes.[4]

Our price stabilization results are also derived under the assumption that unlimited finance or stock is available. That may appear quite unrealistic, especially as Townsend (1977) has shown that any intervention scheme will exhaust its financial or stock endowments in finite time with probability one. However, we can get round that shortcoming by penalizing deviations of the stocks held from some target level by enough to prevent stockout or financial exhaustion. That of course requires multi-target dynamic hedging or stabilization rules, and the necessary generalization is provided in the Appendix.

Finally an assumption which we retain throughout is that supply and demand functions are linear with additive uncertainty and do not depend on price variability. The latter assumption reflects the invariance of market behaviour to interventions and is not relaxed for the reasons given earlier. The linearity assumption is easily relaxed (see Nguyen, 1980) but the effect of departures from linearity is to generate transfers between market participants.[5] However, since the stabilization of earnings, and not income transfers, is our focus, linearity is not a restrictive assumption here. We do in fact consider a wider range of objectives than just variance reduction – for example protection from low prices, restraining price fluctuations directly, raising average earnings etc. – but a full welfare analysis and the extension to models with nonlinear uncertainty is a subject for later work.

2.5   Relations to previous literature

There appears to be little academic work on the scope and merits of attempting to stabilize earnings by hedging or by stockpiling operations. The first comparison of these two strategies was made by McKinnon (1967), who favoured the hedging (market) approach. In later work, Newbery and Stiglitz (1981), Gemmill (1985) and Gilbert (1985) also concluded the market approach would probably be superior, although Gemmill's empirical results reveal the comparisons to be pretty mixed in practice with no clear superiority for hedging. More recently Gilbert (1988) has reassessed these comparisons, dropping the assumption of perfect stabilization and allowing hedging on the options markets, and reached the opposite conclusion: price stabilization appears to be superior.

However, all these studies depend on a crucial but implausible set of assumptions. Those assumptions severely limit the usefulness of the results. The purpose of this paper, therefore, is to relax as many of those restrictions as possible:

(a) Private sector stockholding is accounted for. As pointed out earlier private stockholding would imply skewed, and hence non-normal, price distributions. Moreover it is obvious that most commodity prices are in fact distributed with a strong positive skew (see Tables 8.2 and 8.3, and the tests for the significance of those skews in Table 8.4 below).

(b) Earnings stability, and the optimal hedging and stabilization rules are evaluated here on a *distribution-free* basis. They are also *model-free* in the sense of not depending on econometric estimates of the parameters of particular demand and supply functions.

(c) A procedure is given for testing whether optimal hedging or price stabilization would give a greater reduction in earnings stability in any particular case. Extensions to other targets (e.g. optimizing mean–variance combinations of earnings) and to dynamic rules are possible.

(d) The results also cover the case of inefficient (biased) markets.

3   Operating on the futures markets: optimal hedging strategies

3.1   Unbiased markets

Consider a producer who produces a quantity q of some commodity, which he can sell at a spot price p. However, it takes time to complete the production process, and the actual output level is subject to various shocks. In period 0, he plans to produce $\bar{q}$ in period 1, but the actual output level q is a random variable with mean $\bar{q}$ and variance σ_q^2. Similarly period 1's spot price is a random variable with mean $\bar{p}$ and variance σ_p^2. Nothing further is assumed about the probability distributions of p, q or about their independence.

As an alternative to receiving an uncertain revenue of $y = pq$, the producer can hedge on the futures market by selling (in period 0) a fixed quantity q_f for delivery in period 1 at a known price p_f. If he does that he will be obliged to sell his unhedged output $q - q_f$ (including the supply shock $q - \bar{q}$) at the spot price (including the price surprise $p - \bar{p}$). His hedged revenue is therefore

$$y^h = p(q - q_f) + p_f q_f = pq + (p_f - p)q_f \tag{1}$$

If in addition the market is efficient, so that forward prices are an unbiased predictor of future spot prices, $p_f = \bar{p}$. We retain that assumption for the moment, but relax it later. Thus

$$E(y^h) = E(pq) \tag{2}$$

so that hedging on an efficient market does not change the average revenues. Direct calculation also yields

$$\begin{aligned} V(y^h) &= E[pq - q_f(p - \bar{p})]^2 - [E(pq)]^2 \\ &= E(p^2 q^2) - [E(pq)]^2 - 2q_f(\bar{p}\mu_{11} + \bar{q}\sigma_p^2 + \mu_{21}) + q_f^2 \sigma_p^2 \end{aligned} \tag{3}$$

where $\mu_{ij} = E[(p - \bar{p})^i (q - \bar{q})^j]$ for $i, j \geq 1$ are multivariate moments from the joint density function of p and q. Note that $E(p^2 q^2) - [E(pq)]^2 = V(y^0)$ is the variance of the unhedged revenue. It is convenient to write $\mu_{11} = \rho \sigma_p \sigma_q$ from now on, where ρ is the correlation coefficient between p and q. It is usually assumed that $\rho < 0$ on the argument that a production shock which affects one producer will affect them all, and hence a fall in aggregate supply will lead to higher prices (and vice versa). But there is no guarantee of this since a producer who is differentiated either geographically or in production structure may not suffer the same shocks as others and may even be able to profit from high price periods. For example, a non-unionized mine may plan to increase production during the predictable strike periods when unionized mines renegotiate their wage contracts. Similarly non-OPEC oil producers can exploit the regular cycle of oil production cuts instituted by OPEC members. Nevertheless $\rho < 0$ may still be the usual case. Notice also that if p and q are symmetrically and normally distributed $\mu_{21} = \mu_{12} = 0$; and if they are independent then $\rho = 0$ as well.

From (3) the optimal hedging rule is

$$q_f^* = \rho \bar{p} \sigma_q / \sigma_p + \bar{q} + \mu_{21} / \sigma_p^2 \tag{4}$$

which is the result obtained by McKinnon (1967). If $\rho < 0$, the greater is the output uncertainty relative to price uncertainty, the less should be hedged. Similarly the stronger the negative correlation, the smaller is the quantity that should be hedged, but the greater the (positive) asymmetry the larger the hedge. Notice also that if output variability is large enough, q_f^* may be negative and the producer should *buy* forward. Conversely if $\rho > 0$ and μ_{21} is small, $q_f^* > \bar{q}$. So short or long positions can result from (4). Finally, if the joint density function is symmetric we get the familiar formula

$$q_f^* = \rho \bar{p} \sigma_q / \sigma_p + \bar{q} \tag{5}$$

and if p and q are independent (the 'small' producer case) $q_f^* = \bar{q}$. That also holds as price variability becomes very large or as output variability vanishes.

Under any hedging rule, the variance of revenue can be written as,

$$V(y^h) = E(p^2 q^2) - (Epq)^2 + q_f^2 E(p - \bar{p})^2 - 2q_f E[pq(p - \bar{p})]$$
$$= V(y^0) + [q_f^2 - 2q_f q_f^*] \sigma_p^2$$

using (3) and (4) again, where y^0 is the unhedged earnings. Hence under optimal hedging,

$$V(y^h) = V(y^0) - q_f^{*2} \sigma_p^2 \tag{6}$$

That shows an unambiguous gain, in terms of risk reduction, over doing nothing. The risk reduction increases with increasing uncertainty in prices and quantities (σ_p and σ_q), with greater skewness ($\mu_{21} > 0$), but absolutely lower association between prices and quantity (assuming $\rho < 0$). Thus for given market size ($\bar{q}$) 'smaller' or more differentiated producers may benefit more from trading on the futures markets than would large producers.

3.2 Biased (inefficient) markets or markets with transaction costs

Suppose now there are relatively few or, perhaps, no speculators in the market, or that the price risks are not easily diversifiable. The forward price may then be a biased predictor of future spot prices. Let the *systematic* part of the bias be $k = E(p_f - \bar{p})$. This is a known value in period 0, but it may have either sign. Then (1) continues to hold, but

$$E(y^h) = E(pq) + kq_f \tag{7}$$

which shows a systematic gain (loss) if $k > 0$ ($k < 0$). That suggests that by using the futures markets producers might arbitrage the biases away because by selling (buying) ever greater amounts forward when $k > 0$ ($k < 0$) they can systematically increase their expected earnings. Increased forward sales (purchases) will depress (raise) p_f and will ultimately eliminate k.

If $k \neq 0$ does persist it will be because the market is inefficient, or because of transaction costs and the cost of tying up funds in margin payments. As a result we should expect a small positive value for k. The simplest intertemporal pricing models approximate this as $Ep_f = \bar{p} + r$, where r is the rate of interest (Ghosh *et al.*, 1987). Retracing steps (3) to (6) when $k \neq 0$, we have

$$V(y^h) = E\{pq - q_f(p - p_f) - [E(pq) + kq_f]\}^2$$

by (1) and (7). Hence we can write

$$V(y^h) = E[pq - E(pq)]^2 + q_f^2 E(p - p_f + k)^2$$
$$- 2q_f E\{[pq - E(pq)][p - p_f + k]\} \tag{8}$$

where, at each moment, the *current* forward price is given by $p_f = \bar{p} + k$. Substituting for p_f in (8) yields

$$V(y^h) = V(y^0) + q_f^2 \sigma_p^2 - 2q_f(\mu_{21} + \bar{p}\rho\sigma_p\sigma_q + \bar{q}\sigma_p^2) \tag{9}$$

once again. Hence the optimal hedging rule and the earnings variance reduction are both identical to the unbiased market case; (4) and (6) apply just as before.

Thus market bias or inefficiency does not affect the ability of the hedging strategy to stabilize incomes in any way – at least on this definition of stability. In fact, far from being crucial, the assumption of an unbiased market is quite irrelevant to stabilizing earnings; the same hedge and gain in stability apply whether or not there are many traders/speculators, and whether or not risks are diversifiable. On the other hand, had the mean square error of y^h about $E(y^0)$ been taken as the measure of stability, there would be a greater stability gain from a smaller hedge than is possible in an unbiased market.[6] This mean square error could conceivably be the appropriate criterion because $E(y^0)$ is the unhedged income level expected by the rest of the market, and stability about that figure would be required if the prior welfare analysis assumed at the beginning had indicated that level to be the most desirable.

4   Market intervention strategies

4.1   Optimal price stabilization

Direct price stabilization involves the creation of a buffer stock which will buy some or all of the market's excess supply at some target price (to prevent prices falling further) and sell when there is excess demand at that price (to prevent them rising further). Hence net purchases will be

$$BS = \lambda(q^s - q^d) \tag{10}$$

where q^s = quantity supplied, q^d = quantity demanded, and λ is the proportion of excess demand/supply which is sold/bought at any target price level: $\lambda = 0$ gives no stabilization, $\lambda = 1$ gives perfect stabilization.[7]

The buffer stock manager and producers are likely to have difficulty in measuring excess demand or supply accurately, so it is convenient to reformulate (10) in terms of deviations of actual prices from their target level. A second problem is the choice of target price level.[8] Following Gilbert (1988), we set $\bar{p}$ as the target price level to ensure comparability with hedging in an unbiased market and to ignore all the transfers between market participants which would follow if $\bar{p}$ were not chosen. This is appropriate if earnings stability rather than a full welfare analysis is the objective. Let supply and demand be given by:

$$q^s = \alpha + \beta p + v \quad \alpha, \beta > 0$$

$$q^d = a - bp + u \quad a, b > 0$$

The target price $\bar{p}$ is therefore the expected equilibrium price. Post-stabilization prices, $\tilde{p}$, satisfy $q^d + BS = q^s$, where BS is evaluated at $\bar{p}$. In other words

$$\tilde{p} = \bar{p} + (1 - \lambda)[(u - v)/(b + \beta)] \quad \text{where} \quad \bar{p} = (a - \alpha)/(b + \beta) \tag{11}$$

and $V(\tilde{p}) = (1 - \lambda)^2 V(p) \leq V(p)$ where the inequality holds provided $0 \leq \lambda \leq 2$. Notice that $BS = \lambda[(\beta + b)(\bar{p} - p)]$ is implied by evaluating (10) at $\bar{p}$ and substituting for v and u. Hence the intervention rule actually used would be

$$BS = \gamma(\bar{p} - p) \quad \text{with} \quad \gamma = \lambda(\beta + b). \tag{12}$$

where p is the price that would rule in the absence of stabilization. Now the producers' revenue under price stabilization is

$$y^s = \tilde{p}q = pq - \lambda(p - \bar{p}) q \tag{13}$$

Thus $E(y^s) = (1 - \lambda) E(pq) + \lambda \bar{p}\bar{q}$, or more interestingly

$$E(y^s) - E(y^h) = - \lambda \rho \sigma_p \sigma_q > 0 \tag{14}$$

for the usual ($\rho < 0$) case. Hence, in that case only, price stabilization raises expected earnings above the pre-stabilization or hedging level.[9] This is because producers can sell *all* their output at stabilized prices, whereas they can hedge only their *expected* output at forward prices – the remaining supply shock, being necessarily unhedged, fetches the spot price. (Compare (13) with (1) where $q_f = \lambda \bar{q}$). So stabilization will be superior, in terms of average earnings, if prices are negatively correlated with the supply shocks. That will depend on demand elasticities. Moreover, if $V(y^s)$ is minimized at $\lambda < 1$, there will be a conflict of objectives since $E(y^s)$ increases as $\lambda \to 1$.

Optimal stabilization strategies are considerably more complicated than optimal hedging strategies. From (13) and (14) we have

$$
\begin{aligned}
V(y^s) &= (1 - \lambda)^2 V(y^0) + \lambda^2 \bar{p}^2 \sigma_q^2 + 2\lambda(1 - \lambda)\bar{p}\,\mathrm{Cov}(pq, q) \\
&= V(y^0) + \lambda^2[V(y^0) - \bar{p}^2 \sigma_q^2 - 2(\bar{p}\mu_{12} + \bar{p}\bar{q}\rho\sigma_p\sigma_q)] \\
&\quad + 2\lambda[\bar{p}\mu_{12} + \bar{p}^2 \sigma_q^2 - \bar{p}\bar{q}\rho\sigma_p\sigma_q V(y^0)]
\end{aligned}
\tag{15}
$$

From these, a direct evaluation of $V(y^0)$ yields

$$
\lambda^* = \frac{V(y^0) - \bar{p}\,\mathrm{Cov}(pq, q)}{V(y^0) + \bar{p}^2 \sigma_q^2 - 2\bar{p}\,\mathrm{Cov}(pq, q)} = \frac{A}{B}
\tag{16}
$$

where $B = \mu_{22} - \rho^2 \sigma_p^2 \sigma_q^2 + \bar{q}^2 \sigma_p^2 + 2\bar{q}\mu_{21}$ and $A = B + \bar{p}\mu_{12} + \bar{p}\bar{q}\rho\sigma_p\sigma_q$. Moreover $B > 0$, since it can be written as $E[(pq - Epq) - \bar{p}(q - \bar{q})]^2$. Finally inserting (16) into (15) gives

$$
V(y^s) = V(y^0) - A^2/B
\tag{17}
$$

which shows an unambiguous gain. Now $0 < \lambda^* < 1$ provided $0 < A < B$. That will happen if μ_{12}, μ_{21} and ρ are not too strongly negative (so $A > 0$) and if $\mu_{12} + \bar{q}\rho\sigma_p\sigma_q < 0$ (so $A < B$). So a simple sufficient condition is weakly negative second and third joint moments. But if those moments are positive $\lambda^* > 1$, and if they are strongly negative $\lambda^* < 0$. Thus, as in hedging, positive p and q correlations would require 'over-stabilization', while very strong negative correlations calls for pro-cyclical 'stabilization'. Finally for 'small' producers (where p and q are independent) perfect stabilization is best ($\lambda^* = 1$). Only in the special case where p and q are symmetrically distributed *and* $\rho < 0$ are we sure to have the conventional result $0 < \lambda^* < 1$.

The size of the stabilization gain here is rather complicated. For any given λ value, it clearly increases with both price and quantity uncertainty (but more so with price uncertainty) and also with positive third moments. It falls with the covariance between p and q (assuming $\rho < 0$).

4.2   When is direct stabilization preferable to hedging?

When does direct stabilization produce greater earnings stability than hedging? From (6) and (17) price stabilization will be superior to operating on the futures market if $A^2/B > \mu_{21} + \bar{p}\rho\sigma_p\sigma_q + \bar{q}\sigma_p^2 = x^2$ or if $A^2 > Bx^2$. Unfortunately that yields a test which is far too complicated for analysis:

$$
\begin{aligned}
A^2 - Bx^2 &= (\mu_{22} - \rho^2\sigma_p^2\sigma_q^2 + \bar{q}^2\sigma_p^2 + 2\bar{q}\mu_{21} + \bar{p}\mu_{12} + \bar{p}\bar{q}\rho\sigma_p\sigma_q)^2 \\
&\quad - (\mu_{22} - \rho^2\sigma_p^2\sigma_q^2 + \bar{q}\sigma_p^2 + 2\bar{q}\mu_{21})(\mu_{21}^2 + \bar{p}^2\rho^2\sigma_p^2\sigma_q^2 \\
&\quad + \bar{q}^2\sigma_p^4 + 2\mu_{21}\bar{p}\rho\sigma_p\sigma_q + 2\mu_{21}\bar{q}\sigma_p^2 + 2\bar{p}\bar{q}\rho\sigma_p^3\sigma_q) \quad (18)
\end{aligned}
$$

However, we can take a different approach. Let $q_f = \lambda\bar{q}$ and hence $\lambda_h = q_f^*/\bar{q}$. Define λ^+ as the value of λ for which $V(y^h) = V(y^s)$. Now using (16) and (17),

$$
\begin{aligned}
V(y^h) - V(y^s) &= \lambda^2[\bar{q}^2\sigma_p^2 - B] - 2\lambda[\bar{q}\mu_{21} + \bar{q}\bar{p}\rho\sigma_p\sigma_q + \bar{q}^2\sigma_p^2 - A] \\
&= -\lambda^2[\mu_{22} - \rho^2\sigma_p^2\sigma_q^2 + 2\bar{q}\mu_{21}] \\
&\quad + \lambda[\mu_{22} - \rho^2\sigma_p^2\sigma_q^2 + \bar{q}\mu_{21} + \bar{p}\mu_{12}] \quad (19)
\end{aligned}
$$

So there are just two values of λ such that $V(y^h) - V(y^s) = 0$; they are $\lambda = 0$ and

$$
\begin{aligned}
\lambda^+ &= \frac{[\mu_{22} - \rho^2\sigma_p^2\sigma_q^2 + 2\bar{q}\mu_{21} + \bar{p}\mu_{12}]}{[\mu_{22} - \rho^2\sigma_p^2\sigma_q^2 + \bar{q}\mu_{21}]} \\
&= 1 + (\bar{p}\mu_{12} + \bar{q}\mu_{21})/[\mu_{22} - \rho^2\sigma_p^2\sigma_q^2 + \bar{q}\mu_{21}] \quad (20)
\end{aligned}
$$

Moreover,

$$
\partial[V(y^h) - V(y^s)]/\partial\lambda = \mu_{22} - \rho^2\sigma_p^2\sigma_q^2 + \bar{q}\mu_{21} + \bar{p}\mu_{12} = d \quad (21)
$$

at $\lambda = 0$. Consequently stabilization is superior, i.e. $V(y^s) < V(y^h)$ in a comparison of hedging/stabilization schemes which use the same small positive λ value, if the right hand side of (21) is positive. Hedging would be superior for schemes which use a small negative λ value. Conversely if (21) yields a negative value, hedging is superior for schemes with small $\lambda > 0$ values, and stabilization for small $\lambda < 0$ values. Consequently, since there are only two λ values, $\lambda = 0$ and $\lambda = \lambda^+$, for which the relative effectiveness of hedging and stabilization gets inverted, we have the following test procedure:

Evaluate $\lambda_h = q_f^*/\bar{q}$ by (4); $\lambda_s = \lambda^*$ by (16); λ^+ by (20); and d by (21). Then

(a) When $d > 0$ and $\lambda^+ > 0$; if $0 < \lambda_h < \lambda^+$ use stabilization, but if $\lambda_s \notin (0, \lambda^+)$ use hedging. Otherwise (i.e. if $\lambda_s < \lambda^+ < \lambda_h$ or $\lambda_h < 0 < \lambda_s$) check if $\lambda_s A > \lambda_h^2\bar{q}^2\sigma_p^2$. The latter is equivalent to checking the sign of (18) and, if satisfied, indicates optimal price stabilization should be used. If this inequality is reversed optimal hedging will give better results.

(b) When $d < 0$ and $\lambda^+ < 0$; if $\lambda^+ < \lambda_h < 0$ use stabilization, but if

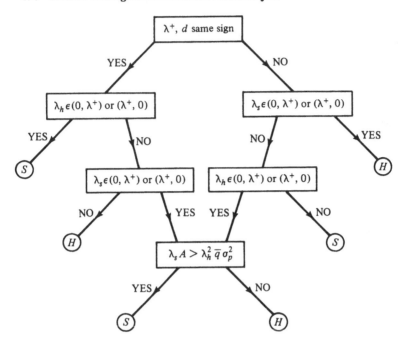

Figure 8.1 Decision tree

$\lambda_s \notin (\lambda^+, 0)$ use hedging. Otherwise use the stabilization rule if $\lambda_s A > \lambda_h^2 \bar{q}^2 \sigma_p^2$, but hedging if not.

(c)   When $d > 0$ and $\lambda^+ < 0$; if $\lambda^+ < \lambda_s < 0$ use hedging, but if $\lambda_h \notin (\lambda^+, 0)$ use stabilization. Otherwise use the stabilization rule if $\lambda_s A > \lambda_h^2 \bar{q}^2 \sigma_p^2$ but hedging if not.

(d)   When $d < 0$ and $\lambda^+ > 0$; if $0 < \lambda_s < \lambda^+$ use hedging, but if $\lambda_h \notin (0, \lambda^+)$ use stabilization. Otherwise use optimal stabilization if $\lambda_s A > \lambda_h^2 \bar{q}^2 \sigma_p^2$, but hedging if not.

This test procedure is summarized in the decision tree given in Figure 8.1. In practice it may be simpler just to check the $\lambda_s A > \lambda_h^2 \bar{q}^2 \sigma_p^2$ condition, but for analytic purposes we need all four cases. $V(y^h)$ and $V(y^s)$ are therefore equal at just two λ values: $\lambda = 0$ and $\lambda = \lambda^+$. If $d > 0$, $V(y^s)$ falls below $V(y^h)$ as λ increases from zero. The test therefore consists of checking whether each scheme's optimal λ value occurs within the interval (say $0, \lambda^+$ or λ^+, ∞) where the sign of d indicates which scheme will produce the lower earnings variance. If it does we have established superiority. But if λ_h and λ_s occur each side of λ^+, we have to check directly if the optimized value of $V(y^h) = $ is smaller than $V(y^s)$ or vice versa. The test for case (a) is illustrated in Figure 8.2.

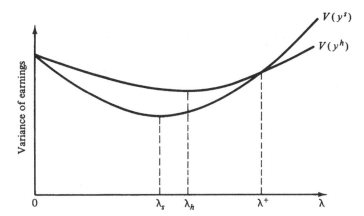

Figure 8.2 An illustration of case (a) with $d > 0$ and $\lambda^+ > 0$

The comparisons are substantially simplified *either* if p and q are independent (the 'small' producer case) *or* if $\mu_{12} = \mu_{21} \approx 0$ (symmetric distributions) since then $\lambda^+ = 1$. In the 'small' producer case $\lambda_h = \lambda_s = 1$ too so there is no distinction between hedging and stabilization; they are equally good. In the symmetric distribution case $\lambda_h = \rho(\sigma_q/\bar{q})/(\sigma_p/\bar{p}) + 1 = e + 1$ where e is the estimated demand elasticity for the product. In fact $(\rho\sigma_p\sigma_q/\sigma_p^2) = \hat{b}$ is just the OLS estimate of b in $q = a - bp + v$. In that case (21) shows $d > 0$, so we have case (a) above and stabilization is the best strategy if $\rho < 0$ *and* demand is inelastic; but hedging will be best if demand is elastic *or* if $\rho \geq 0$. The first half of this result was obtained by Gilbert (1988)[10] but the superiority of hedging when demand is elastic, or when $\rho \geq 0$, was not noted.

These results confirm that, even in the simplest cases, the comparisons can go either way depending on the parameters of the problem, and that no strategy will ever dominate in all circumstances. They also confirm our earlier intuition that the choice of strategy depends on elasticities. Strictly speaking it will always be necessary to check dominance, as in cases (a) to (d) above. But a reasonable rule of thumb is that, unless the skewness and covariance of the price/quantity distributions is rather strong, producers should use price stabilization when they face inelastic demand *and $\rho < 0$*, but operate on the futures markets when demand is elastic *or $\rho > 0$*.

4.3 Can hedging strategies be replicated by stabilization?

Since contingency markets are incomplete for many commodity markets, and since the LDCs have shown a clear preference for stabilization schemes over hedging, it is important to know whether there are circumstances in which stabilization can be used to produce roughly the same revenue stream as hedging would have done when the latter was superior. This is also an important question because most LDCs are severely credit constrained and would probably be unable to adopt the required positions on the futures markets. Stabilization, in contrast, requires an international market authority (financed perhaps by the UN, the World Bank or OECD governments) whose credit rating is much better. Could it replicate the required hedging results?

Complete replication will never be possible because producers' revenue differs between the two schemes to the extent of output shocks. Comparing (1) and (13), where $q_f = \lambda \bar{q}$, the two revenue streams are identical if

$$(p - \bar{p})\bar{q}(\lambda_h - \lambda_s) = \lambda_s(p - \bar{p})v$$

or $$\lambda_s = \lambda_h \bar{q}/(v + \bar{q}) \qquad (22)$$

Hence the λ value needed to replicate the hedging strategy by price stabilization depends on the random output shock. That cannot be computed in advance of setting the stabilization mechanism in motion. But if the output shocks are small relative to the price disturbances, $\lambda_s = \lambda_h$ may approximate to the hedging rule pretty well. More generally

$$E(\lambda_s) = \lambda_h^* E\{1/[(v/\bar{q}) + 1]\} \qquad (23)$$

would have to be used.

It may still be possible to approach the same degree of revenue stability (without attempting to get the same income stream) if $\lambda_h \approx \lambda^+$ when hedging is superior. A stabilization scheme with $\lambda_s = \lambda^+$ would reproduce that stability level. But since one cannot hope to replicate hedging precisely with a stabilization rule when the former is optimal, the main item of interest here will be the proportional gain in $V(y^h)$ over $V(y^s)$. Table 8.6 will provide some empirical results.

5   Some empirical examples

We have examined price and earnings distributions for four commodities which are widely traded internationally and which are predominantly produced in developing countries. From the 29 most important commodities reported in the World Bank's 'Commodity Trade and Price Trends', which also covers UNCTAD's 15 'Core Commodities',[11] we selected Copper, Cocoa, Coffee and Jute to illustrate of the typical price and earnings distributions which primary commodity producers face.

Our selection of these four commodities was governed by two factors: high price variability and a high dependence of LDCs on earnings in those

Commodity	Coefficient of variation of prices	% Trade originating in LDCs (1981–3)
Copper	0.44	63
Cocoa	0.40	92
Jute	0.40	96
Coffee	0.34	91

Table 8.1 Price variability and LDC trade participation rates in 4 commodities (monthly data for 1973–87)

Notes:
Price variability is measured here by the coefficient of variation of the US dollar price per unit (for Jute £ per unit), deflated by the UN's index of export unit values for manufactured goods. The maximum value across all 29 of the major commodities was 0.45. So this group of 4 commodities satisfies our criteria pretty well.

The data used for the calculations reported here was obtained from:
Prices: UN, *Monthly Commodity Price Bulletins* and IMF, *International Financial Statistics.*
Quantities: For Coffee, Cocoa and Jute – FAO *Monthly Bulletins on Agricultural Commodities*. For Copper *Metal Statistics* (Metalgesellschaft A.G., Frankfurt-am-Main). The quantity data was available only as quarterly data. By considering the monthly export volumes of countries which among them hold more than 60–70% of the export markets of the respective commodities, the quarterly output data was converted into monthly data.
Futures Prices: The *Financial Times* 'Commodities Review of the Week' on the first Saturday of the month, January 1973 to December 1987.

markets for their foreign exchange revenues. Rather arbitrarily we chose one metal, one cash crop and two perennials, to ensure roughly a representative 'sample'. The characteristics of our 4 commodities are given in Table 8.1

We use price and quantity data from those markets to demonstrate the asymmetry (non-normality) of the price *and* quantity distributions. We then use the first four moments from the bivariate price–quantity distributions (i.e. $\bar{p}$, $\bar{q}$, σ_p^2, σ_q^2 and μ_{11}, μ_{12}, μ_{21} and μ_{22}) to construct optimal hedging and stabilization strategies for the period of the data (1973–87 inclusive). It is then possible to determine which strategy would have been preferable for stabilizing producers' earnings and hence reducing export instability.

These empirical results are of interest as practical illustrations of our stabilization rules. They are also of interest because the Cocoa and Coffee markets had price stabilization agreements in force at the time. We can check whether the producers in fact chose the right strategy. But, most important, these results allow us to make a rough assessment of the actual

	Mean	Variance	3rd Moment	4th Moment
(a) *Spot Prices* (US$/MT)				
Jute	219.4	2.0896×10^4	9.732×10^6	5.780×10^9
Coffee	2,854	1.159×10^6	769.3×10^6	5.722×10^{12}
Cocoa	2,248	6.099×10^5	280.1×10^6	1.052×10^{12}
Copper	1,604	1.393×10^5	75.89×10^6	9.946×10^{10}
(b) *Export Volume* (000 MT)				
Jute	46.40	521.10	0.8596×10^4	9.465×10^5
Coffee	314.4	5927.0	5.8614×10^4	1.271×10^8
Cocoa	99.80	898.00	2.9457×10^4	3.169×10^6
Copper	255.0	726.00	0.2675×10^4	1.455×10^6
(c) *Earnings* (000 US$)				
Jute	0.898×10^4	2.133×10^7	1.406×10^{11}	2.982×10^{15}
Coffee	89.88×10^4	1.627×10^{11}	3.611×10^{16}	8.325×10^{22}
Cocoa	21.90×10^4	7.319×10^9	4.707×10^{14}	1.943×10^{20}
Copper	40.90×10^4	1.152×10^{10}	1.541×10^{15}	6.570×10^{20}

Table 8.2 Observed moments of the price, quantity and earnings distributions

Note: For Jute prices £/LT, volume 000LT, earnings 000£.

scope for earnings stabilization by operating on the futures markets or price stabilizations. This has not been done before.

5.1 The price and quantity distributions: tests of non-normality

Table 8.2 contains a summary of the estimated moments of the spot price, quantity traded (as exports), and producers' earnings in our 4 commodity markets. In every case, the third moment shows the skew is quite marked and reflects the stockholding behaviour which we argued earlier would produce such a positive asymmetry.

Table 8.3 supports Table 8.2 by reporting the estimated joint moments from the bivariate (p, q) distribution for each commodity. One item of interest there is the signs of the correlation coefficients: only two of the markets show the negative (p, q) correlation which is usually assumed in this sort of analysis. The other two markets show a positive correlation, albeit pretty weak. Nevertheless, this is sufficient to show that stabilization would produce *lower* average earnings for Coffee and Copper producers than a hedging strategy or indeed doing nothing at all – see (14).

Of greater interest perhaps are the third moments, μ_{12} and μ_{21}, where 5

	Jute	Coffee	Cocoa	Copper
ρ	-0.3624	0.0186	-0.2276	0.0683
μ_{21}	-3.86×10^5	-2.685×10^7	-7.81×10^6	-3.79×10^5
μ_{12}	-1258	1.18×10^6	-53830	-26178
μ_{22}	1.34×10^7	6.24×10^9	5.41×10^8	1.52×10^8

Table 8.3 Moments of the joint (p, q) distributions

Note: $\mu_{ij} = E[(p - \bar{p})^i(q - \bar{q})^j]$, and $\mu_{11} = \rho \sigma_p \sigma_q$ where ρ = correlation coefficient.

out of 8 have the signs predicted for them as a result of stockholding behaviour (Section 2.3). The μ_{21} moments are large and have the expected sign. Three of the μ_{12} values are very small and negative, but the one significant value has the expected positive sign. It would be hard to argue that these distributions are symmetric and normal. In fact, if they used the standard analysis which assumes normally distributed price and quantity disturbances (McKinnon, 1967; Gilbert, 1988), producers would think hedging was superior for reducing instability in Coffee and Copper revenues, but price stabilization was better for Jute and Cocoa earnings. But that result is invalid if the non-normality is statistically significant and we in fact reach the opposite conclusion in Table 8.5 below.

The usual test of whether a variable's distribution departs significantly from a normal distribution is either the Kolmogorov–Smirnov test (or one of its variants) or the χ^2 goodness of fit test. But these tests are not very powerful and do not reveal whether the non-normality in the distribution is due to 'skewness' or due to 'kurtosis' (Miller, 1986). As a result Pearson (1963, 1965) recommends the following test statistics be used to detect the non-normality:

Skewness:
$$\delta_1 = 1/n\Sigma(y_i - \bar{y})^3/[1/n\Sigma(y_i - \bar{y})^2]^{3/2} = \mu_3/\sigma^3$$

	Spot prices		Quantities traded	
	δ_1	δ_2	δ_1	δ_2
Jute	3.195	10.046	0.723	0.486
Coffee	0.611	1.208	0.128	0.618
Cocoa	0.583	-0.203	1.095	0.930
Copper	1.448	2.072	0.136	-2.724

Table 8.4 Tests of non-normality in commodity markets

	Hedging: no forward bias		forward biases	MSE criterion*	Price stabilization:			Sign	Dominant strategy
	λ_h	q_i^*	q_i^*	k	λ_2	γ^*	λ^*	d	
Jute	0.330	15.36	14.51	33.9	0.411	0.134	4.073	−	H
Coffee	0.938	295.00	294.70	− 31.5	1.046	0.672	3.306	+	S
Cocoa	0.676	67.37	67.38	9.5	0.737	0.884	4.371	−	H
Copper	1.020	260.20	259.90	12.0	1.027	2.160	− 1.526	+	S

Table 8.5 The optimal hedging and price stabilization strategies

* See Section 3 and footnote 6.
Notes:
(a) S = price stabilization, H = hedging on futures markets.
(b) Units as in Table 8.2.
(c) The γ^* values follow from (12) evaluated using λ_x and the (long-run) price coefficients from the market's supply and demand functions; $(\beta, b) = 0.52$, 1.06; 0.25, 0.07; 0.53, 0.17; and 0.71, 0.22 for Jute, Coffee, Cocoa and Copper respectively.

Kurtosis:
$$\delta_2 = \{1/n\Sigma(y_i - \bar{y})^4/[1/n\Sigma(y_i - \bar{y})^2]^2\} - 3 = [\mu_4/\sigma^4] - 3$$

The calculated values of δ_1 and δ_2 for the price and quantity distributions in our 4 markets are given in Table 8.4.

Using the tabulated values for the distribution functions of δ_1 and δ_2 (with a null hypothesis of normality) we find the 1% significance value for δ_1 with a sample size of 180 is 0.424, and for δ_2 the 1% significance value is 2.49 (Pearson and Hartley, 1966). Thus all four price distributions have third moments which depart significantly from normality (at the 1% level). But only Jute prices show significant kurtosis. The non-normality of the quantity distributions is less marked; Jute and Cocoa supplies show significant skewness and Copper supplies significant kurtosis. Thus *all* the price distributions, and 3 out of 4 quantity distributions, show significant departures from normality, most notably in the asymmetries of the price distributions. Thus we have to check whether hedging or stabilization is superior using the distribution free tests of Section 4.2.

5.2   Hedging versus price stabilization

Table 8.5 contains the result of applying the optimal hedging and price stabilization strategies to minimize the variability aggregate earnings. Our

	Preferred strategy	Reduction in earning variance [as % of $V(y^0)$] by		% gain of stabilization over hedging	$V(y^0)$
		Hedging*	Price stabilization		
Jute	H	23.1	16.8	− 8.3	2.1×10^2
Coffee	S	62.0	69.9	+ 10.9	1.6×10^{11}
Cocoa	H	37.9	37.2	− 1.1	7.3×10^9
Copper	S	81.8	82.4	+ 3.3	1.2×10^{10}

Table 8.6 The potential reduction in earnings variability

* The reductions in MSE of y^* about y^0 were less than 0.1% (1% for Jute) greater than these variance reduction figures.

numerical results therefore reflect a market-wide view, rather than the policies for individual producers within these markets.

5.2.1 Hedging
The first two columns of Table 8.5 show the optimal degree of hedging when it is assumed that the futures market is *unbiased*, i.e. $Ep_f = \bar{p}$. Evidently producers would need to hedge virtually all their expected output in Coffee and Copper markets – in the case of Coffee it is just less than their full expected output, but for Copper they should sell a little more than their expected output forward. These hedging positions are the result of a positive p, q correlation and asymmetries in the (p, q) distribution. If $q < \bar{q}$ and $\rho > 0$, then $p < \bar{p} = p_f$ may be expected. In that case hedging more than $\bar{q}$, and then buying any shortfall on the spot market, will yield extra profit on average. This would be offset by $\mu_{12} > 0$ (as in Coffee, but *not* Copper) since that would reduce the expected fall in p for a given output disturbance. But, on the same argument, this effect would be exaggerated if $\mu_{21} < 0$.

In the other two markets, things are less extreme. Producers would need to hedge one-third of the expected Jute output and two-thirds of the Cocoa output in order to minimize earnings instability. A lower degree of hedging will mean smaller reductions in earnings variances for these two commodities, if price variabilities are about the same as for Coffee and Copper. And this is exactly what happens; see Table 8.6, cols 2 and 3. All these results apply whether the forward markets are biased or not,[12] and the biases noted in Table 8.4 imply changes of less than 1% in average earnings in each case.

5.2.2 Price stabilization
Under this strategy, the market authority should intervene strongly to stabilize Coffee and Copper earnings, somewhat less strongly in the Cocoa market, but only moderately for Jute. Indeed in Coffee and Copper markets they should 'over-stabilize' if they wish to minimize income (export) instability.[13]

The corresponding parameters for the operational (price deviation) form of the intervention rule are given by γ^*. This is evaluated from (12) with the long-run parameters β and b, on the argument that we are considering a one-shot intervention analysis and therefore need to allow for the dynamic consequences of that intervention. But if, more realistically, repeated interventions are possible, smaller interventions would be appropriate in order to avoid having to undo interventions that subsequently appear to have been too strong; γ^* falls to 0.07, 0.13, 0.15, and 0.43 respectively for short term interventions.[14] Which ever is done, a very high degree of price stabilization is involved. Table 8.6 implies that price variability needs to be reduced by 65% in the Jute market, and by 94% or more in the other markets, in order to maximize earnings stability. For Coffee, Cocoa and Copper, that is close to perfect price stabilization. Average earnings also change according to (14) – up by 5% and 2% for Jute and Cocoa, and down by 0.2% for Coffee and Copper. Once again the average earnings versus earnings stability trade-off hardly arises in any of these markets.

5.2.3 Which strategy dominates?
The tests described at the beginning of this section showed that the conventional analysis with normally distributed and negatively correlated price and quantity disturbances, in an unbiased market, would be misleading. The test interval of $(0, \lambda^+ = 1)$ for λ_h and λ_s does not apply in *any* of the four cases, neither does the conclusion that stabilization will dominate because of relatively inelastic demand responses.

According to our test results, it would be best to hedge in the Jute and Cocoa markets but to stabilize prices in the Coffee and Copper markets. Hence it appears that the Cocoa producers would have been better advised to use the futures markets rather than a buffer stock to stabilize their prices. But Coffee producers are indeed right to prefer a buffer stock agreement to hedging.

5.2.4 How large are the variance reductions?
Table 8.6 sets out the gains in revenue stability under the optimal hedging and stabilization strategies.[15] Our preferred strategies would be hedging in the Jute and Cocoa markets, and price stabilization for Coffee and Copper.

The largest gains appear in the Coffee and Copper markets, and that is also where the worst instability problems have arisen (see the last column). These results suggest a 70% reduction is possible in earnings instability for Coffee and an 83% reduction for Copper. Those are strong results, even if subject to a margin of error. But for Cocoa and Jute we could only hope for a reductions of 40%, and 20% respectively. It also happens that the big gains come from price stabilization and the smaller gains from hedging, but there is obviously no generality about that. However, with the possible exception of Coffee, the losses from using the 'wrong' strategy are not large – so it is more important to do something than it is to insist on doing exactly the right thing. That is a comforting conclusion in a world where estimated parameters inevitably introduce an element of approximation and error.

6 Policy conclusions

(a) It is *never* true, either in general or in particular cases, that either a hedging strategy or a price stabilization strategy will always be more effective for stabilizing commodity market earnings, or indeed, the revenues from any market which is subject to significant price or quantity uncertainties. This is because there are always two points where any superiority ranking between the two strategies will be inverted, and those switch points can occur at quite low levels of 'interventions' or at low demand elasticities, as well as in cases where the elasticities have unconventional signs. It is therefore pointless to argue that one or the other strategy is usually superior (as the literature has tended to do), or to favour one particular strategy over the other (as the policy makers have tended to do), whether or not a full set of contingency contracts is available.

(b) It is therefore necessary to test which strategy is superior on a case-by-case basis. This is most efficiently done by determining which strategy offers greatest scope for reducing instability when both are optimized. The relevant test was given in Figure 8.1 and depends on no more than estimates of the first two moments from the marginal distributions for prices and output, together with third and fourth moments from their joint distribution. (The underlying decision rules require the same information). This test procedure will allow producers and policy makers to select the strategy with the greatest potential for stabilizing their (export) earnings, together with the decisions needed to achieve that level of stability.

(c) A rough rule of thumb is to use price stabilization when demand is inelastic *and* prices and quantities are negatively correlated, but to hedge on the futures markets otherwise. However that rule may prove to be misleading if the price and/or quantity distributions depart significantly from normality. That is likely in commodity markets because stockholding implies asymmetries in the price distribution; it may also happen because overshooting, speculative attacks, and interventions by traders with market power, exaggerate disturbances in the price formation process and produce large fourth moments. Thus any such ranking could easily be changed around if there are stockholding asymmetries; if there is a significant possibility of large (price) shocks or if the producers are differentiated (by size, geography, or by market structure, information availability or policy regime). Market bias or inefficiency, however, has no effect on the ability to stabilize earnings by using futures market.

(d) It is also not true that one or other strategy dominates when price or supply uncertainties are small. In fact the difference between them becomes unimportant as *either* σ_q *or* σ_p diminishes. Under *hedging*, $q_f^* \to \bar{q}$ and $V(y^h) \to V(y^0) - \bar{q}^2 \sigma_p^2 = 0$ as $\sigma_q^2 \to 0$. Similarly $q_f^* \to 0$ and $V(y^h) \to \bar{p}^2 \sigma_q^2 \neq 0$ if $\sigma_p^2 \to 0$. But under *stabilization*, $\lambda_s \to 1$ *and* $V(y^s) \to V(y^0) - \bar{q}^2 \sigma_p^2 = 0$ if $\sigma_q^2 \to 0$, while $\lambda_s \to 0$ and $V(y^s) \to V(y^0) - \bar{p}^2 \sigma_q^2 \neq 0$ if $\sigma_p^2 \to 0$. Moreover $[V(y^h) - V(y^s)] \to 0$ if *either* $\sigma_p \to 0$ *or* $\sigma_q \to 0$. Perfect revenue stabilization is therefore possible only if there is no output uncertainty, but the difference between the performance of hedging and stabilization is only slight unless *both* price *and* output fluctuations are strong.[16]

(e) Optimal hedging strategies can never be replicated exactly by price stabilization (unless prices and quantities are independently and symmetrically distributed, when $\lambda_s = \lambda_h = \lambda^+ = 1$), but they can be approximated fairly well if output disturbances are small. Hence the fact that no commodity has a full set of futures markets (and some have none at all) *does* matter – but only for those markets where production is uncertain and hedging would have been the better strategy for stabilizing earnings. That means futures markets would probably be more important for producers of agricultural products and perennial crops, than for producers of metals and other 'hard' commodities. If hedging is also superior in those markets, then policy should be directed at creating and providing access to a sufficient set of futures markets, rather than trying to set up some price stabilization agreement. If hedging is superior but output fluctuations are small, then a compensatory finance (income support) scheme aimed at replicating the hedging outcomes should be used. But if price stabilization is superior, a suitable buffer stock scheme will be needed. This is a very different policy programme from that currently debated.

(f) Hedging has the extra advantage that each producer can operate his own optimal rule. In contrast market stabilization depends on a single intervention parameter, so, unless every producer/country has the same supply distribution, what is optimal for the market will be suboptimal for individual producers (Gemmill, 1985). Our results have to be extended for the individual producers who face different supply conditions (Hughes Hallett and Ramanujam, 1989a). It is also important to extend these results to other markets where hedging is undertaken with options contracts and prices are stabilized within target zones (Hughes Hallett and Ramanujam, 1989b). Although one might argue that options/bandwidth strategies are inferior for stabilizing commodity earnings (Gilbert, 1988), there are obviously significant applications in the currency and financial markets.

(g) These policy conclusions are dependent on earnings stabilization as an objective; they might not survive in a fuller welfare analysis or if the costs of stabilizing earnings were fully accounted for. Things might also change if we dropped the assumptions of behavioural invariance and additive uncertainty. Nevertheless there can be no presumption that one strategy will in fact tend to dominate 'in practical cases'. Two of our four markets showed hedging would dominate, and two showed price stabilization would be better.

APPENDIX: OPTIMAL HEDGING AS A SPECIAL CASE OF RISK-SENSITIVE DECISION MAKING: A MULTI-TARGET DYNAMIC EXTENSION OF THE OPTIMAL HEDGING RULE

Conventional certainty equivalent decision making is risk-neutral, at least in linear–quadratic control problems. Risk-sensitivity requires the decisions to be a function of the second (and possibly higher) moments of the targets' joint density function. Indeed an appropriate linear combination of the moments of the stochastic optimization criterion, w, would define an objective function such that optimizing its expectation produces decisions consistent with any degree of risk-sensitivity; if $\mu_j = E[w - E(w)]^j$ for $j = 2, 3 \ldots$ then $E(w) + \sum_2^k \alpha_j \mu_j$ is the expectation of any standard utility function, $U(w)$ say, given suitable values for $\alpha_j \geqslant 0$ and $k = \infty$. To introduce $E(U)$ as an objective is to specify that the decisions must follow from a von Neumann–Morgenstern utility function which associated utility values with different (risky) outcomes for w and hence the underlying target variables. Truncating the linear combination at $k = 2$ produces the familiar mean–variance decision model, and a *computable* second-order approximation to the von Neumann–Morgenstern utility function (Hughes Hallett, 1984).

An advantage of the mean–variance approach is that α_2 can be adjusted to reflect an increasing preference for avoiding risk; raising α_2 trades greater security (as indexed by $V(w)$) for less ambition (as indexed by $E(w)$) and vice versa if α_2 falls. In our case, varying α_2 traces out the trade-off between higher average earnings and greater stability of earnings.

Section 2.3 argued that price stabilization typically results in lower average prices as well as more stable prices and hence more stable but lower average earnings.[17] A mean–variance criterion provides an opportunity to reduce that conflict. In particular it deals with the objection that to reduce the variance of earnings is a symmetric objective where high prices/earnings are penalized at the same rate as low prices/earnings. Producers, of course, have no difficulty with high prices or earnings, but they do fear periods of low earnings. A mean–variance criterion allows low earnings to be penalized separately via the mean part of the rule and it sets asymmetric penalties on positive and negative deviations of prices or earnings from their desired levels through the skew component in the variance part of the rule (Hughes Hallett, 1984, p. 217–18). It is therefore possible to penalize periods of low earnings or prices, without doing so at the expense of periods of high earnings.

To see the hedging rule as a special case of risk-sensitive decision making, note that the earnings objective $y = pq$ is quadratic while the stochastic 'constraints' $p = p_f + e$ and $q - q_f = \bar{q} - q_f + v$ are linear. So far the goal has been to minimize $V(y)$ rather than to maximize $E(y)$. But we can write any quadratic objective as

$$w = \tfrac{1}{2}\{z'\,Cz + x'\,Dx\} + c'\,z + d'\,x \tag{A1}$$

where z and x are (respectively) vectors of targets and instruments stacked over $t = 1 \ldots T$ decision periods, and expressed as deviations from their desired values; and where C and D are symmetric positive definite matrices of order mT and nT respectively. A dynamic model $z_t = f(z_t, z_{t-1}, x_t, u_t)$ can be rewritten as

$$z = Rx + s \tag{A2}$$

where R is an $mT \times nT$ matrix of dynamic multipliers stacked over T periods. The decisions which minimize $V(w)$ are then

$$x^* = -(R'\,C\phi CR)^{-1}\,R'\,C[\phi(CEs + c) + s^*] \tag{A3}$$

where $\phi = E(\sigma\sigma')$ and $s^* = \tfrac{1}{2}E(\sigma\sigma'\,B\sigma)$ are the second and third moments of the disturbance terms $\sigma = s - Es$.

In our case, stability is defined by $V(y^h)$ where y^h is given in (1) and the 'constraints' on p and q^h were given in the previous paragraph. There is one decision period, and one instrument, q_f. Thus in terms of (A1)

$$w = y^h; \; z = \begin{bmatrix} p \\ q - q_f \end{bmatrix}; \; x = q_f; \; C = \begin{bmatrix} 0 & 1 \\ 1 & 0 \end{bmatrix}; \; D = 0; \; c = \begin{bmatrix} 0 \\ 0 \end{bmatrix}; \; d = p_f$$

The constraints, in the form of (A2) for an unbiased market, are

$$\begin{bmatrix} p \\ q - q_f \end{bmatrix} = \begin{bmatrix} 0 \\ -1 \end{bmatrix} q_f + \begin{bmatrix} p_f + e \\ \bar{q} + v \end{bmatrix} \quad \text{with } Es = \begin{bmatrix} p_f \\ \bar{q} \end{bmatrix} \tag{A4}$$

Hence

$$\phi = \begin{bmatrix} \sigma_p^2 & \rho\sigma_p\sigma_q \\ \rho\sigma_p\sigma_q & \sigma_q^2 \end{bmatrix} \quad \text{and} \quad s^* = E\begin{bmatrix} e^2 & v \\ e & v^2 \end{bmatrix}$$

so that $R'\,Cs^* = \mu_{21}$ follows directly. Inserting all these quantities into (A3) yields

$$q_f^* = -(1/\sigma_p^2)\left[[-\rho\sigma_p\sigma_q - \sigma_p^2]\begin{bmatrix} p_f \\ \bar{q} \end{bmatrix} - \mu_{21}\right]$$

$$= \rho p_f(\sigma_q/\sigma_p) + \bar{q} + \mu_{21}/\sigma_p^2 \tag{A5}$$

which is identical to the optimal hedging rule at (4) if $p_f = \bar{p}$.

This formulation has three important implications:
(a) Optimal hedging combined with other targets is easily undertaken by expanding z and (C, c) to accommodate extra variables and priorities. The

mean–variance criterion can be introduced in the form $E(U) = E(y^h) - \alpha V(y^h)$, $\alpha > 0$, where the minus sign is needed to preserve the concavity of the utility function. $E(y^h)$ is to be maximized, $V(y^h)$ to be minimized. The hedging rule becomes a reparameterization of (A3):

$$x^* = -(R'GR + D)^{-1} R'(Gg + d) \qquad (A6)$$

where $G = C - \alpha C' \phi C$ and $g = c - \alpha C(\phi c + s^*)$. Thus (A3) and (A5) appear as special cases when $\alpha \to \infty$, and certainty equivalence as $\alpha \to 0$.[18] By utilizing α and s^*, and by extending z, we can combine targets such as higher average earnings, price stability, avoiding low earnings or prices, along with revenue stability.

(b) Given equations of motion for p, p_f and q, $\bar{q}$, it is straightforward to reformulate (A4) and substitute the result into (A3) to give an optimal hedging rule. A word of warning however: producers will know that, at every moment, the hedging decisions which still lie in the future will be revised in light of the *latest* information or price and output shocks. That means the hedging rule which minimizes $V(y^h)$ on a static basis *is no longer optimal* for dynamic problems unless p, p_f, q, $\bar{q}$ display no systematic dynamic behaviour (Dixon and Hughes Hallett, 1988). (A3) may nevertheless deliver a good approximation.

(c) Direct comparisons with price stabilization are possible by making up (A1) from (13) rather than (1), where the instrument is λ. To make the comparison we have to replace q_f by $\lambda \bar{q}$ throughout. Placing a penalty on q via the C matrix also allows us to compare optimal hedging with price stabilization where the latter is constrained *not* to exhaust the buffer or financial stock.

NOTES

1 The players would be producers, consumers and the market authority; with any producers or consumers large enough to influence market prices picked out as individual players.

2 In fact, the theory and practice may present rather different pictures. For example, Newbery (1984) uses a theoretical model to show that, if private stocks are suboptimal, the creation of a buffer stock would change overall stockholding and hence the behaviour of market participants. But in an empirical model which attempts to capture such changes in behaviour, Ghosh et al. (1987) found that there was little effect on the ability to stabilize the Copper market.

3 See Ghosh et al. (1987) for an explicit demonstration.

4 This result is a convenient simplification since to give speculators an explicit role would mean adding extra players to the game. That would prevent any analytic comparisons. It also disposes of one of the restrictions said to limit Gilbert's (1988) analysis.

5 Gilbert (1986) demonstrates this result.

6 $MSE(y^h) = E[pq - q_f(p - p_f) - E(pq)]^2$
$\qquad = V(y^0) + q_f[\sigma_p^2 + k^2] - 2q_f[\mu_{21} + \bar{q}\sigma_p^2 + \bar{p}\rho\sigma_p\sigma_q]$
so that $q_f^* = (\bar{p}\rho\sigma_p\sigma_q + \bar{q}\sigma_p^2 + \mu_{21})/(\sigma_p^2 + k^2)$
and $MSE(y^h) = V(y^0) - q_f^{*2}(\sigma_p^2 + k^2)$.

7 This stabilization scheme is taken from Gilbert (1988), who uses (10) as the intervention rule. Nguyen (1980) examined the same problem using (12) with a log-linear model and multiplicative uncertainty.

8 Ghosh et al. (1987) examine this issue in detail.

9 Notice that by evaluating BS at $\bar{p}$ (that is, at the price level that is expected to eliminate

any excess supply), we ensure that the mean post-stabilization price equals the mean pre-stabilization price and that both equal the market clearing price level. It is easily verified that the analysis of this section still goes through if the supply and demand functions are nonlinear, *so long as* uncertainty remains additive. However it will no longer be true that $E(\bar{p}) = \bar{p}$, or that the price which is expected to clear the market (p^*) equals $\bar{p}$, or that $E(\bar{p}) = p^*$. In that case our formulae have to be extended with p^* for $\bar{p}$ and extra terms reflecting the difference between p^* and $\bar{p}$. We have not investigated the sensitivity of our results to those changes. The case of multiplicative uncertainty is more complicated. Expressions for optimal intervention and income stability are given by Nguyen (1980) but they are not directly comparable with the hedging strategy results. The crucial generalization is therefore going to be the case where uncertainties are not additive.

10 Assuming symmetric distributions, $V(y^h) - V(y^s) = \lambda(1 - \lambda)(\mu_{22} - \rho^2\sigma_p^2\sigma_q^2)$, by (19), which is maximized at $\lambda = \frac{1}{2}$. Hence Gilbert's stabilization rule which maximizes buffer stock profit also maximizes the superiority of stabilization. But it does not minimize $V(y)$ or maximize earnings stability even with normally distributed disturbances.

11 The 'core commodities' were those thought by UNCTAD to be prime candidates for stabilization. They were Wheat, Rice, Bananas, Sugar, Coffee, Cocoa, Tea, Rubber, Cotton, Jute, Wool, Iron Ore, Copper, Bauxite and Tin. (*Year-book of International Trade Statistics*, United Nations, New York, 1982, Vol. 2).

12 Testing the null hypothesis that $k = 0$, as the difference between two means, against the alternative that $k > 0$, reveals a significant bias in the Jute, Coffee and Copper markets, but not for Cocoa, at the 5% level. Representing transactions costs by a 3% real rate of interest in the null hypothesis, suggested bias in the Jute and Coffee markets but not in the Cocoa and Copper markets. But these are very crude statistical tests, and bias cannot in any case affect our conclusions (recall Section 3).

13 Since $\lambda \neq \frac{1}{2}$, stabilizing earnings is incompatible with maximizing buffer stock profits.

14. In practice, of course, short-run interventions should be computed using the kind of dynamic decision rule discussed in Ghosh *et al.* (1987).

15 These results are of course independent of any transaction costs in the futures markets. We have not attached any corresponding storage and financing costs to the price stabilization case, since such costs would be paid by the market authority and not by the producers – although they are likely to be large enough to be a significant disadvantage (Ghosh *et al.*, 1987).

16 These results follow from (4), (6), (16) and (17) together with the expression for $V(y^0)$.

17 This result follows directly from the expression for $E(y^s)$ at (14), and by (17) where $\bar{p}$ has been reduced but average pre-stabilization earnings $E(pq) = E(y^0)$ are unaffected and $\lambda > 0$.

18 This reparameterization is established and demonstrated by Hughes Hallett (1984), in an equivalent generalization for the (dynamic) price stabilization rule.

REFERENCES

Dixon, B. L. and A. J. Hughes Hallett (1988) 'Risk Sensitive Decision Making in LQG Problems: Extensions and a Clarification' Department of Agricultural Economics, University of Arkansas and Department of Economics, University of Newcastle.

Gemmill, G. (1985) 'Forward Contracts or International Buffer Stocks? A Study of their Relative Efficiencies in Stabilizing Commodity Export Earnings', *Economic Journal* **95**, 400–17.

Ghosh, S., C. L. Gilbert and A. J. Hughes Hallett (1987) *Stabilizing Speculative Commodity Markets*, Oxford, Oxford University Press.

Gilbert, C. L.(1985) 'Futures Trading and the Welfare Evaluation of Commodity Price Stabilization', *Economic Journal* **95**, 637–61.

Gilbert, C. L. (1986) 'Commodity Price Stabilization: the Massell Model and Multiplicative Disturbances', *Quarterly Journal of Economics* **100**, 635–40.

Gilbert, C. L. (1988) 'Buffer Stocks, Hedging and Risk Reduction', *Bulletin of Economic Research* **40**, 271–86.

Hughes Hallett, A. J. (1984) 'Optimal Stockpiling in a High Risk Commodity: the Case of Copper', *Journal of Economic Dynamics and Control* **8**, 211–38.

Hughes Hallett, A. J. (1986) 'Commodity Market Stabilization and North–South Income Transfers', *Journal of Development Economics* **24**, 293–316.

Hughes Hallett, A. J. and P. Ramanujam (1989a) 'Market Solutions to the Problem of Stabilizing Commodity Earnings' in L. Phlips (ed.), *Commodity, Futures and Financial Markets*, Kluwer Academic Publishers, Boston and Dordrecht, forthcoming.

Hughes Hallett, A. J. and P. Ramanujam (1989b) 'The Stabilizing Properties of Options Contracts and Target Zones', Mimeo, University of Newcastle.

Kawai, M. (1983) 'Spot and Futures Prices of Nonstorable Commodities under Rational Expectations', *Quarterly Journal of Economics* **98**, 235–54.

McKinnon, R. I. (1967) 'Futures Markets, Buffer Stocks, and Income Stability for Primary Producers', *Journal of Political Economy* **75**, 844–61.

Miller Jr. R. G. (1986) *Beyond Anova. Basics for Applied Statistics*, John Wiley & Sons.

Newbery, D. M. G. (1984) 'Commodity Price Stabilization in Imperfect or Cartelized Markets', *Econometrica* **42**, 563–78.

Newbery, D. M. G. and J. E. Stiglitz (1981) *The Theory of Commodity Price Stabilization*, Oxford, Oxford University Press.

Nguyen, D. T. (1980) 'Partial Price Stabilization and Export Earnings Instability', *Oxford Economic Papers* **32**, 340–52.

Pearson, E. S. (1963) 'Some Problems Arising in Approximating to Probability Distributions, Using Moments', *Biometrika* **50**, 95–112.

Pearson, E. S. (1965) 'Tables of Percentage Points of $\sqrt{b_1}$ and b_2 in Normal Samples; A Rounding Off' *Biometrika* **52**, 282–5.

Pearson, E. S. and H. O. Hartley (1966) *Biometrika Tables for Statisticians*, Vol. 1, University Press, Cambridge.

Townsend, R. M. (1977) 'The Eventual Failure of Price-fixing Schemes', *Journal of Economic Theory* **14**, 190–9.

Turnovsky, S. J. (1983) 'The Determination of Spot and Futures Prices with Storable Commodities', *Econometrica* **51**, 1363–87.

Wright, B. C. and J. C. Williams (1982) 'The Economic Role of Commodity Storage', *Economic Journal* **92**, 596–614.

Summary of general discussion

Christopher Gilbert said that he was less and less persuaded that the use of futures markets was a viable alternative to International Commodity Agreements as a price stabilizing measure. This is not to say that the ICAs were desirable, but that futures markets do not stabilize earnings and are not designed, nor intended to do so. For long-term stabilization the roll-over and margin costs rule out the possibility of such a stabilizing role for futures markets; they offer certainty, but not stability. As futures prices follow closely the path of spot prices the transaction costs incurred in going out on such futures contracts for several years would become enormous. Rather than futures contracts he thought that those producers who seek earnings stability via the market should use commodity bonds or commodity-contingent contracts. For example, it was noticeable that gold prices had drifted down in the last two years whereas nearly all other commodity prices had risen; this was possibly attributable to the extensive financing of gold development with commodity-linked bonds, which in turn may have had a stabilizing effect.

Marian Radetzki remarked that an awful lot of attention was being paid to the question of instability, yet the impact of instability on both micro and macroeconomic variables did not seem to indicate any adverse effects. Hughes Hallett responded by saying that in fact there are studies which demonstrate the adverse effect of instability in prices and earnings on welfare variables; they show that many a developing country faced by severe commodity price fluctuations has neither the opportunity to diversify away from them, nor the reserves to service them.[1]

Roland Herrmann noted that the results quoted referred to the stabilization of world export earnings, and not national export earnings, let alone producer export earnings. He also noted that the paper assumed away difficulties of implementation or limitations on buffer stock funds. David Newbery asked how sensitive the results of the analysis were to the assumptions of linearity and separability of risk. Hughes Hallett acknowledged all these questions as ones for research.

NOTE
1 See Dick *et al.* (1983).

REFERENCE
Dick, H., S. Gupta, T. Meyes and D. Vincent (1983) 'The short-run impact of fluctuating commodity prices on three developing economies: Colombia, Ivory Coast and Kenya', *World Development* 11, 405–16.

9 Primary Commodity Prices and Exchange-Rate Volatility*

PAUL KOFMAN, JEAN-MARIE VIAENE and
CASPER G. de VRIES

1 Introduction

It is well known that primary commodity prices show large fluctuations. Their causes and effects have been a matter of interest for a long time. Agricultural economists have focused upon firm-level aspects (like producer's income, planting decisions and the like) whereas development economists directed their attention towards macroeconomic aspects (e.g., welfare measures, changing terms of trade). Crucial in most studies is the question how to lessen the volatility of prices. Futures markets for commodities are usually found to be a stabilizing factor in these markets. Unfortunately, the investigation of interactions between markets (influencing primary commodities trading) has been neglected. A general equilibrium framework where futures prices themselves become endogenous is difficult to deal with. Most analysis in this direction, like Kawai (1983), is too general to provide insight into the specific effects of volatility on output and trade.

Several empirical studies like Chu and Morrison (1984), suggest a large number of economic indicators showing substantial correlation with commodity price volatility. How can one incorporate all uncertainties influencing the primary commodity market into one model? We chose to link the commodity market with the currency market, following Kawai and Zilcha (1986), as these seem to be the two variables of foremost interest. Since most primary commodities are traded internationally and are usually denominated in a few currencies, the exchange rate is believed to be one of the main factors of importance in production decisions.

A typical primary commodity market is often made up of four participants: producers, dealers, speculators and consumers. Most models treat the consumer as a rather passive agent for approximations in comparing welfare properties as far as these consumers are concerned.[1] The introduction of a firm consuming the commodity as an intermediate product, as done by Viaene (1988), is free of these problems. Since very few primary commodities are consumed directly, it also is an empirical improvement.

The forementioned papers by Kawai and Zilcha (1986), and Viaene (1988), present theoretical models dealing with the problem of two-sided uncertainty in the primary commodity market. Since most of primary production is traded internationally, traditional analysis taking only price uncertainty into consideration falls short of empirical facts. Most primary commodity producers are confronted with simultaneous uncertainty, in price and in the exchange rate. Producers and merchants being risk-averse therefore hedge themselves in the forward market for foreign currency as well as in the futures market for the commodity.

Our theoretical model consists of a home producer also acting as merchant of his produce, a foreign primary-consuming producer and a currency speculator. One good, the primary commodity, is produced and traded. To avoid undue complications, no factor markets have been included. The solutions for the producing and consuming firms reflect the theorems of separation and full double hedging as introduced by Kawai and Zilcha (1986). The first theorem states that the production and consumption decisions are determined solely by the futures- and/or forward price[2] while the amount hedged is determined by the utility function and the probability distribution of the random variables. The latter theorem which applies to all three agents, says that under rational expectations the level of output will be equal to the amount hedged in the futures market. In turn, this amount hedged will be fully covered in the forward foreign exchange market. These solutions are quite easy to analyze. Nevertheless, we also analyze other potential solutions of our model. Empirical research seems to be in conformity with this approach.

This paper is published in a period in which the emergence of futures markets seems to have stagnated. The promising risk-reducing aspects of these markets for primary commodity producers are surely underexploited. One important reason for this shortcoming may be found in the interaction between currency and commodity markets. Since most important futures markets are situated in a few countries, these countries acquired some kind of exclusive trading rights on futures markets. Unfortunately, most primary commodities are produced outside these consuming countries. Whereas consumers are able to trade spot as well as forward in their own currencies, the producers have to cope with exchange rate risk.

Previous studies of the welfare aspects of futures markets, e.g. Turnovsky and Campbell (1985), derived their results in isolation from the international trade context. We think that it is extremely important to investigate the links between the foreign exchange market and the commodity futures market. Only in such a way may it become possible to assess the importance of a well-functioning forward exchange market for countries relying on the production of primary commodities. So far, forward exchange markets for non-OECD countries remain quite scarce. It is argued that this is caused by the instability of most non-OECD currencies. We are of the opinion that this same instability might have some roots in the inaccessibility of futures markets for these countries. Thus, some policy oriented preconditions should be established for a smoothly operating futures market.

The paper proceeds as follows. Section 2 gives an outline of our model with the optimization results for all agents. These partial equilibria are transformed into an equilibrium framework with explicit market clearing conditions for the spot, the forward, and the futures markets. This leads to solutions for the forward and futures prices in terms of risk premia over the random exchange rate and the random commodity price. In Section 3 the analytical results are presented as well as a graphical exposition. In turn, this allows us to assess (Section 4) the influence of variability in both prices as well as changing correlation between the two. Some empirical results are presented confirming our theoretical findings. Section 5 ends our paper with some concluding remarks.

2   Partial solutions (the optimizing approach)

Each agent maximizes his/her expected utility. The following symbols will be used throughout our exposition:

Π = Profit for producers, consumers, speculators
$\tilde{p}$ = Random price of primary commodity X
$\tilde{w}$ = Random domestic price of foreign currency
X = Primary commodity production
P_t = Actual spot market price at time t
m = Use of primary product per unit of final product
H = Amount of forward foreign currency bought
K = Volume of commodity futures bought
I = Inventory holdings
Y = Final good production
$E(\cdot)$ = Expectations operator
$\text{Var}(\cdot)$, $\text{Cov}(\cdot)$ = (Co-)variance operator
U = Utility
F = Forward rate of foreign currency
T = Futures price of primary commodity
q = Price of final good

2.1   *Producer cum merchant*

One representative out of n_f identical producers of primary commodity X, has a profit function Π^f and a specified risk attitude embodied in a coefficient α of absolute risk version. Our producer takes his production decisions one period in advance. His output plans will generate a certain output X_{t+1}. At decision time the producer is concerned with price and, since prices are denominated in the foreign currency, exchange-rate uncertainty. His profit function reads:

$$\Pi^f_{t+1} = \tilde{w}\tilde{p}X_{t+1} - \tfrac{1}{2}X^2_{t+1} + (\tilde{w} - F_t)H^f_t + \tilde{w}(\tilde{p} - T_t)K^f_t \qquad (1)$$

The first term $(\tilde{w}\tilde{p}X_{t+1})$ gives his return to be received at time $t + 1$, that is uncertain in price and exchange rate. The producer incurs his costs according to a quadratic cost function, $\tfrac{1}{2}X^2_{t+1}$. His profits are denominated in local currency. It is assumed that the producer has monetary habitat in local currency. He can buy an amount H^f of foreign currency in the forward market to be delivered at time $t + 1$. If foreign currency is bought forward, $H > 0$. If foreign currency is sold forward, as will typically be the case for the producer, $H^f < 0$. A purchaser of forward currency will make a profit if the uncertain spot rate exceeds the locked-in forward rate and vice versa. In the case of the commodity, it can be bought or sold forward. If commodities are bought forward, $K > 0$; if they are sold forward, as will typically be the case for the producer, $K^f < 0$. Nevertheless, there is a difference since the forward currency market is situated in the producing country while the futures market[3] is situated abroad.

It is assumed that the producer maximizes his expected utility:

$$EU^f_{t+1} = \int_0^\infty \int_0^\infty U^f(\Pi^f(\tilde{w}\tilde{p}))f_f(\tilde{w}, \tilde{p})\,d\tilde{w}\,d\tilde{p} \qquad (2)$$

where $U^f(\cdot)$ is a strictly concave von Neumann–Morgenstern utility function characterized by the measure of absolute risk aversion [4] α and f_f is the subjective joint probability density function of $\tilde{w}$ and $\tilde{p}$. The first two moments are assumed to exist such that we can write the following equations:

$$E\Pi^f_{t+1} = X_{t+1}E[\tilde{w}\tilde{p}] - \tfrac{1}{2}X^2_{t+1} + H^f_t(E[\tilde{w}] - F_t)$$
$$+ K^f_t(E[\tilde{w}\tilde{p}] - T_tE[\tilde{w}]) \qquad (2a)$$

$$\mathrm{Var}\,\Pi^f_{t+1} = (X_{t+1} + K^f_t)^2\mathrm{Var}[\tilde{w}\tilde{p}] + (H^f_t - T_tK^f_t)^2\mathrm{Var}[\tilde{w}]$$
$$+ 2(X_{t+1} + K^f_t)(H^f_t - T_tK^f_t)\mathrm{Cov}[\tilde{w}\tilde{p}, \tilde{w}] \qquad (2b)$$

The following short-hand notation has been used:

$$
\begin{array}{lll}
E[\tilde{w}\tilde{p}] = \mu & \mathrm{Var}[\tilde{w}\tilde{p}] = \phi^2 & \mathrm{Cov}[\tilde{w}\tilde{p}, \tilde{w}] = \rho\phi\sigma \\
E[\tilde{w}] = \epsilon & \mathrm{Var}[\tilde{w}] = \sigma^2 & \mathrm{Cov}[\tilde{w}, \tilde{p}] = \rho^*\nu\sigma \\
E[\tilde{p}] = \zeta & \mathrm{Var}[\tilde{p}] = \nu^2 &
\end{array}
$$

Traditional analysis, of this kind, only takes the second covariance expression, $\rho^* v\sigma$, into account. The product of $\tilde{w}$ by $\tilde{p}$, appearing in the producer's profit function is an extension of these traditional analyses. The covariance term $\mathrm{Cov}(\tilde{w}\tilde{p}, \tilde{w})$, therefore, has a different interpretation than the traditional one.

Approximating $U^f(\cdot)$ by a second-order Taylor expansion at μ and maximizing with respect to the endogenous variables X_{t+1}, H_t^f and K_t^f leads to the following first-order conditions shown in matrix notation.

$$
\begin{bmatrix}
1 + \alpha\phi^2 & \alpha\rho\phi\sigma & \alpha\phi^2 - \alpha\rho\phi\sigma T \\
\alpha\rho\phi\sigma & \alpha\sigma^2 & \alpha\rho\phi\sigma - \alpha\sigma^2 T \\
\alpha\phi^2 - \alpha\rho\phi\sigma T & \alpha\rho\phi\sigma - \alpha\sigma^2 T & \alpha\phi^2 + \alpha\sigma^2 T^2 - 2\alpha\rho\phi\sigma T
\end{bmatrix}
\begin{bmatrix}
X_{t+1} \\
H_t^f \\
K_t^f
\end{bmatrix}
$$

$$
=
\begin{bmatrix}
\mu \\
\epsilon - F \\
\mu - T\epsilon
\end{bmatrix}
$$

The determinant of this matrix is easily calculated: $\mathrm{Det} = \alpha^2(1 - \rho^2)\sigma^2\phi^2$ and is positive if $\tilde{w}$ and $\tilde{w}\tilde{p}$ are less than perfectly correlated, $|\rho| < 1$. By Cramer's rule we can solve for X, H and K:

$$X_{t+1} = F_t T_t \tag{3}$$

$$K_t^f = - X_{t+1} + \frac{\mu - T_t F_t}{\alpha(1 - \rho^2)\phi^2} - \frac{\rho(\epsilon - F_t)}{\alpha(1 - \rho^2)\phi\sigma} \tag{4}$$

$$H_t^f = T_t K_t^f + \frac{\epsilon - F_t}{\alpha(1 - \rho^2)\phi^2} - \frac{\rho(\mu - T_t F_t)}{\alpha(1 - \rho^2)\phi\sigma} \tag{5}$$

The producer simultaneously chooses a production level for export, as the total production is exported, and hedges on the futures and forward markets. The full double hedge occurs when rational expectations assure that ϵ and μ are equal to respectively F and TF, i.e. so that the two risk premia are zero. Rewriting equation (5), we get an expression for $[H_t^f - T_t K_t^f]$ which is the amount of speculation. This is the amount of forward currency a producer holds in excess of his future commodity sales.

2.2   Primaries demanding firms

In analogy with the producers, we have a representative foreign firm, out of n_c identical ones, using the storable commodity X as an intermediate input for producing final good Y. It has two possible means of obtaining this input: first, holding inventories (in relation to a desirable inventory level I^r) and second, hedging on the futures market for commodity X. With

K^c positive, this means buying the commodity forward to be delivered at time $t + 1$. Since the primary commodity is quoted in the demanding firm's currency, the firm's profit function is only affected by commodity price randomness. Potential exchange rate risk is eliminated altogether. It is assumed that final good price q is given and constant for the firm. Its profit function looks like:

$$\Pi^c_{t+1} = qY_{t+1} - m\tilde{p}Y_{t+1} - \tfrac{1}{2}Y^2_{t+1} + K^c_t(\tilde{p} - T_t) \\ + I_t(\tilde{p} - rP_t) - \tfrac{1}{2}(I_t - I^c)^2 \tag{6}$$

where $(r - 1)$ is the foreign interest rate. Inventory holding is subject to a quadratic cost function over the gap between actual and desired levels. In addition to this cost, the firm has quadratic production costs. Both are incurred in its own currency. The firm maximizes expected utility:

$$EU^c_{t+1} = \int_0^\infty U^c(\Pi^c(\tilde{p}))f_c(\tilde{p}) d\tilde{p} \tag{7}$$

where $U^c(\cdot)$ is the utility function characterized by the measure of absolute risk aversion α and f_c is the subjective probabiity density function of $\tilde{p}$. The first two moments are assumed to exist such that we can write the following equations:

$$E\Pi^c_{t+1} = qY_{t+1} - mY_{t+1}E[\tilde{p}] - \tfrac{1}{2}Y^2_{t+1} + K^c_t(E[\tilde{p}] - T_t) \\ + I_t(E[\tilde{p}] - rP_t) - \tfrac{1}{2}(I_t - I^c)^2 \tag{7a}$$

and

$$\text{Var}\,\Pi^c_{t+1} = (K^c_t + I_t - mY_{t+1})\text{Var}[\tilde{p}] \tag{7b}$$

Approximating $U^c(\cdot)$ by a second-order Taylor expansion around ζ and maximizing with respect to the consumer's decision variables Y_{t+1}, I_t and K_t gives the following partial solutions:

$$Y_{t+1} = q - mT_t \tag{8}$$

$$I_t = I^c + (T_t - rP_t) \tag{9}$$

$$K^c_t = (mY_{t+1} - I^c) - (T_t - rP_t) + \left(\frac{\zeta - T_t}{\alpha v^2}\right) \tag{10}$$

The consumer's production decision is a function of the futures price and once more stresses the separation theorem. Inventory holding contains a quantity and a price part. If the future price T exceeds the spot price times r (one plus the interest rate which is the opportunity cost) it becomes attractive to hold inventories in portfolio. The solution for K^c stresses the purely speculative nature of futures trading by the demanding firm.

2.3   Currency speculators

Currency speculators are situated in the home country. Domestic producers have no access to foreign forward currency markets. Some kind of government institution can however act as the counterpart, taking over currency risk. Out of n_s identical domestic speculators, in which $n_s \geq 1$, we choose a representative currency speculator who has the following profit function, in domestic currency:

$$\Pi^s_{t+1} = i\Pi^s_t + (\tilde{w} - F_t)H^s_t \tag{11}$$

This speculator only operates on the forward currency market and, as such, is the counterpart of the other forward market actor, the producer in our model. The speculator maximizes expected utility of future wealth:

$$EU^s_{t+1} = \int_0^\infty U^s(\Pi^s(\tilde{w}))f_s(\tilde{w})\,d\tilde{w} \tag{12}$$

where $U^s(\cdot)$ is the utility function characterized by the measure of absolute risk aversion α and f_s is the subjective probability density function of $\tilde{w}$. The first two moments are assumed to exist such that we can write the following equations:

$$E\Pi^s_{t+1} = (i)\Pi^s_t + H^s_t(E[\tilde{w}] - F_t) \tag{12a}$$

and

$$\text{Var}\,\Pi^s_{t+1} = (H^s_t)^2\,\text{Var}[\tilde{w}] \tag{12b}$$

Approximating $U^s(\cdot)$ by a second-order Taylor expansion at ϵ and maximizing with respect to H^s_t gives the optimal amount of forward currency:

$$H^s_t = \frac{\epsilon - F_t}{\alpha\sigma^2} \tag{13}$$

confirming the purely speculative character of this agent.

3   Solving for prices in a general equilibrium framework

Having described each agent's behaviour, in terms of futures and forward prices, we can now turn to the determination of these future prices. Figure 9.1 depicts our model's transaction flows. For each market, supply and demand are confronted in such a way to establish market clearing

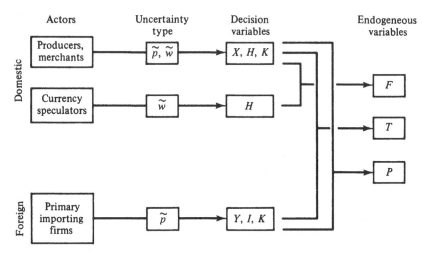

Figure 9.1 Flow chart

equilibria. To that end, we first aggregate the above obtained market relations for fixed numbers of our three agents, i.e. n_f producers, n_c demanding firms and n_s speculators.

In the following sections, Figure 9.1 is explained in detail. One by one, starting with the spot market and proceeding with the forward and futures markets, these relations are presented in an integrated way. This will enable us to analyze graphically what happens when the parameters of the model are allowed to change. The relevant variables for which the model is solved are defined as follows:

$$R = \epsilon - F_t$$

$$R_q = \mu - T_t F_t$$

$$A^* = T_t - rP_t$$

Here, R is the forward risk premium. Hence, we want to know F_t given ϵ. R_q is the two-sided commodity risk premium. We want to know $T_t F_t$ given μ. These two risk premia reflect the *fee* a hedging agent is willing to pay to agents taking speculative *open* positions. The latter are counterparts to the forward hedging. A^* is the excess commodity return. Hence, we want to know P_t for the solved level of T_t.

We employ some useful expressions. First of all we have an expression for the expected value of the term $[\tilde{w}\tilde{p}]$:

$$\mu = \text{Cov}[\tilde{w}, \tilde{p}] + \epsilon\zeta = \rho^* \nu\sigma + \epsilon\zeta \tag{14}$$

where ρ^* $(\neq \rho)$ is the correlation coefficient between the exchange rate and the price. Next, we derive the relation between the different risk premia:

$$F_t R_q^* = R_q - \zeta R - \rho^* \nu\sigma \tag{15}$$

where R_q and R are already introduced and R_q^* is the commodity risk premium:

$$R_q^* = \zeta - T_t \tag{16}$$

3.1 Spot market equilibrium

The aggregated speculative demands are obtained from equations (4) and (10)

$$S_f = \frac{n_f(\mu - T_t F_t)}{\alpha\phi^2(1 - \rho^2)} - \frac{n_f\rho(\epsilon - F_t)}{\alpha\sigma\phi(1 - \rho^2)} \tag{4a}$$

expressing the speculative aggregate demand for commodity futures by producers, or the part of production which is not covered in the futures market and thus arrives on the spot market. And,

$$S_c = n_c\left(\frac{\zeta - T_t}{\alpha\nu^2}\right) - n_c(T_t - rP_t) \tag{10a}$$

which is the aggregate speculative demand for commodity futures by the demanding firms, or the demand which is being exerted on the spot market. Being more specific, this is a demand for futures at time period t which will be sold at the future period $t + 1$ on the spot market to realize the expected profits. Hence, the spot market for the primary commodity is cleared at the current date as follows:

$$S_f(t - 1) + S_c(t - 1) = n_c I_t \tag{17}$$

Making use of equation (9) gives our final expression

$$A^* = T_t - rP_t = \frac{1}{n_c}[S_f(t - 1) + S_c(t - 1)] - I^c \tag{18}$$

Given that the variables on the right hand side are predetermined, the difference between T_t and rP_t remains constant. Thus, a change in T_t leads to a change in rP_t in the same direction. Figure 9.2 has been constructed with this information: the amount NS shows the right hand side of equation (18), or the net supply of storables on the spot market.

3.2 Currency forward market clearing

Recalling that producers and speculators make up the domestic forward currency market, we have the following market clearing condition:

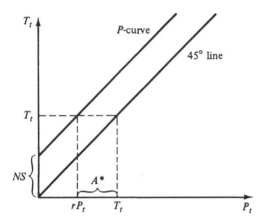

Figure 9.2 Spot market equilibrium

$$n_s H_t^s + n_f H_t^f = 0 \tag{19}$$

The substitution of equations (5) and (13), making use of (4) gives a relationship between $F_t T_t$, F_t and X_{t+1}, where, in order to reach some simple results it is convenient to fix the initial values for T_t and F_t at unity,

$$
F_t T_t - \mu = \left[\frac{\alpha(1 - \rho^2)\,\phi^2\,\sigma}{\rho\phi - \sigma} \right] X_{t+1}
$$
$$
+ \left[\frac{n_s(1 - \rho^2)\,\phi^2 + n_f\phi(\phi - \rho\sigma)}{n_f\sigma(\rho\phi - \sigma)} \right] (F_t - \epsilon) \tag{20}
$$

Leaving X explicit is useful to assess the effect of a change in the supply of storables on forward prices F and T. What this last expression indicates is that for a given R_q that is equal to zero, an increase in X (and, as such, an increase in future returns in domestic currency) leads to an unexpected appreciation in the forward rate F so as to maintain the exchange market in equilibrium. The necessary condition is that:

$$\phi > \rho\sigma \tag{21}$$

Intuitively we should have expected a positive value for the correlation coefficient ρ. If the correlation coefficient ρ^* is equal to zero (or $\mathrm{Cov}[\tilde{w}, \tilde{p}] = 0$) necessarily the correlation coefficient ρ is positive (or $\mathrm{Cov}[\tilde{w}\tilde{p}, \tilde{w}] > 0$). Table 9.1 gives an idea of the *ex post* value for ρ. For most commodities, the correlation coefficient is indeed positive. The model is, however, capable of analyzing volatility and shocks with negative values for ρ as well. It is truly a crucial factor in assessing the effects of these scenarios. Table 9.2 gives the values for standard deviations ϕ and σ for

Primary Commodity	1957.I–1971.IV	1972.I–1979.IV	1980.I–1988.II
Bananas (*Ecuador*)	0.319	n.a.	0.988
Bauxite (*Guyana*)	0.352[a]	0.925	0.823[b]
Beef (*Argentina*)	n.a.	0.948	0.976[c]
Butter (*New Zealand*)	0.248	0.828	0.433
Coal (*Australia*)	− 0.557[d]	0.752	0.570[c]
Cocoa Beans (*Brazil*)	n.a.	0.926	0.999[e]
Cotton (*Egypt*)	0.688	0.795	n.a.
Iron ore (*Brazil*)	n.a.	0.988	0.999[e]
Manganese (*India*)	0.669[f]	0.798	0.909
Newsprint (*Finland*)	0.971[g]	0.011	0.761[h]
Petroleum (*Venezuela*)	0.869[i]	− 0.534	0.717[j]
Plywood (*Philippines*)	0.925[k]	0.400	0.860
Rice (*Thailand*)	− 0.458	− 0.650	− 0.663
Rubber (*Malaysia*)	0.147	− 0.720	− 0.303[c]
Tea (*Sri Lanka*)	n.a.	0.953[l]	0.589[j]
Tin (*Malaysia*)	0.103	− 0.677	− 0.885
Wheat (*Australia*)	0.316[g]	0.219	0.012
Zinc (*Bolivia*)	n.a.	n.a.	0.994[m]

Table 9.1 *Ex post* **correlation coefficients (ρ) between domestic currency prices and the exchange rate**

Data source: International Financial Statistics.

[a]1969.I	[b]1986.IV	[c]1987.II	[d]1966.III	[e]1987.IV	[f]1960.I	[g]1965.I
[h]1987.I	[i]1960.I	[j]1988.I	[k]1963.I	[l]1973.I	[m]1982.IV	

Primary Commodity	1957.I–1971.IV		1972.I–1979.IV		1980.I–1988.II	
	ϕ	σ	ϕ	σ	ϕ	σ
Bananas (Ecuador)	0.153	2.750	n.a.	n.a.	12.043	66.957
Bauxite (Guyana)	6.330[a]	0.025	103.103	0.198	66.794[b]	0.661
Beef (Argentina)	n.a.	n.a.	0.001	0.0001	0.680[c]	0.521
Butter (New Zealand)	0.038	0.077	0.133	0.123	0.212	0.342
Coal (Australia)	0.935[d]	0.014	12.296	0.079	6.862[c]	0.234
Cocoa Beans (Brazil)	n.a.	n.a.	0.013	0.008	13.895[e]	16.485
Cotton (Egypt)	0.047	0.040	0.226	0.101	n.a.	n.a.
Iron ore (Brazil)	n.a.	n.a.	0.219	0.008	896.310[e]	39.041
Manganese (India)	66.895[f]	1.338	299.785	0.639	184.116	0.473
Newsprint (Finland)	54.872[g]	0.474	331.787	0.198	158.427[h]	0.832
Petroleum (Venezuela)	1.215[i]	0.547	19.590	0.020	47.820[j]	3.717
Plywood (Philippines)	1.310[k]	1.019	3.864	0.323	22.593	5.557
Rice (Thailand)	605.488	0.134	2,287.704	0.214	1,688.759	2.196
Rubber (Malaysia)	0.179	0.028	0.255	0.184	0.203[c]	0.134
Tea (Sri Lanka)	n.a.	n.a.	4.874[l]	3.949	6.891[j]	4.381
Tin (Malaysia)	0.903	0.028	3.480	0.184	3.207	0.134
Wheat (Australia)	0.086[g]	0.012	0.855	0.079	0.653	0.234
Zinc (Bolivia)	n.a.	n.a.	n.a.	n.a.	0.365[m]	0.978

Table 9.2 Standard deviations of price/exchange rate and exchange rate

Data source: International Financial Statistics.

[a]1969.I	[b]1986.IV	[c]1987.II	[d]1966.III	[e]1987.IV	[f]1960.I	[g]1965.I
[h]1987.I	[i]1960.I	[j]1988.I	[k]1963.I	[l]1973.I	[m]1982.IV	

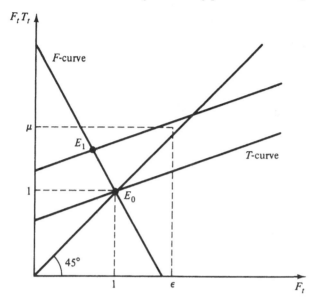

Figure 9.3 Forward/futures market equilibrium

the same commodities. Condition (21) is met for every commodity except for bananas (all periods), cocoa beans (last period) and zinc (last period).

Substituting in equation (20) the producers' solution for X, equation (3) and the expressions for R and R_q we get:

$$F_t T_t = \Pi_1 \mu + \Pi_2 (F_t - \epsilon) \tag{22}$$

where

$$\Pi_1 = (\rho \phi \sigma - \sigma^2)/[\rho \phi \sigma - \sigma^2 - \alpha(1 - \rho^2)\sigma^2 \phi^2] < 0$$

$$\Pi_2 = [((n_s(1 - \rho^2)/n_f) + 1)\phi^2 - \rho \phi \sigma]/[\rho \phi \sigma - \sigma^2 - \alpha(1 - \rho^2)\sigma^2 \phi^2] < 0$$

In Figure 9.3, the relation between FT and T is represented by the downward sloping F-curve. Its slope depends upon the value of Π_2, which is negative if:

$$\rho \phi \sigma - \sigma^2 - \alpha(1 - \rho^2)\sigma^2 \phi^2 < 0$$

which is likely to hold for large values of α, negative values of ρ or low positive values of ρ. A sufficient condition is:

$$\sigma \geq \phi \quad \text{and} \quad \rho < 1$$

3.3   Commodity futures market clearing

The commodity futures market clearing condition reads:

$$n_c K_t^c + n_f K_t^f = 0 \tag{23}$$

Substituting equations (4) and (10) and making use of equations (3) and (8) leads to the following solution for $F_t T_t$:
where

$$F_t T_t = \Omega_1 \mu - \Omega_2 R + \Omega_3 [n_c m(q - m\zeta) - [S_f(t-1) + S_c(t-1)]] \\ - \Omega_4 \rho^* v\sigma \tag{24}^5$$

where

$$\Omega_1 = [n_f v^2 + n_c(1 + \alpha m^2 v^2) \phi^2(1 - \rho^2)]/\Lambda_1$$

$$\Omega_2 = [n_f \rho v^2 + n_c(1 + \alpha m^2 v^2) \sigma\phi(1 - \rho^2)]\phi/\sigma\Lambda_1$$

$$\Omega_3 = \alpha(1 - \rho^2)\phi^2 v^2/\Lambda_1$$

$$\Omega_4 = n_c(1 + \alpha m^2 v^2)\phi^2(1 - \rho^2)/\alpha v^2 \Lambda_1$$

$$\Lambda_1 = n_f \alpha(1 - \rho^2)\phi^2 v^2 + n_f v^2 + n_c(1 + \alpha m^2 v^2)\phi^2(1 - \rho^2)$$

Note that in order to arrive at equation (24), Y_{t+1} in equation (8) has been rewritten as,

$$Y_{t+1} = q + m(\zeta - T_t) - m\zeta \tag{8a}$$

By means of equation (24) we can now draw the T-curve in Figure 9.3. Slope-coefficient Ω_2 is positive if its numerator is positive (the denominator is). This is the case for $\rho \geqslant 0$. For $\rho \to -1$, the slope of T tends to be small and even negative.

Equation (24) can also be presented in a slightly different way, by not substituting for $X_{t+1} = F_t T_t$:

$$F_t T_t = \mu - \Delta_1 R + \Delta_2 \Big[n_c m(q - m\zeta) - n_f X_{t+1}$$

$$- [S_f(t-1) + S_c(t-1)] \Big] - \Delta_3 \rho^* v\sigma \tag{24a}$$

where

$$\Delta_1 = [n_f \rho v^2 + n_c(1 + \alpha m^2 v^2) \sigma\phi(1 - \rho^2)]\phi/\sigma\Lambda_2$$

$$\Delta_2 = \alpha(1 - \rho^2)\phi^2 v^2/\Lambda_2$$

$$\Delta_3 = n_c(1 + \alpha m^2 v^2)\phi^2(1 - \rho^2)/\alpha v^2 \Lambda_2$$

$$\Lambda_2 = n_f v^2 + n_c(1 + \alpha m^2 v^2)\phi^2(1 - \rho^2)$$

Since Δ_2 is positive for $0 < |\rho| < 1$, the output effect is in conformity with what we might have expected, in that an increase in commodity supply leads, *ceteris paribus*, to a drop in commodity prices. From equation (24a) we can immediately read off the elasticity of commodity price with respect to a change in the exchange rate as given by Δ_1. Its sign depends upon ρ and several features are worth of note:

$$1 > \rho > 0 \quad \Rightarrow 1 > \Delta_1 > 0$$

$$\rho = 1 \quad \Rightarrow \Delta_1 > 1 \quad \text{for } \sigma < \phi$$

$$-1 < \rho < 0 \Rightarrow \Delta_1 \text{ can become negative for high negative}$$
$$\text{values of } \rho$$

$$\rho = -1 \quad \Rightarrow \Delta_1 = \frac{-\phi}{\sigma} < -1 \quad \text{for } \sigma < \phi$$

Where this elasticity will be positive with a positive correlation coefficient it will become negative when this correlation coefficient is negative. We know already that for $|\rho| = 1$, the model does not offer an equilibrium solution. As a matter of fact, with $\rho = 1$, the two curves in Figure 9.3 (F and T) will run parallel. Clearly this is a non-feasible solution.

3.4   Simultaneous equilibrium on forward and futures markets

Confronting equations (20) and (24), gives a unique solution for F_t which can be substituted in either of these two equations to solve for $F_t T_t$. In Figure 9.3 we find this solution at point E_0. Here, we have $F_t = F_t T_t = 1$, hence $T_t = 1$. No particular assumptions are made about μ and ϵ. We do, however, assume that $\zeta = 1$. The latter is consistent with $\mu \neq \epsilon$ since $\mu = \rho^* v\sigma + \epsilon\zeta$. If $\zeta = 1$ and $\epsilon > \mu$ then we have $\rho^* v \sigma < 0$. To have this latter term being positive, ϵ should lie to the left of the 45° line. This line indicates whether, after an exogenous shock, $F_t T_t$ moves more than F_t. This is equivalent to an increase in T_t, which in turn has similar implications for P_t.

4   Volatility and shock effects

Having constructed a workable framework in Section 3, we can now proceed to analyze some effects of demand shocks, exchange-rate volatility and changes in expectations. The latter two have to do with the influence the exchange rate exerts on primary commodity prices. In these cases, parameters of importance are ϵ, the expected exchange rate and σ, the exchange rate's standard deviation. We will study the effect of an increase in ϵ (expected depreciation) and a decrease in σ (tending towards zero).[6]

	Base[a]	$\Delta\epsilon = 10\%$	$\Delta q = 10\%$	$\Delta\zeta = 10\%$	$\alpha = 0.5$
F	1.000	1.269	0.975	1.135	1.287
T	1.000	0.565	1.086	0.605	0.586
X	1.000	0.716	1.058	0.686	0.755
Y	0.500	0.718	0.557	0.698	0.707
	Base[a]	$\sigma = 0.01^b$	$\sigma = 0.01^c$	$\nu = 0.01^c$	$\rho = 0.9$
F	1.000	1.492	1.492	1.161	1.490
T	1.000	0.770	1.047	0.749	1.101
X	1.000	1.149	1.548	0.870	1.641
Y	0.500	0.615	0.482	0.626	0.450

Table 9.3 Impact on prices, output and demand of shocks and changes in volatility

[a]Base parameter set: $\alpha = 1$, $m = 0.5$, $n_c = n_f = n_s = 1$, $\sigma = \nu = 1$, $\phi = 3$, $\rho = 0.5$, $\rho^* = 0$, $A^* = 1$.
[b]Without parameter dependency.
[c]With parameter dependency: $\phi = f(\overset{+}{\nu}, \overset{+}{\sigma}, ..)$.

4.1   Demand shock

Figure 9.3 has been used to analyze the effect of a demand shock. Point E_1 shows the result of an increase in the demand of consuming firms. The effect can be measured by interpreting equation (24). Demand is positively related to $F_t T_t$. This will shift the T-curve upwards, leading to a decrease (appreciation) in the forward currency rate. Since it lies to the left of the 45° line, the future commodity rate will rise (compensating the decline in F_t more than proportionally). This leads, according to the one-to-one relation in Figure 9.2, to a rise in the spot commodity price. It is also obvious that, since $F_t T_t$ rises, production X_{t+1} will also rise. Table 9.3, second column of the upper panel, shows the simulation results of a ten percent increase in the final good price q. The chosen base parameter set assures that production X rises even though F falls below 1. Final production Y rises, because the rise in T does not completely offset the original stimulus in q.

4.2   Expected depreciation

Figure 9.4 gives the effect of an expected depreciation of the exchange rate. According to equation (20), where the forward currency market is in equilibrium, the will lead to an outward shift of the F-curve. This is caused

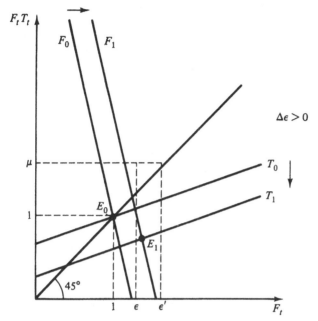

Figure 9.4 A change in the expected exchange rate

by an increase in speculation on the forward market (by speculators as well as producers). Since the futures market is not isolated from the exchange-rate expectation (the producer solution for K), we see what happens by considering equation (24). A downward shift of the T-curve will occur. The combined result is depicted by equilibrium E_1. It is clear that F_t, the forward currency rate, rises. The effect on $F_t T_t$ is ambiguous since we cannot be sure of the amount of each change. Nevertheless, we know that T_t will have decreased since the new equilibrium lies to the right of the 45° line.[7] In Table 9.3, first column of the upper panel, this scenario has been simulated with a ten percent increase in the expected exchange rate ϵ. Production, X, falls since the rise in F is more than offset by a fall in T. This latter fall leads to a substantial rise in final production Y. A somewhat similar expectation change has been simulated for the commodity price, ζ. The results are, though somewhat lower, essentially the same.[8]

4.3 *Decreased volatility*

Figure 9.5 gives an idea of what happens when volatility of the exchange rate declines to zero. Taking the limit ($\sigma \to 0$) is necessary to assess this effect. When this is done in the forward currency market we get a very simple expression:

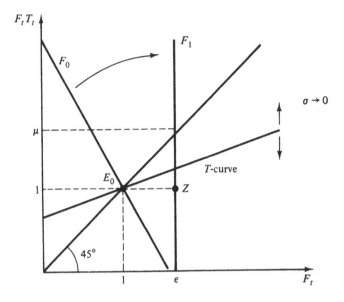

Figure 9.5 A change in the exchange rate's variance

$$\lim_{\sigma \to 0} F_t T_t = \lim_{\sigma \to 0} \Pi_1 \mu + \lim_{\sigma \to 0} \Pi_2 (F_t - \epsilon)$$

leads to

$$F_t = \epsilon$$

or a vertical F-curve as shown in Figure 9.5. When we take the limit ($\sigma \to 0$) of the futures market equilibrium condition, we get,

$$\lim_{\sigma \to 0} F_t T_t = \lim_{\sigma \to 0} \Omega_1 \mu + \lim_{\sigma \to 0} \Omega_2 (F_t - \epsilon) + \lim_{\sigma \to 0} \Omega_3 A^* + \lim_{\sigma \to 0} \Omega_4 \rho^* \nu \sigma$$

It is obvious that it consists of a composition of effects. There are several forces which work in different directions. We are interested whether the new equilibrium E_1 lies above or below point Z, because of the new F-curve at $F_t = \epsilon$:

$$\lim_{\sigma \to 0} \Omega_1 < \Omega_1 \qquad \Rightarrow \text{ direction towards } E_1 \text{ below } Z$$

$$\lim_{\sigma \to 0} \Omega_2 \qquad \Rightarrow \text{ not relevant}$$

$$\lim_{\sigma \to 0} \Omega_3 > \Omega_3 \qquad \Rightarrow \text{ direction towards } E_1 \text{ above } Z$$

$$\lim_{\sigma \to 0} \Omega_4 \rho^* \nu \sigma = 0 \Rightarrow \text{ direction towards } E_1 \text{ above } Z \text{ (for } \rho^* > 0)$$

The T-curve will rotate upon itself (become steeper) and shifts up or down depending upon the various forces at work. So far, the only conclusion we may draw is the rise in F_t at the new equilibrium. This scenario has been tested in two ways, with and without parameter dependency. Taking account of the fact that ϕ is a function of ν and σ, changes in one of these has repercussion effects in our simulations. In the lower panel of Table 9.3, we report for both possibilities. The rotation of the F-curve takes place in both simulations (with F becoming equal to $\epsilon = 1.492$).[9] The effect upon T, however, is ambiguous. Whereas T rises with parameter dependency, it falls without this dependency. Production X, nevertheless, rises in both cases.[10] Analogous to the results for T, is the effect upon the final production Y (higher T leads to lower Y and vice versa). The simulation result for decreasing price variance differs from the above. The slope coefficient for the F-curve will not, unlike the former case, go to infinity. Thus, the forward currency rate, F, will not rise as much. The future commodity rate, T, will fall more than proportionally leading to a decrease in production. Because of the movement in T, consumption Y will fall.

5 Conclusions

In the foregoing analysis we presented a model capable of explaining the effects of exchange-rate volatility on primary commodity prices. This two-country, two-date, three-agent model is solved in a general equilibrium framework. Explicit solutions for market clearing prices have thus been obtained. A first conclusion of the paper is, that it is possible to integrate the commodity market and the exchange market in a comprehensive way without loss of explanatory power of the model.

We introduced three change scenarios in our model, i.e. a demand shock, an expected depreciation and decreased volatility of the exchange rate. The demand shock was easy to analyze in terms of prices and output effects; a rise in the futures commodity price, output and final production with a drop in the forward exchange rate.

Expected depreciation gives straightforward answers for spot, forward and futures prices (a rise in the forward rate and a drop in the futures and spot price) but the output effect can go either way. Model simulations, nevertheless, indicated a drop in primary production and a rise in final production.

In contrast, a change in exchange-rate volatility can lead to price as well as output effects whose sign can not be uniquely defined. However, on the basis of model simulations we discovered that output will rise. This means that the rise in the forward exchange rate offsets a potential drop in the futures commodity price.

NOTES

* We are grateful to A. de Vaal for constructing Table 9.1.

1 Turnovsky and Campbell (1985) combine consumer surplus with producer's and speculator's utility to obtain an overall welfare measure.

2 With complete markets, the production decision becomes independent of the utility function and/or the probability distribution of our two random variables.

3 Both currency and commodity markets are (based upon the transactions' characteristics) in fact forward markets. In this paper we will, nevertheless, use the term commodity *futures* market to prevent confusion.

4 The measure of risk aversion, α, is assumed to be the same for all agents for reasons of simplicity. Introduction of diverse degrees of risk aversion will, however, not harm our equilibrium outcomes.

5 The term between brackets (corresponding to Ω_3) can be rewritten, using equations (8a) and (18) and $\zeta = T$, showing that it is equal to A^*.

6 Shocks in these two parameters cause repercussion effects in the other parameters: in μ according to equation (14), and in ϕ^2 since

$$\phi^2 = \mathrm{Cov}(\omega,\rho) + \sigma^2 \nu^2 + \epsilon^2 \nu^2 + \zeta^2 \sigma^2 - (\rho^* \nu\sigma)^2 - 2\rho^* \nu\sigma\epsilon\zeta.$$

7 In deriving this result, we made use of the assumption of $\rho > 0$.

8 When the degree of risk aversion declines (Table 9.3, upper panel) the same effects will be obtained.

9 Table 9.3 shows that this rotation of the curve will also take place when the correlation coefficient ρ, increases to 1.

10 *F* times *T* becomes equal to $\mu = 1.548$, in the parameter dependent case. R_q, the two-sided commodity risk premium will then be equal to zero.

REFERENCES

Chu, K. Y. and Morrison, T. K. (1984) 'The 1981–82 Recession and Non-Oil Primary Commodity Prices', *IMF Staff Papers* **31**, 93–140.

Kawai, M. (1983) 'Price Volatility of Storable Commodities under Rational Expectations in Spot and Futures Markets', *International Economic Review* **24**, 435–59.

Kawai, M. and I. Zilcha (1986) 'International Trade with Forward- Futures Markets under Exchange Rate and Price Uncertainty', *Journal of International Economics* **20**, 83–98.

Turnovsky, S. J. and R. B. Campbell (1985) 'The stabilizing and welfare properties of futures markets: a simulation approach', *International Economic Review* **26**, 277–303.

Viaene, J. M. (1988) *The Equilibrium Approach to International Commodity Prices*, Erasmus University, Rotterdam.

Discussion

ALASDAIR I. MACBEAN

Many conditions associated with commodity price instability attract policy makers' attention. For producers and users, commodity market instability creates uncertainty, raises costs and may deter investment. From a macroeconomic viewpoint exporting nations suffer unstable export revenues, tax revenues, incomes, and investment. These may result in lower investment and growth; and through ratchet effects, higher inflation. Some observers have alleged that importing nations suffer more inflation as a result of volatile commodity import prices. Clearly policies which cut price fluctuations without incurring high costs would be welcome. What can we draw from Kofman, Viaene and de Vries's paper which is relevant to the objective of moderating price fluctuations or alleviating their effects?

The analytics of the paper explore the relationship between the markets (spot and forward) for foreign exchange and the markets for commodities (spot and futures [forward]). By linking these markets the paper ought to tell us something about the value to commodity price stabilization (or reducing producer and user uncertainty) of hedging currency transactions.

The paper's concern is with the spot or actual price in 'pesos' to the producer/merchant and the 'dollar' price to the user. It investigates the effect of the use of the futures (forward) market for 'copper' to hedge the producers' sales and the use of the forward market for foreign exchange to hedge exchange variation in the peso/dollar exchange rate. The spot price and the spot exchange rate are both treated as *random* variables (i.e. *independent of the actions of the producer or the user*).

This assumes implicitly that our producer/merchant is small in relation to the spot and futures markets, is sufficiently sophisticated to use futures markets to hedge sales, and has access to a *large enough forward market* (with enough speculators) for his national currency to hedge his expected dollar revenues by buying forward pesos. This probably rules out most developing country producers – mainly because there are no forward markets in their currencies and most have exchange rates pegged to their major trading partner's currency.

At present relatively few LDCs currently make use of either market. But the other conditions are rarely met either. Exchange rates are mainly pegged to a major trading partner's currency and controls on currency transactions are stringent. No doubt in the future more LDCs will meet the required conditions. But the supply of forward exchange or futures contracts of adequate lengths is always likely to be a problem for many important crops (or minerals) where the period of production from planting to production is often lengthy.

Despite these problems the model is relevant to producer/merchants in developed countries and some relatively mature developing countries. The producer contracts to deliver x tons of copper at the spot price on the day of delivery in dollars. To hedge against a fall in the copper price he sells x tons in the futures market at the current price there. Then if the spot price falls his gain on the futures contract offsets the low price in the spot market (vice versa if the spot price has risen). Because he wants his revenue in pesos the producer sells forward dollars from the sale of his output. With this double hedge he has eliminated peso price uncertainty. The producer knows the precise price for his product in advance and plans his output accordingly.

But two problems would remain: (1) the hedge is not costless. Particularly if the markets are narrow, and his product large relative to the market, he can affect forward prices, increasing the discount on them and increasing the cost of hedging. There are also transaction costs (fees to be paid). (2) he has not eliminated output uncertainty, i.e. the effects of strikes, etc., on copper sales or nature's impact on harvests.

Analogously the user of copper hedges by buying copper forward in an equal amount to his intended purchase. So both have eliminated the relevant uncertainty, but always at a cost.

The model simultaneously determines spot and forward prices and planned output. Actual output would of course be affected by exogenous and random factors. So producers' revenue, and the nation's exchange earnings would still be uncertain and would fluctuate. So if our objective were to stabilize producers' incomes and foreign exchange earnings we might do better to go down the compensatory financing route both externally and internally.

The model is used to examine the effects of demand shocks, exchange rate volatility and changes in expectations. The prediction is that an increase in demand leads to a rise in the spot price and output. That is certainly what one would expect. Increased demand – increase in expected price – increase in planned output as long as the producer can hedge forward dollars without causing the peso to appreciate so much that it lowers the number of pesos he gets. (So the size of that market and the presence of willing speculators matters.)

Depreciation of the exchange rate one would expect to stimulate production as one gets more pesos per dollar earned. But the model comes up with ambiguous results.

A decrease in exchange rate volatility should reduce uncertainty and so encourage an increase in planned output, but again the model's analytical results are ambiguous.

So I am unsure what the policy messages are.

I have other worries.

(1) What about producers of other crops? If commodity prices tend to be correlated then they may be taking similar positions in the forward exchange market at the same time. Could not that make hedging more expensive?

(2) If commodity markets or exchange markets are subject to destabilizing speculation, e.g. by portfolio investors, then the futures and forward markets may be a poor guide to production decisions.

(3) Hedging currencies will be complicated by having many customers in different countries.

(4) Forward markets will respond to interest differentials in various countries which may increase costs of hedging.

(5) Most of the important primary commodities from the view point of LDCs: coffee, cocoa, tea, palm oil etc. have production lags of 18 months to 6 years from new planting to harvest. Does not this limit severely the explanatory power of this model for production as the existence of hedging facilities for such long periods forward is implausible?

Many of these queries are addressed to much broader issues than those tackled by the paper. Within its chosen limits the paper makes a valuable contribution to a very difficult subject. The authors are to be congratulated for their analytical skill.

DAVID SAPSFORD

I would like to begin by thanking the authors (referred to as KV^2 hereafter) for their presentation of an extremely elegant model which focusses on one of the principal empirically observed determinants of fluctuations in primary commodity prices, namely exchange rate movements. In order to achieve this, the authors take a somewhat novel approach which seeks to link together commodity and currency markets while taking account of both price and exchange rate uncertainties.

When discussing an earlier paper of this conference, Ken Wallis drew the analogy between econometricians and plumbers. In discussing the paper by KV^2 I find myself very much in the role of the plumber confronted with *no* heating system to fix: in the sense that the paper in its present form contains little in the way of formal econometric analysis. I will therefore proceed in my discussions in the time honoured tradition of the 'plumber-economist' in that I will assume the presence of a heating system, the likely features of which I will aim to bring to your attention!

More concretely I will, in the following comments, raise a number of issues relating to points made elsewhere in the conference, while also highlighting some further issues in respect of which the model might be improved and extended. KV^2 rightly point out that in some models of commodity price determination consumers are treated in an essentially passive sense and their explicit treatment of the producer as using primary commodities as intermediate inputs used in the production of some final good is to be welcomed. However, I am less than happy about the specification of the primary commodity producer also acting as merchant for the commodity. While this may be a reasonable assumption for some primary commodities, I must admit to having serious reservations regarding the plausibility of this assumption in the context of (say) third world agriculture. Although it may perhaps be argued that some form of marketing board fills this role in the context of third world agriculture, I must admit to being less than happy about the implied assumption that the same degree of risk aversion is displayed in both roles: an assumption which seems to go against the spirit of much of the economic analysis of third world countries, including the well known Lewis two-sector type of model. It would be particularly interesting to know how the model would perform if these two roles were separated and assigned differing degrees of risk aversion. I also note that KV^2 do not appear to have given any thought to the ways in which foreign currency rationing might influence the workings of their model. In addition, it is necessary to draw your attention once again to a point made earlier by David Newbery: namely that what matters is the price which producers actually receive in their hands, so that the omission from this model of both taxes and subsidies is to be regretted.

In Section 2.2 I encountered a further worry: namely that KV^2 assume that by tradition the primary commodity is traded in the demanding firm's currency, hence eliminating potential exchange rate risks from the demanding firm's viewpoint. However, this surely cannot be accepted as a general rule, since a range of major primary commodities have prices which are traditionally quoted in US$ and major consumers which include countries other than the USA. Are KV^2 therefore implicitly assuming for such consuming countries the existence in their model of some form of wholesaler who bears the exchange risk on this side of the market? In addition, it might further be argued that the model contains an additional significant omission in that it includes a currency speculator but not a commodity speculator. The potential importance of the latter having been clearly illustrated in discussion earlier in the conference regarding the speculative demand for commodity stocks.

Central to the model's properties is the precise value taken by the parameter ρ, the correlation coefficient between the domestic price of the commodity and the exchange rate. Table 9.1 reports some estimated values of ρ, commodity by commodity. If we accept the sub-periods selected for this exercise (although we are not told exactly how they were arrived at) I would draw attention to the marked period to period variations evident in the case of certain commodities, newsprint and petroleum to name only two. This volatility raises a number of questions and specifically, would seem to raise some reservations regarding the model's potential empirical performance and suggest the presence of potential problems of the structural instability sort. However such volatility would seem to provide one reasonably plausible explanation for the lack of robustness in the exchange rate-commodity price relationship (both across time and between different commodities and commodity groups) typically found in empirical studies, including the cited paper by Chu and Morrison (1984). The authors are careful to point out in their paper that the model fails to yield an equilibrium solution in the case where $|\rho| = 1$. It is, however, somewhat alarming to notice that of the forty-six correlations reported in Table 9.1 over 25 per cent are in excess of 0.9, while around 10 per cent are in excess of 0.987! Clearly there is scope for further refinement of the model.

All things considered the KV^2 model is a welcome addition to the literature which illustrates that once general equilibrium considerations are taken into account it is possible to integrate the commodity and exchange markets together in a meaningful and instructive manner.

Summary of general discussion

Andreas Köttering made two points at the beginning of the general discussion. Firstly, he argued that as the model is based on the mean–variance approach but ran into problems of deriving this given the occurrence of a product of two random variables both of which are assumed normal, rendering the product of the two non-normal, why not circumvent these difficulties by simply asserting the mean–variance model as the point of departure for the analysis? To what extent this may be a robust approximation may then be tested. In any case Newbery had offered two alternative ways out of the dilemma; the first of these involved stating that the mean–variance model holds true as a second-order approximation to the general case, and the second made use of the exact calculation provided by M. Bray (1981). The second point raised by Köttering concerned the reliance of the model on the so-called Separation Theorem. He reported his own research which had shown that this result no longer holds if basis risk is introduced into the analysis. Basis risk is usually ignored in these models, whereas in reality the whole point about futures markets is that they offer the substitution of basis risk for the higher price risk. Köttering found from numerical optimization exercises that the Separation result vanishes rapidly as even small amounts of basis risk are introduced into the analysis.

David Newbery added to this that the Separation Theorem also depends on the assumption that no output risk, or at least no multiplicative output risk, is present; an assumption which is clearly at odds with reality for the case of agricultural commodities. Newbery further noted that models which look at the use of futures hedging are usually placed in a partial equilibrium framework. Thus the extension in this model to a general equilibrium context should be welcomed. However, he was not certain whether this was ideal in this case as it required the use of some very strong assumptions. For example, there was an assumption that exchange rate changes do not affect the domestic price of the good. This appears somewhat unrealistic. The need to close the market model allows only primary producers to be considered as affecting the exchange rate; yet, there are many other actors in LDC economies whose activities bear on the level of the exchange rate. Newbery proposed the following alternative modelling strategy: construct a domestic futures market and have the producers hedge their output in the local currency; then consider how they tackle the problem of exchange rate volatility separately.

Stephen Dunn pointed out that it is incorrect to say that commodity users such as commercial processors do not need to take account of the exchange rate. In fact for the case of cocoa, many producers take out a currency option as cocoa is priced in US dollars. Anthony Bird remarked that commodity prices are mostly quoted in US dollars. He considered it important to recognize that as a producer, one cannot always adjust the output price in response to a change in the exchange rate.

Viaene responded by stressing the fact that this model is only a stylized reflection of actual markets; its intention is to shed light on the link between commodity prices and the exchange rate. Viaene acknowledged that the exchange rate had not been taken account of in the profit function of the processor, but thought this legitimate when considering expectations. He also agreed that no explicit account had been taken in this model of terms of trade effects. Finally, Viaene noted that there may not exist a forward currency rate for a particular developing country, but many of these are part of the French franc zone, for example, and thus do enjoy access to such hedging opportunities.

REFERENCES
Bray, M. (1981) 'Futures Trading, Rational Expectations and the Efficient Market Hypothesis', *Econometrica* **49**, 579–96.

10 Commodity policy: price stabilization versus financing*

ROLAND HERMANN, KEES BURGER and
HIDDE P. SMIT

1 Introduction

The instability of world commodity markets has been a central issue in the North-South dialogue for more than two decades now. The proponents of policy intervention argue that excessive market price fluctuations cause negative micro- and macro-economic consequences which can be avoided by stabilization measures.[1] Price stabilization policies, based on buffer stocks as intended by the Integrated Programme on Commodities (IPC) or export quotas, and compensatory financing schemes were primarily discussed as international measures to stabilize export earnings and to counter the negative consequences of world market instabilities.

Until recently, the analytical literature on price stabilization dealt primarily with commodity initiatives which fulfil their primary objectives perfectly. Analyses of price stabilization assumed that hypothetical buffer stock schemes stabilize prices successfully as intended by the decision-maker (Behrman, 1978; Nguyen, 1980). They concentrated on the consequential effects of successful price stabilization on other goals. On the basis of this approach, an argument for buffer stock schemes is that pure price stabilization can increase the aggregate welfare of all market participants. Moreover, price stabilization is expected to reduce earnings instability in many cases (Nguyen, 1980) and, hence, contribute to economic growth (Lim, 1976). In another branch of the literature, it is argued that compensatory financing systems are superior to buffer stocks and export quotas. Again, those results are based on the assumption of a perfectly stabilizing compensatory financing scheme (Newbery and Stiglitz, 1981, p. 299; Bird, 1987). It was put forward that compensatory financing can stabilize national export earnings directly, whereas price stabilization does so only under specific conditions. However, a general argument for compensatory financing is that no market intervention is

240

needed. Hence, compensatory financing can avoid the aggregate welfare losses associated with price-changing commodity agreements.

The approach of this paper is different. We do not impose on our analysis that commodity agreements stabilize prices or that compensatory financing stabilizes export earnings. In a quantitative analysis it is investigated whether existing commodity initiatives fulfilled their primary objectives. Four important commodity policies are selected which are often evaluated positively in the literature. The two major export earnings stabilization schemes are investigated first – the Compensatory Financing Facility (CFF) of the IMF and the STABEX system laid down in the Convention of Lomé. Then, two international commodity agreements are examined which are often seen as the only success stories among commodity agreements – the International Coffee Agreement (ICA) and the International Natural Rubber Agreement (INRA). The efficiency of these commodity initiatives is evaluated and policy conclusions are drawn.

2   Economic evaluation of existing compensatory financing schemes

Two important compensatory financing systems are implemented in order to stabilize export earnings: the IMF's CFF and the STABEX scheme laid down in the Lomé Convention. In the following, a brief survey of each of these systems will be given. Then, a quantitative analysis will be presented in order to assess whether the systems have reached their primary goal – earnings stabilization. Additionally, quantitative analyses are reviewed which deal with side effects of the compensatory financing schemes, e.g. with their redistributive consequences.

2.1   The IMF's Compensatory Financing System

2.1.1 Basic rules of the system
The IMF's CFF was established in 1963.[2] Its major objective is to provide timely financial assistance to member countries which experience shortfalls of their aggregate export earnings. Export earnings from commodities and manufactured goods are covered and earnings from workers' remittances and tourism can be included since 1979 if a country wishes. The CFF has been extended twice. Since 1981, excesses in the cost of cereal imports are covered additionally in order to meet the stabilization needs of poor developing countries. Members can either request a purchase under the older rules or the new rules which integrate excesses in cereal import costs and export earnings shortfalls. Most recently, in August 1988, the

Compensatory and Contingency Financing Facility was founded. The new contingency element is that members with Fund-supported adjustment programmes can borrow *ex ante* in order to cope with various external shocks.

Export earnings shortfalls and excesses in the costs of cereal imports are compensated after a member country's application, given that some conditions are met. The disturbance has to be temporary and largely beyond the member's control. The maximum time-lag between the end of the compensation year and the application is 6 months. The compensation year does not need to be a calendar year. Advance payments are possible during the year of compensation. In order to calculate the amount of compensation, the actual value of export earnings is subtracted from the geometric mean of export earnings for a five-year period, centred on the shortfall year. The IMF estimates the values of the two years following the shortfall by means of qualitative considerations. A full compensation of the shortfalls is subject to quota limitations and limits on outstanding drawings. Drawings under the CFF are credits which have to be repaid fully within five years, usually in fixed quarterly amounts between the third and fifth years. There is no binding linkage between repayments and excesses in export earnings. The drawings are conditional; the member must be willing to cooperate with the IMF in an effort to find appropriate solutions for its balance-of-payments problems.

Besides these rules, which are crucial for the stabilizing impact, the CFF contains redistributive elements. Interest is charged for credits under the CFF, but it is far below market rates. The grant elements involved in the stabilization payments are only lowered by a service charge of 0.5 per cent of the amount of the credit.

2.1.2 Did the IMF system stabilize export earnings? New estimates for the period 1963–87

The following empirical measurement of the stabilization effects of the IMF system is based on a broad country basis and a comprehensive period of analysis. 92 of the 95 countries[3] which have received compensatory financing payments under the IMF system up to 1987 are taken into account. The period of analysis is 1963–87.[4] It is analyzed whether export earnings with compensatory financing by the IMF are more or less stable than without it. The impacts of drawings under the CFF and of the countries' repayments are calculated separately. Additionally, the aggregate effect of all transactions under the facility is presented. In order to compute stabilization effects, yearly data on national export earnings[5] from the IMF's *International Financial Statistics* were utilized.

Methodologically, the measurement of instability is based on the trend-corrected coefficient of variation (v^*) as derived by Cuddy and Della Valle (1978):

$$v^* = v \cdot \sqrt{(1 - \bar{R}^2)} \tag{1}$$

with v = coefficient of variation of the time series; $\bar{R}^2$ = adjusted coefficient of determination of the trend function with the best fit to the data. Generally, linear and loglinear trend functions are compared as in the original studies of Cuddy and Della Valle (1978) and Della Valle (1979) and v^* includes a correction for the appropriate trend.[6] Compensatory financing may change the trend of export earnings and not only the instability around the trend. Therefore, equation (1) was applied to export earnings with and without compensatory financing respectively. If instability as defined in (1) is an indicator for uncertainty, this implies that a policy-induced change in the trend does not affect uncertainty whereas a policy-induced change of fluctuations around the trend does.

Table 10.1 shows the results. The instability of export earnings and the stabilizing impact of the CFF are presented for 92 recipient countries. The findings can be summarized as follows:

(1) Export earnings instability varies widely across countries. It ranges between 10.4 per cent (Portugal) and 67 per cent (Lao, PDR) with an arithmetic mean of 24.5 per cent and a median instability of 21.9 per cent. The measurement of instability is mostly based on the coefficient of variation corrected for a loglinear trend. This means that export earnings of many countries grew exponentially and the coefficient of variation had to be strongly corrected downwards.[7]

(2) The overall impact of the IMF's compensatory financing systems on export earnings instability tends to be small. The median shows a destabilizing impact for the payments from the IMF (+ 0.10 per cent) as well as for the repayments to the IMF (+ 0.41 per cent). The median effect of payments and repayments combined on export earnings instability is a destabilizing one: + 0.63 per cent. This implies that the CFF induced destabilizing influences for most of the drawing countries.

(3) The payments from the IMF were only in 43 out of 92 cases export-earnings stabilizing. When stabilizing effects existed, they were mostly low. They were for 12 countries higher than 3 per cent and only for five countries higher than 5 per cent: Côte d'Ivoire, Nepal, Zaire, Argentina and Dominica. The clear success case is Côte d'Ivoire where export-earnings instability was reduced by some 47 per cent. This country received relatively high payments in 1976 and 1981 when

Instability of selected variables[a]

Percentage change in export earnings

Countries	Export earnings (1)	Export earnings and payments from the IMF (2)	Export earnings minus repayments to the IMF (3)	Export earnings and payments from the IMF minus repayments to the IMF (4)	Instability[b] due to — Payments from the IMF (5)	Repayments to the IMF (6)	Payments from the IMF minus repayments to the IMF (7)
Afghanistan[c]	22.80	22.67	22.98	22.85	−0.59	+0.79	+0.22
Argentina	22.73	21.56	24.46	23.16	−5.15	+7.64	+1.91
Australia	12.74	12.86	12.69	12.81	+0.93	−0.38	+0.56
Bangladesh[d]	14.71	15.27	15.67	16.06	+3.81	+6.51	+9.14
Barbados	37.76	37.63	38.52	38.39	−0.36	+2.00	+1.66
Belize	19.91	19.82	20.15	20.07	−0.43	+1.22	+0.81
Bolivia[e]	26.58	25.70	26.85	25.95	−3.33	+1.02	−2.40
Brazil	16.98	17.26	17.46	17.74	+1.63	+2.83	+4.47
Burma	38.62	38.92	40.55	40.87	+0.77	+5.01	+5.83
Burundi	31.41	32.02	31.75	32.38	+1.92	+1.09	+3.08
Cameroon[c]	22.03	21.98	21.92	21.87	−0.24	−0.50	−0.73
Central African Republic[c]	19.21	18.47	18.99	18.22	−3.86	−1.16	−5.13
Chad[i]	24.85	25.13	24.81	24.95	+1.12	−0.16	+0.41
Chile	17.39	17.06	17.58	17.26	−1.90	+1.09	−0.72
Colombia	15.16	15.06	15.22	15.13	−0.61	+0.43	−0.16
Congo[g]	59.29	59.02	59.30	59.04	−0.45	+0.02	−0.43
Costa Rica	17.64	17.74	17.75	17.85	+0.56	+0.63	+1.19
Côte d'Ivoire[c]	31.20	16.59	16.46	16.61	−46.84	−47.24	−46.77

Cyprus	17.58	17.76	17.41	17.59	+ 0.99	− 0.96	+ 0.06
Dominica[g]	31.57	29.97	30.63	29.08	− 5.08	− 3.00	− 7.89
Dominican Rep.	25.76	25.78	26.53	26.59	+ 0.08	+ 2.99	+ 3.21
Ecuador	26.50	26.33	26.89	26.73	− 0.62	+ 1.47	+ 0.87
Egypt	15.60	15.48	15.91	15.78	− 0.75	+ 1.98	+ 1.14
El Salvador[c]	21.76	21.58	22.38	22.22	− 0.84	+ 2.85	+ 2.09
Ethiopia[c]	12.37	12.90	12.50	13.12	+ 4.26	+ 1.00	+ 5.99
Fiji[c]	19.72	19.90	19.74	19.93	+ 0.92	+ 0.11	+ 1.07
Gambia[c]	26.02	25.47	27.60	26.46	− 2.13	+ 6.05	+ 1.66
Ghana	41.68	42.50	43.50	44.09	+ 1.95	+ 4.35	+ 5.78
Greece	15.70	15.80	15.65	15.75	+ 0.66	− 0.31	+ 0.36
Grenada	19.58	19.81	19.49	19.75	+ 1.17	− 0.45	+ 0.87
Guatemala	21.03	21.26	21.42	21.65	+ 1.06	+ 1.82	+ 2.92
Guinea Bissau[g]	38.22	39.34	38.21	39.54	+ 2.93	− 0.03	+ 3.45
Guayana	24.47	25.06	24.16	24.77	+ 2.42	− 1.27	+ 1.24
Haiti	23.16	23.27	23.74	23.87	+ 0.45	+ 2.51	+ 3.06
Honduras[c]	13.21	13.25	13.44	13.49	+ 0.29	+ 1.72	+ 2.09
Hungary[h]	12.47	12.59	12.60	12.71	+ 0.90	+ 1.01	+ 1.90
Iceland	19.96	19.45	20.01	19.52	− 2.53	+ 0.25	− 2.22
India	16.01	15.99	16.14	16.13	− 0.12	+ 0.79	+ 0.74
Indonesia	31.02	30.82	31.05	30.84	− 0.66	+ 0.08	− 0.58
Iraq	45.31	45.30	45.33	45.31	− 0.03	+ 0.03	+ 0.00
Israel	10.69	10.86	10.59	10.76	+ 1.57	− 0.93	+ 0.66
Jamaica	22.00	22.20	22.52	22.64	+ 0.92	+ 2.37	+ 2.93
Jordan	24.31	23.43	24.75	23.84	− 3.62	+ 1.82	− 1.94
Kenya	19.60	19.95	19.93	20.27	+ 1.77	+ 1.66	+ 3.40
Korea	20.10	20.12	20.12	20.14	+ 0.07	+ 0.09	+ 0.17
Lao, PDR[i]	67.01	78.95	78.93	90.45	+ 17.82	+ 17.78	+ 34.97
Liberia	19.84	20.19	19.89	20.25	+ 1.75	+ 0.23	+ 2.04
Madagascar[c]	15.76	16.47	16.72	17.44	+ 4.50	+ 6.06	+ 10.62
Malawi[k]	15.70	16.37	16.06	16.71	+ 4.25	+ 2.24	+ 6.42

Table 10.1 (*cont.*)

Countries	Instability of selected variables[a]				Percentage change in export earnings Instability[b] due to		
	Export earnings (1)	Export earnings and payments from the IMF (2)	Export earnings minus repayments to the IMF (3)	Export earnings and payments from the IMF minus repayments to the IMF (4)	Payments from the IMF (5)	Repayments to the IMF (6)	Payments from the IMF minus repayments to the IMF (7)
Malaysia	19.61	19.65	19.58	19.63	+ 0.20	− 0.12	+ 0.08
Mali	24.88	24.90	24.78	24.81	+ 0.11	− 0.37	− 0.25
Mauritania	25.18	24.93	25.22	24.94	− 1.00	+ 0.15	− 0.93
Mauritius[c]	25.70	25.02	25.34	24.66	− 2.66	− 1.43	− 4.05
Morocco	16.88	17.09	17.06	17.29	+ 1.26	+ 1.10	+ 2.44
Nepal	19.60	18.04	19.76	18.30	− 7.96	+ 0.79	− 6.66
New Zealand	13.41	13.10	13.42	13.12	− 2.34	+ 0.10	− 2.18
Nicaragua	32.82	33.23	32.86	33.27	+ 1.24	+ 0.11	+ 1.39
Niger[g]	39.94	40.49	39.94	40.49	+ 1.39	+ 0.00	+ 1.39
Pakistan	24.12	23.92	23.87	23.70	− 0.82	− 1.03	− 1.73
Panama	14.04	15.00	14.89	15.94	+ 6.83	+ 6.08	+ 13.53
Papua New Guinea	18.94	19.98	18.91	18.98	+ 0.22	− 0.16	+ 0.20
Peru	24.36	24.53	24.34	24.51	+ 0.68	− 0.11	+ 0.61
Philippines	17.23	17.13	17.36	17.24	− 0.56	+ 0.72	+ 0.04
Portugal	10.44	10.07	10.31	9.95	− 3.52	− 1.28	− 4.67
Romania[c]	12.25	12.49	12.27	12.52	+ 2.00	+ 0.18	+ 2.20

St. Lucia[c]	22.25	22.38	22.22	22.36	+ 0.57	− 0.16	+ 0.46
St. Vincent[f]	43.83	44.47	43.83	44.47	+ 1.46	+ 0.00	+ 1.46
Senegal[c]	35.58	34.83	35.77	35.04	− 2.10	+ 0.55	− 1.51
Sierra Leone	15.05	14.36	14.68	14.09	− 4.59	− 2.48	− 6.35
Solomon Islands[c]	21.14	21.27	21.15	21.26	+ 0.58	+ 0.03	+ 0.54
Somalia[g]	37.85	40.40	37.85	40.40	+ 6.74	+ 0.00	+ 6.74
South Africa	19.31	19.35	19.51	19.55	+ 0.21	+ 1.01	+ 1.24
Spain	12.94	12.97	12.93	12.95	+ 0.18	− 0.08	+ 0.08
Sri Lanka	23.00	22.12	23.88	22.99	− 3.80	+ 3.81	− 0.05
Sudan[c]	21.93	22.35	23.00	23.39	+ 1.92	+ 4.86	+ 6.65
Swaziland	21.84	21.93	22.09	22.18	+ 0.40	+ 1.13	+ 1.55
Syria[c]	31.28	31.02	31.27	31.01	− 0.83	− 0.03	− 0.86
Tanzania	21.40	22.40	21.41	22.43	+ 4.65	+ 0.01	+ 4.80
Thailand	17.07	17.21	17.04	17.18	+ 0.87	− 0.16	+ 0.67
Togo[g]	24.54	24.37	24.32	24.15	− 0.68	− 0.89	− 1.56
Trinidad/Tobago	38.88	38.88	38.88	38.88	+ 0.00	+ 0.00	+ 0.00
Tunisia	24.27	23.86	24.20	23.79	− 1.67	− 0.29	− 1.95
Turkey	21.87	21.31	22.00	21.43	− 2.57	+ 0.59	− 2.04
Uganda[f]	20.82	20.57	21.47	21.20	− 1.21	+ 3.13	+ 1.81
Uruguay	19.78	19.27	20.19	19.70	− 2.56	+ 2.04	− 0.41
Vietnam[f]	64.86	65.96	65.12	66.26	+ 1.69	+ 0.40	+ 2.15
Western Samoa	32.30	31.62	33.34	32.41	− 2.41	− 2.89	+ 0.05
Yemen, PDR[f]	55.70	55.62	55.71	55.63	− 0.14	+ 0.01	− 0.13
Yugoslavia[c]	11.92	11.91	11.86	11.87	− 0.01	− 0.43	− 0.41
Zaire	29.63	27.60	30.99	29.04	− 6.85	+ 4.56	− 1.99
Zambia[c]	24.74	23.85	24.99	23.97	− 3.59	+ 1.05	− 3.08
Zimbabwe[m]	19.83	19.66	20.16	20.00	− 0.86	+ 1.69	+ 0.86
Arithmetic mean	24.52	24.49	24.75	24.84	− 0.42	+ 0.69	+ 0.76
Standard deviation	11.25	11.89	11.85	12.54	5.81	5.69	6.96
Median	21.86	21.57	21.96	22.03	+ 0.10	+ 0.41	+ 0.63

Table 10.1 Effects of the IMF's Compensatory Financing System on the instability of export earnings of 92 recipient countries in the period 1963–87

[a]On the computation of the measures of instability see the text. Export earnings are expressed in mill. SDR. For Lao, PDR, and Zimbabwe, the uncorrected coefficient of variation was used. A linear trend correction was utilized for Burma, Guinea Bissau, Hungary, Mauritius, Papua New Guinea, Vietnam, Yemen, PDR, and Zimbabwe. In all other cases, a loglinear trend correction was used. [b]The percentage changes were computed from the non-rounded values underlying the instabilities of columns (1) to (4). [c]The calculations refer to the period 1963–86. [d]1972–87. [e]1966–87. [f]1963–85. [g]1963–84. [h]1970–87. [i]1963–81. [k]1964–87. [l]1963–82. [m]1964–86.

Source: Own computations. Data on export earnings are from IMF (1988). The payments of the IMF up to 1979 were taken from Goreux (1980), pp. 52 *et seq.*, and the additional payments of 1980 and 1981 from IMF (a), February 1980, 1981 and 1982. The repayments up to 1975 were taken from IMF (a), February 1976, p. 15. For the following years, the repayments were calculated by using data on payments and 'net compensatory drawings' of subsequent February issues of IMF (a).

its export earnings were clearly below the exponential trend. The payments from the CFF were for the majority of countries, 49, export-earnings destabilizing. These destabilizing effects exceeded 3 per cent for eight countries and 5 per cent for three countries: Lao, PDR, Panama and Somalia.

(4) With regard to the stabilization of export earnings, repayments to the IMF performed even worse. In less than a third of all recipient countries, 28, export earnings were stabilized. In all cases except Côte d'Ivoire, these stabilizing effects were lower than 3 per cent. On the other hand, destabilizing effects of the repayments exceeded 3 per cent in 12 countries and 5 per cent in the following seven countries: Lao, PDR, Argentina, Bangladesh, Panama, Madagascar, Gambia and Burma.

(5) Consequently, the overall impact of both payments from the IMF and repayments to the IMF was for 30 countries stabilizing on export earnings and for 62 countries destabilizing. The stabilizing effect was higher than 3 per cent for eight countries and it exceeded 5 per cent only for the following five countries: Côte d'Ivoire, Dominica, Nepàl, Sierra Leone and the Central African Republic. On the other hand, export earnings were destabilized by more than 3 per cent in 17 countries and by more than 5 per cent in the following ten countries: Lao, PDR, Panama, Madagascar, Bangladesh, Somalia, Sudan, Malawi, Ethiopia, Burma and Ghana. Destabilization was more than 10 per cent for the first three countries.

The overall performance of the IMF's compensatory financing scheme can be generalized when transactions up to 1987 are regarded as a representative sample for the future performance of the scheme. Then, given a 99 per cent level of statistical significance and a two-sided test, confidence intervals for the median stabilization effects can be computed.[8] These confidence intervals are

$$- 0.59 \leqslant 100 \cdot (\Delta v^*/v^*) \leqslant + 0.66 \tag{2}$$

for payments from the IMF,

$$+ 0.01 \leqslant 100 \cdot (\Delta v^*/v^*) \leqslant + 1.01 \tag{3}$$

for repayments to the IMF and

$$+ 0.05 \leqslant 100 \cdot (\Delta v^*/v^*) \leqslant + 1.24 \tag{4}$$

for the sum of payments from the IMF and repayments to the IMF. This implies:

(1) Given the historical performance of the CFF, it can be expected that

compensatory financing will lead to a median effect on export earnings instability which is destabilizing and lies between 0.05 and 1.24 per cent. The median effect of the repayments alone can be expected to be destabilizing within a range of 0.01 to 1.01 per cent. Payments under the CFF can be expected to induce a median effect on export earnings instability which ranges between stabilization by 0.59 per cent and destabilization by 0.66 per cent. Generally, the probability of a destabilizing effect is higher than that of a stabilizing one.

(2) Without a significant change in the system it is very unlikely that payments from the IMF, repayments to the IMF or all transactions under the CFF will have a strong effect on export earnings instability for many countries. Stabilization effects in the magnitude of 10 per cent or more are far outside the confidence intervals for the median impacts.

What are the reasons for this relatively poor performance of the CFF with regard to its primary objective – export earnings stabilization? Four reasons are important:

(1) The compensation payments are not timely enough to effectively stabilize national export earnings.
(2) Forecast errors led in some cases to destabilization of national export earnings.
(3) Repayments often lead to destabilization of national export earnings as they are not linked to excesses in export earnings.
(4) The fact that stabilization payments are limited to a share of the national quota lowers the CFF's potential for stabilizing export earnings.

On (1): An analysis of the time-lags between the end of the shortfall years and the compensation payments under the CFF shows that these were relatively long in the period 1963–80 (Herrmann, 1983, section 2.2). The mean time-lag was slightly above four months, and less than 10 per cent of compensation payments were advance payments. This pattern has not significantly changed since then. In 1985, e.g., the mean time-lag was 4.7 months and only one out of 13 cases was an early drawing within the shortfall year. These time-lags in the compensation payments have caused destabilizing effects on export earnings of several countries under the CFF. This holds true, e.g., for Somalia and Panama where destabilizing effects of compensation payments were higher than 5 per cent. Payments to those countries in the 1980s were disbursed in the year following the export earnings shortfall. The payments arrived in years of 'high' export earnings and thus had destabilizing impacts.

On (2): In other cases, payments were disbursed in the calendar year in which the shortfall year ended but were still destabilizing. Panama, which experienced a noticeable destabilization effect of drawings under the CFF, received in 1976 a payment for a shortfall in that year. However, Panama's export earnings in 1976 were higher than the short-run trend of export earnings as implied in the IMF's calculation of shortfalls, and clearly higher than the medium-run trend as implied in the instability measurement used here. Forecasting errors occurred and they led in this case to destabilizing payments. Similar cases were payments to Bangladesh in 1972 and 1976, which were excessive given the actual trend values of export earnings in these years.

On (3): From the stabilization perspective, the rule that payments have to be repaid between the third and fifth years is unsatisfactory. It leads in many cases to a destabilizing impact on the current account since repayments are often made in a period of 'low' export earnings. Argentina, e.g., a country with relatively strong destabilization effects of the repurchases, repaid major parts of its debt in years of low export earnings: 1986 and 1987. The same holds true for Bangladesh in 1986 and 1987.

On (4): An essential cause for the relatively low magnitude of the CFF's stabilization or destabilization effects is the limitation of drawings to a share of the national quota. This was an especially binding rule in the first years. Individual credits were not allowed under the 1966 decision of the IMF to exceed 25 per cent of the quota. 63 per cent of the drawings under the CFF touched this 25 per cent limit (Goreux, 1980, pp. 37 *et seq.*).

The empirical analysis presented basically confirms the earlier results of Finger and DeRosa (1980). For their smaller sample of countries which had drawn until 1979 they also found minimal stabilization effects of the CFF. This study as well as that of Finger and DeRosa has focussed on the direct effects of the CFF on export earnings instability. The conceptual question could be raised whether it is appropriate to concentrate on these direct effects and to ignore indirect effects of the CFF on export earnings instability. To the extent that compensation payments under the CFF become predictable for the user countries and for the banking sector, the willingness of the banking sector to give short-term credits to potential CFF users could increase. In such cases, optimal adjustments of the users with debt-management operations could lead to export earnings stabilization even if the direct effects of the CFF are destabilizing. This would be an indirect and uncertainty-reducing effect of the CFF which might lead to a significantly more positive evaluation of the CFF from the stabilization point of view.

A study by the IMF (Kumar 1988) is based on this argument. Kumar distributes the drawings over the shortfall and the drawing year. Consequently, the stabilization effects Kumar calculates are more favourable than those computed here. Of course, positive indirect effects are possible.

There is no empirical evidence, however, that they actually exist. Hence, our procedure to measure the direct effects of the CFF on earnings instability seems superior to the approach adopted by Kumar. He imposes the existence of the indirect effects on his model, whereas we do not. Some other arguments cast some doubt on the existence of the indirect effects and the necessity to deal with them. First, it is the philosophy of compensatory financing schemes that they ought to stabilize export earnings directly. It is not their philosophy that countries should adjust optimally to destabilizing compensation and secure stability for themselves. Secondly, it seems impossible to predict compensation payments exactly. The country does not know how the IMF predicts future earnings and the country's willingness to cooperate. Thirdly and more importantly, payments from the IMF are cheap credits and this provides a major incentive to use the facility irrespective of whether the CFF succeeds in its primary goal of earnings stabilization.

2.1.3 Other effects of the IMF system
As mentioned already, the CFF is not a pure stabilization scheme. It also induces a substantial income transfer towards the borrowing nations. This can be explained as follows. The benchmark situation, against which the CFF has to be evaluated, is a situation without this policy. In the benchmark situation, a country with export earnings shortfalls would have to demand foreign exchange on the international credit market. The conditions for a drawing under the CFF are more favourable than those for a commercial credit from the banking system. A uniform interest rate across countries is charged which is clearly lower than the market rate. Income transfers towards the user of the CFF arise. The transfers are higher the larger the credit, the later it is repaid and the higher the opportunity interest rate of the individual borrower.

In a quantitative analysis on all drawings under the CFF in the period 1963–80, the hidden income transfers were measured (Herrmann 1983). This analysis rests on the assumption of a uniform interest rate, since country-specific interest rates were not available. The credit costs of the World Bank were utilized as an opportunity interest rate. Based on these assumptions, the average grant ratio in fully repaid drawings from the CFF in the period 1963–80 amounted to about 10 per cent. Income transfers were distributed to richer as well as poorer countries and not in all cases to developing countries. The allocation of aid under the CFF showed a positive correlation with per-capita income. 'Richer' recipient countries were clearly favoured and, thus, the hidden aid seems arbitrary from a distributive point of view.

2.2   The STABEX system of the Lomé Convention

2.2.1   Basic rules of STABEX

The STABEX system was introduced in 1975 under the first Lomé Convention (1975–79). It remained a major element of the second (1980–84) as well as the third Lomé Convention (1985–89), which is currently valid for the 12 EC countries and 66 African, Caribbean and Pacific (ACP) countries. STABEX is the major commodity-related export earnings stabilization scheme in force. It is the declared aim of STABEX to remedy 'the harmful effects of the instability of export earnings and to help the ACP States overcome one of the main obstacles to the stability, profitability and sustained growth of their economies, to support their development efforts and to enable them in this way to ensure economic and social progress for their peoples by helping to safeguard their purchasing power . . .' (Art. 1470).[9] Compensation is granted for short-falls in export earnings of products on which the ACP economies are dependent. 48 agricultural products are covered by the scheme. The system applies to export earnings in trade with the EC or, upon request, to export earnings to all destinations or to other ACP countries (Art. 150). Apart from modifications of STABEX in the course of the Lomé Convention, a parallel system of compensation for loss of export earnings was established in 1987 for least-developed countries not signatory to the Lomé Convention (Commission of the EC, 1987).

Export earnings shortfalls are calculated for calendar years, the so-called application years. The reference levels are the average export earnings during the preceding four calendar years (Art. 158). The difference between the reference level and actual export earnings, plus 2 per cent for statistical errors and omissions, constitute the transfer basis. The following conditions must be fulfilled in order to give entitlement to a transfer:

(1)   The dependence threshold must be reached. This is given when exports to all destinations represent at least 6 per cent of all exports during the preceding year (Art. 161). The percentage is lower for sisal (4.5 per cent).

(2)   The fluctuation threshold must be reached, i.e. earnings have to be at least 6 per cent below the reference level. For the least-developed, landlocked and island ACP states, the dependence and fluctuation threshold is lower (1.5 per cent).

(3)   The request has to be presented before 31st March of the year following the application (Art. 163).

(4)   There is no compensation for export earnings shortfalls caused by the trade policy of the ACP country (Art. 163).

Given that the resources of STABEX are sufficient in an application year and the above conditions are fulfilled, the loss of earnings is to be compensated fully. If the amount of resources available is lower than the total amount of the transfer bases, each transfer basis can be reduced. The reduction of each transfer shall not exceed 30 per cent for the least-developed countries (LLDCs) and the landlocked countries, and 40 per cent for the other ACP countries (Art. 155, §3).

In order to reach the stabilization objective, the ACP states and the Commission shall make sure that compensation payments are made rapidly. Advance payments are possible (Art. 170).

STABEX contains a strong redistributive element, too. First, the least-developed ACP states do not have to repay the compensation payments (Art. 172). Secondly, STABEX payments for all other ACP countries are interest-free loans. These loans have to be repaid (Art. 172) given that the following three conditions are fulfilled simultaneously: the export price has to be higher, the export quantity has to be equal to or higher and export earnings have to be at least 6 per cent higher than the average values of the respective variables in a reference period. The reference period is the four years prior to the shortfall year (Art. 173). The repayment shall then occur after a two-year deferment period in five equal annual instalments (Art. 174). These are rather soft repayment conditions.

2.2.2 Did STABEX stabilize export earnings of the ACP countries? Quantitative results for the period 1975–87

The following empirical analysis of the stabilizing effects of STABEX is based on aggregate export earnings. It is comprehensive countrywise as well as periodwise.[10] Out of 51 countries,[11] which received STABEX payments since the beginning of the Lomé Convention in 1975 up to 1987, 48 are covered. Export earnings instability is analyzed for the whole period 1975–87. Since information on the extent and timing of repayments is not regularly published by the EC and most ACP countries do not have to repay STABEX transfers, only the stabilization effects of disbursements from the EC are considered. The empirical analysis concentrates again on the direct effects of STABEX on export earnings instability.[12] The measurement of instability is based on equation (1) and it is investigated whether the ACP countries' export earnings were more or less stable with STABEX payments than without them.

Table 10.2 shows the results for 48 ACP countries:

(1)   Export earnings instability varied strongly between ACP countries

which used the STABEX scheme. Instabilities ranged between 18 per cent (Senegal) and 62.6 per cent (Sao Tomé & Principe). The arithmetic mean of instabilities was 34.7 per cent and the median 31.6 per cent. This implies that the average export earnings instability of STABEX users was higher than for users of the IMF's CFF. The instabilities shown in Table 10.2, which are calculated for export earnings denominated in ECU, are in most cases based on the uncorrected coefficient of variation. Export earnings of many ACP countries showed no statistically significant growth in the period 1975–87.

(2) The qualitative result on the stabilization effects of STABEX is similar to that reported for the IMF's CFF. The overall impact of STABEX was weak. Table 10.2 reveals that the median effect arising from STABEX payments on export earnings of recipient countries was slightly stabilizing (− 0.21 per cent). For 20 countries, a destabilizing effect on export earnings occurred, and for 28 countries a stabilizing one. The magnitude of the effects in either direction was low. Not a single stabilization effect was larger than 10 per cent. All destabilizing impacts were smaller than 10 per cent, too. Export earnings instability was reduced by more than 3 per cent for only five countries and by more than 5 per cent for only two countries – Western Samoa and Tonga. The destabilizing effect was higher than 5 per cent in only one country, Senegal. Interestingly, STABEX payments destabilized export earnings in all four countries which received the highest STABEX transfers: Côte d'Ivoire, Senegal, Sudan and Papua New Guinea.

The overall performance of the STABEX scheme can be generalized when the payments from 1975 to 1987 are treated as a representative sample for the future success of the system. Then, a median test can be applied in order to derive confidence intervals for the stabilizing effects of STABEX disbursements. Given a 99 per cent level of statistical significance and a two-sided test, this confidence interval is

$$- 0.93 \leqslant 100 \cdot (\Delta v^*/v^*) \leqslant + 0.11 \tag{5}$$

This implies:

(1) Starting from the performance of STABEX in the first 13 years of the Lomé Convention, it can be expected that STABEX will induce a median effect on export earnings instability that lies between stabilization by 0.93 per cent and destabilization by 0.11 per cent. Consequently, the median effect can be evaluated as rather negligible.

(2) Without any significant policy change, it is very unrealistic that STABEX will affect export earnings instability of ACP countries strongly. Stabilizing effects of 10 per cent or more are clearly outside the confidence interval for the median impact.

Countries	Instability of selected variables[a] Export earnings (1)	Export earnings and STABEX payments (2)	Percentage change in export earnings instability due to STABEX payments (3)
Belize	31.33	31.31	− 0.05
Benin*	35.00	34.30	− 1.99
Burkina Faso*	52.57	52.17	− 0.78
Burundi*	29.05	28.80	− 0.86
Cameroon	31.06	30.91	− 0.50
Cape Verde*	47.76	47.04	− 1.50
Central African Republic*	32.08	32.68	+ 1.87
Chad*	28.05	28.66	+ 2.16
Congo, PDR	34.14	34.11	− 0.08
Côte d'Ivoire	29.07	29.10	+ 0.12
Djibouti*	22.06	22.10	+ 0.15
Dominica*	42.50	41.80	− 1.66
Equatorial Guinea*	30.57	31.00	+ 1.40
Ethiopia*	23.88	23.66	− 0.93
Fiji	34.23	23.13	− 0.29
Gabon	37.97	38.00	+ 0.06
Gambia*	33.49	33.50	+ 0.03
Ghana	31.70	31.29	− 1.28
Grenada*	29.66	28.28	− 4.65
Guinea Bissau*	42.59	43.56	+ 2.27
Jamaica	30.08	30.09	+ 0.02
Kenya	25.71	25.64	− 0.27
Lesotho[b]*	61.69	61.51	− 0.29
Liberia	30.81	30.85	+ 0.11
Madagascar	29.95	29.87	− 0.26
Malawi*	28.13	28.14	+ 0.04
Mali*	44.33	44.03	− 0.68
Mauritania*	25.83	25.33	− 1.93
Mauritius	40.47	40.59	+ 0.29
Mozambique*	54.74	54.20	− 0.99
Niger*	54.62	53.78	− 1.54
Papua New Guinea	28.71	28.98	+ 0.91
Rwanda*	21.95	22.25	+ 1.38
St. Lucia[b]*	29.31	29.44	+ 0.45
St. Vincent*	26.55	26.84	+ 1.08
Sao Tomé & Principe*	62.62	59.71	− 4.65
Senegal	17.96	19.48	+ 8.49
Sierra Leone*	41.30	40.39	− 2.21
Solomon Islands*	32.33	31.81	− 1.58

Table 10.2 (*cont.*)

| Countries | Instability of selected variables[a] | | Percentage change in export earnings instability due to STABEX payments |
	Export earnings (1)	Export earnings and STABEX payments (2)	(3)
Somalia*	38.29	38.25	− 0.11
Sudan*	28.84	29.35	+ 1.76
Swaziland*	35.82	35.76	− 0.16
Tanzania*	27.41	27.22	− 0.71
Togo*	42.15	40.81	− 3.18
Tonga*	32.10	29.91	− 6.80
Uganda*	31.54	31.99	+ 1.43
Vanuatu*	28.96	29.87	+ 3.16
Western Samoa*	34.93	31.98	− 8.45
Arithmetic mean:	34.71	34.47	− 0.44
Standard deviation:	9.91	9.57	2.51
Median:	31.62	31.30	− 0.21

Table 10.2   Effects of the STABEX scheme on export earnings instability of 48 ACP countries

* indicates countries which do not have to repay STABEX disbursements.
[a]On the computation of the measures of instability see the text. Export earnings are expressed in ECU. A linear trend correction was used for Benin, Djibouti and Equatorial Guinea, a loglinear one for Burundi, Cameroon, Cape Verde, Congo, PDR, Dominica, Rwanda, St. Lucia, St. Vincent, Sao Tomé & Principe, Solomon Islands, Tanzania and Vanuatu. In all other cases, the F-values of the regressions were insignificant at the 5 per cent level and the uncorrected coefficient of variation was used. [b]The calculations refer to the period 1975–86.

Source: Own computations. Data on export earnings are from IMF (b). Data on STABEX payments are taken from Commission of the EC (1988). The information on the dates of disbursement is from Commission of the EC (a, b, 1981).

Three reasons are responsible for the low success of the STABEX scheme in stabilizing ACP countries export earnings:

(1) Compensation payments are usually granted after a delay in the year following the shortfall. Requests for compensatory payments can be made up to 3 months after the shortfall year. Assuming a three-months duration for the consideration of the request, the time lag between the middle of the shortfall year and the disbursement may

be as much as 12 months. In this case, stabilization effects are coincidental, as they depend on the level of export earnings in the year following the earnings shortfall. An empirical analysis of delays in STABEX payments indicates that this is an important point. Under Lomé I, the mean time lag between the end of the shortfall year and the compensation payment was higher than nine months (Commission of the EC, 1981; Herrmann, 1983, Table 2). Hence, STABEX transfers were much less timely than transfers under the IMF's CFF. This is also indicated by the fact that less than 1 per cent of all STABEX disbursements under Lomé I were given as advance payments.

(2) The EC compensates commodity-related export earnings short-falls which need not be correlated positively with national export earnings shortfalls. Destabilizing effects on national export earnings may occur. A case in point is Senegal where national export earnings were destabilized the most by STABEX payments. Senegal is the country which experienced the lowest export earnings instability of all STABEX users. However, substantial earnings instability existed in its groundnut sector and gave rise to large STABEX payments. Falls in export earnings for groundnuts were overcompensated in various years by booming petroleum exports and, thus, STABEX payments for earnings shortfalls in groundnuts destabilized Senegal's national export earnings. Another aspect matters in this context. The computation of the reference value is oriented at past values and does not take into account that a trend might underly the time series of export earnings. Due to the overestimation or underestimation of the 'normal' value which includes the time trend, a destabilizing effect may occur for an ACP country that plans on the basis of detrended earnings.

(3) Additionally, STABEX payments may be insufficient to compensate export earnings shortfalls fully. This problem is the most severe when international coffee and cocoa prices fall drastically and many ACP coffee and cocoa exporters apply for compensation within the same year. In such cases, STABEX funds proved to be too low to stabilize export earnings effectively. This was the case in 1980 and 1981. For the application year 1980, only shortfalls in the magnitude of under 1 mill. ECU were compensated fully. 59.5 per cent of the higher shortfalls were covered for the least developed ACP countries and 47.5 per cent for all other ACP countries. For the application year 1981, export earnings shortfalls of the ACP countries exceeded STABEX funds even more and the transfer bases had to be cut more severely than in 1980 (Commission of the EC, b). In such years, the stabilization potential of STABEX is obviously very limited.

In a comprehensive evaluation of the STABEX system it has to be borne in mind that these different reasons for the low stabilization success often occur together. The limited STABEX transfers for the export earnings shortfalls in 1980 and 1981, e.g., were disbursed in the years following the shortfalls. It had to be decided discretionarily how to allocate the available funds to the ACP countries with earnings shortfalls. Additionally, a decision was taken in 1986 to compensate that part of the shortfalls in 1980 and 1981 which had been still uncompensated until then (Commission of the EC, 1988, pp. 16 *et seq.*). Of course, compensation payments of this kind are purely coincidental in their stabilization effect. The discretionary character of decisions under STABEX indicates that STABEX is not primarily a stabilization scheme. It is regarded by the EC Commission as a kind of insurance system which transfers resources to ACP countries after a discretionary decision process, given that commodity-related export earnings shortfalls exist.

2.2.3 Other effects of the STABEX scheme
The STABEX system is not purely an instrument of stabilization, but also contains substantial elements of redistribution. Compared with a hypothetical situation without STABEX, redistributive effects are induced both between the EC and the ACP countries and within the group of ACP countries themselves. In the non-STABEX situation, ACP countries would have to demand foreign exchange in the international credit market in order to stabilize their ability to meet their import needs. There exists a differential grant ratio in STABEX payments for different country groups:

(1) There is a grant ratio of 100 per cent in STABEX payments to the least-developed ACP countries. These countries, marked by * in Table 10.2, do not have to repay STABEX payments.

(2) There is a grant ratio, usually of less than 100 per cent, in all other STABEX payments. However, it is still substantial as very soft repayment conditions are granted. The grant ratio is much higher than in the CFF. One difference from the CFF is that STABEX credits bear no interest. There is also a two-year grace period before credits have to be repaid. Moreover, debts arising from STABEX credits can be cancelled when the reference values of export quantities, export price and export earnings are not reached within seven years following the shortfall.

The empirical evidence shows for the period 1975–87 that 49 per cent of all STABEX payments were pure grants. They went to the least-developed ACP countries. Under Lomé I, this share had even been higher with nearly 70 per cent. The declining share under Lomé II and III is due to the fact that coffee and cocoa, the main agricultural export crops of the ACP countries, caused a relatively large share of the transactions under Lomé II and III. Major coffee and cocoa exporting ACP countries do not belong to the group of the least-developed ACP states. In a quantitative analysis of all individual transfers until 1983, which were in principle repayable, the grant ratios were measured (Koester and Herrmann, 1987, Appendix 7.6). They were calculated as actual grant ratios for already repaid STABEX payments and as minimum grant ratios for all other STABEX credits. Again, the credit costs of the World Bank were used as opportunity interest rate. The analysis showed an average grant ratio in repayable STABEX credits of 61 per cent. If we assume that the grant ratio remained constant, the STABEX payments up to 1987 included an average grant ratio of 80.2 per cent. When the allocation of these implicit transfers to ACP countries is considered, it is striking that the transfers are uncorrelated with neediness. The correlation coefficient between per-capita income transfers and per-capita GNP, both measured in ECU, is − 0.01.

What makes the system even more attractive for users is that no conditionality exists for STABEX payments. The Lomé Convention says that payments shall be devoted to economic and social development either in the shortfall sector or elsewhere (Art. 147, §2). This, however, cannot be enforced and STABEX grants are basically a form of untied aid.

3   Economic evaluation of existing international commodity agreements

The empirical evidence on international commodity agreements shows that they have been much less important than intended by UNCTAD's IPC. It had been the objective of the IPC to stabilize real prices of ten core commodities on the basis of international buffer stock schemes. Right now, only two buffer stock agreements exist, the INRA and the International Cocoa Agreement (ICCA). The ICA, which is also in force, is based on an export quota scheme. Moreover, there is ample evidence that various agreements were rather unsuccessful in reaching their objectives (Gilbert, 1987). The International Tin Agreement and the ICCA of 1980 broke down. Prices were enforced which exceeded the medium-run equilibrium price and the commodity authorities ran out of funds. The International Sugar Agreement has never been an effective market stabilizer as major producing countries do not participate.

The following quantitative analysis on the impacts of commodity agreements concentrates on two of the three existing agreements – the ICA and the INRA. These are often pointed to as the success stories. A brief overview of both agreements will be given. Then, a quantitative analysis will be presented in order to judge the effectiveness of both agreements in reaching their primary objectives. It will be argued that the ICA is primarily oriented at price support, i.e. income redistribution, and the INRA at price stabilization.

3.1 The International Coffee Agreement

3.1.1 Basic rules of the ICA and its performance in the 1980s

The stated objective of the Fourth ICA of 1983 are diverse.[13] Generally, the ICA is supposed to achieve a reasonable balance between world supply and demand on a basis which will assure adequate supplies of coffee at fair prices to consumers and markets for coffee at renumerative prices to producers and which will be conducive to long-term equilibrium between production and consumption (Art. 1, §1). Additional goals of the ICA are

- to avoid excessive fluctuations in the levels of world supplies, stocks and prices which are harmful to both producers and consumers (Art. 1, §2);
- to contribute to the development of productive resources and to the promotion and maintenance of employment and income in member countries, thereby helping to bring about fair wages, higher living standards and better working conditions (Art. 1, §3);
- to increase the purchasing power of coffee-exporting countries by keeping prices in accordance with §1 and by increasing consumption (Art. 1, §4);
- to promote and increase the consumption of coffee by every possible means (Art. 1, §5).

The 1983 ICA is based on an export quota scheme, as were the earlier agreements of 1962, 1968 and 1976. The quota system is valid for the market of the importing member countries. No quotas exist for the market of the importing non-member countries. The first market is called the member market; the second one is the non-member market. The International Coffee Council sets a global annual export quota for all exporting member countries as the maximum to be sold in the member market (Art. 34). Annual national quotas are fixed, too, and allocated as quarterly quotas (Art. 35–37). Annual national export quotas contain a fixed part, determined by the historical basic quota of each member, and a variable part, which is allocated among exporting members according to the share of the individual member's stocks in all exporting members' stocks. The fixed part shall constitute 70 per cent and the variable part 30 per cent of the annual quotas (Art. 35). Various smaller countries are exempt from basic quotas and have a joint 4.2 per cent share of the global annual quota or individually fixed quotas like Burundi and Rwanda (Art. 31; Annex 2). The quota scheme is controlled at the borders of importing member countries. These countries have to make sure that each coffee export of a member is covered by a valid certificate of origin (Art. 43). The introduction, continuation or suspension of the quota scheme is bound by price rules. A crucial element of these price rules is whether the composite indicator price of the agreement, defined as the arithmetic mean of the indicator prices for Other Mild Arabicas and Robustas, is higher or lower than minimum prices fixed by the International Coffee Organization (Art. 33, 38).

The history of the ICAs shows that there was an active quota policy in the 1960s, but no intervention by the International Coffee Organization occurred from 1972 to 1980, partly due to high world coffee prices. In September 1980, coffee quotas were reintroduced and remained in force until February 1986. Since October 1987, the quota system has again been in force. The introduction of quotas in 1980 caused a market separation between the member and the non-member market with clearly higher prices in the quota market (Pieterse and Silvis, 1988, p. 79). Exporting members sold parts of their quota-induced oversupply in the non-member market and depressed prices there. The International Coffee Organization responded in 1985 to this situation with Resolution 336, saying that exporting members shall not accept any sales contracts for coffee to be exported to non-members at a price which is lower than that applying to coffee with the same specifications sold to a member country. However, the parallel-market problem is still unresolved and it shows up again each time the quota system is in operation.

Some authors conclude from the ICA's objective that it is primarily a price-stabilizing agreement (Pieterse and Silvis, 1988, p. 47). This view is misleading, however. The instruments of the ICA work towards a price increase in the member market compared with a liberalized world coffee market. The quota mechanism is a price-support instrument in periods of 'low' world price, but the ICA has no instrument to drive down prices in 'boom' periods. Therefore, it is argued here that the ICA is rather a price-support than a price-stabilization scheme and we will concentrate in the following on an analysis of the redistributive consequences of this price-support scheme.

3.1.2 The allocative and redistributive consequences of price support under the ICA
The short-run allocative and redistributive consequences are modelled for two typical years when the quota system was in operation: 1982 and 1983.

First, the ICA's aggregate impact on the world market and the consequential welfare implications for country groups are shown. Beneficiaries and losers from the ICA will be determined in aggregate terms.
Then, it will be investigated how hidden income transfers under the ICA
are allocated among 94 exporting and importing countries and policy
conclusions will be drawn. The analysis is based on an econometric
world coffee market model which is used to model the hypothetical
non-quota situation (Hermann, 1986) and on the procedure outlined in
Herrmann (1988a).

Table 10.3 summarizes the ICA's aggregate impacts for 1982 and 1983.
Impacts arising from the quota policy on the world market price, on trade,
on export earnings and import expenditures and on economic welfare of
major country groups are presented. The following aggregate redistributive and allocative effects occurred:

(1) Export quotas under the ICA raised the import price on the market
of the importing member countries compared with a liberalized world
coffee market. The price-increasing effect was 47 per cent in 1982, 17 per
cent in 1983 and some 30 per cent on average for both years. This led to a
reduction in the imports of member countries by 7 per cent and, due to low
price elasticity of import demand in this market segment (− 0.28), to an
increase in import expenditures by 21 per cent. The price rise on the quota
market implies that income redistribution occurs under the ICA away
from the importing member countries.

(2) The effect arising from the ICA's quota policy in the market of the
importing non-members was opposite to the effect in the quota market.
Oversupply was transmitted to this parallel market and depressed the
price by about 10 per cent compared with a liberalized world coffee
market. Importing non-members raised their imports by 1.5 per cent and
their import share by nearly 10 per cent. Due to a price-inelastic import
demand in the non-member market (− 0.13), import expenditures fell by
some 10 per cent in spite of increased imports. As a consequence of the
price fall in the parallel coffee market, the ICA leads to a redistributive
impact in favour of importing non-member countries.

(3) Nearly all coffee exporters are members of the ICA. Hence, the
coffee exporters were affected twofold by the export quota policy. They
experienced a price support for their quotas on the markets of the
importing members, and sold surpluses at a reduced price on the parallel
market, compared with a uniform price in a liberalized world coffee
market respectively. Due to the large share of the member market in the
aggregate world coffee market, the price-support element dominated.
Although total exports declined, coffee exporters increased their export
earnings by 17 per cent as a consequence of the ICA. The rise in the

Variables	Existing situation with ICA	Hypothetical situation without ICA	Impact of the ICA
Price on the member market of the ICA ($/mt):	2,774	2,130	+ 30%
Price on the non-member market of the ICA ($/mt):	1,912	2,130	− 10%
Price ratio between the member and the non-member market (%)[b]:	69	100	− 31%
Trade on the member market (1000 mt):	3,337	3,605	− 7%
Trade on the non-member market (1000 mt):	591	582	+ 2%
Total world coffee trade (1000 mt):	3,928	4,187	− 6%
Relative size of the non-member compared with the member market (%)[b]:	18	16	+ 10%
Import expenditures on the member market ($m):	9,256	7,651	+ 21%
Import expenditures on the non-member market ($m):	1,123	1,244	− 10%
Export earnings of all exporting countries ($m):	10,379	8,895	+ 17%
Economic welfare of importing member countries ($m):	—	—	− 2,239
Economic welfare of importing non-member countries ($m):	—	—	+ 140
Economic welfare of all importers ($m):	—	—	− 2,099
Economic welfare of exporters on the member market ($m):	—	—	+ 1,991
Economic welfare of exporters on the non-member market ($m):	—	—	− 58
Economic welfare of all exporters ($m):	—	—	+ 1,932
Economic welfare on the member market ($m):	—	—	− 249
Economic welfare on the non-member market ($m):	—	—	+ 82
Aggregate welfare of all exorters and importers ($m):	—	—	− 167

Table 10.3 Aggregate short-run impacts of price support under the ICA on world prices, trade, export earnings, import expenditures and economic welfare, average of 1982 and 1983[a]

[a]The member market is the market of the importing member countries of the ICA, the non-member market is the market of the importing non-member countries of the ICA.
[b]Average price and trade ratios were calculated as a geometric mean.

Source: Various tables in Herrmann (1988a, chapter 3) and the data sources cited therein.

average export price implies that the group of exporting members of the ICA received a hidden income transfer due to the quota system.

(4) Table 10.3 also records the magnitude of income transfers which was involved in the ICA's export quota policy. Implications of the ICA for economic welfare in Marshallian terms is measured for various country groups. The importing member countries were welfare losers with an aggregate loss of $2,239m. Welfare gainers were the exporting members with an aggregate gain of $1,932m and the importing non-member countries with $140m. The exporting member countries gained $1,991m in the member market and lost $58m in the non-member market.

(5) As is well-known from theory, an export quota policy does not represent a zero-sum game in welfare terms. The welfare loss of importing member countries exceeded the combined welfare gains of the exporting members and the importing non-members. This implies that the ICA induced an aggregate welfare loss for all exporters and importers in the world coffee market. The magnitude of this welfare loss was $167m. When the parallel market is ignored, the net welfare loss in the quota market due to the ICA amounted to some $250m. This represents the negative short-run allocation effect arising from the ICA's price-support policy. It results from the fact that coffee production is too high and world coffee consumption too low from the worldwide efficiency point of view.

These redistributive and allocative impacts seem inconsistent with the goals of the ICA for the following reasons:

(1) In general, the price-support character of the quota policy is not consistent with declared objectives of the ICA as it decreases consumption in the member market and also world coffee consumption. Art 1, §6 says, however, that coffee consumption shall be increased by every possible means.

(2) It does not conform with the objectives of the ICA that importing non-member countries are net beneficiaries of the agreement. These countries realized lower import prices and import expenditures and a welfare gain in Marshallian terms. Several articles of and resolutions on the agreement indicate that welfare gains of non-members are undesired (Art. 45, Resolution 336). The parallel-market problem and the welfare

gains of non-members provide an incentive for importing members to leave the agreement and, therefore, endanger the stability of the agreement.

One might argue, however, that most coffee exporters are developing countries and the implicit transfer of the ICA might be justified from a redistributive point of view. The validity of this argument was tested in a quantitative analysis for 94 importing and exporting countries. On the basis of the aggregate price effects shown in Table 10.3, and econometrically estimated price elasticities of import demand and export supply for individual countries, the implicit aid flows under the ICA were determined.[14]

Table 10.4 shows that large importing members like the USA and West Germany were the most important welfare losers in absolute terms. Countries with the highest per-capita consumption – Finland, Denmark and Sweden – experienced the highest welfare losses in per-capita terms. Analogously, the highest welfare gains in absolute terms went to large coffee exporters like Brazil and Colombia and in per-capita terms to countries with particular high per-capita exports. El Salvador, Côte d'Ivoire and Costa Rica. Within the group of importing non-member countries, the highest welfare gains were realized in absolute and per-capita terms by the largest coffee importers, Algeria and East Germany. The correlation analysis presented in Table 10.4 shows that welfare effects in either direction increase with a country's net coffee trade position. This is consistent with theory: large importers are affected more negatively than small importers by a given price increase due to the ICA, and large exporters gain more than small exporters. It can also be seen in Table 10.4 that the welfare gains arising from the ICA are negatively correlated with per-capital income as far as the total country sample is concerned.

Does the negative correlation of per-capital welfare gains and per-capita income imply that the ICA leads to a redistribution of income towards poor countries? The negative correlation coefficient for the total country sample implies that relatively rich coffee importers transfer hidden aid to relatively poor coffee exporters. However, neediness does not matter when the major economic determinants of the ICA's welfare impacts are also introduced into a regression model. This can be seen in the following regression equation which was estimated for all 94 countries in order to explain the cross-country distribution of welfare gains and losses due to the ICA:

$$\Delta WC = 0.9593 + 0.4163 \; ESC + 1.4238 \; D1 - 2.0518 \; D2$$
$$(3.74) \quad\;\; (27.95) \qquad\quad (3.10) \qquad (-5.13)$$
$$- 6.1314 \cdot 10^{-5} GNPC$$
$$(-1.44) \tag{6}$$

$$(\bar{R}^2 = 0.94; \ F = 377.04)$$

ΔWC is the per-capita welfare change in $ due to the ICA, ESC is the net export status measured by average net coffee exports in kg per capita for 1966–81, $GNPC$ is the per-capita gross national product in $. $D1$ is a dummy variable indicating whether the country is exporting ($D1 = 1$) or importing coffee ($D1 = 0$). $D2$ is a dummy variable showing whether the country is a member of the ICA ($D2 = 1$) or not ($D2 = 0$). WC and $GNPC$ are average values for 1982 and 1983. Values in parentheses are t values.

Equation (6) shows that the magnitude of the ICA's impact on a country's economic welfare depends on whether the country is an importing member country, an importing non-member country or an exporting member country. Within each group, the welfare impacts were stronger the higher the country's coffee imports or exports. After having introduced these major determinants of the ICA's welfare impact, per-capita income does not contribute significantly to the explanation of the cross-country distribution of welfare gains and welfare losses.

The result becomes even clearer when the distribution of trade-tied aid among the exporting member countries is analyzed in more detail. The following regression equation was estimated for this country group:

$$\Delta WC = 0.4296 + 0.4057 \ ESC - 0.80698 \cdot 10^{-4} GNPC$$
$$ (1.68) \quad (24.68) \qquad (-0.58) \tag{7}$$

$$(\bar{R}^2 = 0.93; \ F = 306.69)$$

Equation (7) shows that the most important determinant of a welfare gain due to the ICA is net coffee exports. An increase in per-capita coffee exports by one kilogram led to a rise in the per-capita welfare gain by $0.41. Neediness does not matter for the cross-country allocation of hidden aid to exporting member countries. This finding confirms empirically the well-known view from the economics of aid that trade-tied aid is inferior to a well-targeted financial aid. The ICA redistributes income according to the size of the coffee export sector which is uncorrelated with neediness.

It can be summarized that the ICA contains strong redistributive elements. Income transfers are given as a form of trade-tied aid, and this is a clearly suboptimal redistributive policy compared with targeted financial aid. Due to the price-support effect, the ICA leads also to aggregate efficiency losses in the world coffee economy.

Indicator	Welfare effects – Magnitude and correlations	
Highest welfare losses of importing member countries:		
– in absolute terms ($m):	711.0	(USA)
	341.8	(FR Germany)
	216.4	(France)
	162.9	(Italy)
	123.2	(Japan)
– in per-capita terms ($):	8.50	(Finland)
	7.82	(Denmark)
	7.72	(Sweden)
	6.94	(Netherlands)
	6.85	(Belgium)
Highest welfare gains of exporting member countries:		
– in absolute terms ($m):	581.6	(Brazil)
	332.0	(Colombia)
	151.0	(Côte d'Ivoire)
	94.4	(Uganda)
	87.3	(El Salvador)
– in per-capita terms ($):	16.93	(El Salvador)
	16.41	(Côte d'Ivoire)
	15.16	(Costa Rica)
	12.19	(Colombia)
	8.23	(Guatemala)
Highest welfare gains of importing non-member countries:		
– in absolute terms ($m):	24.0	(Algeria)
	20.6	(East Germany)
	9.4	(Hungary)
	9.3	(Czechoslovakia)
	8.0	(Poland)
– in per-capita terms ($):	1.22	(East Germany)
	1.19	(Algeria)
	1.08	(Israel)
	0.88	(Hungary)
	0.68	(Jordan)
Correlation between per-capita welfare gains and GNP per capita:		
– All countries:	– 0.603*	(90)
– Exporting members:	– 0.083 (n.s.)	(91)
Correlation between per-capita welfare gains and net coffee exports in per-capita terms:		
– All countries:	0.929*	(43)
– Exporting members:	0.926*	(44)

Table 10.4 The international allocation of welfare gains and losses under the ICA, 94 countries, average of 1982 and 1983[a]

* Statistically significant at the 99.9 per cent level; n.s. indicates not significant at the 90 per cent level. All tests are two-sided. The numbers in parentheses are degrees of freedom.
[a]Welfare effects are calculated for 1982 and 1983 in Marshallian terms with the procedure outlined in Hermann (1988b). Net coffee exports are calculated on average for 1961–81 with data from FAO and GNP per capita on average for 1982 and 1983 with data from World Bank.

Source: Herrmann (1988b), various tables, and the sources cited therein.

3.1.3 Other effects of the ICA
Price support and redistribution towards the exporting countries were regarded here as primary objectives of the ICA. This paper as well as another recent study (Palm and Vogelvang, 1988) indicate that a substantial redistribution occurred in the first half of the 1980s. Besides this, the ICA's impacts on price stability and the long-run redistributive consequences are of special interest. A recent study by Akiyama and Varangis (1988) concluded that the quota system contributed to price stability in the early 1980s, but will not be successful in redistributing income towards the exporting members in the medium run. Their basic argument is that price support in the quota market will increase supply and reduce coffee prices in the years when the quota system is not in operation. More work has to be done to clarify these issues, however. The linkage between the member and non-member markets is not modelled by Akiyama and Varangis and this linkage is crucial for the price-stabilization and long-run redistributive impact of the ICA.

3.2   The International Natural Rubber Agreement

3.2.1 The natural rubber market
Total world rubber consumption (i.e. natural plus synthetic rubber) increased dramatically in the past decades. The tyre sector consumed between 40 per cent and 70 per cent of total rubber consumption. Specific non-tyre end-uses for rubber number in the thousands. To mention a few: footwear, window strips, engine mouldings, conveyor belts, hoses, rubber gloves and condoms.

Until 1940 natural rubber (NR) was the only source of rubber (see Table 10.5). Large scale production of synthetic rubber (SR) emerged when, during the Second World War, supply of NR was insufficient, largely due to blocked supply lines. In the fifties and sixties production of SR increased dramatically because demand, particularly in the automotive sector, grew much faster than supply of NR, thus creating a reduction in

	Total rubber consumption	Natural rubber consumption	% Share natural rubber	Singapore S$/mt	New York US$/mt
1900	53	53	100		1,277
1910	102	102	100		2,267
1920	302	302	100		943
1930	722	722	100	422	226
1940	1,127	1,127	100	828	439
1950	2,339	1,750	75	2,393	906
1960	4,400	2,095	48	2,383	841
1970	8,625	2,990	35	1,244	463
1975	10,395	3,370	32	1,346	659
1980	12,540	3,760	30	3,079	1,625
1985	13,295	4,355	33	1,665	924
1987	14,415	4,805	33	2,072	1,113

Table 10.5 World total rubber consumption and natural rubber consumption (000 mt) and prices of NR in Singapore and New York (RSS1)

Sources: Allen *et al.* (1973); *Rubber Statistical Bulletin*, International Rubber Study Group, various issues.

the share of NR from 75 per cent in 1950 to 30 per cent in 1980. This was feasible owing to technological improvements in SR, enabling SR to take over from NR. However, the decline in the share of NR was gradually stopped because certain end-uses, in particular radial tyres and commercial vehicle tyres still need a large share of NR, which cannot be replaced commercially by an SR substitute. On average, about 1/3 of rubber in passenger car tyre is NR while approximately 2/3 is required in a heavy truck tyre. On a world scale, NR takes some 10–15 per cent in non-tyre end-uses. The price elasticity decreased owing to an increasingly strong emphasis on technology.

Hevea Brasiliensis emerged as the only source of NR, because of such advantageous properties as high yield of latex over a sustained period and resistance to disease and insect pests. Although a plantation crop, most production of NR is considered to come from smallholders. Of the major producing countries, only Malaysia and Indonesia have substantial estate sectors, accounting for one-third of these countries' total NR production. The share of Malaysia, the leading producer, increased from 36 per cent at the end of the 1950s to 44 per cent in 1979. Since 1980, however, it has declined to 32 per cent in 1988. Production in Indonesia declined to a minimum in 1960, recovered considerably in the following decade, remained on a plateau between 1970 and 1977, to grow fairly rapidly again after 1977 to reach a share in total world production of 25 per cent in 1987. Thailand shows the fastest growth of all larger producing countries, its production increasing by 600 per cent since 1955; her share in 1987 was 20 per cent.

Different types of NR have different prices. Two important groups are sheet rubber, which is the traditional type and technically specified rubber, which is the modern type. Sheet rubber is divided into grades of which RSS1 and RSS3 are the most commonly used in price quotation. RSS stands for ribbed smoked sheet. Table 10.5 gives a review of price developments during this century. Instability in the prices of NR is obviously present and increasingly so, because of less substitutability on the demand side. For such reasons an international price stabilization scheme has been established, as will be discussed below.

3.2.2 The International Natural Rubber Agreement of 1979

This brief description of the price stabilization side of INRA (1979) is given to act as a basis for the further analysis in this report. We have drawn heavily on UNCTAD (1985). UNCTAD at its Fourth Session in Nairobi in May 1976, adopted Resolution 93 (IV) containing the IPC. Pursuant to that resolution, UNCTAD convened a series of meetings to prepare for negotiation of a natural rubber agreement. At the end of the Fourth Session, on 6 October 1979, the text of the INRA (1979) was established. Thus this Agreement became the first new International Commodity Agreement successfully negotiated under the IPC.

Selected main features of the Agreement as regards stabilization are:

(1) The objectives of the agreement are spelled out in Art. 1; selected sub-articles regarding price stabilization are as follows:

(a) to achieve a balanced growth between the supply of and demand for natural rubber, thereby helping to alleviate the serious difficulties arising from surpluses or shortages of natural rubber;

(b) to achieve stable conditions in natural rubber trade through avoiding excessive natural rubber price fluctuations, which adversely affect the long-term interest of both producers and consumers, and to stabilize these prices without distorting long-term market trends, in the interests of producers and consumers;

(c) to help to stabilize the export earnings from natural rubber of exporting members, and to increase their earnings based on expanding natural rubber export volumes at fair and remunerative prices, thereby helping to provide the necessary incentives for a dynamic and rising rate of production and the resources for accelerated economic growth and social development;

(d) to seek to ensure adequate supplies of natural rubber to meet the requirements of importing members at fair and reasonable prices and to improve the reliability and continuity of these supplies.

(2) In order to achieve the objectives of the agreement, an international natural rubber buffer stock of 550,000 tonnes was established. This buffer stock consists of a normal buffer stock of 400,000 tonnes and a contingency buffer stock of 150,000 tonnes and shall be the sole instrument of market intervention for price stabilization in the Agreement.

(3) For the operations of the buffer stock, the Agreement has established a price range consisting of a reference price and three price levels above and three price levels below it. The reference price that applied on the entry into force of the Agreement was set at 210 Malaysian/Singapore cents per kilogram. The upper and lower intervention prices are calculated as plus or minus 15 per cent of the reference price. The upper and lower trigger action prices are calculated as plus and minus 20 per cent of the reference price. For the first 30 months after the entry into force of the Agreement, the upper and lower limits of the price range have been set at 270 and 150 Malaysian/Singapore cents per kilogram respectively. The upper limit is called the upper indicative price and the lower limit is called the lower indicative price.

(4) A daily market indicator price (DMIP) was established which is a composite weighted average of daily official current-month prices on the Kuala Lumpur, London, New York and Singapore markets in respects of three grades, namely, RSS1, RSS3 and TSR20. Depending on the level of 5-day average of DMIP the buffer stock manager is forbidden, allowed or forced to intervene in the market.

(5) Under Art. 28 of the Agreement, members commit themselves to financing the total costs of the international buffer stock of 550,000 tonnes. The financing of both the normal and contingency stock shall be shared equally between exporting and importing categories of member. The total costs of the normal buffer stock of 400,000 tonnes are to be paid in cash.

(6) The Agreement is for a period of five years, unless extended or terminated in accordance with the provisions of the Agreement.

The Agreement entered into force provisionally on 23 October 1980 and definitively on 15 April 1982. It expired 5 years later and was extended for 2 more years until 22 October 1987. In March 1987, a second international agreement has been reached on continuation of the previous agreement under roughly the same terms. The new agreement entered into force on 29 December 1988.

A graph showing the DMIP and the – twice revised – price ranges is

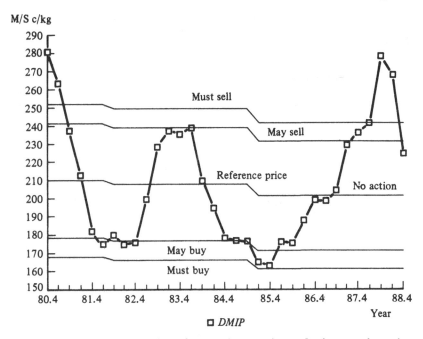

M/S c/kg

□ DMIP

Figure 10.1 The DMIP and the reference, intervention and trigger action prices (Malaysian/Singapore cents/kg)

presented in Figure 10.1. The area between the upper two lines is called the 'may-sell' range, while at the bottom, a similar area is the 'may-buy' range. The top line shows the 'must-sell' price and the bottom line the 'must-buy' price. Early in 1980, prices had peaked; they fell to the 'may-buy' level in 1981, stayed there in 1982, rose to the 'may-sell' level in 1983, fell again in 1985 and gradually rose afterwards to a level in mid-1988 above the upper bound of the Agreement. The last quarter of 1988 gave prices which were again in the 'no-action' range. The BSM intervened in 1982 and 1985 and in September 1987 the buffer stock contained 362,000 tonnes. Later in the year prices rose to the 'may-sell' level, and just before the expiration date of the first agreement some rubber could be sold by the BSM. Also after 22nd October 1987, substantial quantities of natural rubber have been sold by the BSM. Only some 25,000 tonnes was believed to be left in the buffer stock by the end of 1988.

3.2.3 A summary of the natural rubber market model
The complete model used to evaluate the INRA consist of
– the long-term analysis of total rubber demand, which is one of the long-term pillars of the short-term analysis;

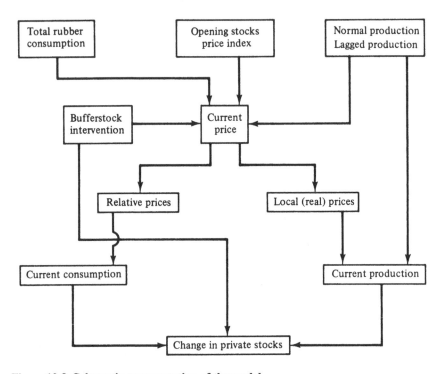

Figure 10.2 Schematic representation of the model

– the long-term analysis of natural rubber supply, which is the other long-term pillar for the short-term analysis;
– the quarterly model which is developed to describe short-term reactions of demand, supply and prices to each other, as well as in relation to behaviour of the Buffer Stock Manager (BSM) in the market.

Details of the long-term analysis are described in Smit (1984). An elaborate summary of the quarterly model can be found in Burger and Smit (1989). Schematically the model is depicted in Figure 10.2.

3.2.4 Performance of the International Natural Rubber Agreement, 1982–88
Results on the impact that buffer stock interventions in the period 1982–88 have had on the NR market are arrived at by comparing a dynamic simulation for all 28 quarters, in the case of buffer stock intervention according to the official rules with the same in the event of no BS intervention. As the equations were estimated on data up to 1987, 1988 is *ex ante* simulated, but with actual values – as far as known – for the exogenous variables. Two assumptions need to be discussed first. One is the choice of the BS intervention rule. The official BS-intervention rule is

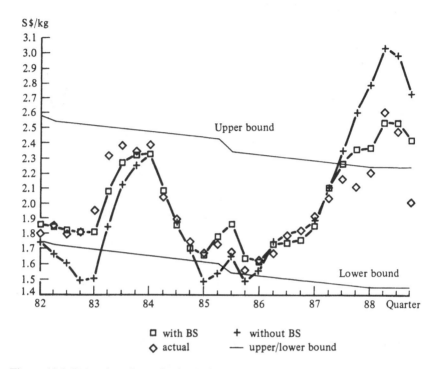

Figure 10.3 Prices in a dynamic simulation with and without a buffer stock

based on the DMIP, the Daily Market Indicator Price, consisting of prices in various currencies and of various qualities of NR. The model covers only the price of RSS1 and a relationship between the DMIP and RSS1 price was used to transform the 'must buy' and 'must sell' prices into the corresponding level of RSS1 price. From a static simulation, i.e. forecasting only one quarter ahead, was derived whether the BSM defended the 'must-buy' and 'must-sell' level or the 'may-buy' and 'may-sell' levels. BSM behaviour appeared to correspond to defending the 'may-buy' price in 1982 and a slightly lower price in 1985 (when there was a danger of the buffer stock reaching its upper-limit) and rubber sales were triggered by the 'must-sell' price. The rule for buffer stock intervention 'not to disrupt the orderly marketing of NR' was incorporated in the model by binding the changes in the buffer stock to a maximum of 100,000 tonnes per quarter.

A second assumption involves the disturbances that occur in the established relationships, particularly the supply and demand equations. The main results for the differences caused by the INRA will be assessed assuming that the disturbances as found in static simulation will also

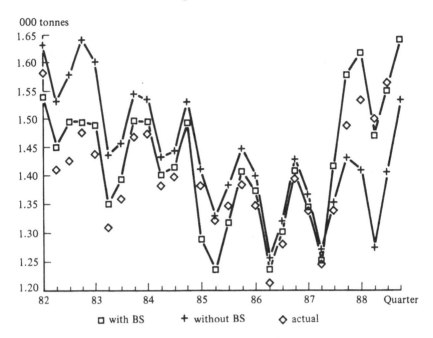

Figure 10.4 **Private stocks of natural rubber in dynamic simulations with and without a buffer stock**

occur in the dynamic simulation. This is similar to the procedure followed by Chu & Morrison (1986). Finally, in the paragraph on short-term stabilization, we will report on stochastic simulation.

The main results on the effects of the buffer stock are depicted in Figures 10.3 and 10.4. Figure 10.3 shows what the price is estimated to have been in a dynamic simulation with and without buffer stock intervention and can be compared with the actually observed price. In 1982.1, the first quarter to be compared, the BSM is estimated to buy 98,000 tonnes (actual purchases were 56,000), thus increasing the price to S\$ 1,861 per tonne, i.e. 7 per cent more than without intervention; production responds in the same quarter by a mere + 5,400 tonnes, together bringing private stocks down by 92,000 tonnes. In the following quarters estimated BS purches of 0, 21 and 90,000 tonnes, respectively, bring prices at the end of 1982 to an estimated level of S\$ 1,812 per tonne (actually 1,807) to be compared with S\$1,491 in case of no intervention. By this time cumulative additional production equals 56,000 tonnes and consumption over the year is 9,000 less than without intervention.

The various sources for the buffer stock purchases, more production, less consumption or less in private stocks, are displayed in Figure 10.5.

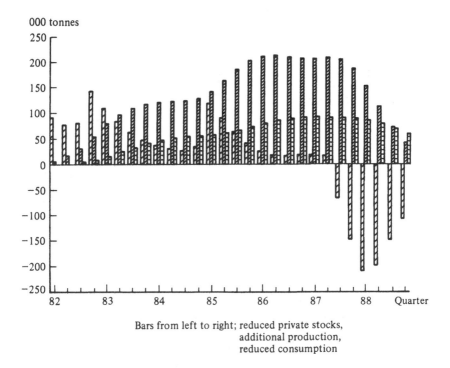

Bars from left to right; reduced private stocks,
additional production,
reduced consumption

Figure 10.5 Composition of the buffer stock by source 1982–8 (000 tonnes)

Private stocks, shown separately in Figure 10.4, are down by 144,000 tonnes at the end of 1982, but gradually return toward their free-market level, which is reached by mid-1984. Thus, although initially the effect of intervention is an increase in sales by private stockholders, the final impact is distributed among consumers and producers.

The next interventions are estimated to take place in the last quarter of 1984 and the first of 1985, which is two quarters earlier than actually happened. By mid-1986, hardly any difference in private stocks is left when comparing simulations with and without BS intervention. When the BSM starts selling in 1987.3 and 1987.4 (estimated at 86,000 plus 100,000 tonnes, whereas actual sales were about 20,000 in 1987.3 and 100,000 tonnes in 1987.4), private stocks first increased by 83,000, then by an additional 73,000 tonnes. Later estimated sales by the BSM in 1988.1 and 1988.2 (of 100,000 and 36,000 tonnes) should have increased private stocks to a level of 200,000 tonnes higher than in the case of no intervention. Prices in 1988.2 are estimated to have been reduced by 16 per cent, but this is not enough to keep the prices from rising above the upper

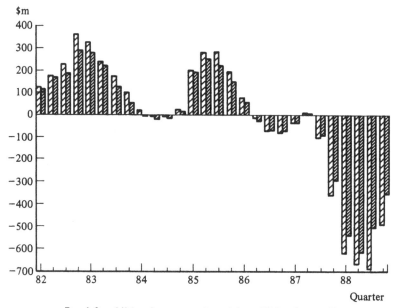

Bars left: additional revenues; bars right: additional expenditure

Figure 10.6 Producer revenues and consumer expenditures induced by INRA

bound of the agreement. Production in 1988 should have decreased by 143,000 tonnes, consumption increased by 30,000 tonnes.

Summed over the whole period 1982.1–1988.4, production was 44,000 tonnes higher and consumption 61,000 tonnes lower due to the buffer stock intervention. Prices in 1988.4 are estimated to be 11 per cent lower but this difference is expected to fade away by the end of 1989. When production and consumption are evaluated at current quarter's prices, producers' cumulative benefits have at one time been as high as 2.8 billion S$, but are estimated to have been washed away by the end of 1988. Cumulative extra payments by consumers have peaked at 2.4 billion, but are more than fully compensated at the end of 1988. Figure 10.6 shows the revenues to producers and payments by consumers as caused by the INRA for all quarters.

The BSM should have made a profit by purchasing at low and selling at high prices. Assuming that the rubber was sold at 10 per cent discount, direct profits were 220m Malaysian dollars. This exceeded the storage costs, which assuming 2.3 Malaysian sen per kg per quarter, amounted to 159 million M$, but was not enough to cover the interest and administration costs.

What redistribution effects were caused by the INRA? By the end of

1988, the NR Buffer Stock was (almost) exhausted. As indicated in the previous paragraph, during and shortly after buffer stock purchases there has been a considerable redistribution of income from consumers (through higher prices) and tax payers (through the BS purchases) to producers, but these transfers were returned at the end of the period by BS sales and lower prices. Because the traded quantities were larger at the end of the period, more has been transferred to consumers than to producers, but the differences are fairly small. Producers have benefitted from the fact that rubber has to be bought by a buffer stock before it can be sold, thus leading to additional revenues for producers preceding additional losses due to BS sales and, hence, to interest revenues for the producers. To the extent that the composition of the group of producers is different for high and low prices, there may have been a transfer of income within the group of producers. High cost producers who are not producing at the lower end of the price range, see some of their revenues transferred to low cost producers. Producers whose capacity has grown in this period are relatively disadvantaged in comparison to producers with constant or decreasing capacity. Thus, Thailand has received much less in 1982–86 than they paid in 1987 and 1988, and vice versa for Malaysian estates, whose production declined in this period. Private stockholders, incorporated here as intermediaries between producers and the BS and between the BS and the consumers, have benefitted from the Agreement by the extent to which their turnover has been larger, i.e. twice the maximum size of the buffer stock. As BS purchases prevented a price fall in 1982 and dampened a price rise in 1988, the effect on 'speculative' profits must have been rather neutral. Initially, synthetic rubber producers have sold more too, because the NR not consumed, due to BS-induced higher NR prices, is assumed to be replaced by SR. The price of SR, however, was not influenced by this additional demand, nor by the reduced demand for SR in 1988, when NR prices were lowered.

The important question for buffer stock operations is whether it has been able to stabilize prices and/or incomes. Three aspects of *stabilization* are considered here.

(1) Long-term stabilization:

The long-term outlook for a commodity like natural rubber critically depends on long-term demand in its turn determined by car sales and income, and on planting policies. Rubber trees remain immature for a period of some 6 years and returns to investments in rubber are typically dependent on the average price levels in 10 to 30 years from the year of planting. As the model shows, after market intervention the prices of NR rather quickly return to the levels that would rule in a free market situation. Given the uncertainty about a continuation of any agreement

	1980	1985	1990
Forecast low growth		13,486	15,178
medium growth		14,356	17,422
high growth		15,288	19,920
Actual	12,445	13,295	15,200*

Table 10.6 Total world rubber consumption

* Expected (see Burger and Smit, 1989)

Source: Smit (1982).

after the 5 or 7 years for which such agreements are made, and the uncertainty about the price ranges if there were to be any continuation, it would be hard to assume that INRA would have any impact on the long-term outlook for the NR market.

(2) Medium-term stabilization:

For a shorter period, say 5 to 10 years ahead, a buffer stocking agreement would have an appreciable impact on the stability of the market if it was able to cope with most of the changes in the relevant factors in the market. In the case of the NR market, these are medium-term prospects for overall rubber consumption and planting and therefore production capacity. What were these prospects at the time INRA was negotiated, i.e. in 1980? As derived in Smit (1982) forecasts for total world rubber consumption at that time were as shown in Table 10.6.

If one of these projections had come true, and if the other relevant variables would have been as they were in the past, the agreement would only in the case of 'low growth' and only after 1985 have had an effect on prices and would have prevented prices from falling below the lower bound of the agreement.

The range of forecasts by various authors for NR production, available in 1980, for the period until 1990 is enormous (Smit, 1982: Table 7.16) and runs from 4.5 to 5.8 million tonnes for NR production in 1985 and from 5 to 6.6 million tonnes in 1990. This is the more surprising given that these trees should already have been planted by that time. Smit (1982, Table 8.36) forecasted 4.34 and 4.74 million tonnes respectively for 1985 and 1990. Actual production in 1985 was 4.34 million and for 1990 5 million tonnes seems likely. What is important here is, that the buffer stock would never have been able to keep the prices within any reasonable range for all of these estimates. With the above mentioned 'medium growth' scenario for total rubber demand, production capacity should have been in a comparatively narrow range between 4.4 and 4.8 million tonnes to have a

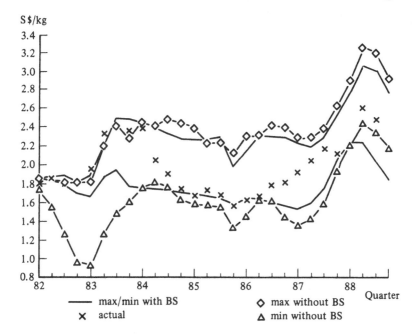

Figure 10.7 Possible price ranges with and without a buffer stock

reasonable chance of yielding prices within the range of the Agreement in 1985. Thus, even medium-term uncertainty about the prices of NR is hardly reduced by adopting INRA.

(3) Short-term stability:

For the short-term, say for the period 1982 until 1988, what stability was offered by the Agreement? As could be seen from Figure 10.3, NR prices have been increased by buffer stock interventions when they would have been low and were reduced when they were high. Some stability of prices was, therefore, achieved. Over this period the standard deviation of quarterly prices was reduced by 37 per cent, that of quarterly revenues of the producers by 34 per cent and that of the value of NR consumption was reduced by 31 per cent. Considerable uncertainty about the prices remains, however. Even with total rubber demand given and using all information contained in the model, the error terms included in the supply equations and the demand equation give rise to uncertainty about the prices. Figure 10.7 shows the range of prices resulting from 25 simulations with the quarterly model using error terms for the world supply and demand taken from a homogeneous distribution corresponding to their actual distribution in this period. Clearly, the range of prices in 1982 under the buffer stock regime is fairly small, which can be ascribed to the 'almost

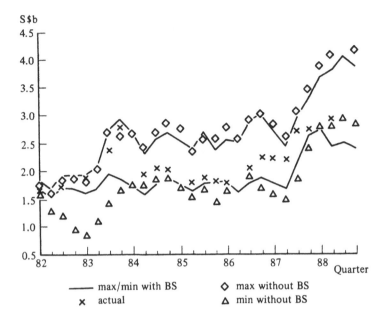

Figure 10.8 Possible revenue ranges with and without a buffer stock

certain' intervention in that period. After 1983, however, the price range
under the BS-regime and that under the free trade regime almost coincide.
In 1987, when the BS starts to sell, the free-market price range lies above
the BS-price range, but is not much wider. Even given the model,
uncertainty about prices, as given by the price spread in any quarter after
1982 is not so much reduced by the Agreement, even though the average
price is influenced. It is noteworthy that the free-market price range is
about as wide as the range afforded by the Agreement, i.e. 15 per cent on
either side of the mean.

Figure 10.8 shows the range for producers' revenues. The interpretation
is that even when all exogenous variables would have been known at the
end of 1981 and even when the error term of the price equation would have
been zero throughout the period, the uncertainty resulting from the
disturbances in supply and demand is such that revenues show a spread of
some 20 per cent on either side of the mean expected value. This spread by
itself is rather independent of whether or not there is an Agreement on
market intervention.

3.2.5 Financial costs of the agreement
As mentioned already, in the period considered the BS has more or less
broken even: its profits from selling at high prices and buying at low prices

approximately covered the costs of storing the NR in the period between. Its effect on money transferred in the NR market has been enormous. The spending of about 350 million US $ during the two purchasing periods in 1982 and 1985 has triggered a transfer from consumers to producers of about 1.2 billion US $ (assuming all trade is done at RSS1 prices). Similarly, selling 400 million $ worth of NR in 1987 and 1988 caused a transfer of about $1.2 billion in these years in the other direction and its effect has not yet finished.

These multiplier effects are mainly due to the lagged effects of BS intervention on stocks, prices and quantities produced and consumed. Once private stocks have been reduced by BS purchases, these stocks tend to be low in the next quarter leading to higher prices in that or the subsequent quarter even in the absence of BS intervention. These lagged effects, that amount to 'overshooting' could be limited by allowing the BSM to sell rather soon after he made his purchases. The present regulations, however, forbid him to intervene as soon as the prices are within the range.

Often, direct financial transfers are discussed as an alternative option for stabilizing incomes. Putting production equal to exports, total export revenues of the producing countries could have been kept above the present revenues at minimum prices by transferring a total amount equal to US $ 580 million during the quarters in which free market prices fell below the INRA lower bound. In this situation, production is assumed to follow the (low) free market prices and the transfer is assumed not to affect production. If, however, such a subsidy would be passed on to the producers within the producing countries, it would be interpreted as a price increase and lead to higher production and even lower world market prices. In some quarters, prices would fall by 15 per cent compared to the present free market scenario. Thus, only when transfers would not affect production, is the consideration of financial transfers worthwhile. But even then, the financial expenditures involved would be higher than the present expenditures under the buffer stocking agreement.

4   Summary and policy conclusions

The analytical literature on stabilization has dealt primarily with policies which fulfil their primary objectives successfully. The focus was on hypothetical stabilization schemes. As far as existing commodity initiatives were analyzed, the studies were in most cases non-quantitative. In contrast it was the objective of this contribution to evaluate the most important existing commodity agreements and compensatory financing schemes on the basis of a quantitiative analysis of their effects. The findings can be summarized and lessons for commodity policy can be drawn as follows:

(1) In principle, it is well known from theory that compensatory financing schemes are superior to buffer stock or export quota policies when export earnings are to be stabilized. Compensatory financing can stabilize national export earnings directly, whereas market price stabilization does so only under specific conditions. No intervention in international commodity markets is necessary and, hence, compensatory financing can avoid the aggregate welfare losses associated with price-changing commodity agreements. Although true in principle, this general view is not very helpful for the evaluation of existing commodity initiatives when existing price stabilization and financing schemes are suboptimal in a theoretical sense.

(2) The findings of this paper challenge some widespread views on commodity stabilization:

(i)   Existing compensatory financing schemes are far from being perfect export-earnings stabilizers.

(ii) One important commodity agreement, the ICA, is rather a redistributive than a price-stabilizing scheme. Redistributive effects are not well-targeted.

(iii) The experience of the INRA in the 1980s shows that buffer stocks may contribute to price and earnings stability and outperform imperfect compensatory financing schemes. A pre-condition is that the buffer stock manager concentrates on price stabilization as opposed to price support and does not fail in forecasting the medium-run equilibrium price.

(3) In many cases, existing compensatory financing schemes did not stabilize national export earnings as a consequence of substantial time lags in the compensation payments. When stabilizing effects occurred, they were often small. Although compensation under the IMF's CFF is more timely than under the STABEX system, the overall impact of payments and repayments under the CFF was more often destabilizing than stabilizing. The median effect on export earnings instability was + 0.63 per cent. Besides time lags, unsatisfactory stabilization effects were due to quota limitations, to the delinking of repayments and stabilization goals and in individual cases to forecast errors. The median impact of STABEX payments on export earnings instability was − 0.21 per cent. Besides time lags, an important reason for the weak stabilization success of STABEX was limited funds in years of depressed coffee and cocoa prices. Without significant policy changes, it can be expected that the median stabilization effect of the existing compensatory financing schemes will remain negligible.

(4) Another problem in this context is that existing compensatory financing schemes are not pure stabilization systems but contain strong redistributive elements. Credits are given under more favourable conditions than on commercial markets. Significant grant elements are involved in the EC scheme where earnings shortfalls are generally compensated with interest-free payments and, for many countries, even without a repayment duty. The grant ratios in the IMF scheme are lower but still important. The high grant elements in compensatory financing provide an incentive to apply for the cheap credits irrespective of the stabilization effects.

(5) A straightforward policy conclusion from the performance of the CFF and STABEX would be to concentrate more on earnings stabilization and less on earnings support. The stabilizing role of the existing facilities could be improved by improving their stabilizing role. An increased use of the advance-payments rule could help to fulfil this goal as well as increased funds under a re-oriented policy. The concentration on the stabilization objective implies that the grant elements in the compensation schemes should be reduced. Right now, implicit income transfers are distributed under both schemes independent of indicators of need. From a redistributive point of view, targeted and visible aid oriented at indicators of need seems clearly superior to hidden aid through compensatory financing.

(6) It is well elaborated in the literature that international commodity agreements have been rather unsuccessful in the past. Hence, only those two agreements were analyzed in more detail which are often pointed to as success cases – the ICA and the INRA. The export quota policy under the ICA is designed for price support in periods of 'low' prices, but it does not provide a mechanism to drive down prices in 'boom' periods. It was shown that the ICA led to a substantial price increase in the quota market (+ 30 per cent) and depressed prices in the non-quota market by 10 per cent. It led to welfare losses of the importing members which were on average for 1982 and 1983 in the magnitude of $2,200m and to short-run welfare gains of the exporting members and the importing non-members. Thus, income is redistributed under the ICA as a form of trade-tied aid for coffee exporters and free riders among the coffee importers. These income transfers are determined by the magnitude of coffee trade, but not by the neediness of countries as indicated by per-capita income. Hence, the implicit transfers under the ICA are an inefficient tool of redistribution compared with a targeted aid policy. The allocative effects of the ICA also seem undesirable given the agreement's goals. The increasing price in the member market decreases consumption in this market segment and aggregate world coffee consumption. Moreover, the price rise leads to a

net welfare loss in the world coffee economy as the welfare losses of importing members are higher than the welfare gains of exporting members and importing non-members.

(7) In the period 1982 to 1988, the INRA achieved some price stability. Prices were increased by buffer stock interventions when they would have been low and were reduced when they would have been high. The standard deviation of quarterly prices was reduced by 37 per cent, that of quarterly revenues of the producers by 34 per cent and that of the value of natural rubber consumption by 31 per cent. The buffer stock has more or less broken even: its profits from selling at high prices and buying at low prices approximately covered the costs of storing natural rubber in that period. Its effect on money transferred in the rubber market has been enormous. The spending of about 350 million US$ during the two purchasing periods in 1982 and 1985 has triggered a transfer from consumers to producers of about 1.2 billion US$ (assuming all trade is done at RSS1 prices). Similarly, selling 400 million $ worth of natural rubber in 1987 and 1988 caused a transfer of about $1.2 billion in these years in the other direction and its effect has not yet finished. The stabilization success of the INRA can, however, not serve as a general example for other commodities. Natural rubber, being a perennial crop with a slight seasonal pattern, has a rather stable level of output which can be adjusted to changes in prices. In particular, a low level of prices will induce a reduction in supply, which can materialize within one or two months. This gives a stabilization scheme a greater chance for success if the price range is chosen properly. Moreover, the Bufferstock Manager of the INRA and the members after all have been most fortunate with the initial choice of the price range, because a higher price range would have caused flooding of the buffer stock. Hence, the performance of the INRA has to be regarded as a limited success in a relatively short period for a commodity with specific characteristics.

NOTES

* Thanks are due to participants of the conference for their very helpful comments on the conference Paper, especially to P. Daniel and J. Spraos as discussants and to D. Sapsford for his written comments. The editorial suggestions of J. Black are also much appreciated.
1 Whether commodity price instability causes micro- and macroeconomic damage in developing countries, is extensively discussed in Behrman (1987). A review of the literature on commodity price stabilization is given in Schmitz (1984). See also Ghosh et al. (1987), MacBean and Nguyen (1987) and the literature cited therein.
2 Detailed information on the CFF can be found in Goreux (1980) and Kaibni (1986). A quantitative analysis of the stabilizing and redistributive effects of the CFF up to 1980 can be found in Herrmann (1983). Green and Kirkpatrick (1982)

discuss the extension of the CFF in 1981. The role of the IMF's financial facilities for the food deficit countries is elaborated in Kaibni (1988). The extension in 1988 to a CFFF is discussed in Pownall and Stuart (1988). The existing compensatory financing schemes are evaluated in Expert Group (1985).

3 Equatorial Guinea, Guinea and Kampuchea are excluded since no data on export earnings were available.

4 Herewith, the analysis is much more comprehensive than earlier studies. Herrmann (1983) analyzed the stabilization effects in the period 1967–80 for 20 recipient countries, which had received either the largest or the most compensatory financing payments up to 1980. Finger and deRosa (1980) refer to all countries which made purchases through January 1979 on the basis of data for the period 1961–77. The study of Kumar (1988) is based on all countries which made purchases from the CFF between 1975 and 1985.

5 The compensation years of the IMF, partly diverging from calendar years, could not be used since data were not available.

6 The presented measure of instability is selected as follows. If at least one F-value of the two regression equations is significant at the 5 per cent level, the trend-corrected coefficient of variation is chosen on the basis of the functional form with the higher F-values. If the F-value of both regression equations is insignificant at the 5 per cent level, the uncorrected coefficient of variation is used.

7 In no case was the 'best' trend of export earnings changed by transactions under the CFF.

8 On the method, see Sachs (1984), p. 201.

9 All the cited articles refer to Lomé III. For details on STABEX see Commission of the EC (1985). An overview of the transactions under STABEX is given in Commission of the EC (1981, 1988). Economic impacts of STABEX on various goals are investigated in Koester and Herrmann (1987), Section 7, and Hewitt (1983).

10 Earlier calculations on the stabilizing impacts of STABEX on export earnings were much less comprehensive. The analysis in Herrmann (1983, pp. 19–22) refers to a selection of 19 ACP countries, which received the highest or most payments under Lomé I, and to the relatively short period 1974–80. Bachou (1986, chapter 5) reports some similar computations but he restricts himself to 12 ACP countries and covers the period 1975–83.

11 For the Comoros, Kiribati and Tuvalu, data on export earnings were insufficient. Hence, these countries were excluded.

12 The concentration on the direct effects of STABEX seems even more justified than in the analysis on the IMF's CFF. The magnitude and timing of STABEX payments is hardly predictable given the limited resources in years of low world commodity prices. Additionally, the grant element under STABEX is so high that ACP countries have a strong incentive to use the system as a source of untied aid irrespective of its stabilization effects.

13 For details on the 1983 ICA, see International Coffee Organization (1982). Various ICAs are discussed in Pieterse and Silvis (1988).

14 The following empirical analysis draws heavily upon Herrmann (1988b) where the international allocation of aid under the ICA is elaborated in much more detail.

REFERENCES

Akiyama, T. and P. Varangis (1988) 'Impact of the International Coffee Agreement's Export Quota System on the World Coffee Market'. Paper presented at the XXVth International Conference of the Applied Econometrics Association on International Commodity Market Modeling, World Bank, Washington, D.C., October 24–26.

Allen, P. W., P. O. Thomas and B. C. Sekhar (1973) *The Techno-economic Potential of Natural Rubber in Major End-uses*. (Malaysian Rubber Research and Development Board, Monograph No. 1), Kuala Lumpur.

Bachou, S. A. (1986) 'An Evaluation of Trade Preference and Compensatory Financing Arrangements in the Framework of the Lomé Regime'. Ph.D. Thesis, University of Notre Dame, Notre Dame, Indiana.

Behrman, J. R. (1978) *Development, The International Economic Order, and Commodity Agreements*. (Perspectives on Economics Series), Reading, Mass.

Behrman, J. R. (1987) 'Commodity Price Instability and Economic Goal Attainment in Developing Countries'. *World Development* 15, 559–73.

Bird, G. (1987) 'Commodity Price Stabilisation and International Financial Policy,' in H. W. Singer, N. Hatti and R. Tandon (eds), *International Commodity Policy (Part II)*, New Delhi: Ashish Publishing House.

Burger, K. and H. P. Smit (1989) 'Short-term and Long-term Analysis of the Natural Rubber Market'. *Weltwirtschaftliches Archiv*, Vol. 125, forthcoming.

Chu, K.-Y. and T. K. Morrison (1986) 'World Non-oil Primary Commodity Markets. A Medium-term Framework of Analysis'. *IMF Staff Papers* 33, 139–84.

Commission of the EC (a) *Gesamtbericht über die Tätigkeit der Europäischen Gemeinschaften*. Various years, Brussels, Luxembourg.

Commission of the EC (b) *Bericht der Kommission an den Rat über das Funktionieren des mit dem AKP-EWG-Abkommen und dem Beschluß über die Assoziation der ÜLG mit der EWG eingeführten Systems zur Stabilisierung der Ausfuhrerlöse*. Brussels, various years.

Commission of the EC (1981) *Zusammenfassender Bericht über das mit dem Abkommen von Lomé eingeführte System zur Stabilisierung der Ausfuhrerlöse in den Anwendungsjahren 1975 bis 1979*. SK (81) 1104, Brussels.

Commission of the EC (1985) *Stabex User's Guide*. Third ACP–EEC Convention. Brussels.

Commission of the EC (1987) Council Regulation (EEC) No 428/87 of 9 February 1987. Setting up a System of Compensation for Loss of Export Earnings for Least-developed Countries not Signatory to the Third ACP–EEC Convention. *Official Journal of the European Communities*, February 13.

Commission of the EC (1988) STABEX-Relevé des Transferts Effectués au Titre des Années d'Application 1975–1987. Brussels.

Cuddy, J. D. A. and P. A. Della Valle (1978) 'Measuring the Instability of Time Series Data'. *Oxford Bulletin of Economics and Statistics* 40, 79–85.

Della Valle, P. A. (1979) 'On the Instability Index of Time Series Data: A Generalization'. *Oxford Bulletin of Economics and Statistics* 41, 247–48.

Expert Group (1985) 'Compensatory Financing of Export Earnings Shortfalls. Report of the Expert Group'. UNCTAD TD/B/1029/Rev. 1, New York.

FAO, *FAO Trade Yearbook* Rome, various issues.

Finger, J. M. and D. A. DeRosa (1980) 'The Compensatory Financing Facility and Export Instability'. *Journal of World Trade Law* 14, 14–22.

Ghosh, S., C. Gilbert and A. Hughes Hallett (1987) *Stabilizing Speculative Commodity Markets*. Oxford.

Gilbert, C. L. (1987) 'International Commodity Agreements: Design and Performance'. In: Maizels, A. (ed.), *Primary Commodities in the World Economy: Problems and Policies*. Special issue of *World Development* 15, 591–616.

Goreux, L. M. (1980) *Compensatory Financing Facility*. (IMF Pamphlet Series No. 34, International Monetary Fund), Washington, D.C.

Green, C. and C. Kirkpatrick (1982) 'The IMF's Food Financing Facility'. *Journal of World Trade Law* 16, 265–73.

Herrmann, R. (1983) *The Compensatory Financing System of the International Monetary Fund. An Analysis of its Effects and Comparisons with Alternative Systems*. (Forum, No. 4), Kiel.

Herrmann, R. (1986) 'Free Riders and the Redistributive Effects of International Commodity Agreements: The Case of Coffee'. *Journal of Policy Modeling* 8, 597–621.

Herrmann, R. (1988a) *Internationale Agrarmarktabkommen. Analyse ihrer Wirkungen auf den Märkten für Kaffee und Kakao*. (Kieler Studien, No. 215), Tübingen.

Herrmann, R. (1988b), 'The International Allocation of Trade-tied Aid: A Quantitative Analysis for the Export Quota Scheme in Coffee.' *Weltwirtschaftliches Archiv* 124, 675–700.

Hewitt, A. (1983) 'Stabex: An Evaluation of the Economic Impact over the First Five Years'. *World Development* 11, 1005–27.

International Coffee Organization (1982) *International Coffee Agreement 1983*. Copy of the authenticated text. London. October.

International Monetary Fund (a) *International Financial Statistics*. February issues, various years, Washington, D.C.

International Monetary Fund (b) *Direction of Trade Statistics: Yearbook*. Various issues, Washington, D.C.

International Monetary Fund (1988) *International Financial Statistics: Yearbook 1988*. Washington, D.C.

International Rubber Study Group (IRSG) *Rubber Statistical Bulletin*. Various issues, London.

International Rubber Study Group (1986) *World Rubber Statistics Handbook*. Volume 3, 1960–1985. London.

Kaibni, N. M. (1986) 'Evolution of the Compensatory Financing Facility'. *Finance and Development* 23, 24–27.

Kaibni, N. M. (1988) 'Financial Facilities of the IMF and the Food Deficit Countries'. *Food Policy* 13, 73–82.

Koester, U. and R. Herrmann (1987) *The EC–ACP Convention of Lomé*. (Forum-Reports on Current Research in Agricultural Economics and Agribusiness Management, No. 13), Kiel.

Kumar, M. S. (1988) 'The Stabilizing Role of the Compensatory Financing Facility: Empirical Evidence and Welfare Implications'. (IMF Working Paper, WP/88/108, Research Department), Washington, D.C.

Lim, D. (1976) 'Export Instability and Economic Growth: A Return to Fundamentals. *Oxford Bulletin of Economics and Statistics* 38, 311–22.

MacBean, A. I. and D. T. Nguyen (1987) *Commodity Policies: Problems and Prospects*. London, New York, Sydney: Croom Helm.

Newbery, D. M. G. and J. E. Stiglitz (1981) *The Theory of Commodity Price Stabilization. A Study in the Economics of Risk*. Oxford.

Nguyen, D. T. (1980) 'Partial Price Stabilization and Export Earning Instability'. *Oxford Economic Papers* **32**, 340–52.

Palm, F. C. and E. Vogelvang (1988) 'Policy Simulations Using a Quarterly Rational Expectations Model for the International Coffee Market'. Paper presented at the XXVth International Conference of the Applied Econometrics Association on International Commodity Market Modeling, World Bank, Washington, D.C., October 24–26.

Pieterse, M. Th. A. and H. J. Silvis (1988) *The World Coffee Market and the International Coffee Agreement.* (Wageningse Economische Studies No. 9), Wageningen.

Pownall, R. and B. Stuart (1988) 'The IMF's Compensatory and Contingency Financing Facility'. *Finance and Development* **25**, 9–11.

Sachs, L. (1984) *Angewandte Statistik. Anwendung statistischer Methoden.* Sixth edition, Berlin, Heidelberg, New York, Tokyo.

Schmitz, A. (1984) 'Commodity Price Stabilization. The Theory and Its Applications'. (World Bank Staff Working Papers, No. 668), Washington, D.C.

Smit, H. P. (1982) 'The World Rubber Economy to the Year 2000'. Unpublished Ph.D. Thesis, Free University, Amsterdam.

Smit, H. P. (1984) *Forecasts for the World Rubber Economy to the Year 2000.* (Globe Report No. 2), London, MacMillan.

UNCTAD (1985) *International Natural Rubber Agreement, 1979: An Analysis of its Development and Effectiveness. Contribution by the International Natural Rubber Organisation.* (UNCTAD TD/B/C.1.260), Geneva, 5 Feburary.

World Bank World Bank Atlas. Washington, D.C., various years.

Discussion

PHILIP DANIEL*

Herrmann, Burger and Smit (HBS) have produced a thorough quantitative analysis of two compensatory financing schemes and two commodity agreements. Their results come as no real surprise, but add some quantitative weight to the body of *a priori* scepticism about such arrangements. This note concentrates on the implications of their results and in particular, on how individual developing countries or groups of countries might respond to these results.

In brief:

(1) The IMF's Compensatory Financing Facility (CFF) has, on balance, destabilized export earnings, while providing limited financial subsidies to drawers.

* At the time of the conference Philip Daniel was Special Adviser (Economic), Technical Assistance Group, Commonwealth Secretariat.

(2)   The European Community (Lomé Convention) STABEX system has had insignificant impact on export earnings stability, but has provided substantial 'trade-linked aid'.
(3)   The International Coffee Agreement (ICA) has functioned as a price support rather than price stabilizing system, and again, has produced significant income transfers to producers.
(4)   The International Natural Rubber Agreement, a buffer stock arrangement, has succeeded in stabilizing prices to some degree, with income transfer effects viewed as neutral over time. But this is regarded as a special case because of the characteristics of the rubber crop.

The HBS approach is to analyze each of these schemes in terms of its own objectives, and, where there is failure in those terms, to evaluate indirect or subordinate effects in terms of optimal criteria for such effects. It is a valid approach, but produces a paradox from another perspective. The three schemes which (to whatever limited degree) have effected income transfers from consuming countries to producing countries – in this case from countries with higher per capita income to those with lower ones – have 'failed', whereas that which has not resulted in such transfers has 'succeeded', albeit in special circumstances and to a limited degree.

In examining this paradox, I wish, first, to leave aside the problem of possible misallocation of such income transfers by the criteria of need (which HBS contentiously equate with the ranking of average per capita income).

HBS correctly point out that untied financial aid is recognized in the economics of aid as superior to trade-tied aid. But when there is insufficient untied financial aid (or suitably allocated debt relief) there is a case for maintaining even third-best income transfer systems in place until they can be traded for something better.

The income transfers resulting from the CFF and STABEX have a number of advantages over other forms of aid. They are not tied to specific projects, they are not tied to procurement from particular donors and they are available for budgetary use. The welfare contribution of the transfers is, therefore, not constrained from the donor side, only by the allocation procedures of the recipient and the return on funds in the recipient economy.

The transfers resulting from the ICA may have fewer advantages in that they accrue to producers and/or marketing boards in the first instance, with the accrual to public revenue dependent on the effective marginal tax burden on income and expenditure. Nonetheless, there is likely to be some increase in availability of deficit-reducing freely-allocable resources to the budget.

The question, therefore, is whether in the absence of these schemes:

(1)   There would be substitute resources of equivalent benefit available to developing countries; and
(2)   Possible international efficiency gains from the abolition of such schemes would outweigh, over time, the income loss to beneficiaries.

The first is basically a political question, while the second might be amenable to quantitative simulation. However, it is suggested that, in the present state of the world, the answer to the first question is almost certainly negative, while the answer to the second question may well be negative too.

The answer to the question about efficiency gains depends in part on whether the welfare effects of inter-country income transfers are to be judged in the light of some weighting of the relative need of recipients. This raises the more basic issue of whether aid from rich countries to poor countries is itself desirable on both equity and efficiency grounds. Since this is not the forum, and a discussant is not allocated the time, for argument about such a matter, I simply assert that there is a strong body of theory and evidence to suggest that such aid *is* desirable. If so, then the income transfer effect of the schemes under review is central to their utility, whatever their official objectives.

In analyzing the CFF and STABEX, HBS concentrate their quantitative attention on the effects on stability of recipient countries' export earnings. For the ICA they go further (using a more sophisticated framework) in analyzing net welfare gains and losses for groups of countries. For all the schemes, however, the impacts examined stand as proximate indicators of whether general equity and efficiency objectives are served by them. Following Newbery and Stiglitz (1981), welfare effects are ultimately measured not by the effects of the schemes on price levels and fluctuations, or even export earnings levels and their fluctuations, but on the level and variability of consumption over time. HBS have gone some way towards this, but the complete picture requires integration of the income transfer and efficiency effects over time.

This, of course, is extremely difficult to undertake since, within each producer economy, the effects of stabilization schemes can be either mitigated or exaggerated by domestic economic policy and by interaction with other schemes (given that many producers, and most countries, are not limited to one scheme or one crop). This is not to argue that individual schemes cannot be evaluated on *ceteris paribus* assumptions or even with repercussion effects incorporated. It is rather to reinforce the suspicion that whether or not the individual scheme is stabilizing or destabilizing is potentially irrelevant if the income transfer is sufficient, there is no better politically feasible way of making the income transfer and other (domestic) means, are in place to provide the required degree of stability.

The primacy of the transfer role of these schemes, in the absence of better mechanisms, can be illustrated by a country case. Papua New Guinea has been a substantial recipient under CFF and STABEX and is also a member of the ICA. Its government has, fairly consistently, maintained a domestic stabilization strategy for more than a decade aimed straightforwardly at aligning domestic expenditure with the medium-term outlook for the terms of trade and exogenous investment, and taking the rule of thumb that the non-mineral economy can grow in real terms at 3–4 per cent per annum without triggering intractable inflation or balance of payments problems. It has maintained currency convertibility and avoided 'permanent' government borrowing from the banking system Papua New Guinea's four domestic agricultural commodity stabilization funds dampen the amplitude of swings in growers' receipts by about 50 per cent, the principal benefit of which is to smooth the flow of indirect tax payments to government.

For a country such as this, the CFF simply strengthens reserves and, if necessary, increases the capacity of the Central Bank to lend to Government without net deterioration in the external position. STABEX funds are directly received by the government and may or may not be allocated to the sectors which triggered them.

The operations of the ICA are mediated through the coffee stabilization fund (whose balances are not appropriated by Government, but may be used to purchase surplus output when quotas are imposed). Insofar as the ICA increases export receipts over time it increases both grower receipts and government tax revenue; any stabilizing effect simply reduces the extent of operations undertaken by the domestic fund.

For Papua New Guinea, and perhaps for many other countries, the potential net income gain is the main incentive for participation in these schemes. Meeting the stabilization criteria for each scheme (in the case of CFF or STABEX drawings) is an administrative procedure and is endured.

We return, therefore, to HBS' criticism of the income transfer content of CFF, Stabex and the ICA. They find for the CFF, for example, that the allocation of aid under the scheme showed a positive correlation with *per capita* income and describe it as arbitrary from a distributional point of view. It is difficult to disagree with such criticism. Nevertheless, few, if any, donors allocate aid on the criterion of relative per capita income alone. Apart from trade, military or political considerations it has become widely regarded as appropriate (not only by donor governments but in substantial measure by proponents of aid) to allocate on grounds of efficiency of aid use (a function of both expected project returns and the economic policy framework) as well as relative poverty. Using these wider criteria, the allocation that results from stabilization schemes will still be arbitrary, but not perhaps as unambiguously wrong as the authors suggest.

The apparent failure of three out of four of these schemes to stabilize export earnings, and the net world welfare loss calculated for the ICA (in any case calculated *without* weighting for the relative income positions of gainers and losers), does not immediately permit the conclusion that they should be scrapped. Reform in their mechanisms may be appropriate, but unless they are traded for alternative mechanisms of direct financial aid to developing countries then a significant group of low and middle income countries may become worse off without a compensating improvement in resource availability to the developing world as a whole.

This conclusion requires modification if, as is sometimes argued in the case of STABEX, the allocations to such schemes are made at the expense of allocations to other forms of aid. Even if it is true that STABEX allocations are part of a fixed overall sum from the European Development Fund (EDF) a shift from STABEX towards project or programme aid (for example) may not represent an unambiguous improvement when the conditions of project and programme transfers are more restrictive than those of STABEX.

REFERENCE

Newbery, D. M. G. and J. E. Stiglitz (1981) *The Theory of Commodity Price Stabilisation*, Oxford.

JOHN SPRAOS

Herrmann has been a pioneer of quantified assessments of compensatory financing schemes and he and his colleagues have been substantial contributors to the quantitative literature on primary commodities. Their present paper extends some of their earlier work and brings many of the parts under one roof. It is very welcome on both these counts, and also for its great clarity of exposition. Following my co-discussant, I shall refer to the three authors as HBS.

I will group my comments in two parts. One part will cover what for lack of a better collective noun I shall call points of method – mostly points of detail, not of broad principle. The other part will cover issues of welfare economics, more specifically issues of efficiency and distribution.

1   Method

Unsurprisingly, the assessment of all the schemes involves a comparison between situations with and without the scheme. Usually this requires the econometric conjuring of a counterfactual without-situation to serve as a benchmark. In the present state of the art and, I would guess, in the foreseeable future, 'conjuring' is frequently an apt expression. I therefore welcome the absence of elaborate counterfactuals in the assessment of the financing schemes – the IMF's CFF and the EEC's STABEX.

In both cases the without-situation consists simply of recorded export earnings, while the with-situation consists of export earnings plus disbursements associated with the scheme. In the case of the CFF, disbursements in both directions are taken into account, i.e. repayments as well as receipts. In the case of STABEX, only receipts are taken into account because repayments are negligible. A measure of instability is then applied to the respective time series for each of 92 countries in the case of the CFF and each of 48 countries in the case of STABEX. 25 annual observations are used for the CFF (1963–87) and 13 annual observations for STABEX (1975–87). The measure used is the root mean squared deviation, with a detrending provision.

I start with a very small point. Results can be sensitive to the instability index used. So it might have been worth telling us what difference, if any, it makes when a mean absolute deviation is employed as an index.

A more important point relates to the choice of trend for detrending. I have no sovereign recipe for the choice of trend. But I am fairly certain that for a country which has made a CFF drawing only once or twice over the 25-year period, an undifferentiated 25-year least squares-estimated time trend is not right both for the neighbourhood of the drawing and for other times. If so, the calculated instability can be misleading. Instead of imposing a single trend, it may be better to break up the total period into subperiods, each with a more homogeneous trend, estimated, perhaps, by piece-wise regression.

The HBS findings for the CFF can be summarized in two propositions: (i) with a few exceptions, the effect on export earnings instability is very small; (ii) the effect is on balance destabilizing as shown by the excess of the destabilized over the stabilized countries and also by the median country and by the unweighted mean of all countries.

I take serious note of both findings. I have, however, reservations on both. My reservation on the first is that it derives from a macroscopic impression, obtained by an undifferentiated viewing of the 25 years as a whole. At some point this needs to be supplemented by a more microscopic examination. A country which made a single drawing could experience substantial and welcome stabilizing effects in the relevant period, while the effect, when diluted over 25 years, shows up as very small.

The second finding is really surprising. It is true that repayments of CFF drawings have to be made over a specified time span regardless of the state of export earnings. But if the sample was unbiased, the expected value of the stabilizing effect of repayments would be zero. However, a bias due to non-random historical occurrences (or due to errors of measurement arising from factors alluded to earlier) could give rise to a recorded dominance of destabilization from repayments. The really surprising thing is that this should be big enough to offset the stabilizing effect exerted, one imagines, by the initial cash flow from the CFF drawing. I say 'one imagines' because, in fact, HBS separate drawings from repayments and find that even the effect of drawings alone is on balance destabilizing. (One of the three measures, the arithmetic mean, points in the opposite direction, but this too falls into line when one very extreme observation – the Ivory Coast – is taken out.) This is not just anti-intuitive, it is anti-definitional. Consider what happens. Countries experience export earnings shortfalls, they make a CFF drawing to compensate for them and instead, on balance, they exacerbate the instability of their export earnings even before the time comes for repayment. As the authors point out, the export earnings shortfall occurs in one calendar year and often the CFF drawing takes place the next year. And so the instability index, calculated on annual data, can register an increase of instability. But while the solar system dictates the calendar year, it does not have to dictate our instability index and, if it does, we do not have to believe what it says. The expectation I have is that if biennial data were used, the recorded effect would not be one of destabilization. HBS do have a point when they say that the time lag between export earnings shortfall and receipt of compensation does create a problem and that one cannot take for granted that bridging loans will be available from commercial banks. But there are a number of other dimensions along which a country can manoeuvre to patch things up in the interim if it can confidently anticipate that it will have access to compensating funds within a year – for example reducing foreign exchange reserves by more than would otherwise be prudent or postponing for a year lumpy imports associated with on-going infrastructural projects. Of course, the confidence with which a CFF drawing could be anticipated was substantially dented when severe conditionality started being attached to CFF loans in 1983. But the transformation of the

CFF into CCFF in 1988 should, in principle, be a great improvement on that. For the practice we shall have to wait and see.

One last point of detail on the instability calculations in the CFF case. Since compensation has also been obtainable for excessive outgoings on imports of cereals, such compensation, when added to export earnings, biases the instability index used and must be netted out.

As with the CFF, the impact of STABEX on export earnings instability comes out as being small but, unlike the CFF, it is on balance stabilizing for total export earnings. As it happens, if STABEX had turned out to be destabilizing, it would not have been an unbelievable outcome, for STABEX is a gross scheme, i.e. compensation is triggered when one or more of the designated commodities shows a shortfall regardless of the net position for all commodities combined and, of course, regardless of non-commodity visible exports.

I now turn briefly to the two commodity agreements which HBS cover – coffee and natural rubber. They involve econometrically estimated counterfactuals and are therefore subject to all the reservations to which such things are subject. The results are, however, intuitively appealing. This is, I think, a criterion which has some force despite the fact that it is subjective and that, if carried to its logical limit, it renders the econometrics redundant.

The Natural Rubber Agreement is assessed for its effects on price instability and is found to be stabilizing. The authors' accompanying commentary is designed to rub off some of the gloss from this finding. But one could argue that the buffer stock was even more stabilizing than appears in Figure 10.3, because the econometrically derived path without the buffer stock, which serves as a benchmark, inevitably cuts out certain price extremes, such as those associated with bandwagon effects, which Keynes (1936, p. 156) likened to newspaper beauty competitions and which are now increasingly referred to as bubbles.

The coffee agreement is labelled by the authors as a price-raising, not a price-stabilizing, agreement because export quotas are the instrument through which price is controlled. For this reason it is not assessed for its effects on price instability. It is assessed only as a price enhancer, by concentrating on a couple of years (1982–83) when export restrictions were in operation. Others (for example Gilbert, 1987) also share the view that the coffee agreement is both in design and in practice a price-raising one. But I would like to emphasize that this view, in so far as it rests on the export quotas, is not well founded. If production is not restricted, export restrictions imply national stock accumulation which, when liquidated in the high-price phase of the cycle, has price-lowering effects. Binding production restrictions to accompany the mandatory export restrictions of the coffee agreement have never been instituted though there have been exhortations. By focusing on years when export restrictions are in operation and observing that these have price-raising effects, one cannot derive any underpinning for the proposition that the coffee agreement is a net price-raiser over the cycle. A restriction of production practiced independently by a country which is a big producer would have had a price-raising effect, but this is another story.

This is not to say that the results HBS obtain for the two price-raising years are not interesting. *Inter alia*, they obtain estimates of the gain accruing to producers and of the deadweight loss accruing to the world economy. For later reference I note, in particular, that the gain of producers is estimated as 12 times the size of the deadweight loss, which is of course what one would expect when elasticities are low.

2　Welfare

I now turn to issues of efficiency and of distribution between producers and consumers.

More than once the authors say that compensatory financing schemes are known to be (Pareto) superior to price stabilization by buffer stock or export quotas. Here again they are in very good company. But since, typically, compensatory financing schemes are not designed to percolate directly to the micro level of the individual producer – STABEX has some provisions to the contrary but they are thought to be weak – like is not being compared with like and the proposition is not correct. At the level of the individual producer, price stabilization, normally accompanied by income stabilization when demand is price inelastic, has two welfare-enhancing effects: a static one, through risk-averse producers having to face a less unstable price (Newbery and Stiglitz, 1981) and a dynamic one, through making the yield on investment in primary production less uncertain (Kaldor, 1983). Whether these welfare gains will or will not outweigh any losses from price distortion is not a question to be resolved here. Suffice to make the point that it is an open question. If all national governments of exporting countries operated a counter-cyclical export tax or a price-stabilizing marketing board strategy, the beneficial microeconomic effects would be present anyway. But this is an 'if' on which one may not wish to depend. A qualification needs to be added, however. The microeconomic efficiency effects, since they are output-raising, would have redistributive consequences adverse to producers, since demand is typically inelastic, unless combined with output-restricting measures. In principle, the latter may be so designed as to be efficiency-preserving (see below).

HBS identify transfer components in both the CFF and STABEX as well as in the coffee agreement. In STABEX the transfer element is pronounced because the bulk of the compensation payments end up as outright grants. In the CFF the transfer element consists of an interest rate lower than the cost of borrowing from alternative sources. The severe conditionality operated since 1983 weighs on the other side. But, in any event, does the transfer aspect not come second, perhaps by a long way, to the efficiency-enhancing role? The argument underlying such a role is powerful and of long standing. Precipitate and drastic responses by countries suffering from an exogenous balance of payments shock have disruptive effects on the world economy. Private sources would not provide adequate bridging finance because they could not appropriate the systemic gains associated with more measured adjustment. The IMF was initially designed to bridge this gap between private and social benefits arising from financing a transitory deficit (Spraos, 1988). If the CFF was providing finance on concessionary terms, it would be doing no more than fulfilling the role for which the IMF was set up.

The authors remark, with respect to each of the schemes which they identify as having transfer implications, that viewed as transfer mechanisms they are inferior to straight aid targeted according to some poverty index. As an academic principle this is fine. As a practical point it does not carry much weight because, as my codiscussant has remarked, alternative forms of aid would not be expected, if one is to go by the evidence of history, to correlate better with an index of poverty. And if the alternative was bilateral aid, it would be tied aid to boot.

Specifically with regard to the transfer estimated to have been effected by the coffee agreement in 1982–83, HBS point critically to the deadweight loss associated with it. But, as I noted earlier, the ratio of the deadweight loss to the gain accruing to producers comes out as one to twelve. That is a cheap price by any standard. With the low price elasticities which typically prevail in primary commodities, the transfer element overwhelmingly dominates the deadweight loss. That is why I have never found convincing the appeal to the deadweight loss as an argument against cartelisation of primary commodities. More serious as a source of inefficiency are the rigid production structures maintained through cartel quotas. But Kaldor (1964) had proposed an ingenious scheme that would gradually adjust the quotas towards the globally cost-minimizing position.

One last point. The authors, in concluding their examination of the Natural Rubber Agreement (end of section 3), consider the financial cost

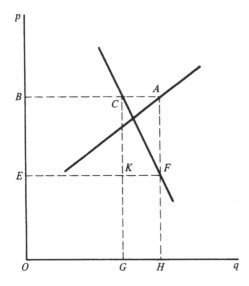

Figure 10A.1 The financial cost of raising producers' revenue. (Financial cost of raising producers' revenue to *OBAH* by (a) subsidy = *EBAF* (b) stockpiling = *GCAH*. Inelastic demand implies that *OBCG* > *OEFH* thus *OBAH* – *OEFH* > *OBAH* – *OBCG* thus (a) > (b).

of raising producers' revenue by deficiency payments as against price support by stockpiling. In this context it is perhaps worth saying that, given inelastic demand, the cost of buying for stock is always less than the cost of a subsidy per unit of output which yields the same total revenue to producers. The intuition is straightfoward. Buying for stock raises market price. Per unit subsidization of output lowers price. Inelastic demand means that consumers spend more in the former case than in the latter and hence a lesser amount needs to be added in the former case to attain a given revenue for producers. This is demonstrated in Figure 10A.1 (suggested by John Black).

For a small increase in producers' total revenue one can be more precise: the financial cost of stockpiling is a fraction of the cost of a per unit subsidy, the fraction being equal to the price elasticity of demand. The mathematics of this are as follows.

Demand (*D*) and supply (*S*) are a function of price (*p*) and the market-clearing equation is

$$D(p) + K = S(p) \tag{1}$$

when stockpiling (*K*) is in operation and

$$D(p) = S(p + \pi) \tag{2}$$

when a per unit subsidy (π) is in operation.

Differentiating (1) and (2) and solving for the price change, assuming initially

$$K = 0 \quad \text{and} \quad \pi = 0,$$

$$dp = dK/[(S/p)(\eta - e)] \tag{3}$$

$$dp = - \eta d\pi/(\eta - e) \tag{4}$$

where $\eta \equiv$ elasticity of supply and $e \equiv$ elasticity of demand.

Producers' revenue in the stockpiling case is

$$R_1 \equiv pS \tag{5}$$

and in the subsidy case

$$R_2 \equiv (p + \pi)D \tag{6}$$

Differentiating (5) and (6),

$$dR_1 = S(\eta + 1)dp \tag{7}$$

$$dR_2 = D[(1 + e)dp + d\pi] \tag{8}$$

The financial cost (X) of stockpiling is $dX_1 = pdK$ and of subsidizing $dX_2 = Dd\pi$, whence

$$dK = dX_1/p \tag{9}$$

$$d\pi = dX_2/D \tag{10}$$

Using (9) to eliminate dK from (3) and using the resulting expression to eliminate dp from (7), we obtain

$$dR_1 = [(1 + \eta)/(\eta - e)]dX_1 \tag{11}$$

and using analogously (10) and (4), we transform (8) into

$$dR_2 = - [e(1 + \eta)/(\eta - e)]dX_2 \tag{12}$$

It can be seen immediately that the expressions in square brackets in (11) and (12) differ only by a factor $- e$.

REFERENCES

Gilbert, C. L. (1987) 'International Commodity Agreements: Design and Performance', *World Development* **15**, 591–616.

Kaldor, N. (1964) 'Stabilising the Terms of Trade of Underdeveloped Countries' in N. Kaldor, *Essays in Economic Policy II*, London: Duckworth, pp. 112–30.

Kaldor, N. (1983) 'The Role of Commodity Prices in Economic Recovery', *Lloyds Bank Review*, No. 149, 21–34.

Keynes, J. M. (1936) *The General Theory of Employment, Interest and Money*, London: Macmillan.
Newbery, D. M. G. and J. E. Stiglitz (1981) *The Theory of Commodity Price Stabilization*, Oxford: Oxford University Press.
Spraos, J. (1988) 'Restoring the IMF to its Old Purpose' in S. Dell (ed.), *Policies for Development*, Basingstoke: Macmillan.

Summary of general discussion

Jim Rollo opened the discussion by making the point that the STABEX arrangement is part of the overall development assistance provided by the European Community. Mirza Jahani wanted to know what alternative there is to replace these schemes with, having diagnosed a failure to achieve their objectives. He expressed scepticism about a market based approach as many LDCs, especially the smaller ones, face dependence on export earnings from just one cash crop, where even small fluctuations may have severe effects on their economy. Finally, Jahani pointed out the problems of the average hiding the specific; if the average transfer of these schemes looked like having only little impact on the instability of export earnings, there may still be instances of substantial effects for an individual economy.

John Spraos argued that a price stabilization scheme affects individual producers on the micro level by enabling risk-averse producers to increase output; in addition there is a dynamic effect on investment which would be expected to be welfare enhancing. He argued that all of these beneficial welfare effects may in the end not offset the price distorting effects of the stabilization scheme. However, the overall welfare effect is not clear, as these transfer benefits need to be properly taken account of. The IMF had created the CFF, Spraos said, in order to provide a means to appropriate the macro benefits from such earnings stabilization.

Alan Winters noted the fact that the compensatory financing facility of the IMF was a cheap source of income and that the STABEX system offered unconditional funds. He wondered, however, whether any evidence exists to suggest that such schemes induced any change in the policy behaviour of recipients. He asked whether the economies that receive earnings stabilization assistance actually alter their macroeconomics.

In reply to these questions Roland Herrmann gave the following responses. With respect to the argument that an export quota agreement such as that for coffee leads to the accumulation of national stocks which exert a price stabilizing influence in boom periods, he argued that it should be recognized that this is not true if there exists a secondary parallel market. He argued that under such circumstances, as is indeed for the case for coffee, these excess stocks tend to be loaded off onto that secondary market immediately rather than being stored, thus depressing the price in that market. Therefore, the conclusion that the coffee export quota scheme is not so much a price stabilizing initiative as a price support scheme for the participating producer members still holds true.

Herrmann also wished to make clear once again that while it is true that conditionality may limit the freedom of action for the recipient countries, the STABEX system only requires a report on how the funds were used, without laying down any rules on how they may be allocated. They are in fact totally free for use by the recipient country, i.e. it is an untied form of aid and in that sense superior to the IMF scheme. In addition, the STABEX system offers a high grant ratio, albeit without considering measures of need and is instead determined by applications for earnings shortfall compensation.

Herrmann went on to assert that it is not generally true that compensatory facilities are superior to buffer stock schemes; arguing that it depends on how the individual producer is affected, i.e. on impact at the microeconomic level. Herrmann agreed that the apparent divergence between goals and achievements of these schemes can be traced back to the specifications of the rules and argued that these could also be changed, given the political will. He acknowledged that the averages have hidden some specific results, but argued that the general conclusion still holds.

Index

Printed in the United States
By Bookmasters